X-MEN LEGACY

S0-BRU-184

FIVE MILES SOUTH OF THE UNIVERSE

WRITER: Mike Carey

ISSUES #254-256 & #258
PENCILER: Steve Kurth
INKERS: Jay Leisten (#254-255), Craig Yeung (#255-256)
& Ed Tadeo (#256 & #258) with Jeff Huet (#256)
COLORISTS: Brian Reber with Rachelle Rosenberg (#256)

ISSUES #257 & #259-260
PENCILER: Khoi Pham
INKERS: Tom Palmer with Ed Tadeo (#260)
COLORISTS: Brian Reber (#257) & Antonio Fabela (#259-260)

LETTERER: VC's Cory Petit with Clayton Cowles (#248)
COVER ART: Mico Suayan with Marte Gracia & Sonia Oback (#254-258)
and Clay Mann & Seth Mann with Christina Strain & Morry Hollowell (#259-260)
ASSISTANT EDITOR: Sebastian Girner
EDITOR: Daniel Ketchum
GROUP EDITOR: Nick Lowe

COLLECTION EDITOR: Jennifer Grünwald • ASSISTANT EDITORS: Alex Starbuck & Nelson Ribeiro
EDITOR, SPECIAL PROJECTS: Mark D. Beazley • SENIOR EDITOR, SPECIAL PROJECTS: Jeff Youngquist
SENIOR VICE PRESIDENT OF SALES: David Gabriel
SVP OF BRAND PLANNING & COMMUNICATIONS: Michael Pasciullo

EDITOR IN CHIEF: Axel Alonso • CHIEF CREATIVE OFFICER: Joe Quesada
PUBLISHER: Dan Buckley • EXECUTIVE PRODUCER: Alan Fine

X-MEN LEGACY: FIVE MILES SOUTH OF THE UNIVERSE. Contains material originally published in magazine form as X-MEN LEGACY #254-260. First printing 2012. Hardcover ISBN# 978-0-7851-6067-0. Softcover ISBN# 978-0-7851-6068-7. Published by MARVEL WORLDWIDE, INC., a subsidiary of MARVEL ENTERTAINMENT, LLC. OFFICE OF PUBLICATION: 135 West 50th Street, New York, NY 10020. Copyright © 2011 and 2012 Marvel Characters, Inc. All rights reserved. Hardcover: $19.99 per copy in the U.S. and $21.99 in Canada (GST #R127032852). Softcover: $15.99 per copy in the U.S. and $17.99 in Canada (GST #R127032852). Canadian Agreement #40668537. All characters featured in this issue and the distinctive names and likenesses thereof, and all related indicia are trademarks of Marvel Characters, Inc. No similarity between any of the names, characters, persons, and/or institutions in this magazine with those of any living or dead person or institution is intended, and any such similarity which may exist is purely coincidental. **Printed in the U.S.A.** ALAN FINE, EVP - Office of the President, Marvel Worldwide, Inc. and EVP & CMO Marvel Characters B.V.; DAN BUCKLEY, Publisher & President - Print, Animation & Digital Divisions; JOE QUESADA, Chief Creative Officer; DAVID BOGART, SVP of Business Affairs & Talent Management; TOM BREVOORT, SVP of Publishing; C.B. CEBULSKI, SVP of Creator & Content Development; DAVID GABRIEL, SVP of Publishing Sales & Circulation; MICHAEL PASCIULLO, SVP of Brand Planning & Communications; JIM O'KEEFE, VP of Operations & Logistics; DAN CARR, Executive Director of Publishing Technology; SUSAN CRESPI, Editorial Operations Manager; ALEX MORALES, Publishing Operations Manager; STAN LEE, Chairman Emeritus. For information regarding advertising in Marvel Comics or on Marvel.com, please contact John Dokes, SVP Integrated Sales and Marketing, at jdokes@marvel.com. For Marvel subscription inquiries, please call 800-217-9158. **Manufactured between 1/16/2012 and 2/13/2012 (hardcover), and 1/16/2012 and 8/13/2012 (softcover), by R.R. DONNELLEY, INC., SALEM, VA, USA.**

10 9 8 7 6 5 4 3 2 1

PREVIOUSLY:

After receiving an intergalactic distress call from wayward X-Man Marvel Girl, Rogue was determined to go to her aid...but had no means to reach her stranded teammates on the other side of the galaxy. But upon coming into contact with fellow X-Man Legion — a mutant with a near infinite catalog of mutant powers at his disposal — Rogue discovered he possessed a teleportation ability, and hastily borrowed it using her own mutant gift to temporarily acquire the powers and memories of others.

Now, Rogue and her small team of X-Men are hurtling through space, hoping that they've reached Marvel Girl, Havok and Polaris before it's too late...

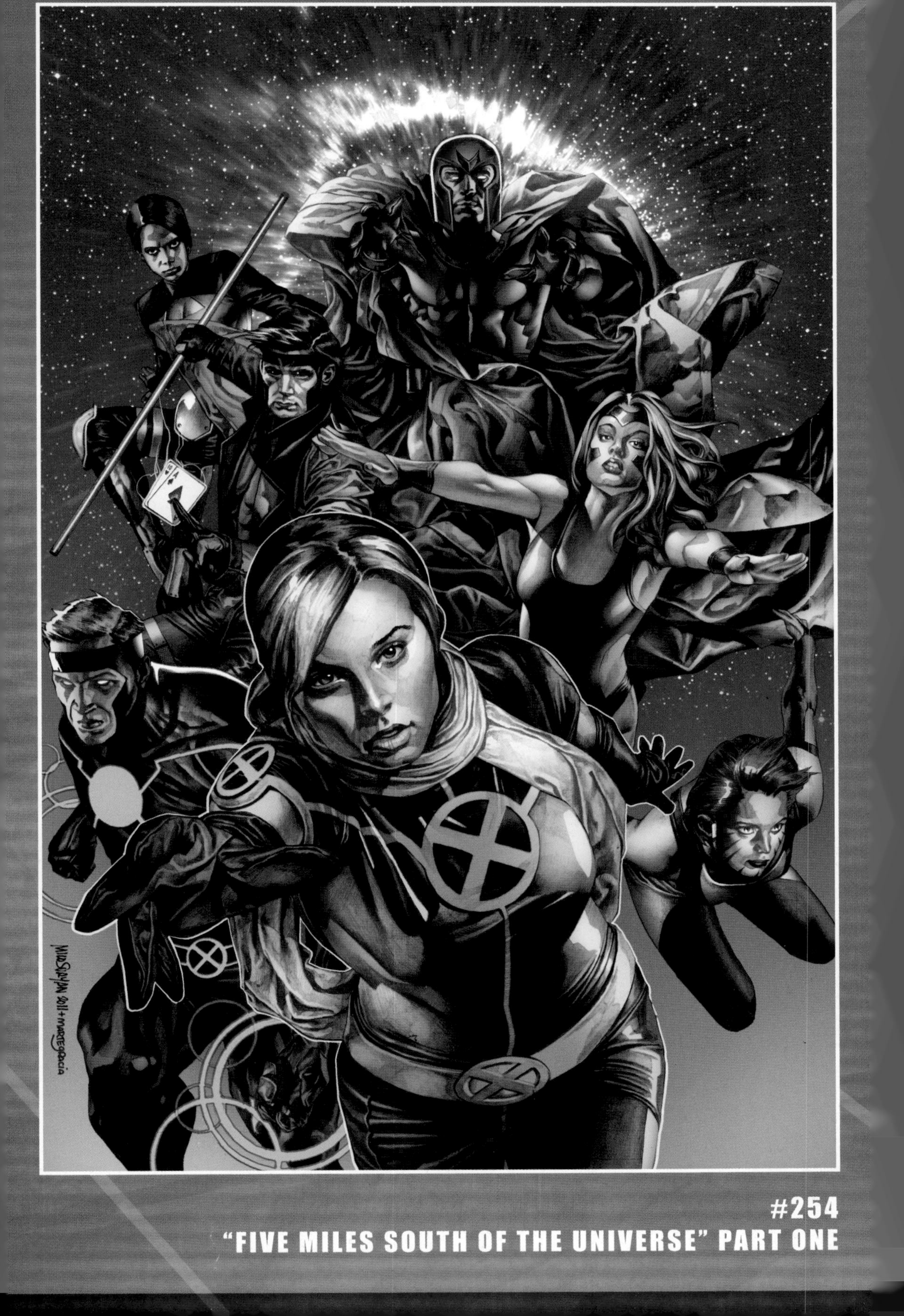
MIRCO SUAYAN 2011 + MARTEGRACIA

#254
"FIVE MILES SOUTH OF THE UNIVERSE" PART ONE

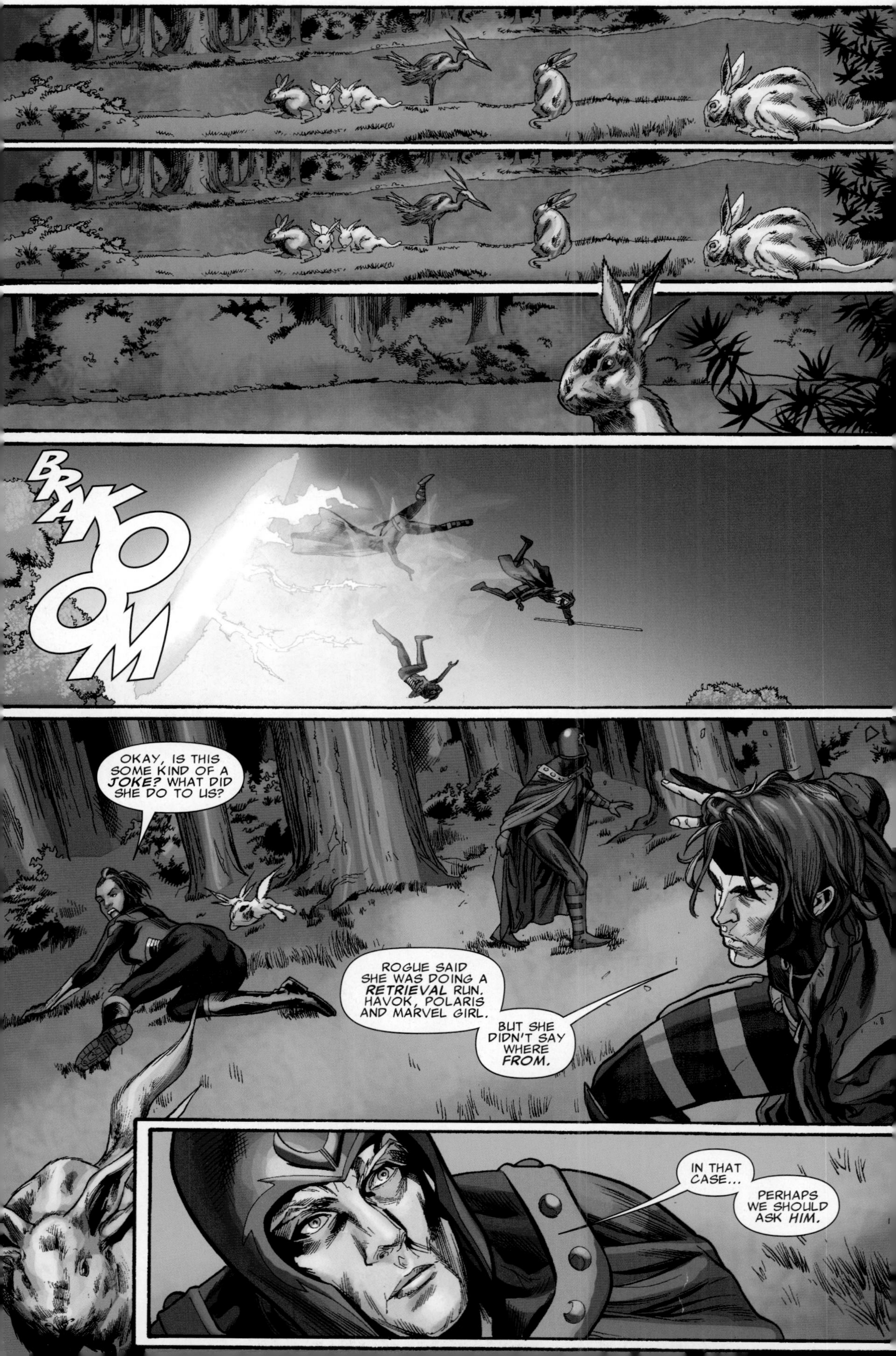
BRAKOOOM
OKAY, IS THIS SOME KIND OF A JOKE? WHAT DID SHE DO TO US?
ROGUE SAID SHE WAS DOING A RETRIEVAL RUN. HAVOK, POLARIS AND MARVEL GIRL.
BUT SHE DIDN'T SAY WHERE FROM.
IN THAT CASE...
PERHAPS WE SHOULD ASK HIM.

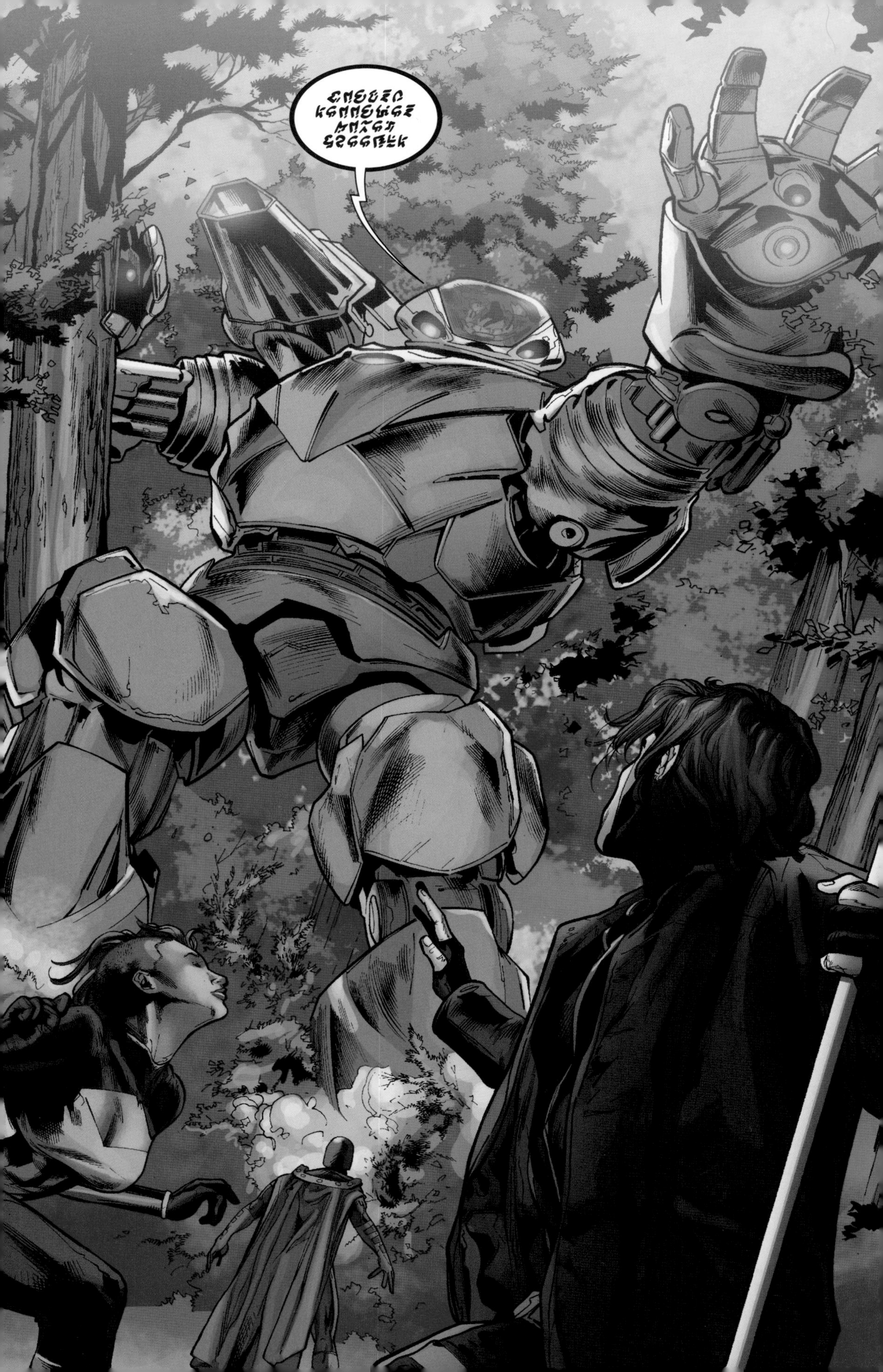

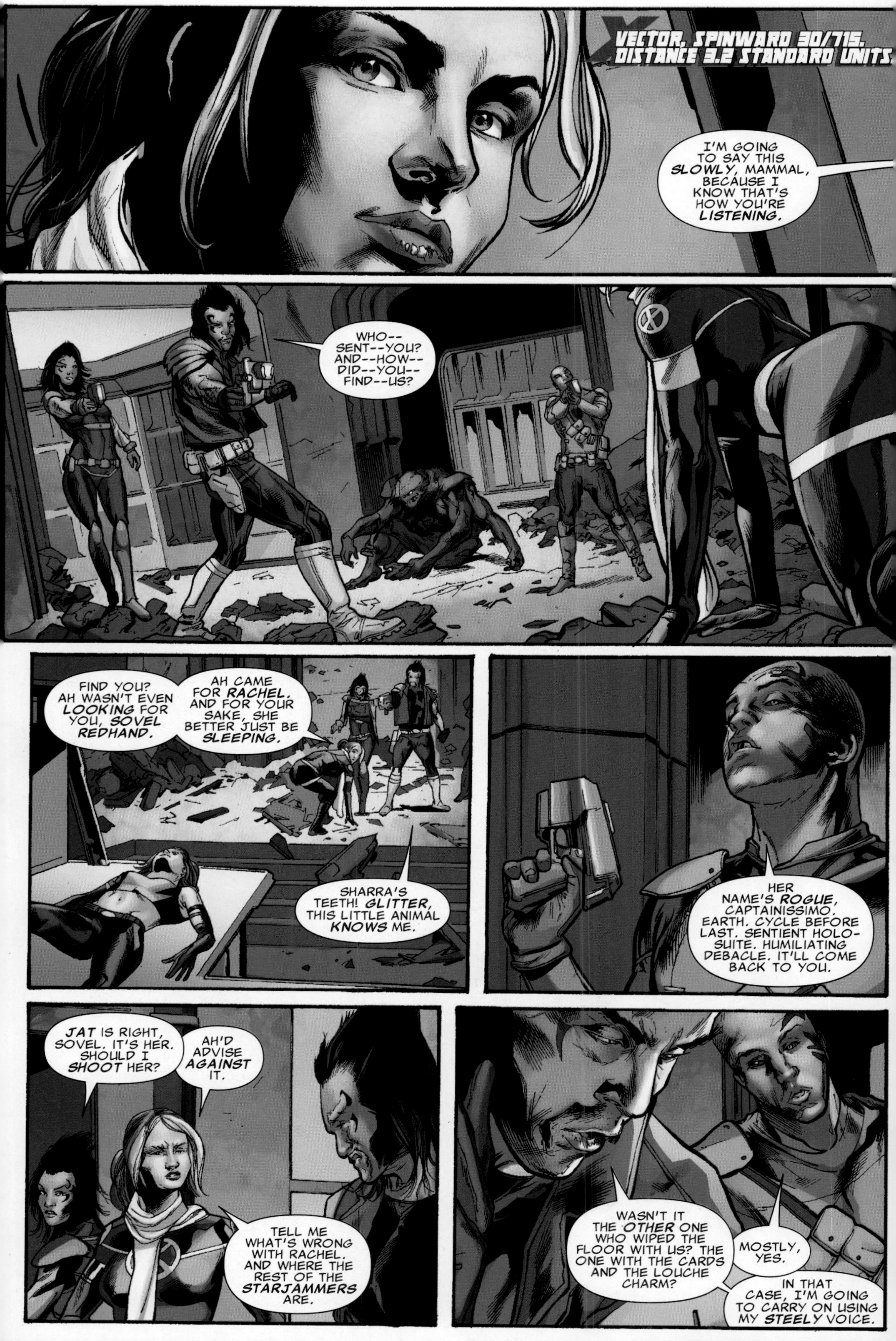
VECTOR, SPINWARD 30/715. DISTANCE 3.2 STANDARD UNITS.
I'M GOING TO SAY THIS SLOWLY, MAMMAL, BECAUSE I KNOW THAT'S HOW YOU'RE LISTENING.
WHO--SENT--YOU? AND--HOW--DID--YOU--FIND--US?
FIND YOU? AH WASN'T EVEN LOOKING FOR YOU, SOVEL REDHAND.
AH CAME FOR RACHEL, AND FOR YOUR SAKE, SHE BETTER JUST BE SLEEPING.
SHARRA'S TEETH! GLITTER, THIS LITTLE ANIMAL KNOWS ME.
HER NAME'S ROGUE, CAPTAINISSIMO. EARTH. CYCLE BEFORE LAST. SENTIENT HOLO-SUITE. HUMILIATING DEBACLE. IT'LL COME BACK TO YOU.
JAT IS RIGHT, SOVEL. IT'S HER. SHOULD I SHOOT HER?
AH'D ADVISE AGAINST IT.
TELL ME WHAT'S WRONG WITH RACHEL, AND WHERE THE REST OF THE STARJAMMERS ARE.
WASN'T IT THE OTHER ONE WHO WIPED THE FLOOR WITH US? THE ONE WITH THE CARDS AND THE LOUCHE CHARM?
MOSTLY, YES.
IN THAT CASE, I'M GOING TO CARRY ON USING MY STEELY VOICE.

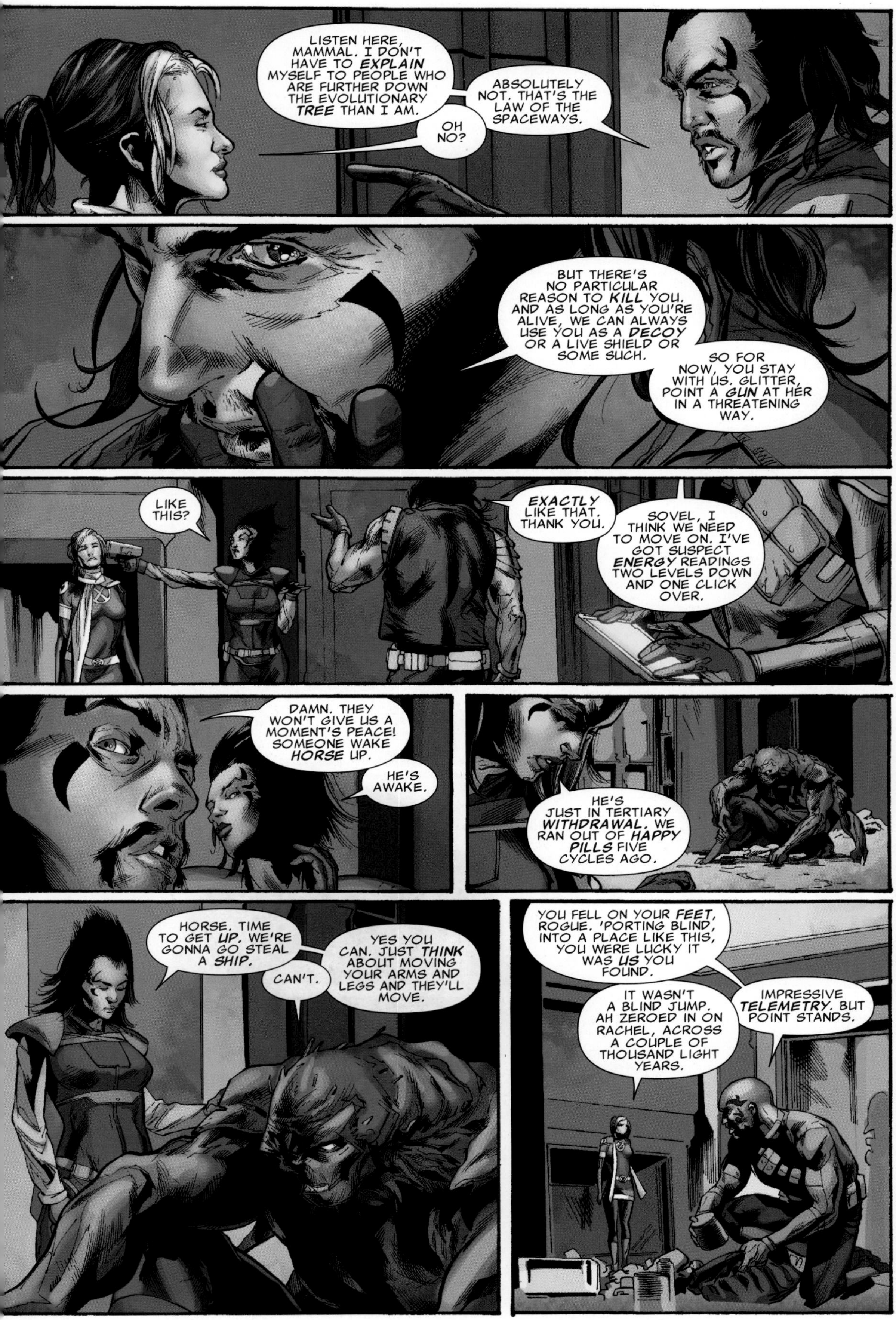
LISTEN HERE, MAMMAL. I DON'T HAVE TO EXPLAIN MYSELF TO PEOPLE WHO ARE FURTHER DOWN THE EVOLUTIONARY TREE THAN I AM.
OH NO?
ABSOLUTELY NOT. THAT'S THE LAW OF THE SPACEWAYS.
BUT THERE'S NO PARTICULAR REASON TO KILL YOU. AND AS LONG AS YOU'RE ALIVE, WE CAN ALWAYS USE YOU AS A DECOY OR A LIVE SHIELD OR SOME SUCH.
SO FOR NOW, YOU STAY WITH US. GLITTER, POINT A GUN AT HER IN A THREATENING WAY.
LIKE THIS?
EXACTLY LIKE THAT. THANK YOU.
SOVEL, I THINK WE NEED TO MOVE ON. I'VE GOT SUSPECT ENERGY READINGS TWO LEVELS DOWN AND ONE CLICK OVER.
DAMN. THEY WON'T GIVE US A MOMENT'S PEACE! SOMEONE WAKE HORSE UP.
HE'S AWAKE.
HE'S JUST IN TERTIARY WITHDRAWAL. WE RAN OUT OF HAPPY PILLS FIVE CYCLES AGO.
HORSE. TIME TO GET UP. WE'RE GONNA GO STEAL A SHIP.
CAN'T.
YES YOU CAN. JUST THINK ABOUT MOVING YOUR ARMS AND LEGS AND THEY'LL MOVE.
YOU FELL ON YOUR FEET, ROGUE. 'PORTING BLIND, INTO A PLACE LIKE THIS, YOU WERE LUCKY IT WAS US YOU FOUND.
IT WASN'T A BLIND JUMP. AH ZEROED IN ON RACHEL, ACROSS A COUPLE OF THOUSAND LIGHT YEARS.
IMPRESSIVE TELEMETRY. BUT POINT STANDS.

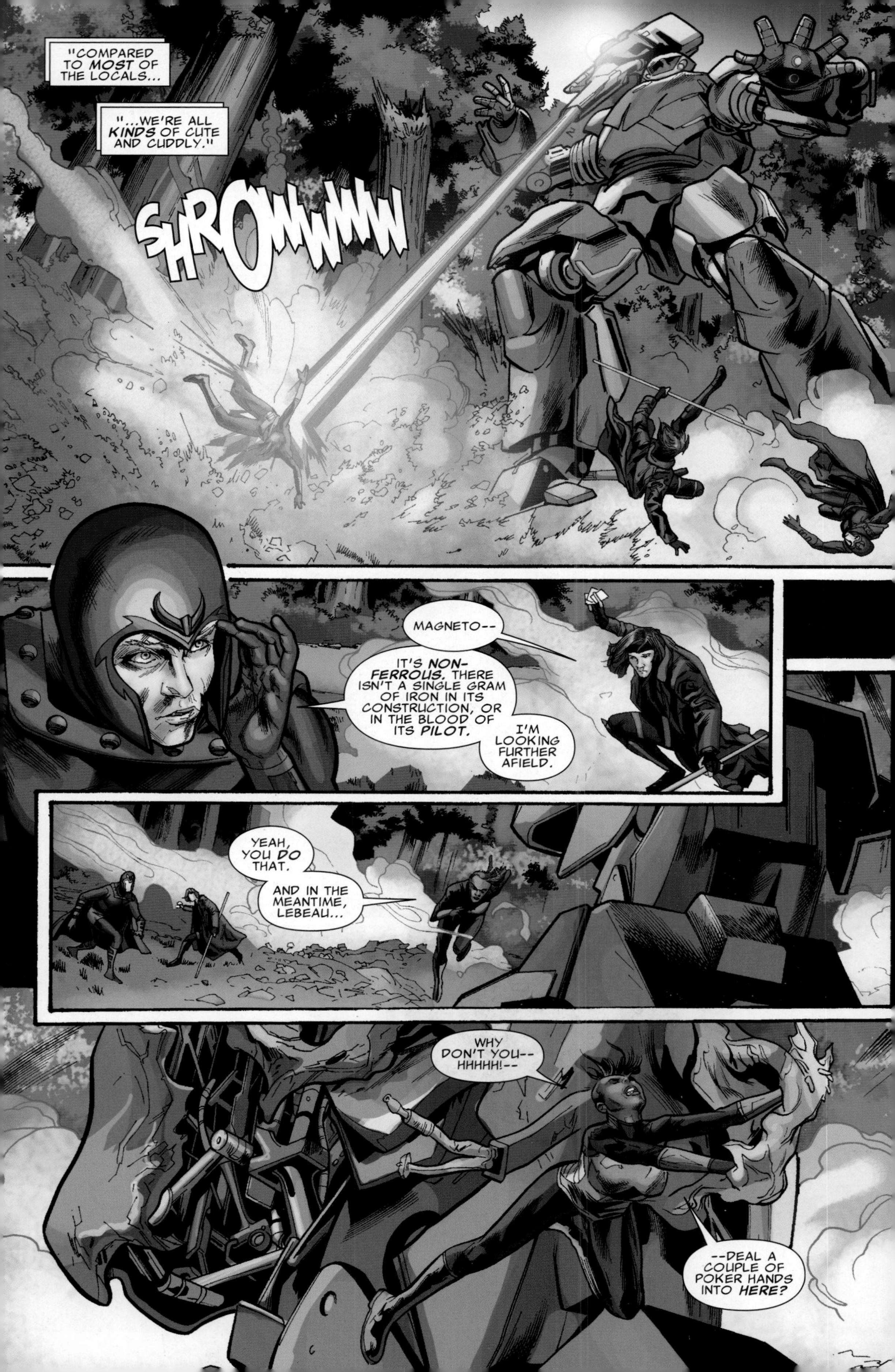
"COMPARED TO MOST OF THE LOCALS...
"...WE'RE ALL KINDS OF CUTE AND CUDDLY."
SHROWWWWW
MAGNETO--
IT'S NON-FERROUS. THERE ISN'T A SINGLE GRAM OF IRON IN ITS CONSTRUCTION, OR IN THE BLOOD OF ITS PILOT.
I'M LOOKING FURTHER AFIELD.
YEAH, YOU DO THAT.
AND IN THE MEANTIME, LEBEAU...
WHY DON'T YOU--HHHHH!--
--DEAL A COUPLE OF POKER HANDS INTO HERE?

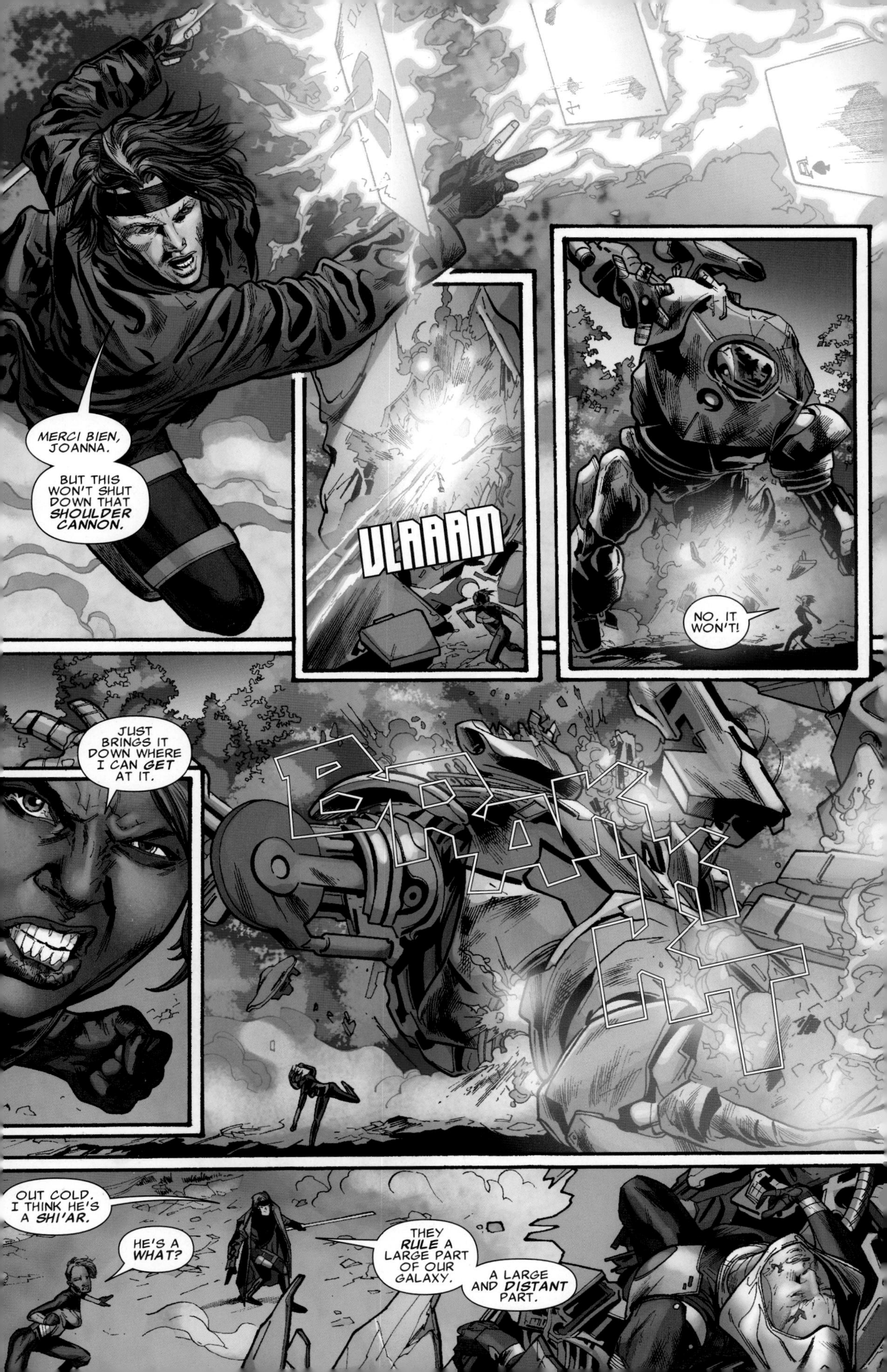
MERCI BIEN, JOANNA.
BUT THIS WON'T SHUT DOWN THAT SHOULDER CANNON.
VLAAAM
NO, IT WON'T!
JUST BRINGS IT DOWN WHERE I CAN GET AT IT.
BRAKKT
OUT COLD. I THINK HE'S A SHI'AR.
HE'S A WHAT?
THEY RULE A LARGE PART OF OUR GALAXY.
A LARGE AND DISTANT PART.

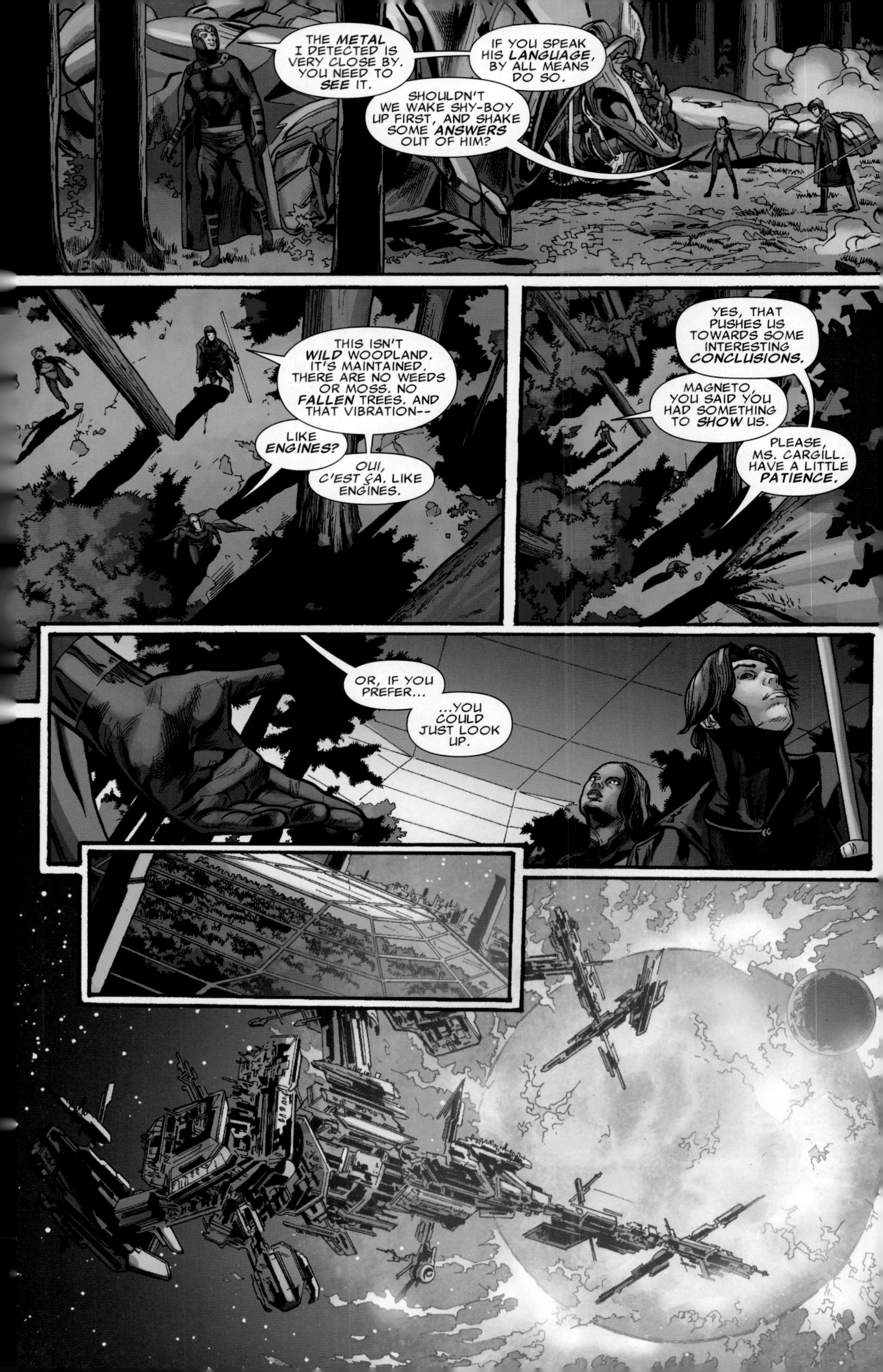

THE METAL I DETECTED IS VERY CLOSE BY. YOU NEED TO SEE IT.
IF YOU SPEAK HIS LANGUAGE, BY ALL MEANS DO SO.
SHOULDN'T WE WAKE SHY-BOY UP FIRST, AND SHAKE SOME ANSWERS OUT OF HIM?
THIS ISN'T WILD WOODLAND. IT'S MAINTAINED. THERE ARE NO WEEDS OR MOSS. NO FALLEN TREES. AND THAT VIBRATION--
LIKE ENGINES?
OUI, C'EST ÇA. LIKE ENGINES.
YES, THAT PUSHES US TOWARDS SOME INTERESTING CONCLUSIONS.
MAGNETO, YOU SAID YOU HAD SOMETHING TO SHOW US.
PLEASE, MS. CARGILL. HAVE A LITTLE PATIENCE.
OR, IF YOU PREFER...
...YOU COULD JUST LOOK UP.

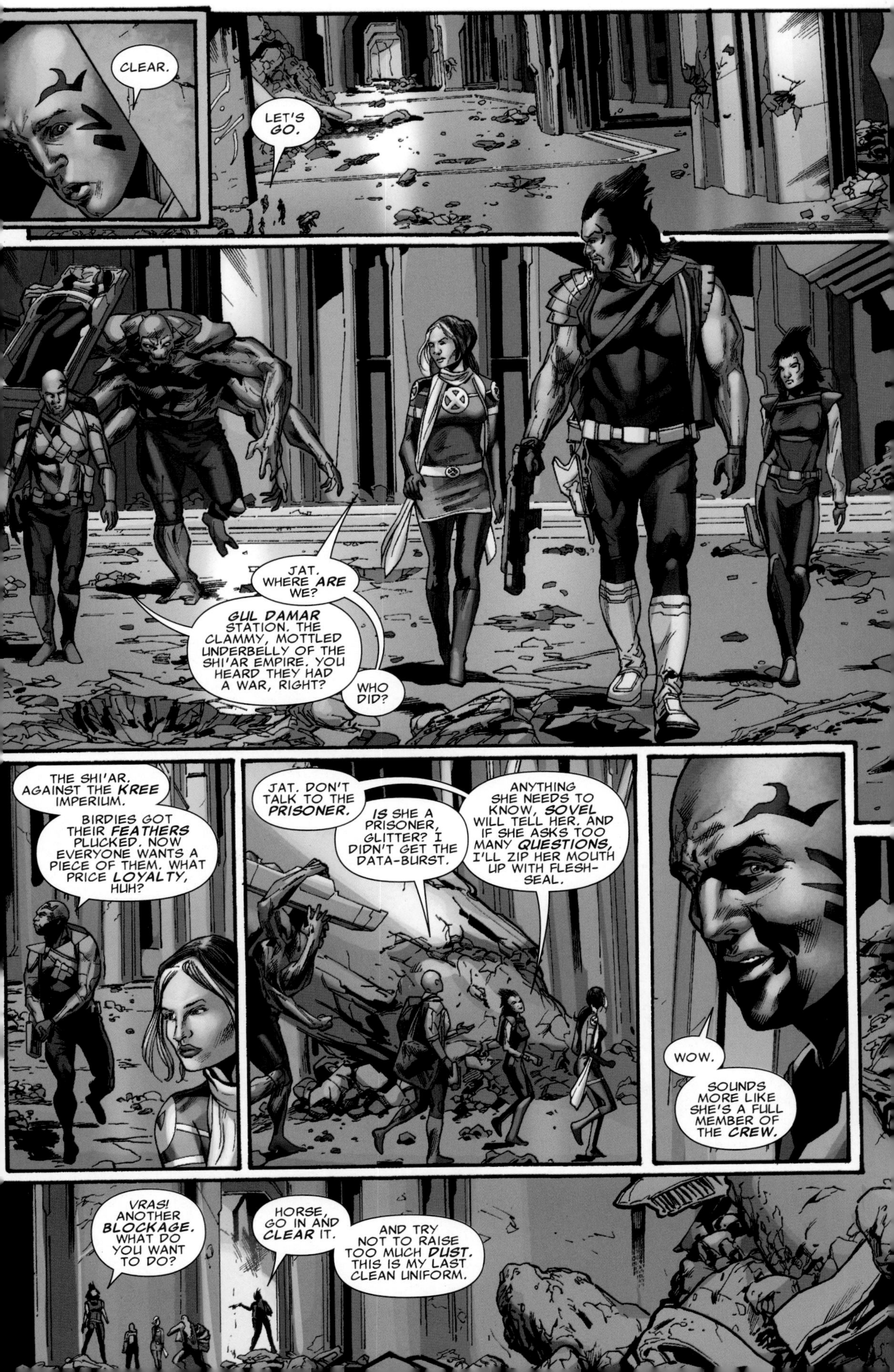
CLEAR.
LET'S GO.
JAT. WHERE ARE WE?
GUL DAMAR STATION. THE CLAMMY, MOTTLED UNDERBELLY OF THE SHI'AR EMPIRE. YOU HEARD THEY HAD A WAR, RIGHT?
WHO DID?
THE SHI'AR. AGAINST THE KREE IMPERIUM.
BIRDIES GOT THEIR FEATHERS PLUCKED. NOW EVERYONE WANTS A PIECE OF THEM. WHAT PRICE LOYALTY, HUH?
JAT. DON'T TALK TO THE PRISONER.
IS SHE A PRISONER, GLITTER? I DIDN'T GET THE DATA-BURST.
ANYTHING SHE NEEDS TO KNOW, SOVEL WILL TELL HER. AND IF SHE ASKS TOO MANY QUESTIONS, I'LL ZIP HER MOUTH UP WITH FLESH-SEAL.
WOW.
SOUNDS MORE LIKE SHE'S A FULL MEMBER OF THE CREW.
VRAS! ANOTHER BLOCKAGE. WHAT DO YOU WANT TO DO?
HORSE, GO IN AND CLEAR IT.
AND TRY NOT TO RAISE TOO MUCH DUST. THIS IS MY LAST CLEAN UNIFORM.

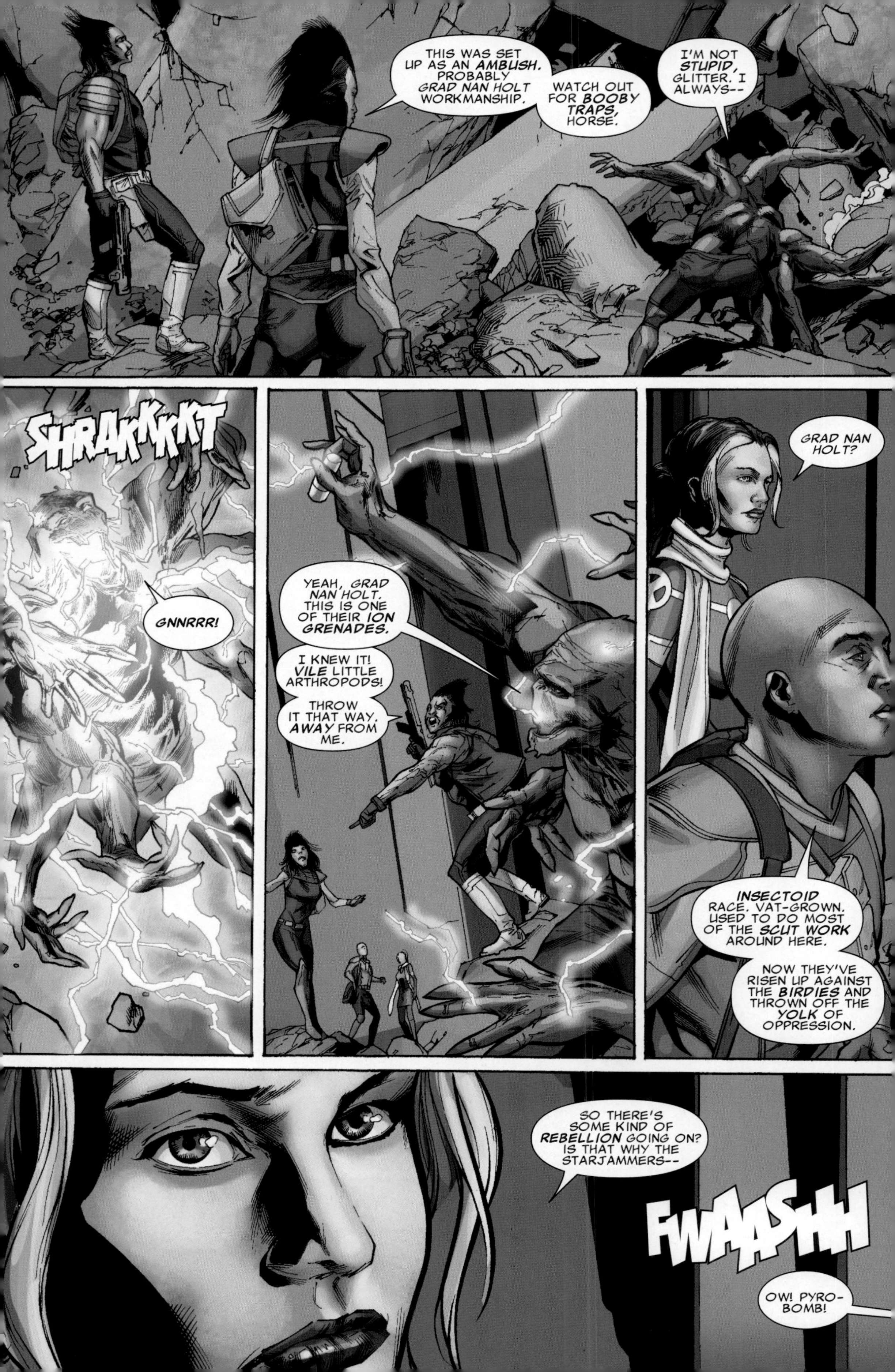
THIS WAS SET UP AS AN AMBUSH. PROBABLY GRAD NAN HOLT WORKMANSHIP.
WATCH OUT FOR BOOBY TRAPS, HORSE.
I'M NOT STUPID, GLITTER. I ALWAYS--
SHRAKKKKT
GNNRRR!
YEAH, GRAD NAN HOLT. THIS IS ONE OF THEIR ION GRENADES.
I KNEW IT! VILE LITTLE ARTHROPODS!
THROW IT THAT WAY. AWAY FROM ME.
GRAD NAN HOLT?
INSECTOID RACE. VAT-GROWN. USED TO DO MOST OF THE SCUT WORK AROUND HERE.
NOW THEY'VE RISEN UP AGAINST THE BIRDIES AND THROWN OFF THE YOLK OF OPPRESSION.
SO THERE'S SOME KIND OF REBELLION GOING ON? IS THAT WHY THE STARJAMMERS--
FWAASHH
OW! PYRO-BOMB!

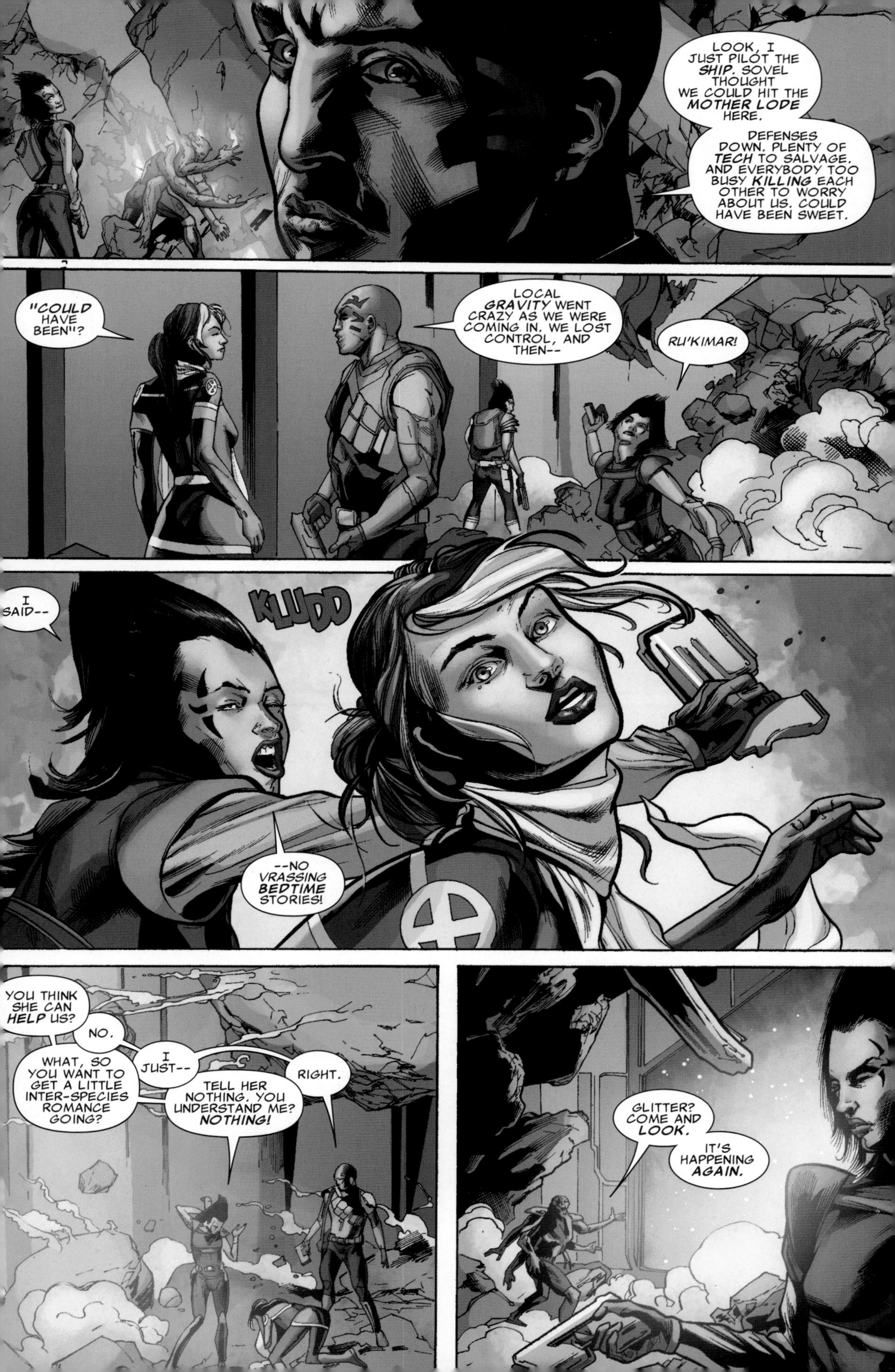
LOOK, I JUST PILOT THE SHIP. SOVEL THOUGHT WE COULD HIT THE MOTHER LODE HERE.
DEFENSES DOWN. PLENTY OF TECH TO SALVAGE. AND EVERYBODY TOO BUSY KILLING EACH OTHER TO WORRY ABOUT US. COULD HAVE BEEN SWEET.
"COULD HAVE BEEN"?
LOCAL GRAVITY WENT CRAZY AS WE WERE COMING IN. WE LOST CONTROL, AND THEN--
RU'KIMAR!
I SAID--
KLUDD
--NO VRASSING BEDTIME STORIES!
YOU THINK SHE CAN HELP US?
NO.
WHAT, SO YOU WANT TO GET A LITTLE INTER-SPECIES ROMANCE GOING?
I JUST--
TELL HER NOTHING. YOU UNDERSTAND ME? NOTHING!
RIGHT.
GLITTER? COME AND LOOK.
IT'S HAPPENING AGAIN.

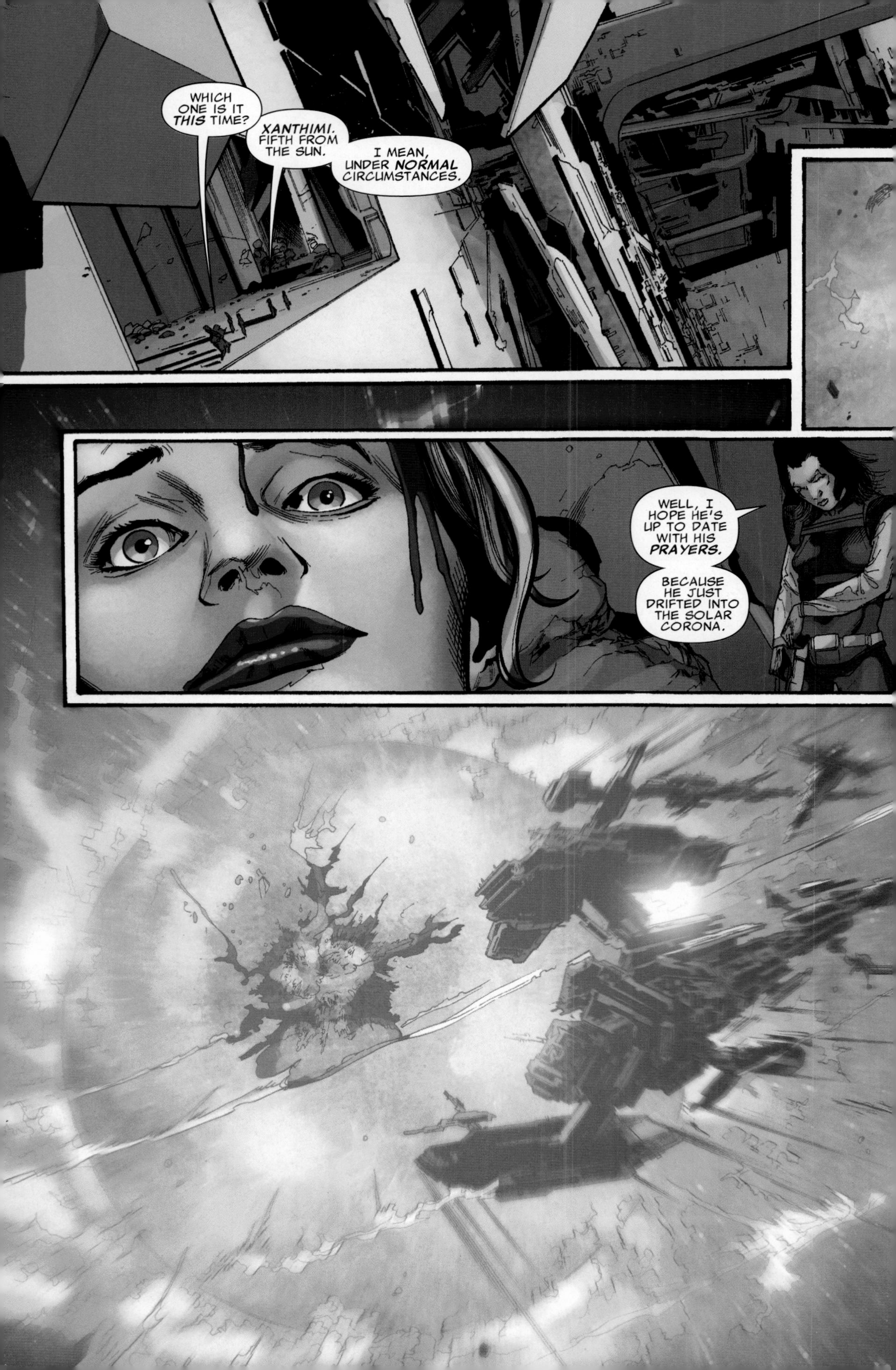
WHICH ONE IS IT THIS TIME?
XANTHIMI. FIFTH FROM THE SUN.
I MEAN, UNDER NORMAL CIRCUMSTANCES.
WELL, I HOPE HE'S UP TO DATE WITH HIS PRAYERS.
BECAUSE HE JUST DRIFTED INTO THE SOLAR CORONA.

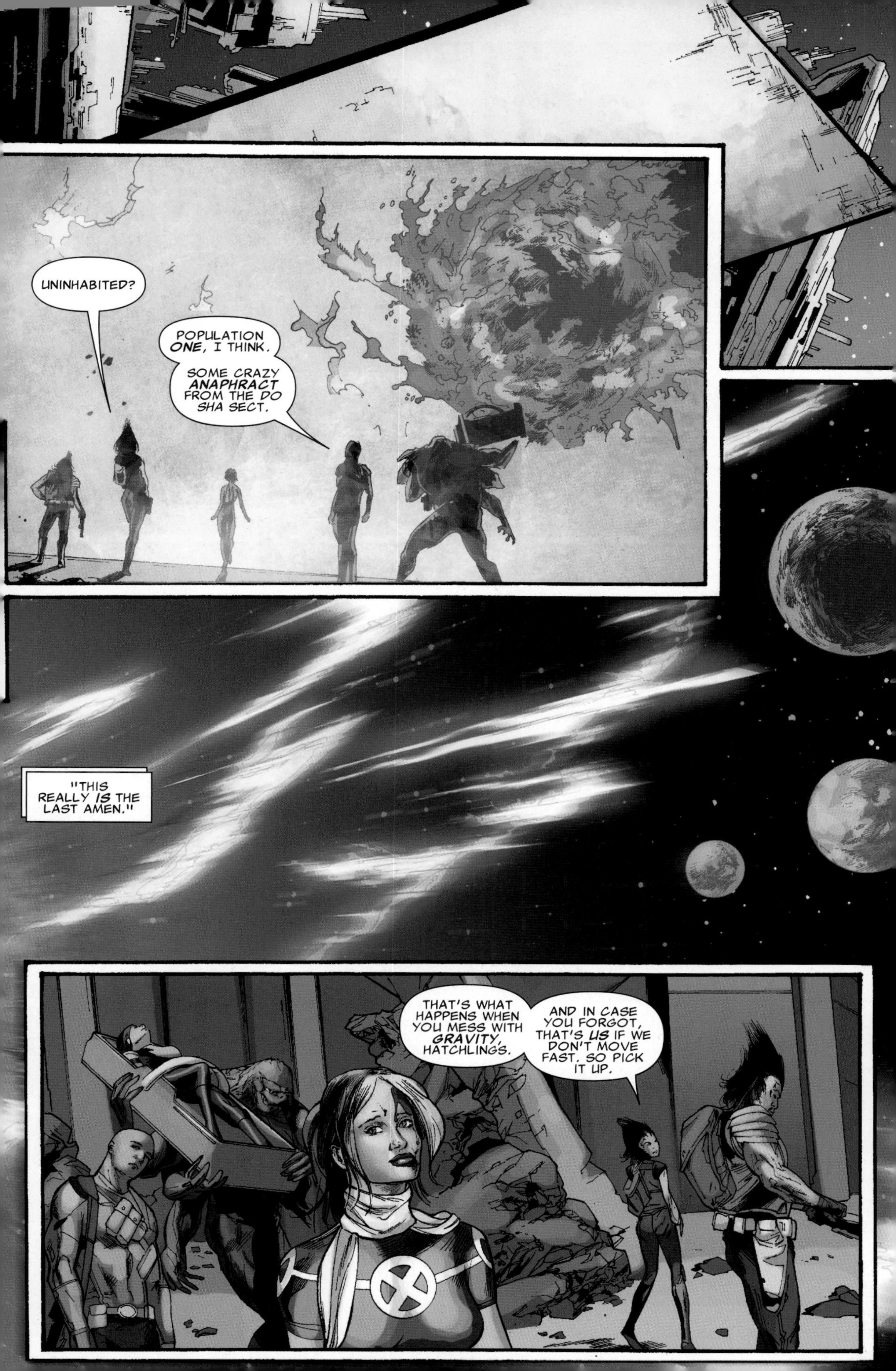
UNINHABITED?
POPULATION ONE, I THINK.
SOME CRAZY ANAPHRACT FROM THE DO SHA SECT.
"THIS REALLY IS THE LAST AMEN."
THAT'S WHAT HAPPENS WHEN YOU MESS WITH GRAVITY, HATCHLINGS.
AND IN CASE YOU FORGOT, THAT'S US IF WE DON'T MOVE FAST. SO PICK IT UP.

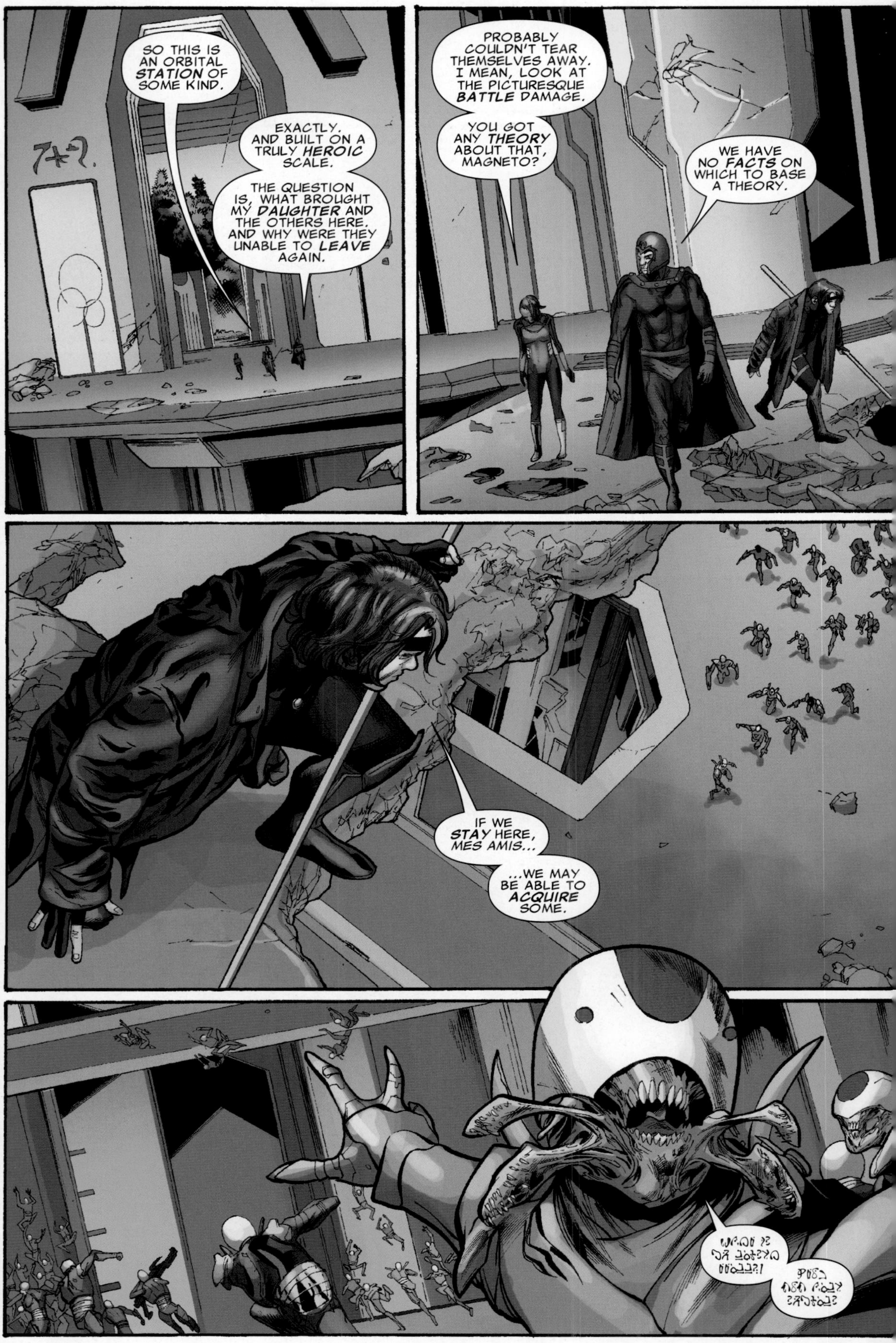
SO THIS IS AN ORBITAL STATION OF SOME KIND.
EXACTLY. AND BUILT ON A TRULY HEROIC SCALE.
THE QUESTION IS, WHAT BROUGHT MY DAUGHTER AND THE OTHERS HERE. AND WHY WERE THEY UNABLE TO LEAVE AGAIN.
PROBABLY COULDN'T TEAR THEMSELVES AWAY. I MEAN, LOOK AT THE PICTURESQUE BATTLE DAMAGE.
YOU GOT ANY THEORY ABOUT THAT, MAGNETO?
WE HAVE NO FACTS ON WHICH TO BASE A THEORY.
IF WE STAY HERE, MES AMIS...
...WE MAY BE ABLE TO ACQUIRE SOME.

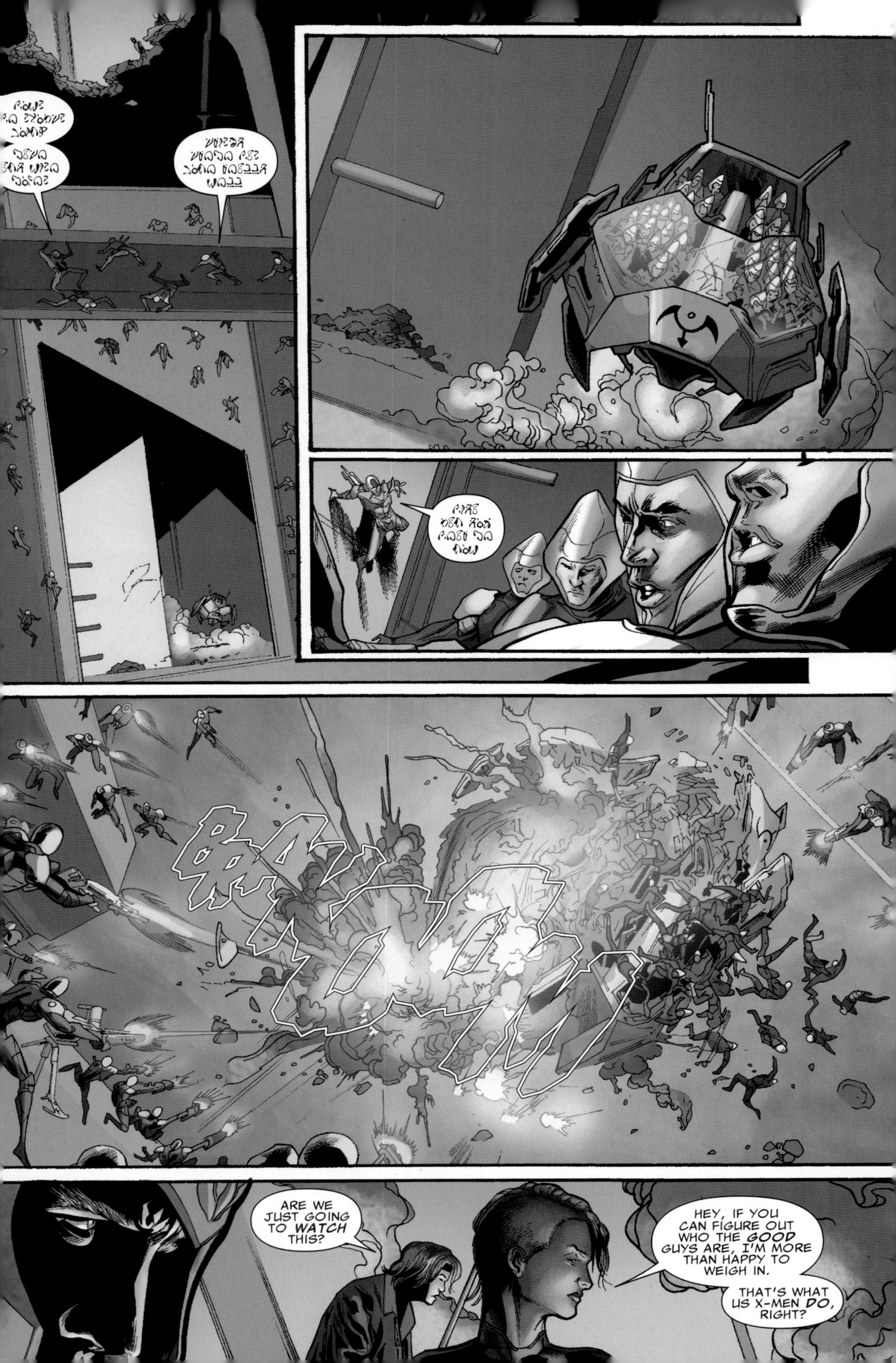
ARE WE JUST GOING TO WATCH THIS?
HEY, IF YOU CAN FIGURE OUT WHO THE GOOD GUYS ARE, I'M MORE THAN HAPPY TO WEIGH IN.
THAT'S WHAT US X-MEN DO, RIGHT?

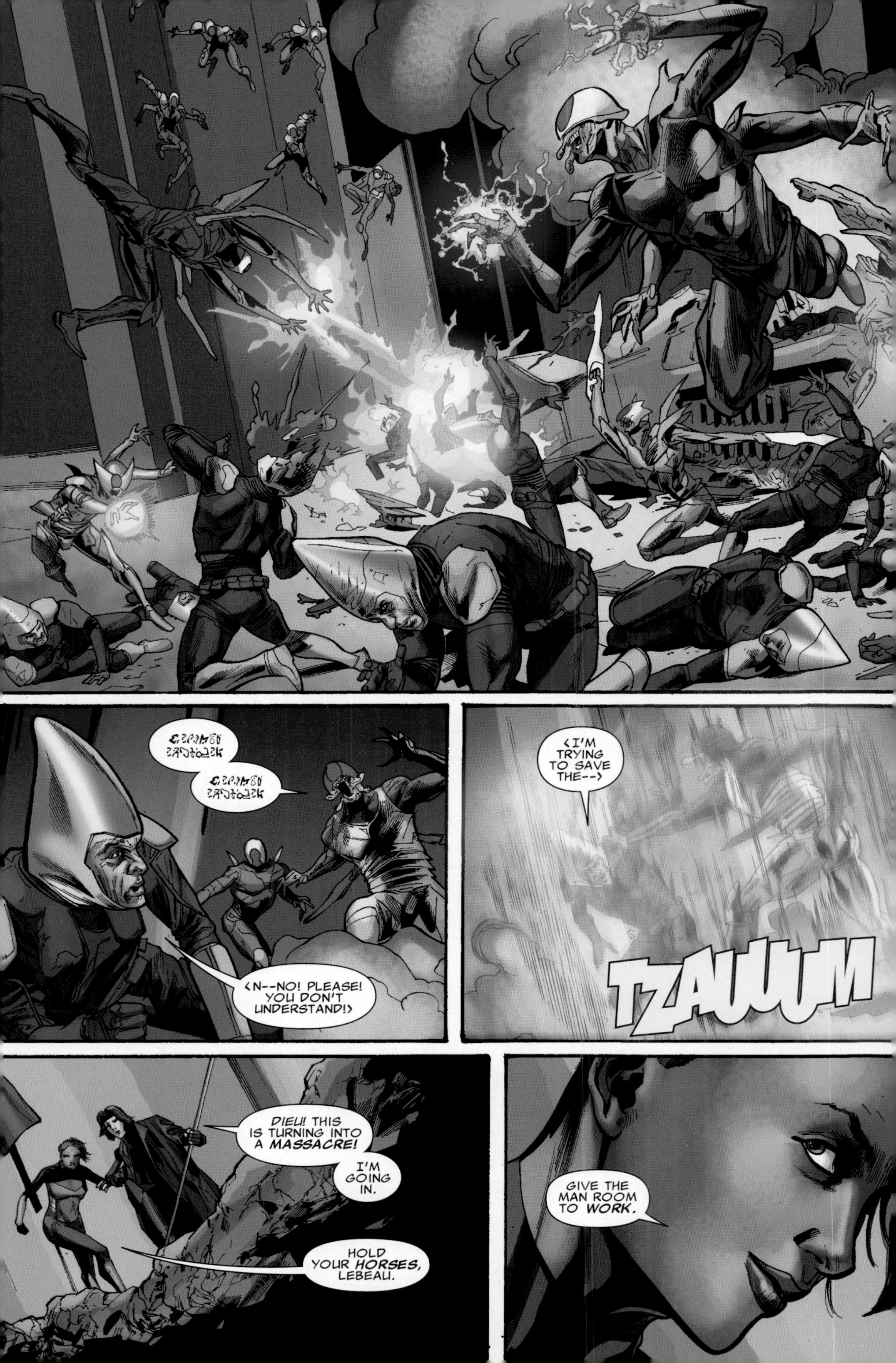
<N--NO! PLEASE! YOU DON'T UNDERSTAND!>
<I'M TRYING TO SAVE THE-->
TZAUUUM
DIEU! THIS IS TURNING INTO A MASSACRE!
I'M GOING IN.
HOLD YOUR HORSES, LEBEAU.
GIVE THE MAN ROOM TO WORK.

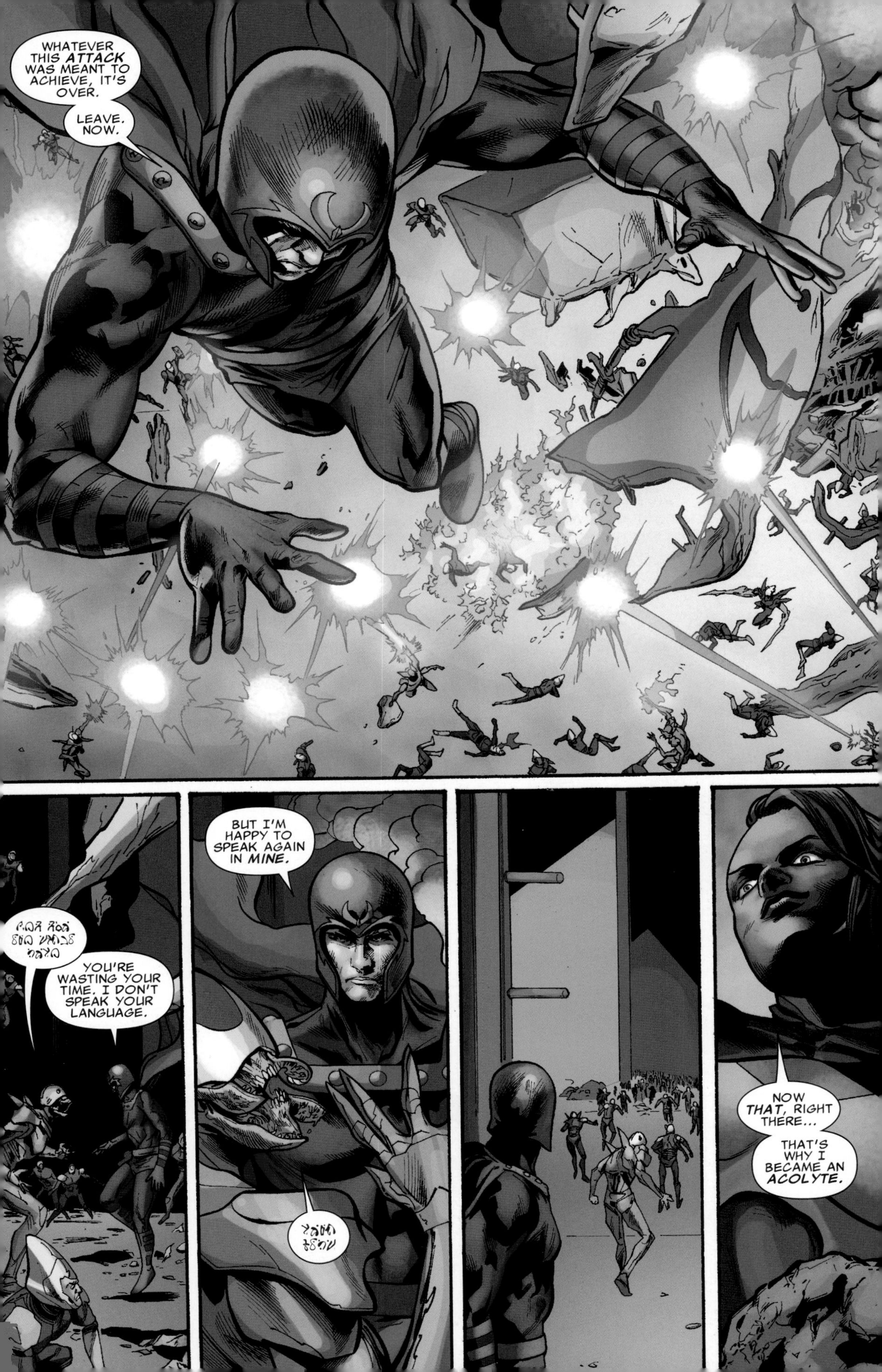
WHATEVER THIS ATTACK WAS MEANT TO ACHIEVE, IT'S OVER.
LEAVE. NOW.
YOU'RE WASTING YOUR TIME. I DON'T SPEAK YOUR LANGUAGE.
BUT I'M HAPPY TO SPEAK AGAIN IN MINE.
NOW THAT, RIGHT THERE...
THAT'S WHY I BECAME AN ACOLYTE.

LIFT TUBE IS *DEAD*, CAPTAINISSIMO.

THIS ONE, *TOO.*

BUT THERE'S NO DAMAGE TO THE *INDUCTION* CIRCUITRY. I'LL SEE IF I CAN DIVERT SOME *POWER* INTO IT.

JAT.

VRAS, ROGUE! I'M NOT SUPPOSED TO *TALK* TO YOU.

AH KNOW IT. AH JUST WANT TO MAKE SURE AH'M GETTING THIS *RIGHT.*

WE JUST WATCHED A *PLANET* FALL INTO THE SUN AND GET SWALLOWED UP.

WHAT COULD *DO* THAT?

GUL DAMAR IS POWERED BY GRAVITIC *FLUX.* IF THE GENERATOR TOOK SOME DAMAGE, THIS IS WHAT YOU'D LIKELY SEE.

THE SUN'S GRAVITY FIELD SPIKING, PULLING EVERYTHING IN.

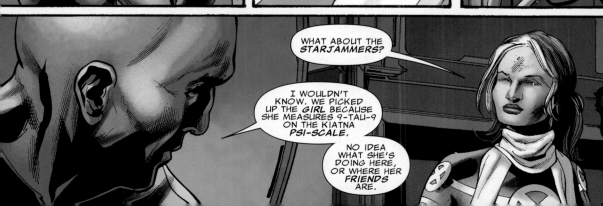

WHAT ABOUT THE *STARJAMMERS?*

I WOULDN'T KNOW. WE PICKED UP THE *GIRL* BECAUSE SHE MEASURES 9-TAU-9 ON THE KIATNA *PSI-SCALE.*

NO IDEA WHAT SHE'S DOING HERE, OR WHERE HER *FRIENDS* ARE.

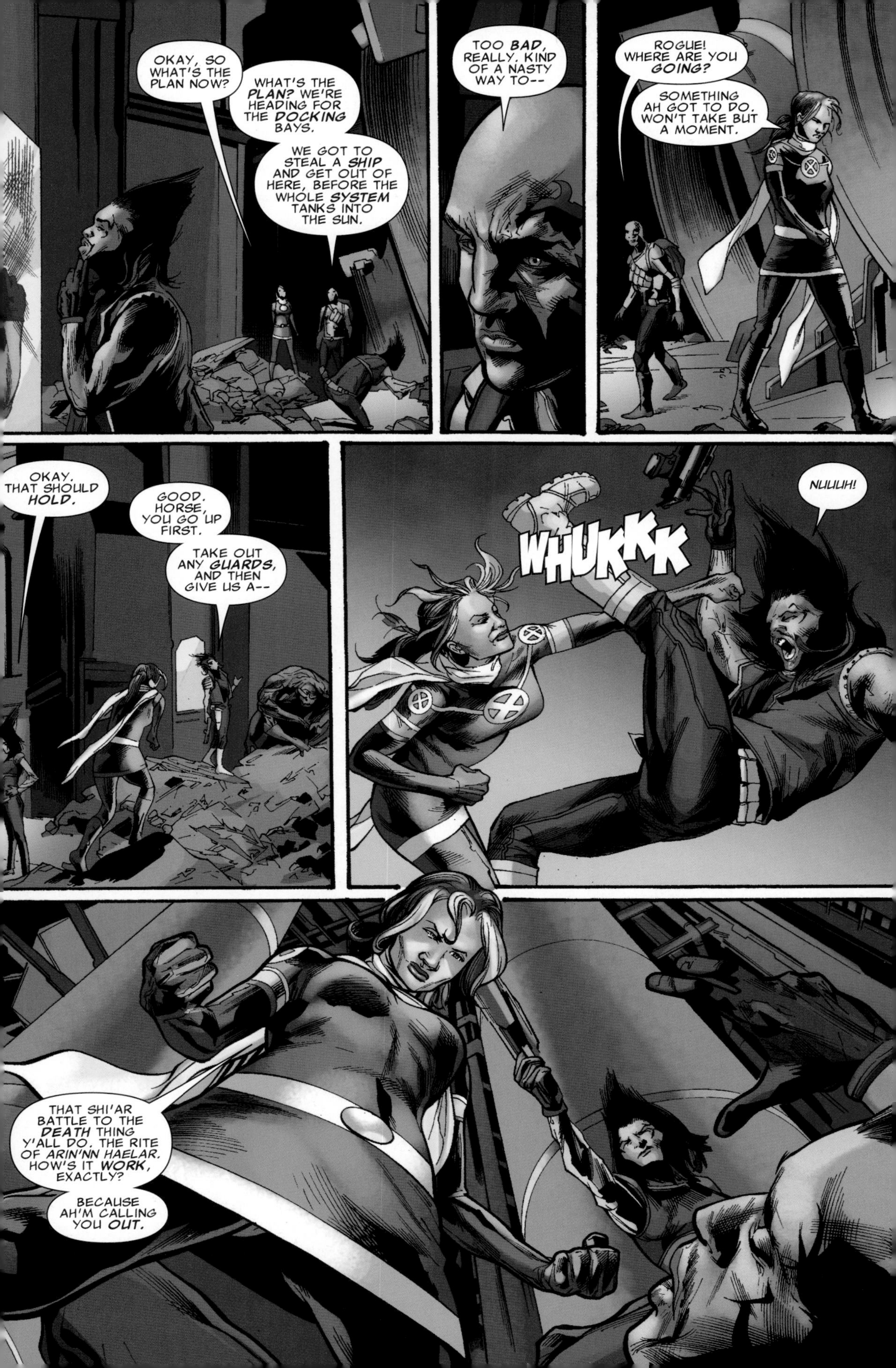

OKAY, SO WHAT'S THE PLAN NOW?
WHAT'S THE PLAN? WE'RE HEADING FOR THE DOCKING BAYS.
WE GOT TO STEAL A SHIP AND GET OUT OF HERE, BEFORE THE WHOLE SYSTEM TANKS INTO THE SUN.
TOO BAD, REALLY. KIND OF A NASTY WAY TO--
ROGUE! WHERE ARE YOU GOING?
SOMETHING AH GOT TO DO. WON'T TAKE BUT A MOMENT.
OKAY. THAT SHOULD HOLD.
GOOD. HORSE, YOU GO UP FIRST.
TAKE OUT ANY GUARDS, AND THEN GIVE US A--
WHUKKK
NUUUH!
THAT SHI'AR BATTLE TO THE DEATH THING Y'ALL DO. THE RITE OF ARIN'NN HAELAR. HOW'S IT WORK, EXACTLY?
BECAUSE AH'M CALLING YOU OUT.

CRETZME GYCI KENSK CRETZME GYCI KENSK CRETZME GYCI KENSK UNDERSTAND ME NOW?

YES. WE **UNDERSTAND** YOU.

EXCELLENT. THANK YOU FOR YOUR **ASSISTANCE.**

YOU ARE **LOYAL** TO THE SHI'AR IMPERIUM, AND TO THE MAJESTOR?

NO, WE'RE **NONALIGNED,** IN THIS STRUGGLE.

WE ARE FROM **EARTH.** TERRA. AND ANY BUSINESS WE HAVE HERE IS **UNRELATED** TO YOUR CONFLICT.

FROM **EARTH!** I SAID AS MUCH, DID I NOT?

THAT HIS ORIGIN MIGHT BE THE SAME AS THE OTHERS, GIVEN THAT HE HAS THE SAME **BODY PLAN** AND SKIN COLORATION.

THE OTHERS? **WHAT** OTHERS?

WE SAW SOME IN THE RANKS OF THE **GRAD NAN HOLT** WHO WERE LIKE **YOU.**

FORCE WIELDERS, MOST **FORMIDABLE,** WHO HAVE DONE TERRIBLE DAMAGE TO THIS STATION AND **KILLED** MANY.

DESCRIBE THEM.

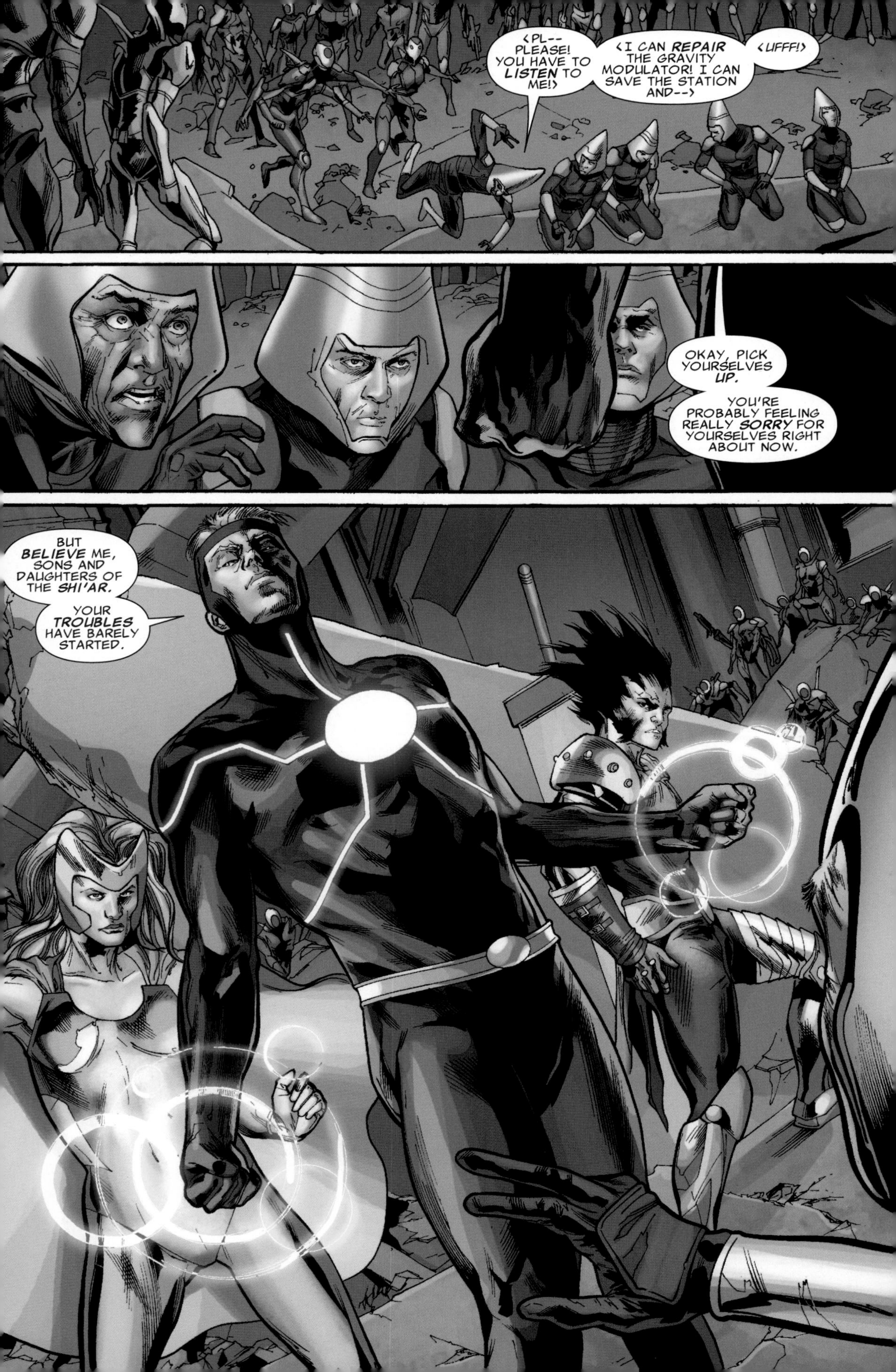

‹PL-- PLEASE! YOU HAVE TO LISTEN TO ME!›
‹I CAN REPAIR THE GRAVITY MODULATOR! I CAN SAVE THE STATION AND--›
‹UFFF!›
OKAY, PICK YOURSELVES UP.
YOU'RE PROBABLY FEELING REALLY SORRY FOR YOURSELVES RIGHT ABOUT NOW.
BUT BELIEVE ME, SONS AND DAUGHTERS OF THE SHI'AR.
YOUR TROUBLES HAVE BARELY STARTED.

#255

"FIVE MILES SOUTH OF THE UNIVERSE" PART TWO

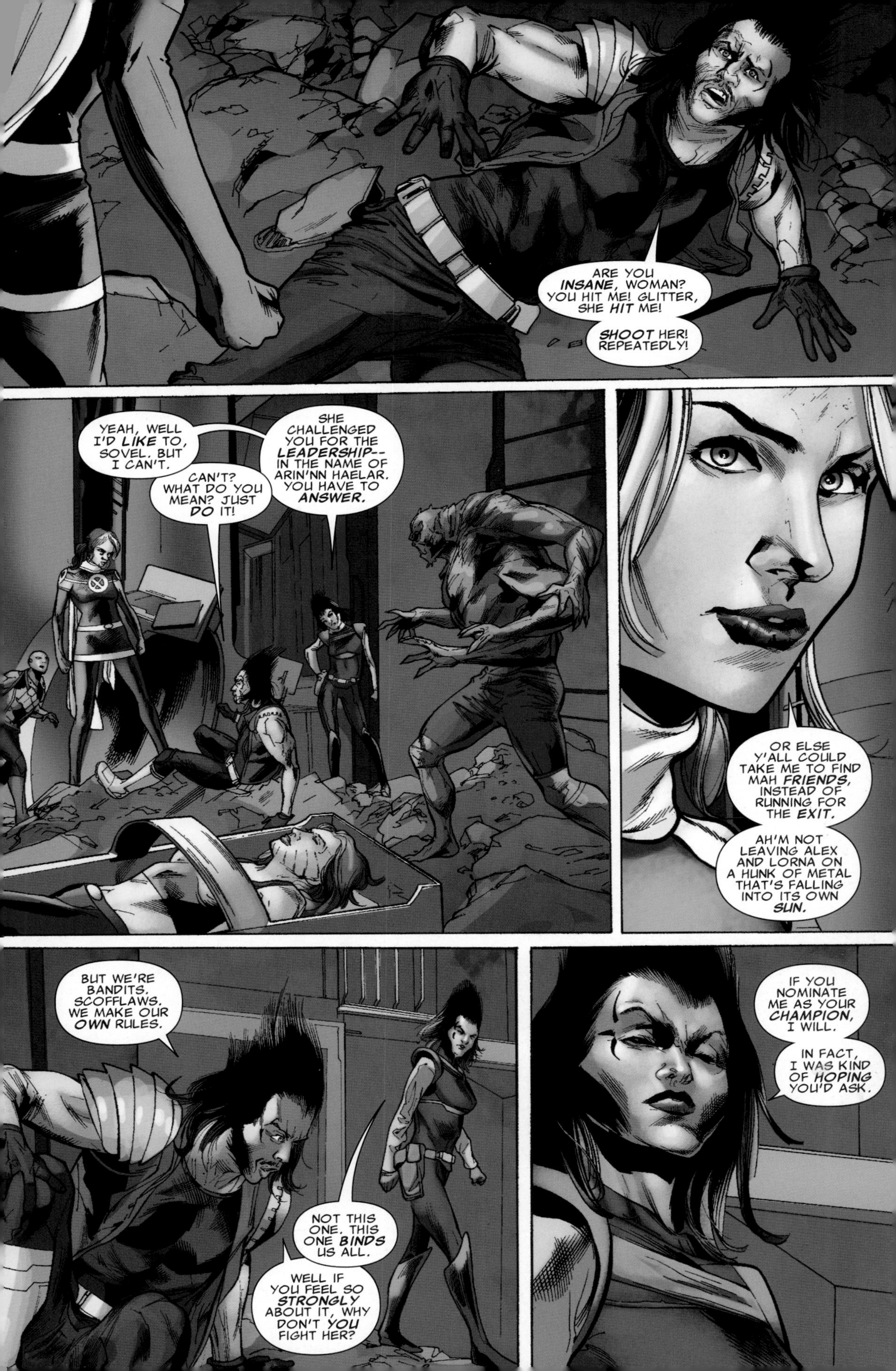
ARE YOU INSANE, WOMAN? YOU HIT ME! GLITTER, SHE HIT ME!
SHOOT HER! REPEATEDLY!
YEAH, WELL I'D LIKE TO, SOVEL. BUT I CAN'T.
CAN'T? WHAT DO YOU MEAN? JUST DO IT!
SHE CHALLENGED YOU FOR THE LEADERSHIP-- IN THE NAME OF ARIN'NN HAELAR. YOU HAVE TO ANSWER.
OR ELSE Y'ALL COULD TAKE ME TO FIND MAH FRIENDS, INSTEAD OF RUNNING FOR THE EXIT.
AH'M NOT LEAVING ALEX AND LORNA ON A HUNK OF METAL THAT'S FALLING INTO ITS OWN SUN.
BUT WE'RE BANDITS, SCOFFLAWS. WE MAKE OUR OWN RULES.
NOT THIS ONE. THIS ONE BINDS US ALL.
WELL IF YOU FEEL SO STRONGLY ABOUT IT, WHY DON'T YOU FIGHT HER?
IF YOU NOMINATE ME AS YOUR CHAMPION, I WILL.
IN FACT, I WAS KIND OF HOPING YOU'D ASK.

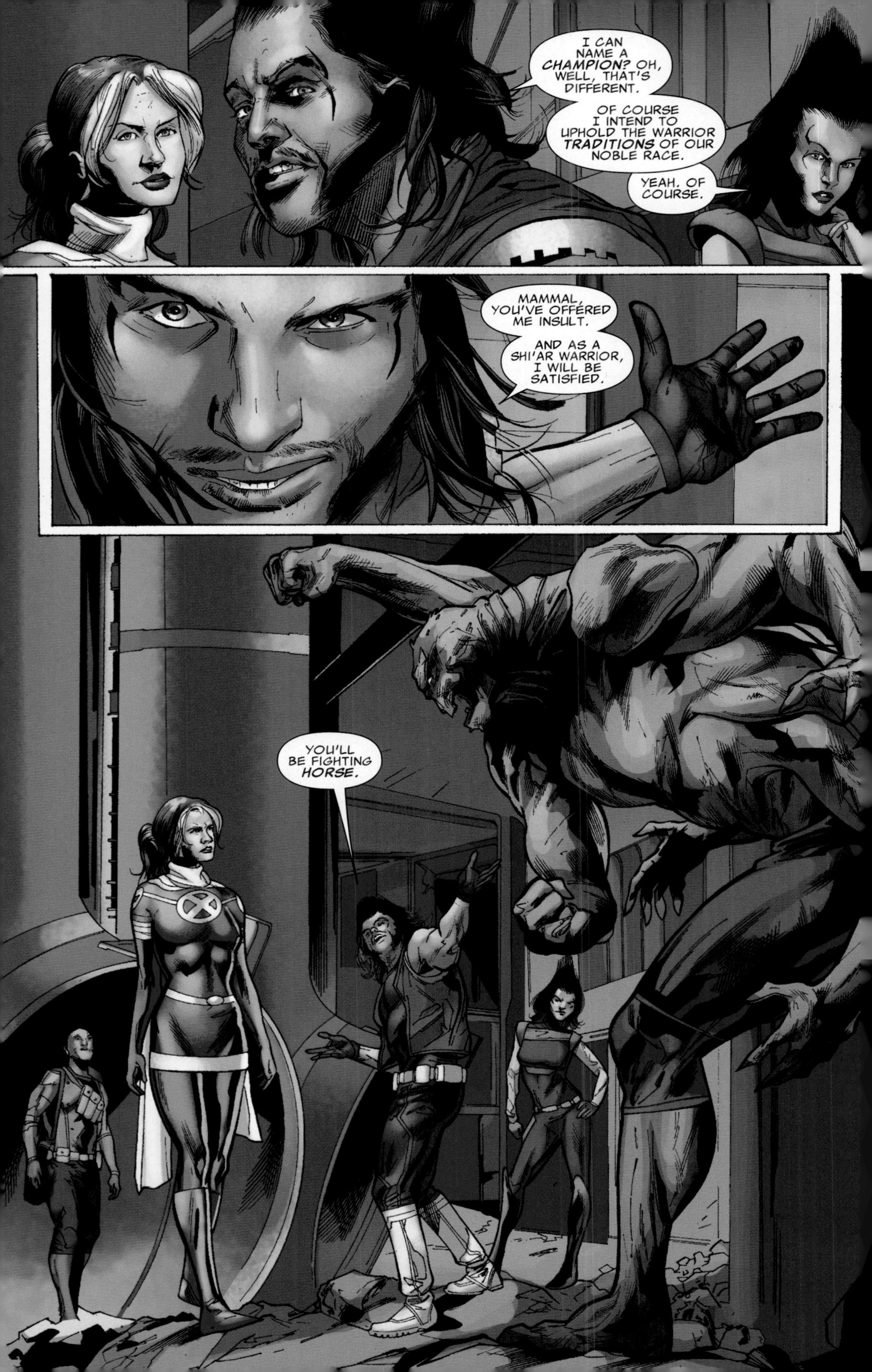
I CAN NAME A CHAMPION? OH, WELL, THAT'S DIFFERENT.
OF COURSE I INTEND TO UPHOLD THE WARRIOR TRADITIONS OF OUR NOBLE RACE.
YEAH. OF COURSE.
MAMMAL, YOU'VE OFFERED ME INSULT.
AND AS A SHI'AR WARRIOR, I WILL BE SATISFIED.
YOU'LL BE FIGHTING HORSE.

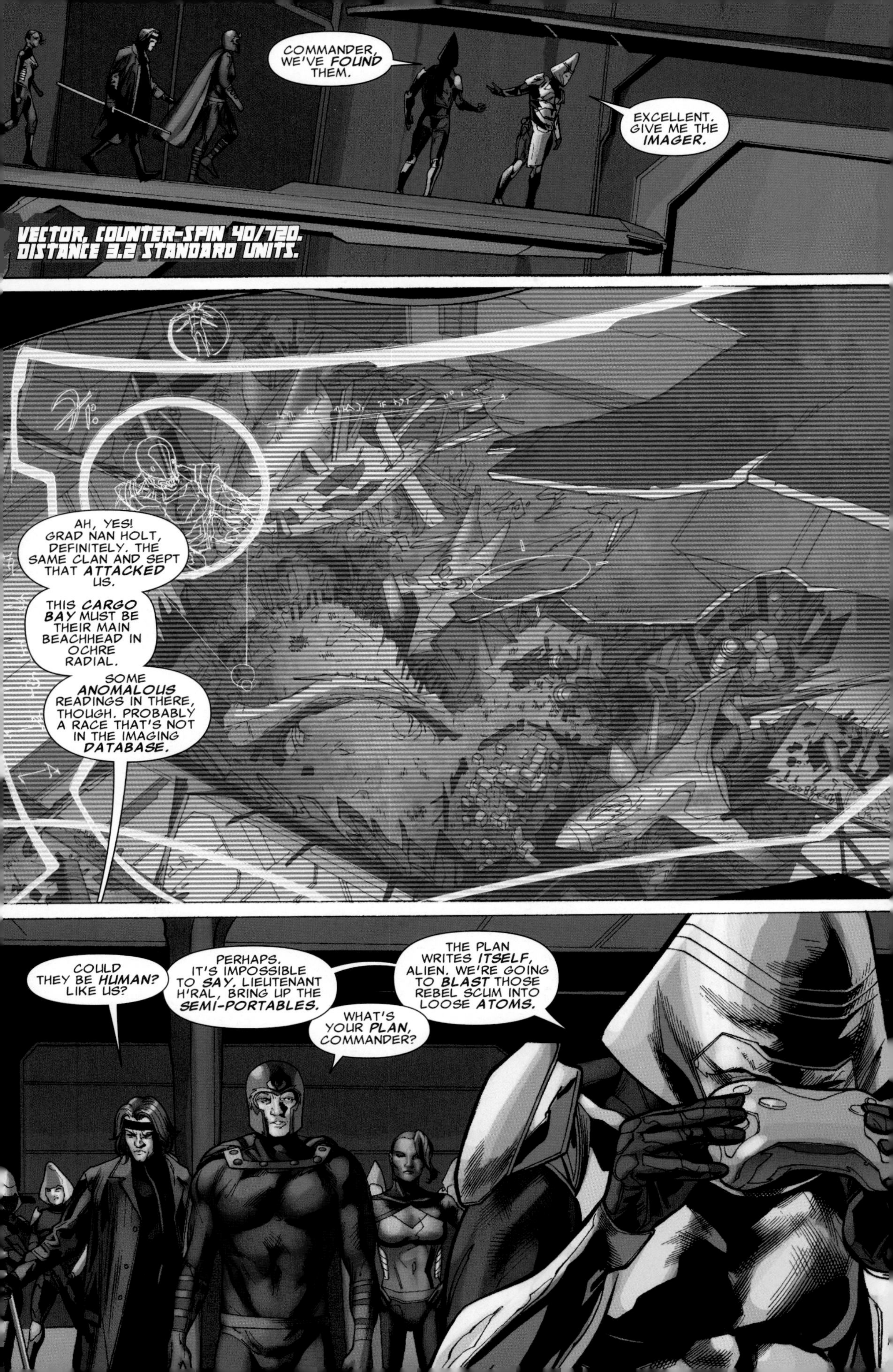

COMMANDER, WE'VE FOUND THEM.
EXCELLENT. GIVE ME THE IMAGER.
VECTOR, COUNTER-SPIN 40/720. DISTANCE 3.2 STANDARD UNITS.
AH, YES! GRAD NAN HOLT, DEFINITELY. THE SAME CLAN AND SEPT THAT ATTACKED US.
THIS CARGO BAY MUST BE THEIR MAIN BEACHHEAD IN OCHRE RADIAL.
SOME ANOMALOUS READINGS IN THERE, THOUGH. PROBABLY A RACE THAT'S NOT IN THE IMAGING DATABASE.
COULD THEY BE HUMAN? LIKE US?
PERHAPS. IT'S IMPOSSIBLE TO SAY. LIEUTENANT H'RAL, BRING UP THE SEMI-PORTABLES.
WHAT'S YOUR PLAN, COMMANDER?
THE PLAN WRITES ITSELF, ALIEN. WE'RE GOING TO BLAST THOSE REBEL SCUM INTO LOOSE ATOMS.

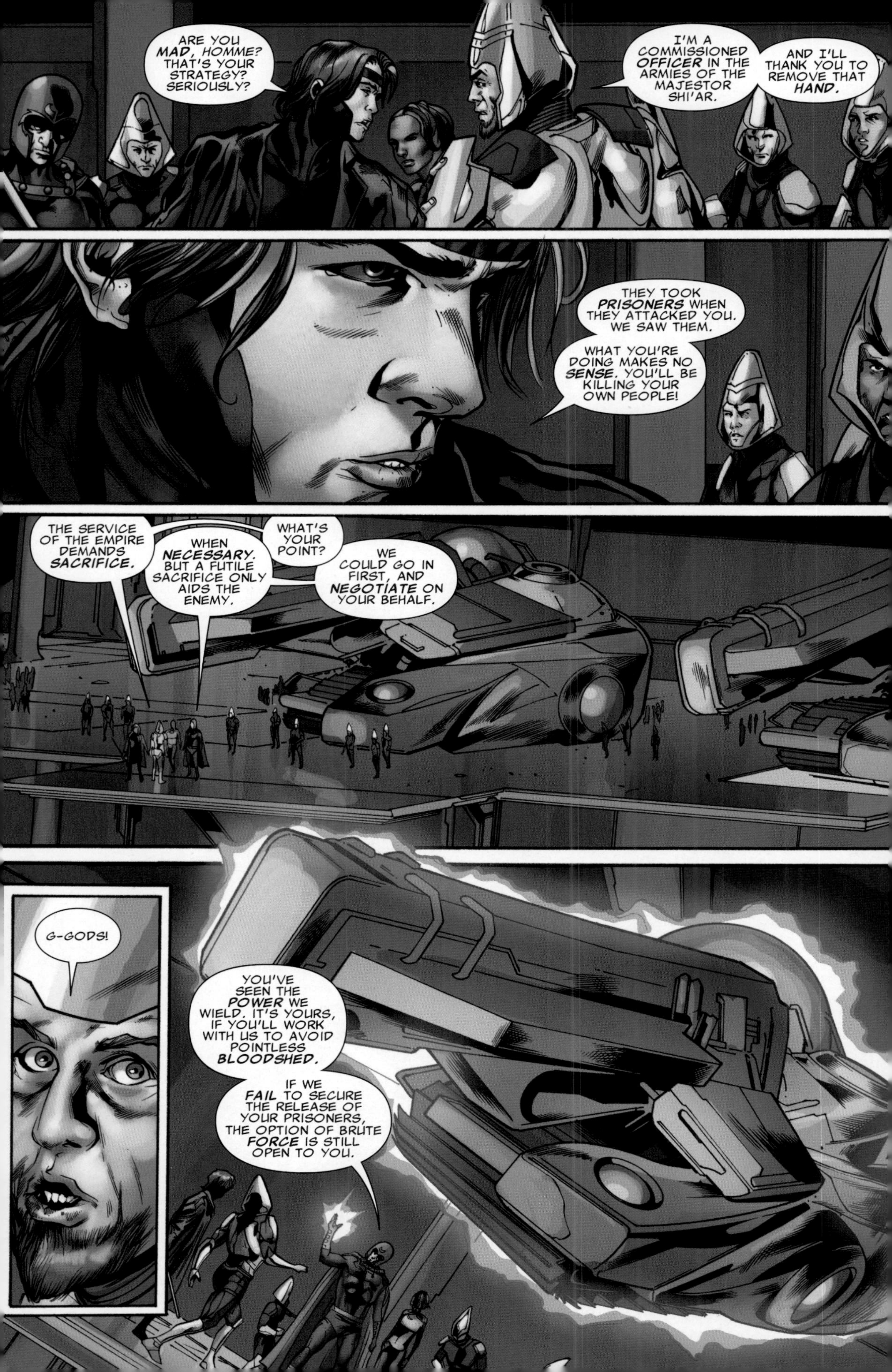

ARE YOU MAD, HOMME? THAT'S YOUR STRATEGY? SERIOUSLY?
I'M A COMMISSIONED OFFICER IN THE ARMIES OF THE MAJESTOR SHI'AR.
AND I'LL THANK YOU TO REMOVE THAT HAND.
THEY TOOK PRISONERS WHEN THEY ATTACKED YOU. WE SAW THEM.
WHAT YOU'RE DOING MAKES NO SENSE. YOU'LL BE KILLING YOUR OWN PEOPLE!
THE SERVICE OF THE EMPIRE DEMANDS SACRIFICE.
WHEN NECESSARY. BUT A FUTILE SACRIFICE ONLY AIDS THE ENEMY.
WHAT'S YOUR POINT?
WE COULD GO IN FIRST, AND NEGOTIATE ON YOUR BEHALF.
G-GODS!
YOU'VE SEEN THE POWER WE WIELD. IT'S YOURS, IF YOU'LL WORK WITH US TO AVOID POINTLESS BLOODSHED.
IF WE FAIL TO SECURE THE RELEASE OF YOUR PRISONERS, THE OPTION OF BRUTE FORCE IS STILL OPEN TO YOU.

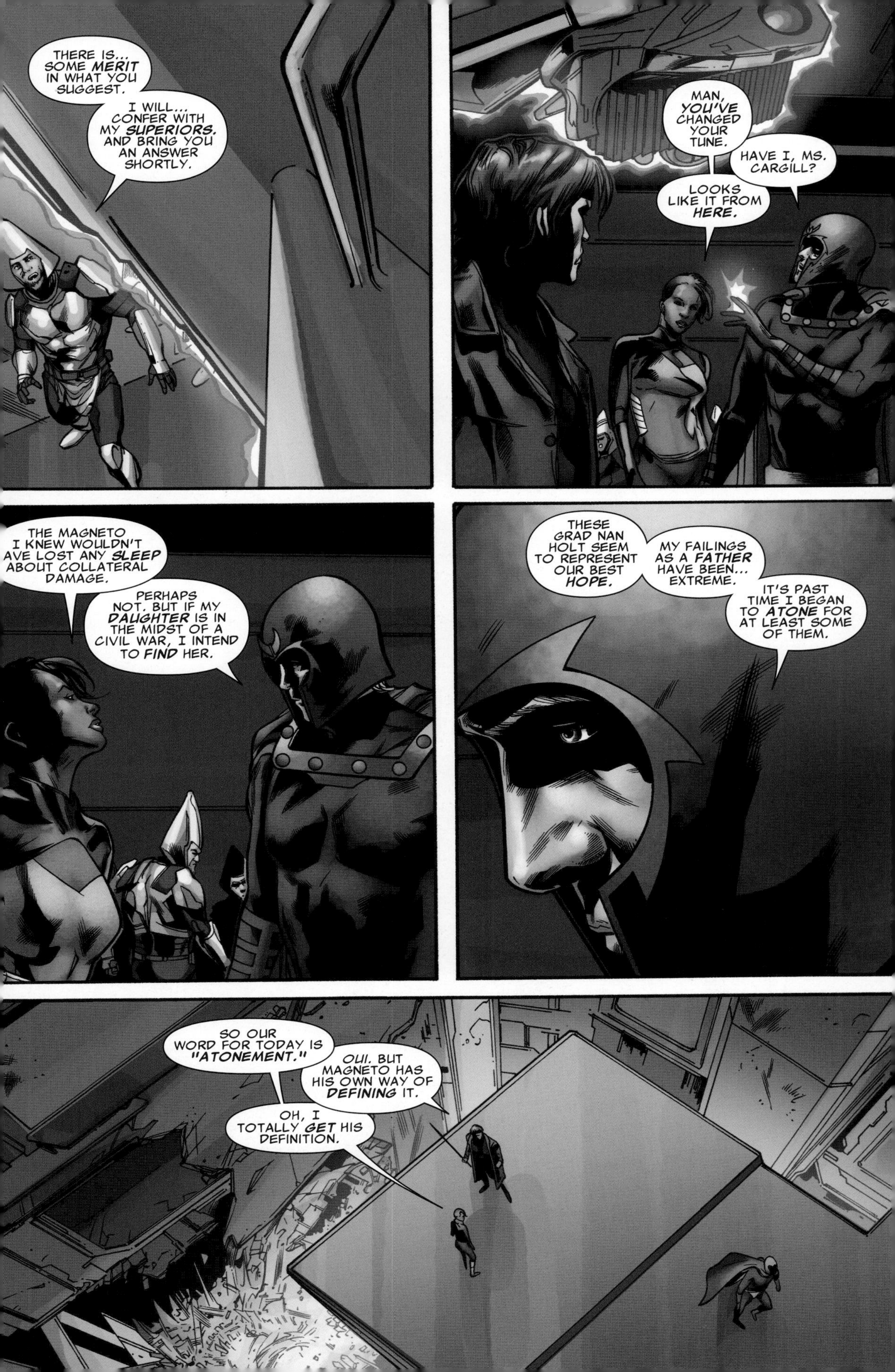
THERE IS... SOME MERIT IN WHAT YOU SUGGEST.
I WILL... CONFER WITH MY SUPERIORS. AND BRING YOU AN ANSWER SHORTLY.
MAN, YOU'VE CHANGED YOUR TUNE.
HAVE I, MS. CARGILL?
LOOKS LIKE IT FROM HERE.
THE MAGNETO I KNEW WOULDN'T AVE LOST ANY SLEEP ABOUT COLLATERAL DAMAGE.
PERHAPS NOT. BUT IF MY DAUGHTER IS IN THE MIDST OF A CIVIL WAR, I INTEND TO FIND HER.
THESE GRAD NAN HOLT SEEM TO REPRESENT OUR BEST HOPE.
MY FAILINGS AS A FATHER HAVE BEEN... EXTREME.
IT'S PAST TIME I BEGAN TO ATONE FOR AT LEAST SOME OF THEM.
SO OUR WORD FOR TODAY IS "ATONEMENT."
OUI. BUT MAGNETO HAS HIS OWN WAY OF DEFINING IT.
OH, I TOTALLY GET HIS DEFINITION.

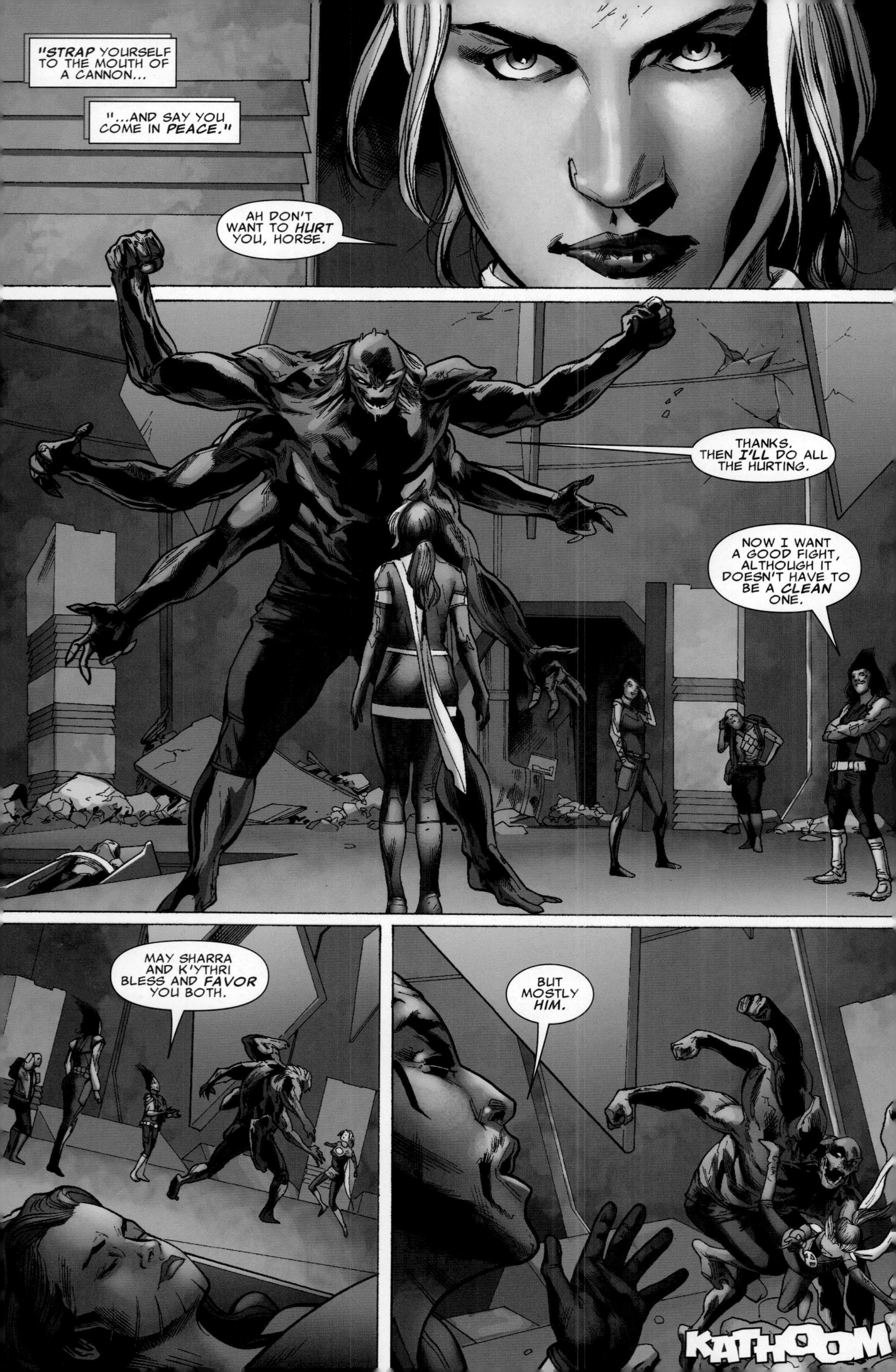
"STRAP YOURSELF TO THE MOUTH OF A CANNON...
"...AND SAY YOU COME IN PEACE."
AH DON'T WANT TO HURT YOU, HORSE.
THANKS. THEN I'LL DO ALL THE HURTING.
NOW I WANT A GOOD FIGHT, ALTHOUGH IT DOESN'T HAVE TO BE A CLEAN ONE.
MAY SHARRA AND K'YTHRI BLESS AND FAVOR YOU BOTH.
BUT MOSTLY HIM.
KATHOOOM

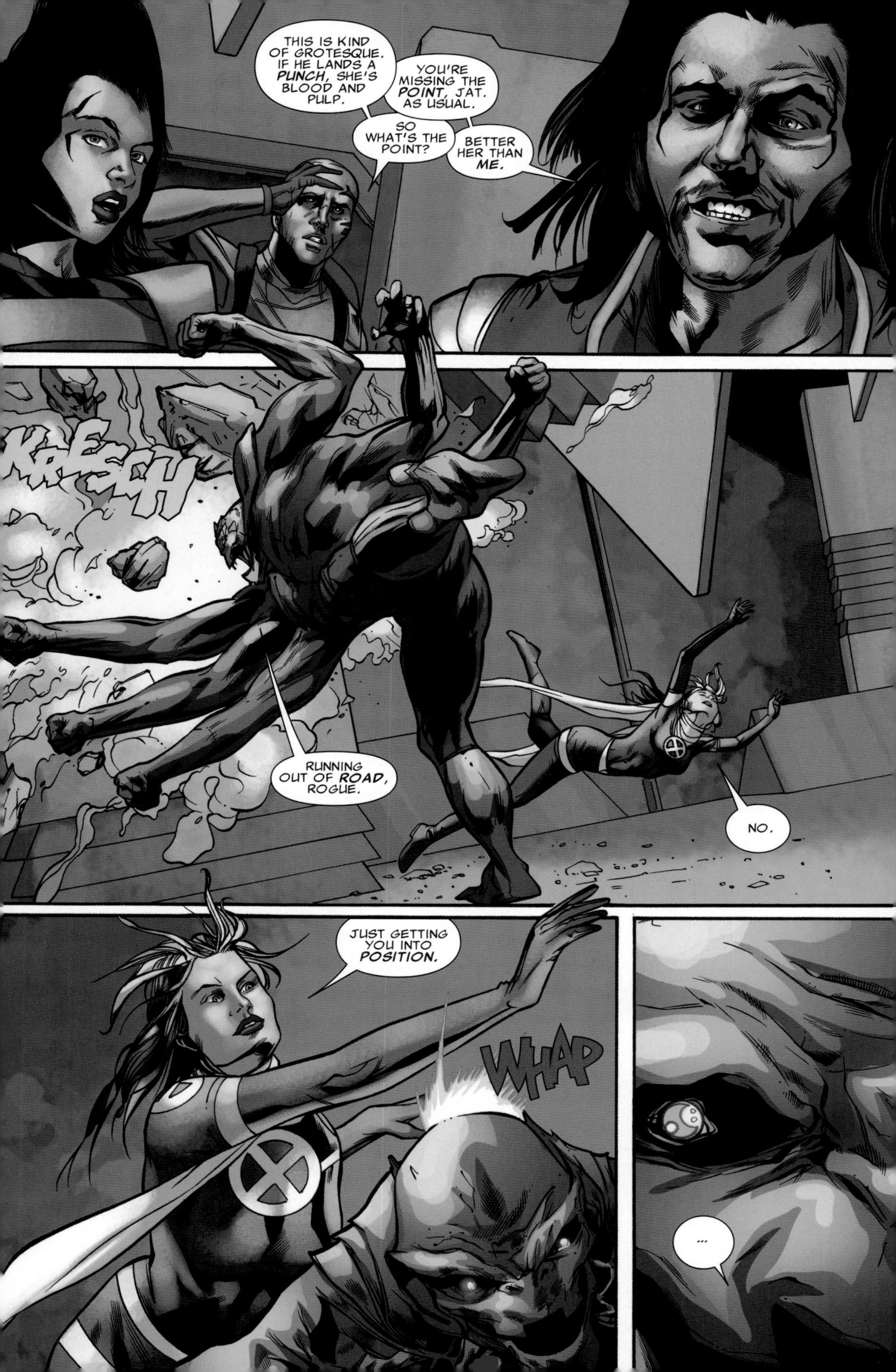
THIS IS KIND OF GROTESQUE. IF HE LANDS A PUNCH, SHE'S BLOOD AND PULP.
YOU'RE MISSING THE POINT, JAT. AS USUAL.
SO WHAT'S THE POINT?
BETTER HER THAN ME.
KRESCH
RUNNING OUT OF ROAD, ROGUE.
NO.
JUST GETTING YOU INTO POSITION.
WHAP
...

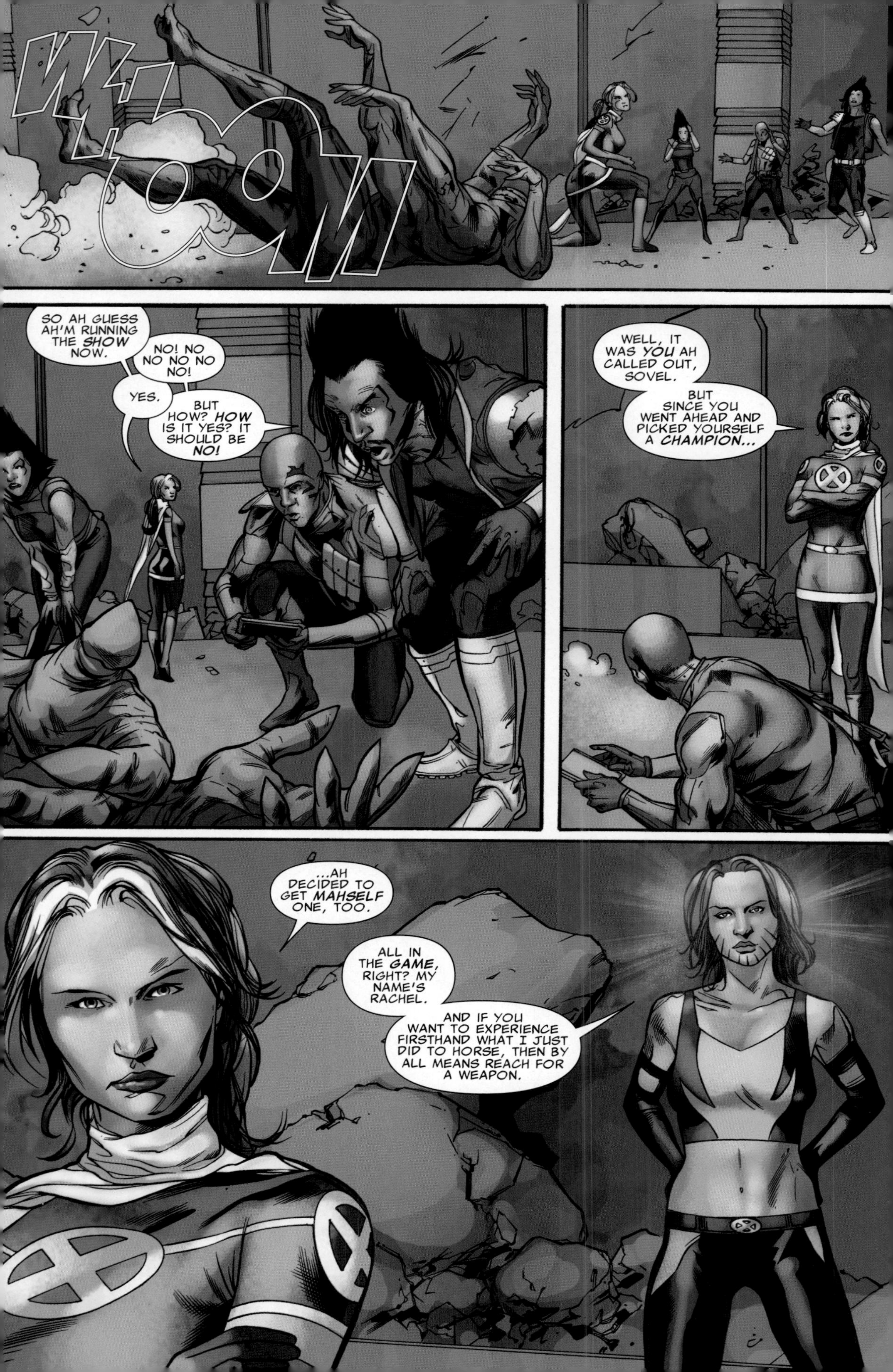
WHOOM
SO AH GUESS AH'M RUNNING THE SHOW NOW.
NO! NO NO NO NO NO!
YES.
BUT HOW? HOW IS IT YES? IT SHOULD BE NO!
WELL, IT WAS YOU AH CALLED OUT, SOVEL.
BUT SINCE YOU WENT AHEAD AND PICKED YOURSELF A CHAMPION...
...AH DECIDED TO GET MAHSELF ONE, TOO.
ALL IN THE GAME, RIGHT? MY NAME'S RACHEL.
AND IF YOU WANT TO EXPERIENCE FIRSTHAND WHAT I JUST DID TO HORSE, THEN BY ALL MEANS REACH FOR A WEAPON.

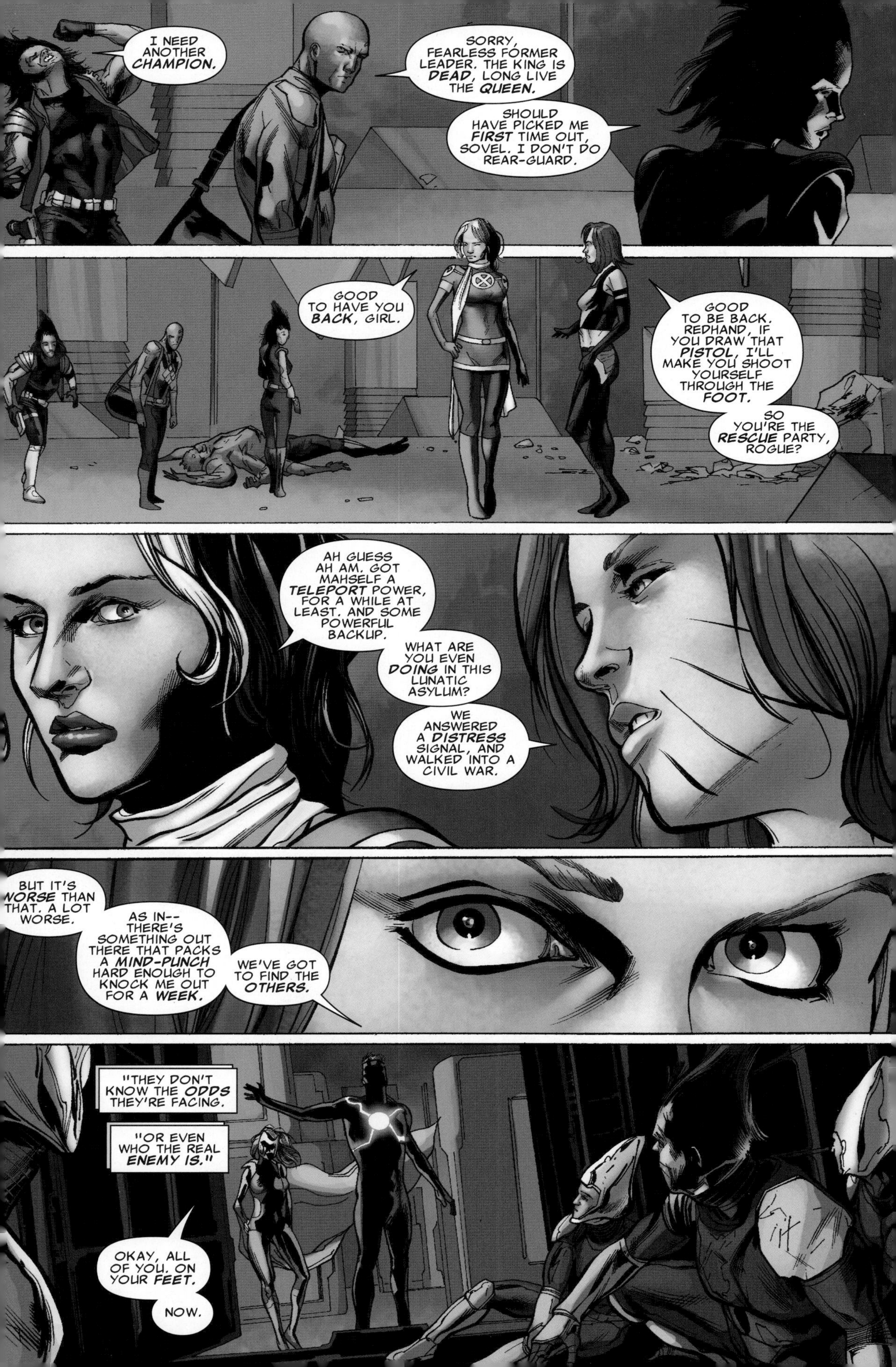
I NEED ANOTHER CHAMPION.
SORRY, FEARLESS FORMER LEADER. THE KING IS DEAD, LONG LIVE THE QUEEN.
SHOULD HAVE PICKED ME FIRST TIME OUT, SOVEL. I DON'T DO REAR-GUARD.
GOOD TO HAVE YOU BACK, GIRL.
GOOD TO BE BACK. REDHAND, IF YOU DRAW THAT PISTOL, I'LL MAKE YOU SHOOT YOURSELF THROUGH THE FOOT.
SO YOU'RE THE RESCUE PARTY, ROGUE?
AH GUESS AH AM. GOT MAHSELF A TELEPORT POWER, FOR A WHILE AT LEAST. AND SOME POWERFUL BACKUP.
WHAT ARE YOU EVEN DOING IN THIS LUNATIC ASYLUM?
WE ANSWERED A DISTRESS SIGNAL, AND WALKED INTO A CIVIL WAR.
BUT IT'S WORSE THAN THAT. A LOT WORSE.
AS IN-- THERE'S SOMETHING OUT THERE THAT PACKS A MIND-PUNCH HARD ENOUGH TO KNOCK ME OUT FOR A WEEK.
WE'VE GOT TO FIND THE OTHERS.
"THEY DON'T KNOW THE ODDS THEY'RE FACING.
"OR EVEN WHO THE REAL ENEMY IS."
OKAY, ALL OF YOU. ON YOUR FEET.
NOW.

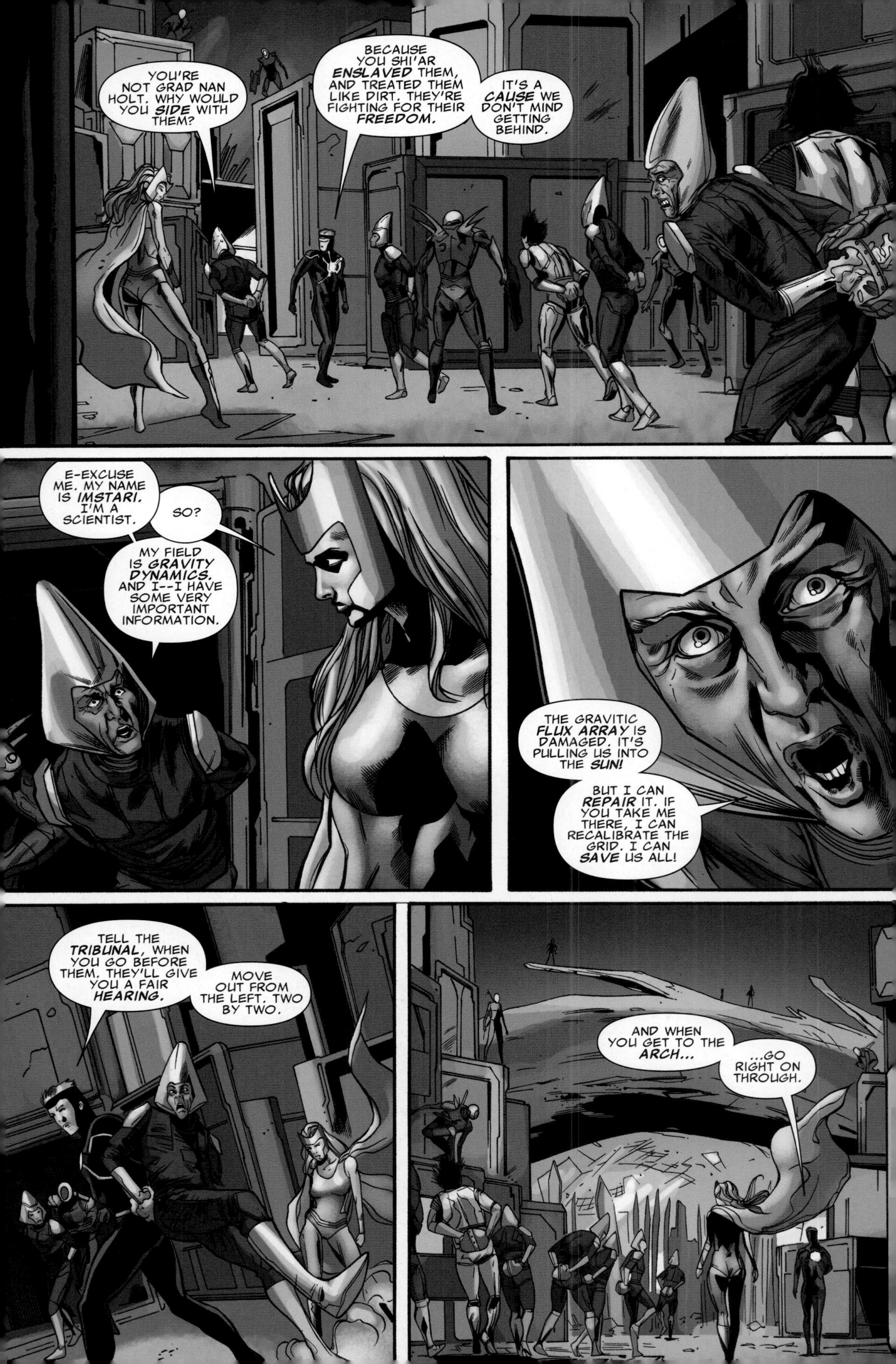

YOU'RE NOT GRAD NAN HOLT. WHY WOULD YOU SIDE WITH THEM?
BECAUSE YOU SHI'AR ENSLAVED THEM, AND TREATED THEM LIKE DIRT. THEY'RE FIGHTING FOR THEIR FREEDOM.
IT'S A CAUSE WE DON'T MIND GETTING BEHIND.
E-EXCUSE ME. MY NAME IS IMSTARI. I'M A SCIENTIST.
SO?
MY FIELD IS GRAVITY DYNAMICS. AND I--I HAVE SOME VERY IMPORTANT INFORMATION.
THE GRAVITIC FLUX ARRAY IS DAMAGED. IT'S PULLING US INTO THE SUN!
BUT I CAN REPAIR IT. IF YOU TAKE ME THERE, I CAN RECALIBRATE THE GRID. I CAN SAVE US ALL!
TELL THE TRIBUNAL, WHEN YOU GO BEFORE THEM. THEY'LL GIVE YOU A FAIR HEARING.
MOVE OUT FROM THE LEFT. TWO BY TWO.
AND WHEN YOU GET TO THE ARCH...
...GO RIGHT ON THROUGH.

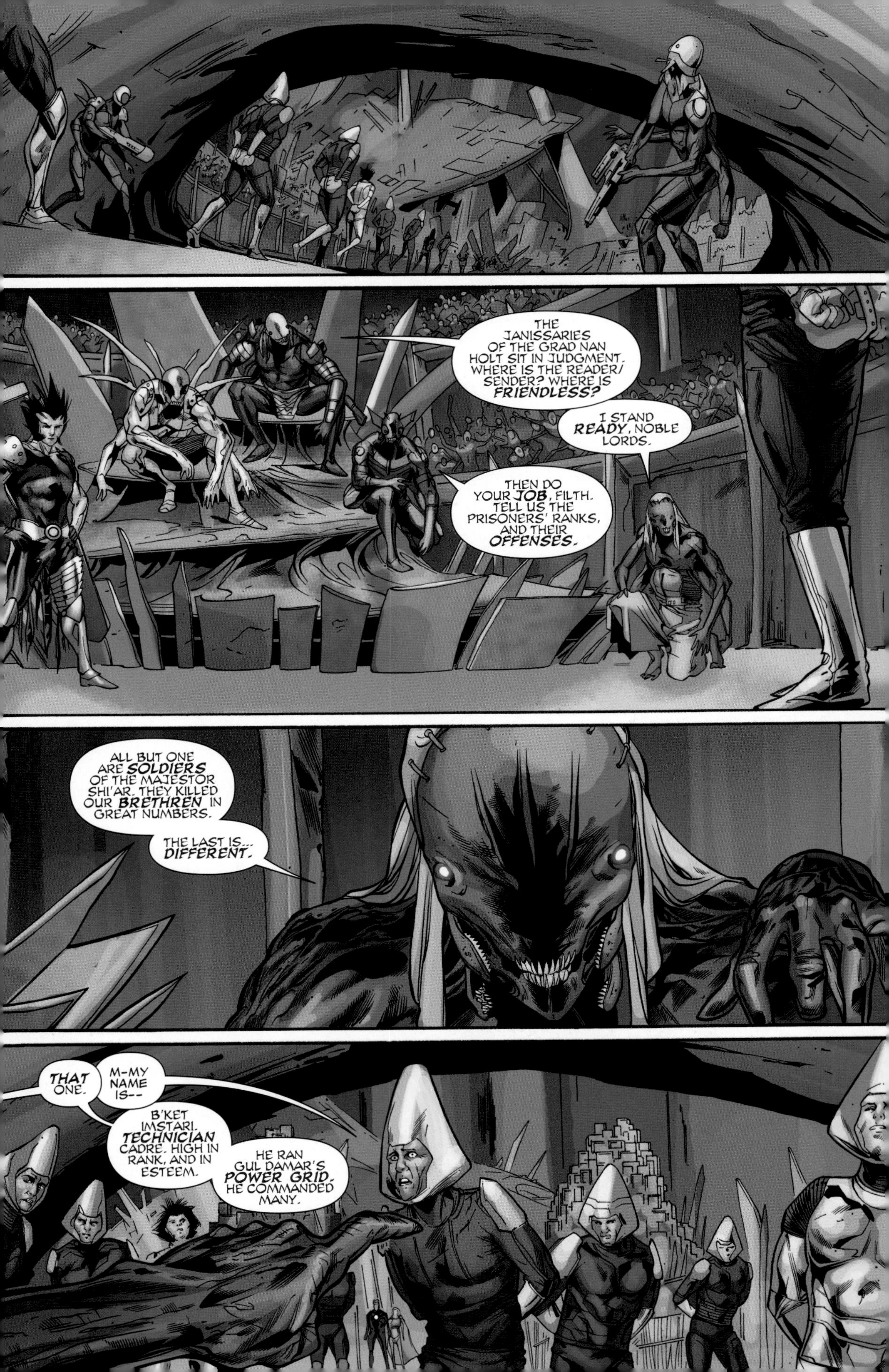

THE JANISSARIES OF THE GRAD NAN HOLT SIT IN JUDGMENT. WHERE IS THE READER/SENDER? WHERE IS FRIENDLESS?
I STAND READY, NOBLE LORDS.
THEN DO YOUR JOB, FILTH. TELL US THE PRISONERS' RANKS, AND THEIR OFFENSES.
ALL BUT ONE ARE SOLDIERS OF THE MAJESTOR SHI'AR. THEY KILLED OUR BRETHREN IN GREAT NUMBERS.
THE LAST IS... DIFFERENT.
THAT ONE.
M-MY NAME IS--
B'KET IMSTARI. TECHNICIAN CADRE. HIGH IN RANK, AND IN ESTEEM.
HE RAN GUL DAMAR'S POWER GRID. HE COMMANDED MANY.

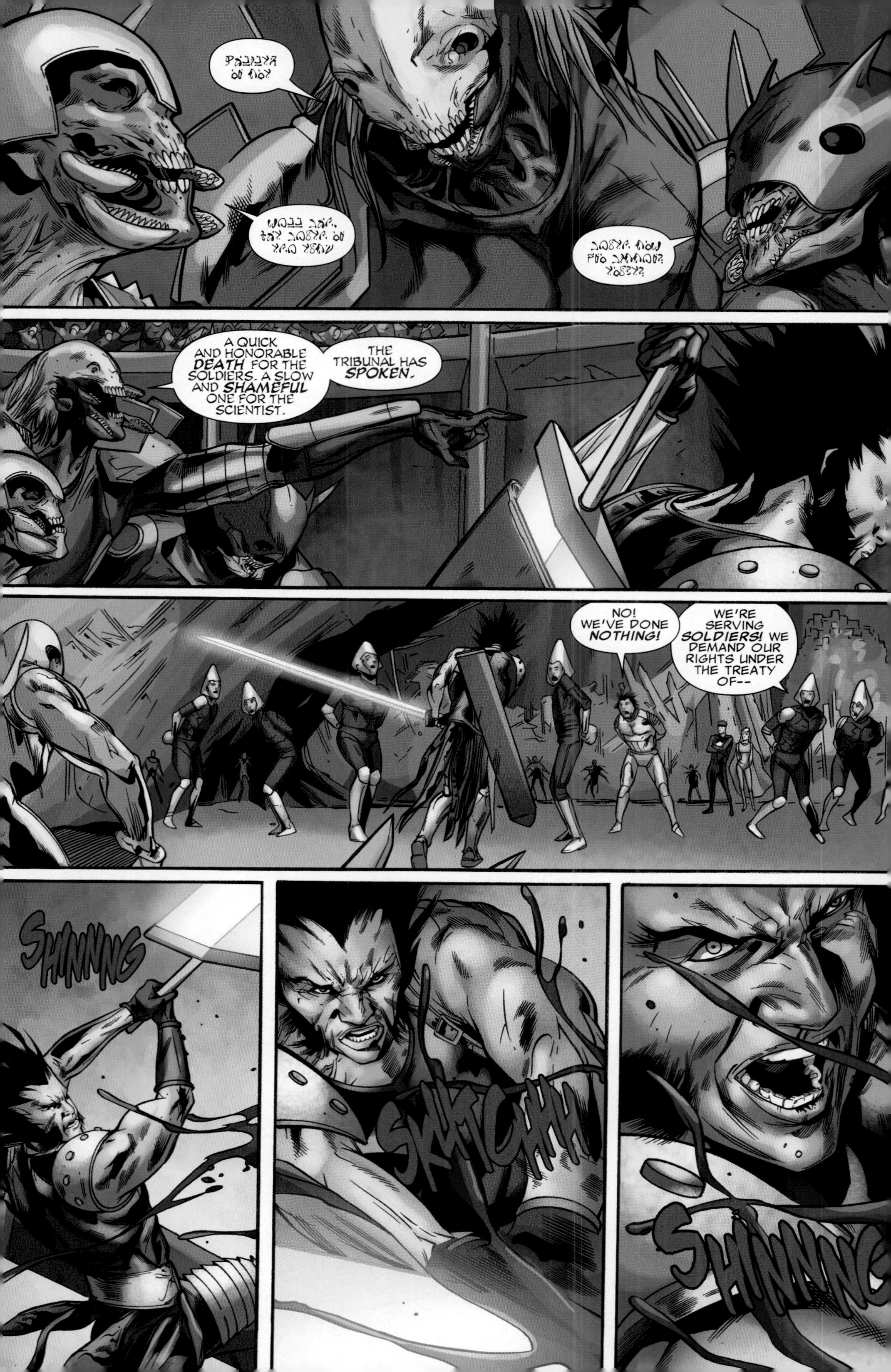
A QUICK AND HONORABLE DEATH FOR THE SOLDIERS. A SLOW AND SHAMEFUL ONE FOR THE SCIENTIST.
THE TRIBUNAL HAS SPOKEN.
NO! WE'VE DONE NOTHING!
WE'RE SERVING SOLDIERS! WE DEMAND OUR RIGHTS UNDER THE TREATY OF--
SHINNNG
SKTCHHH
SHINNNG

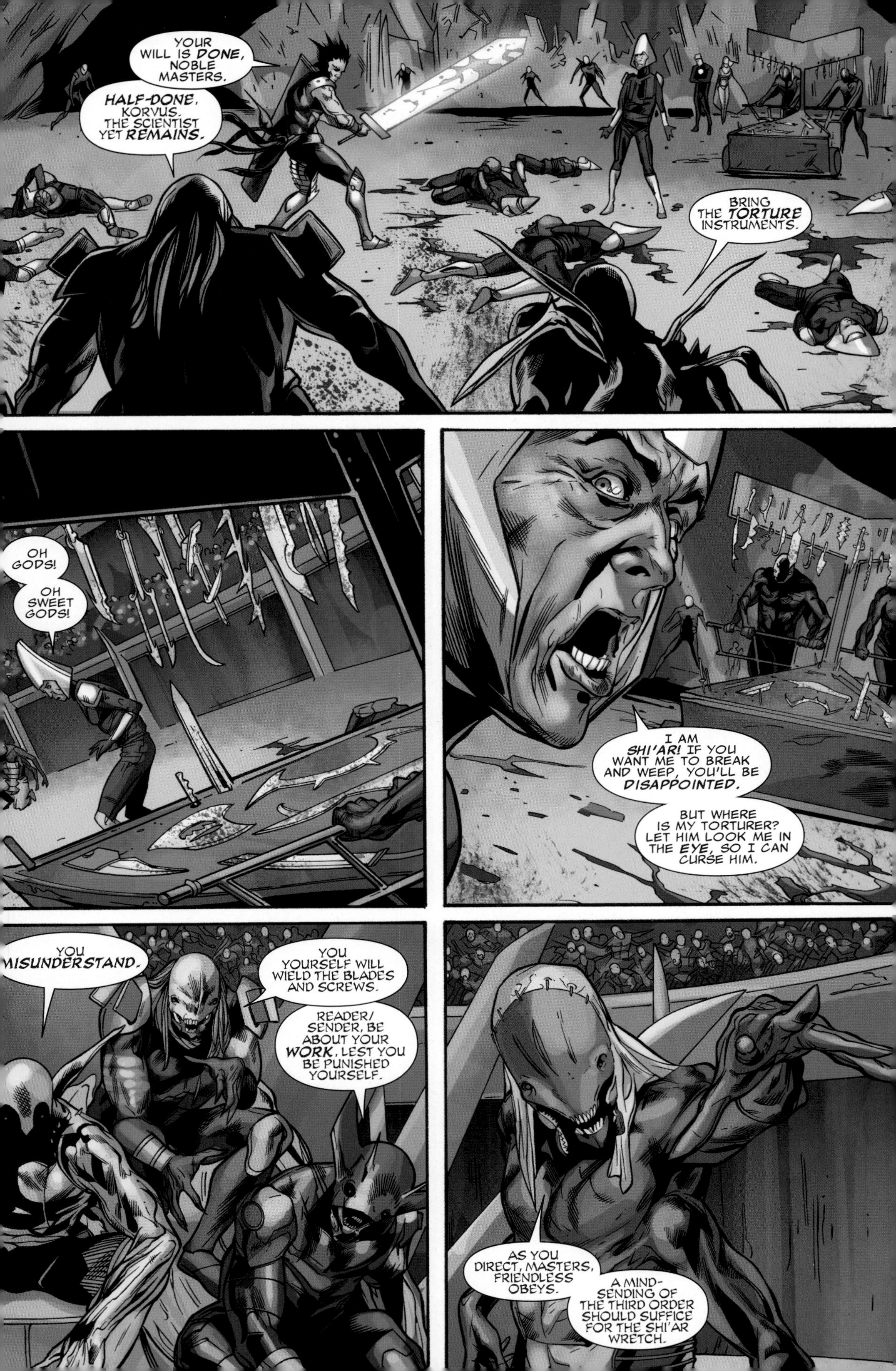
YOUR WILL IS DONE, NOBLE MASTERS.
HALF-DONE, KORVUS. THE SCIENTIST YET REMAINS.
BRING THE TORTURE INSTRUMENTS.
OH GODS!
OH SWEET GODS!
I AM SHI'AR! IF YOU WANT ME TO BREAK AND WEEP, YOU'LL BE DISAPPOINTED.
BUT WHERE IS MY TORTURER? LET HIM LOOK ME IN THE EYE, SO I CAN CURSE HIM.
YOU MISUNDERSTAND.
YOU YOURSELF WILL WIELD THE BLADES AND SCREWS.
READER/ SENDER, BE ABOUT YOUR WORK, LEST YOU BE PUNISHED YOURSELF.
AS YOU DIRECT, MASTERS, FRIENDLESS OBEYS.
A MIND-SENDING OF THE THIRD ORDER SHOULD SUFFICE FOR THE SHI'AR WRETCH.

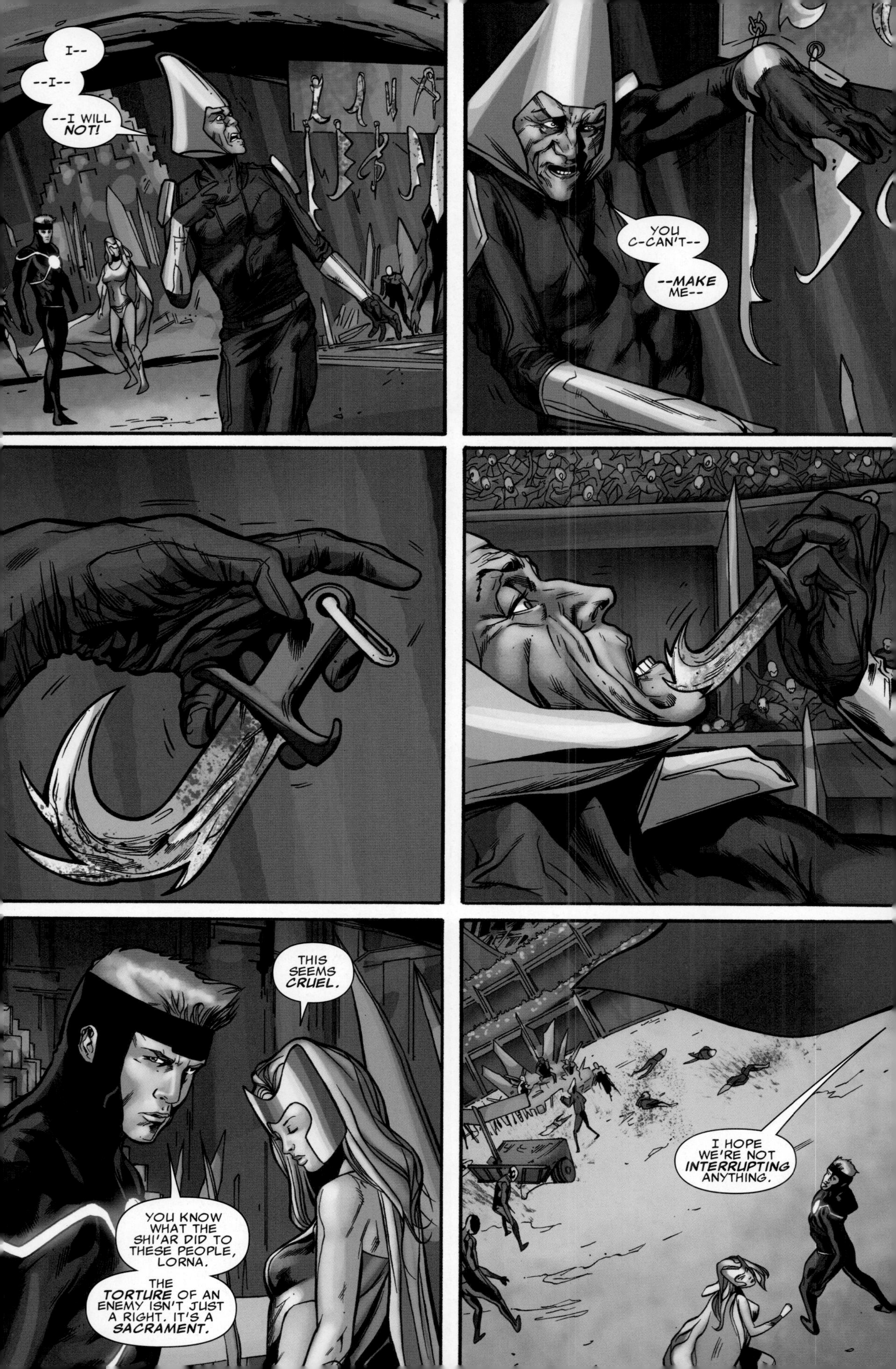
I--
--I--
--I WILL NOT!
YOU C-CAN'T--
--MAKE ME--
THIS SEEMS CRUEL.
YOU KNOW WHAT THE SHI'AR DID TO THESE PEOPLE, LORNA.
THE TORTURE OF AN ENEMY ISN'T JUST A RIGHT. IT'S A SACRAMENT.
I HOPE WE'RE NOT INTERRUPTING ANYTHING.

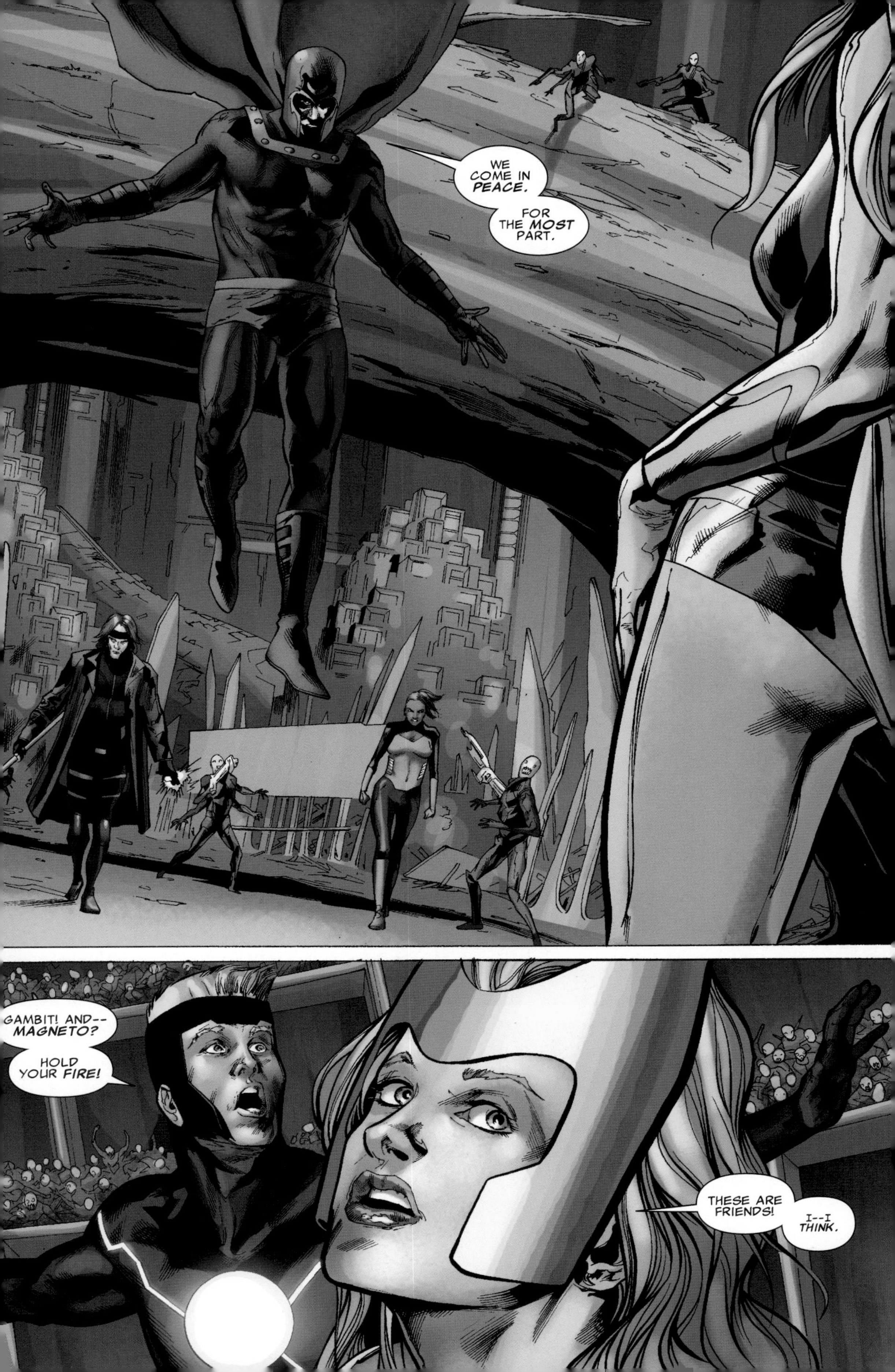
WE COME IN PEACE.
FOR THE MOST PART.
GAMBIT! AND-- MAGNETO?
HOLD YOUR FIRE!
THESE ARE FRIENDS!
I--I THINK.

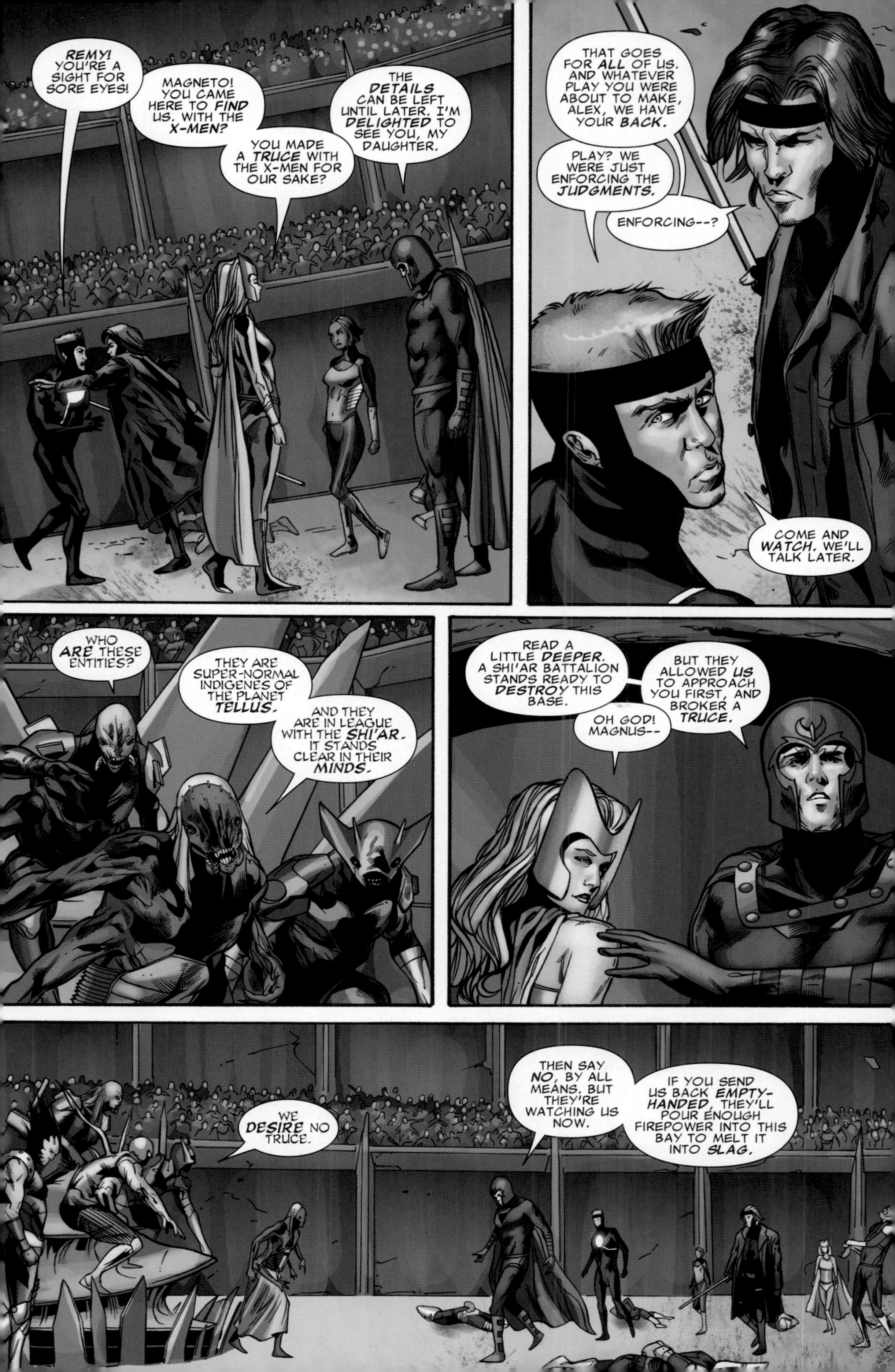
REMY! YOU'RE A SIGHT FOR SORE EYES!
MAGNETO! YOU CAME HERE TO FIND US. WITH THE X-MEN?
YOU MADE A TRUCE WITH THE X-MEN FOR OUR SAKE?
THE DETAILS CAN BE LEFT UNTIL LATER. I'M DELIGHTED TO SEE YOU, MY DAUGHTER.
THAT GOES FOR ALL OF US. AND WHATEVER PLAY YOU WERE ABOUT TO MAKE, ALEX, WE HAVE YOUR BACK.
PLAY? WE WERE JUST ENFORCING THE JUDGMENTS.
ENFORCING--?
COME AND WATCH. WE'LL TALK LATER.
WHO ARE THESE ENTITIES?
THEY ARE SUPER-NORMAL INDIGENES OF THE PLANET TELLUS.
AND THEY ARE IN LEAGUE WITH THE SHI'AR. IT STANDS CLEAR IN THEIR MINDS.
READ A LITTLE DEEPER. A SHI'AR BATTALION STANDS READY TO DESTROY THIS BASE.
BUT THEY ALLOWED US TO APPROACH YOU FIRST, AND BROKER A TRUCE.
OH GOD! MAGNUS--
WE DESIRE NO TRUCE.
THEN SAY NO, BY ALL MEANS. BUT THEY'RE WATCHING US NOW.
IF YOU SEND US BACK EMPTY-HANDED, THEY'LL POUR ENOUGH FIREPOWER INTO THIS BAY TO MELT IT INTO SLAG.

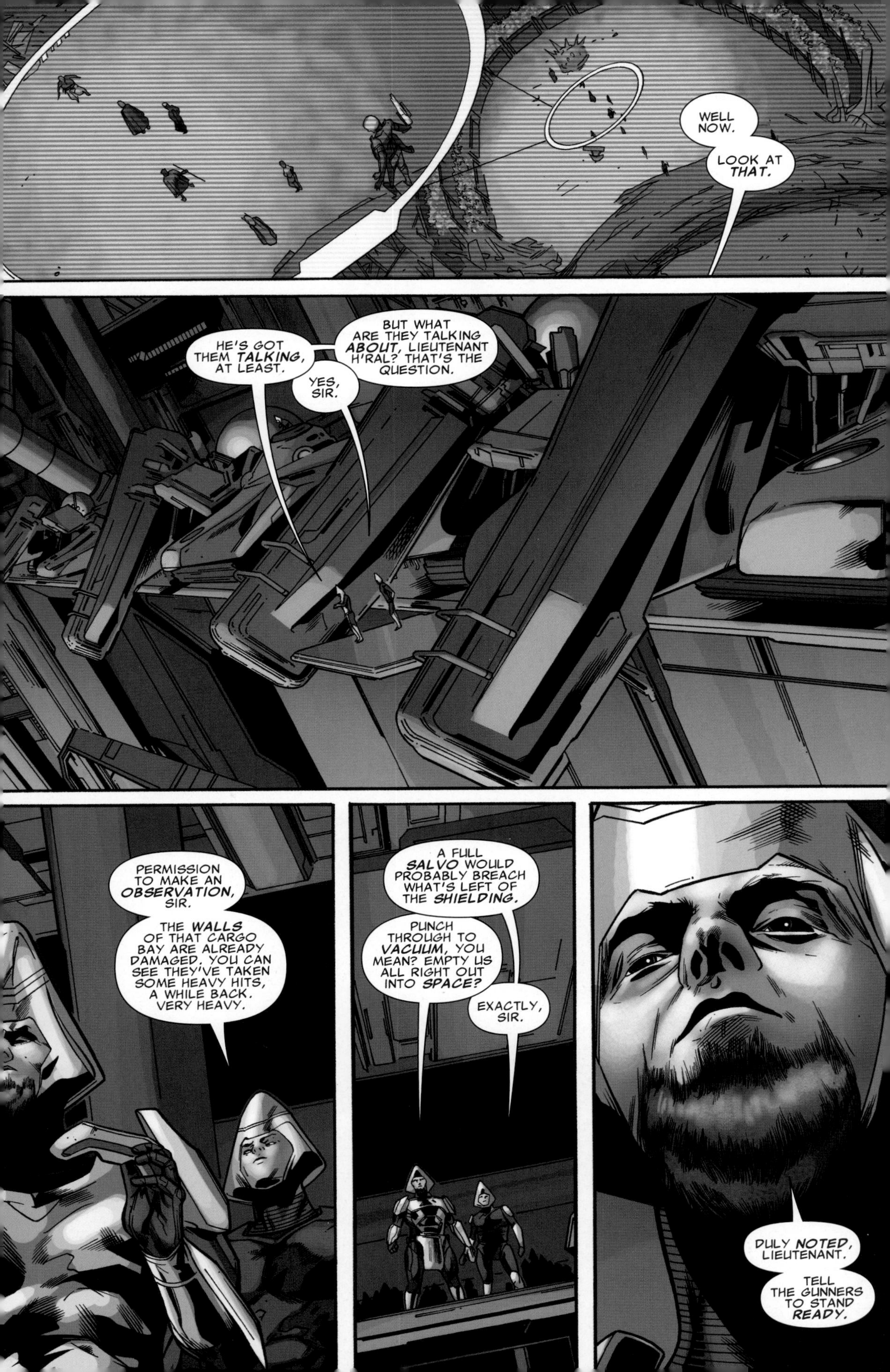
WELL NOW.
LOOK AT THAT.
HE'S GOT THEM TALKING, AT LEAST.
BUT WHAT ARE THEY TALKING ABOUT, LIEUTENANT H'RAL? THAT'S THE QUESTION.
YES, SIR.
PERMISSION TO MAKE AN OBSERVATION, SIR.
THE WALLS OF THAT CARGO BAY ARE ALREADY DAMAGED. YOU CAN SEE THEY'VE TAKEN SOME HEAVY HITS, A WHILE BACK. VERY HEAVY.
A FULL SALVO WOULD PROBABLY BREACH WHAT'S LEFT OF THE SHIELDING.
PUNCH THROUGH TO VACUUM, YOU MEAN? EMPTY US ALL RIGHT OUT INTO SPACE?
EXACTLY, SIR.
DULY NOTED, LIEUTENANT.
TELL THE GUNNERS TO STAND READY.

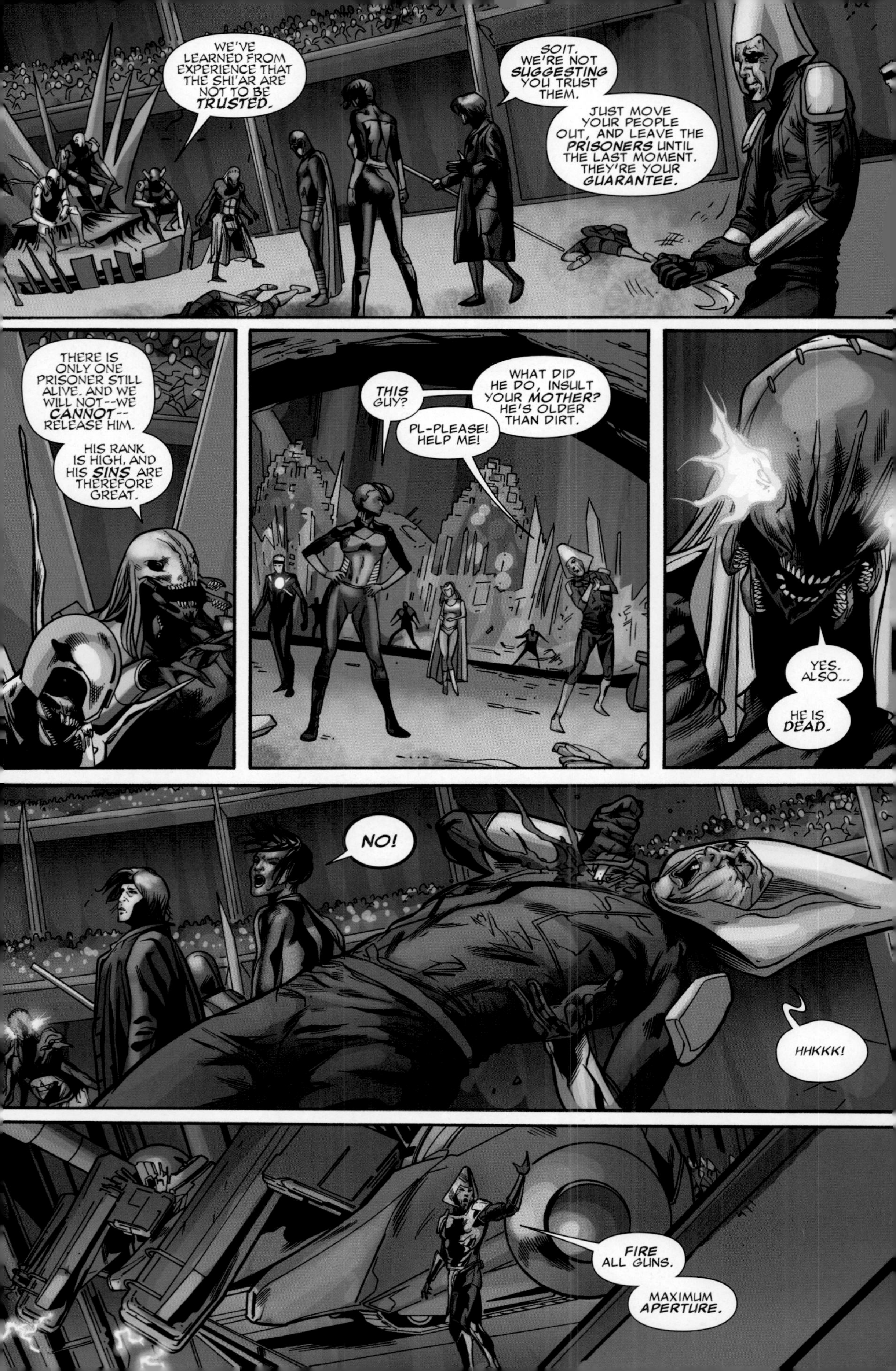
WE'VE LEARNED FROM EXPERIENCE THAT THE SHI'AR ARE NOT TO BE TRUSTED.
SOIT. WE'RE NOT SUGGESTING YOU TRUST THEM.
JUST MOVE YOUR PEOPLE OUT, AND LEAVE THE PRISONERS UNTIL THE LAST MOMENT. THEY'RE YOUR GUARANTEE.
THERE IS ONLY ONE PRISONER STILL ALIVE. AND WE WILL NOT--WE CANNOT--RELEASE HIM.
HIS RANK IS HIGH, AND HIS SINS ARE THEREFORE GREAT.
THIS GUY?
WHAT DID HE DO, INSULT YOUR MOTHER? HE'S OLDER THAN DIRT.
PL-PLEASE! HELP ME!
YES. ALSO...
HE IS DEAD.
NO!
HHKKK!
FIRE ALL GUNS.
MAXIMUM APERTURE.

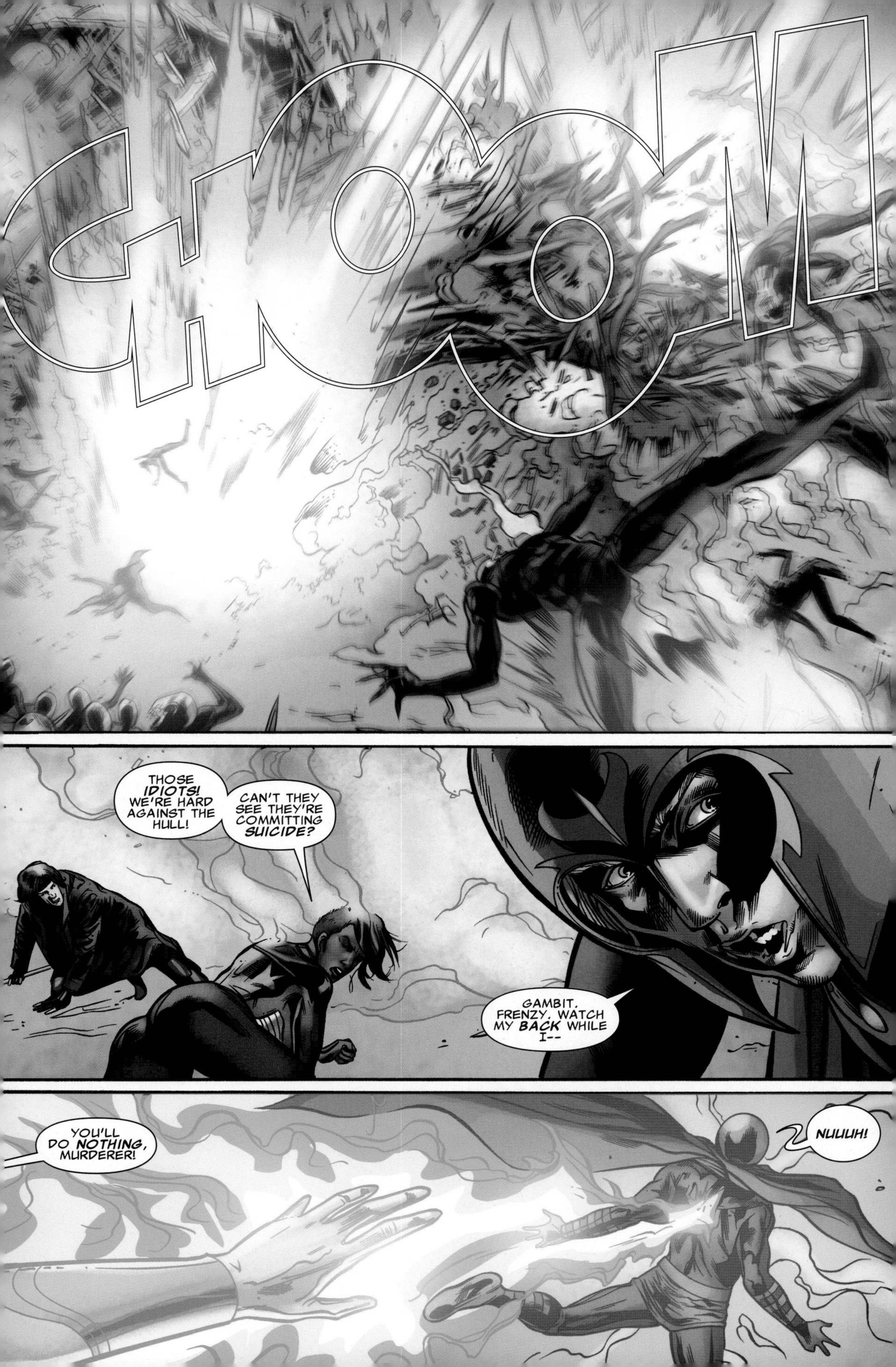
CHOOOM
THOSE IDIOTS! WE'RE HARD AGAINST THE HULL!
CAN'T THEY SEE THEY'RE COMMITTING SUICIDE?
GAMBIT. FRENZY. WATCH MY BACK WHILE I--
YOU'LL DO NOTHING, MURDERER!
NUUUH!

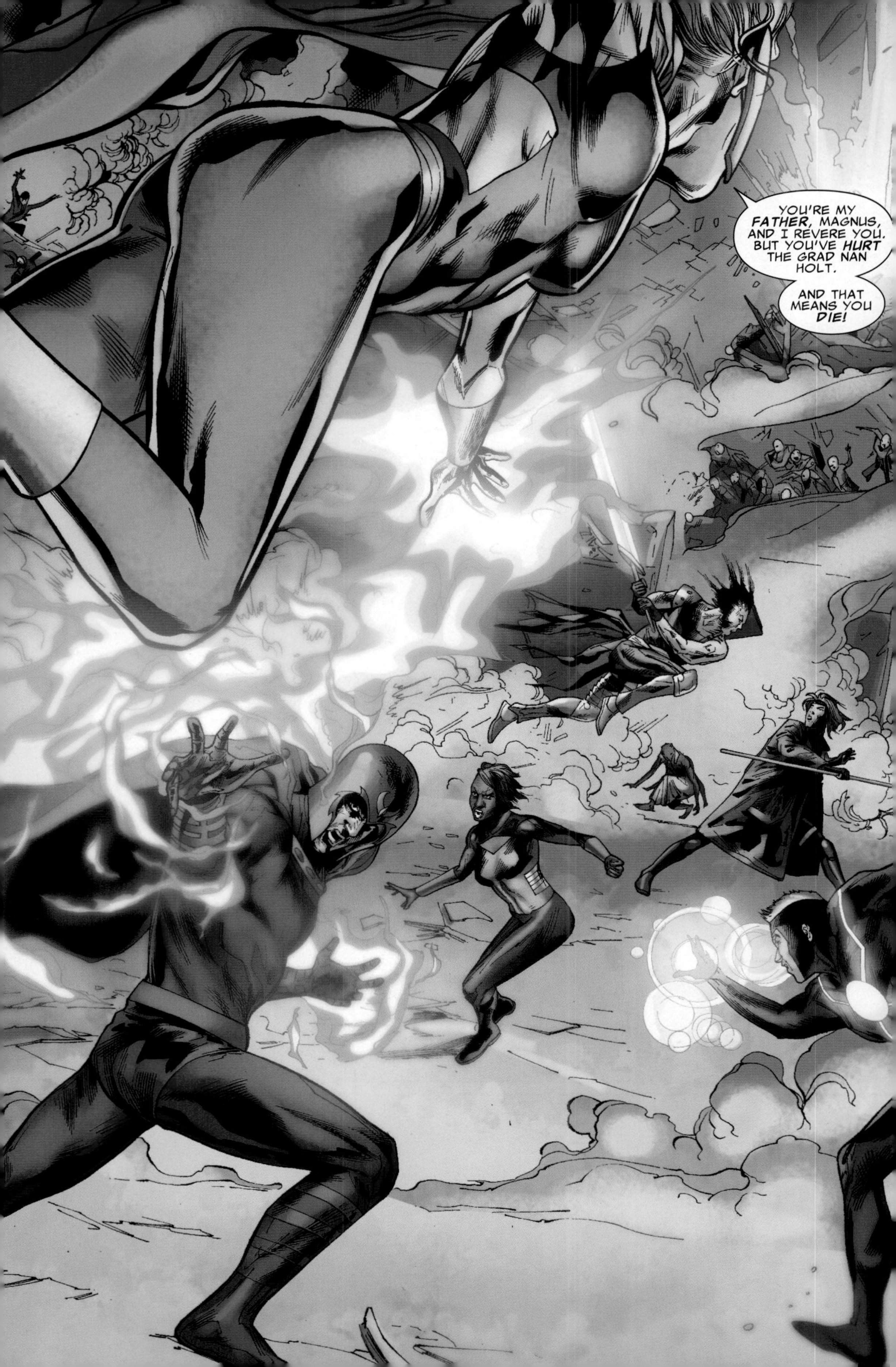
YOU'RE MY **FATHER,** MAGNUS, AND I REVERE YOU. BUT YOU'VE **HURT** THE GRAD NAN HOLT.
AND THAT MEANS YOU **DIE!**

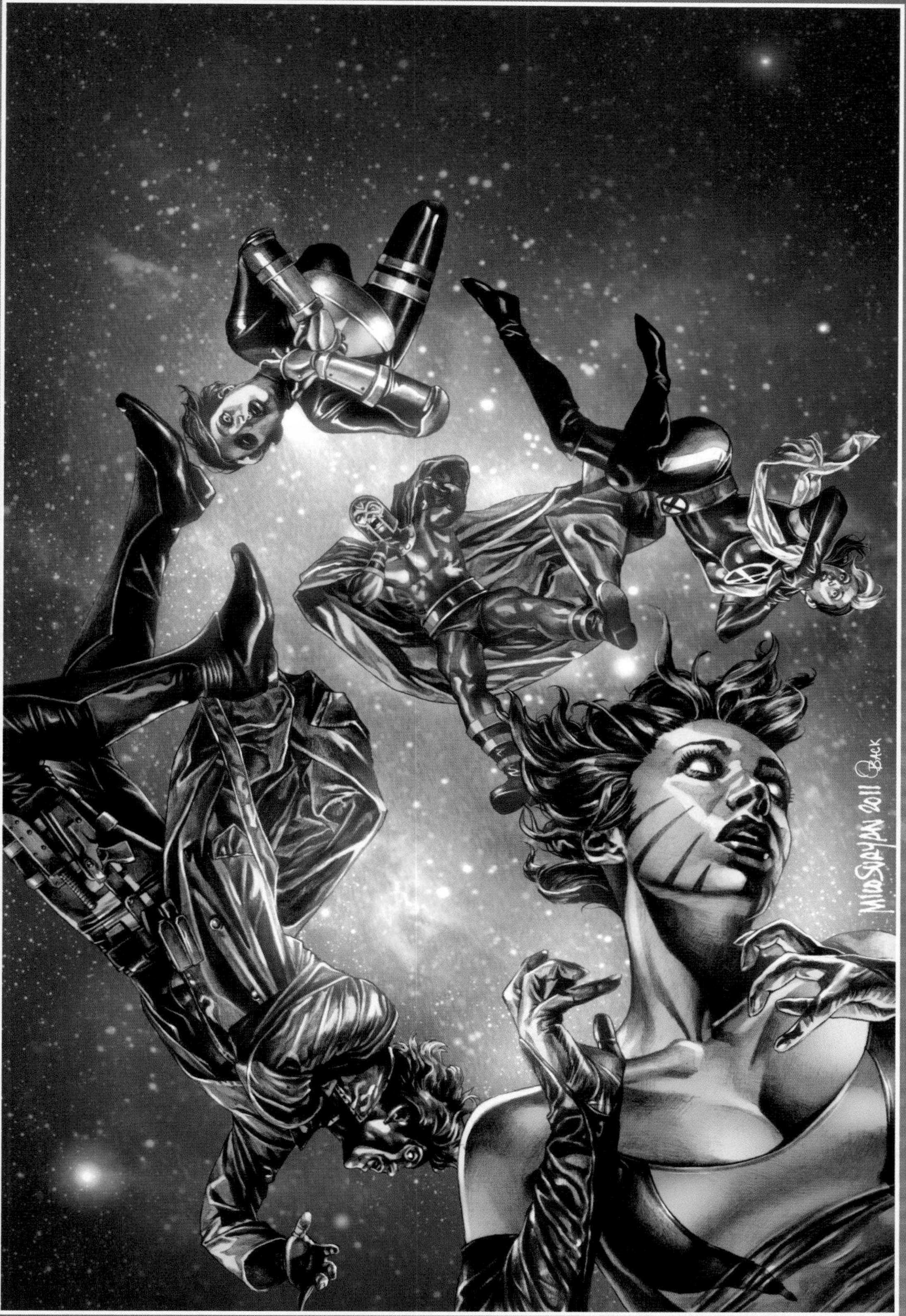

#256
"FIVE MILES SOUTH OF THE UNIVERSE" PART THREE

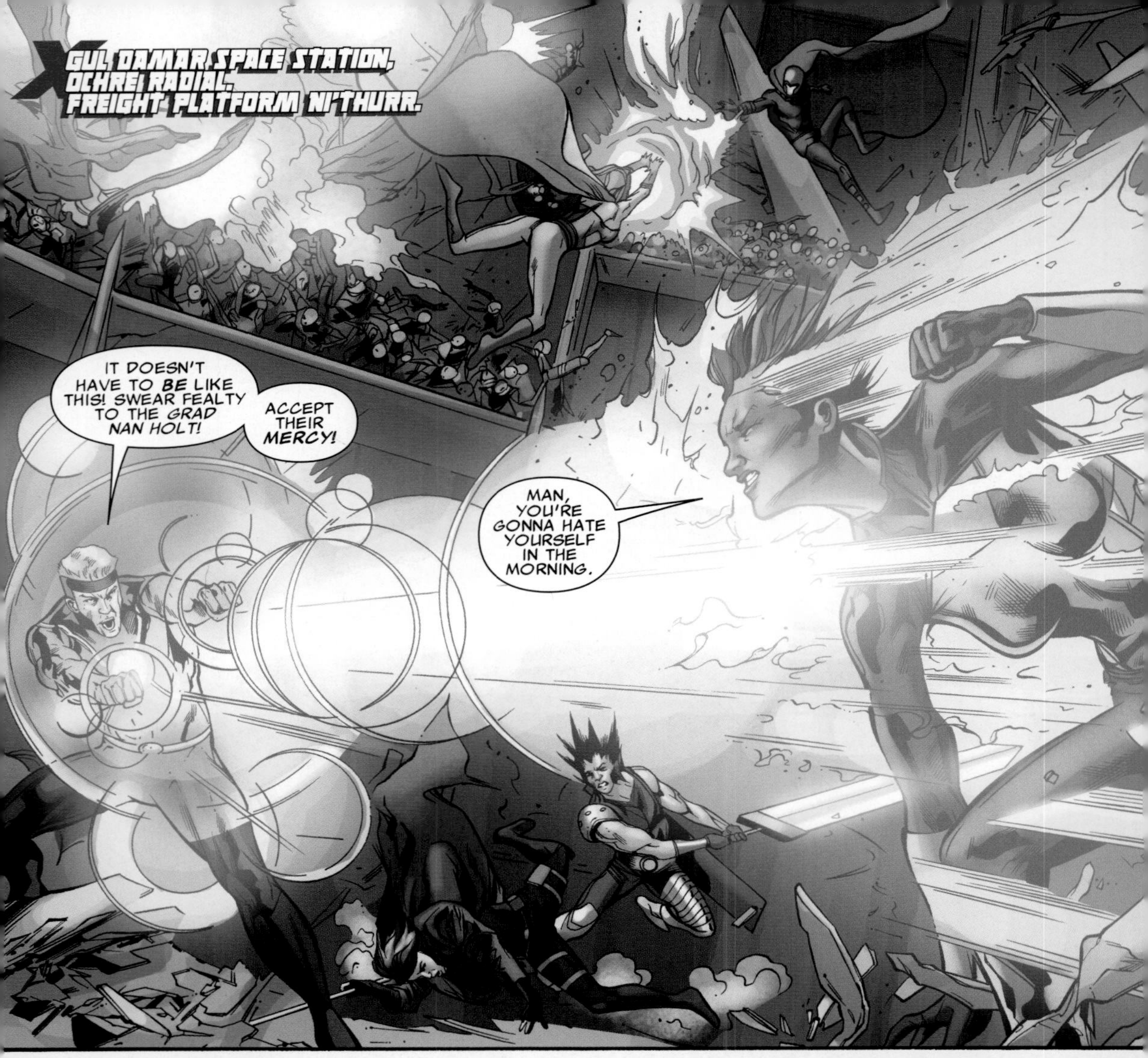
GUL DAMAR SPACE STATION, OCHRE RADIAL. FREIGHT PLATFORM NI'THURR.
IT DOESN'T HAVE TO BE LIKE THIS! SWEAR FEALTY TO THE GRAD NAN HOLT!
ACCEPT THEIR MERCY!
MAN, YOU'RE GONNA HATE YOURSELF IN THE MORNING.

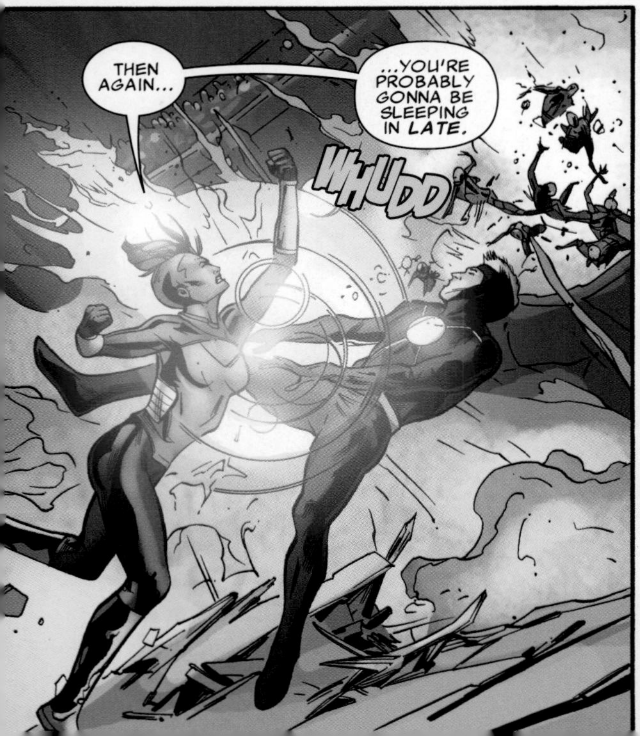
THEN AGAIN...
...YOU'RE PROBABLY GONNA BE SLEEPING IN LATE.
WHUDD

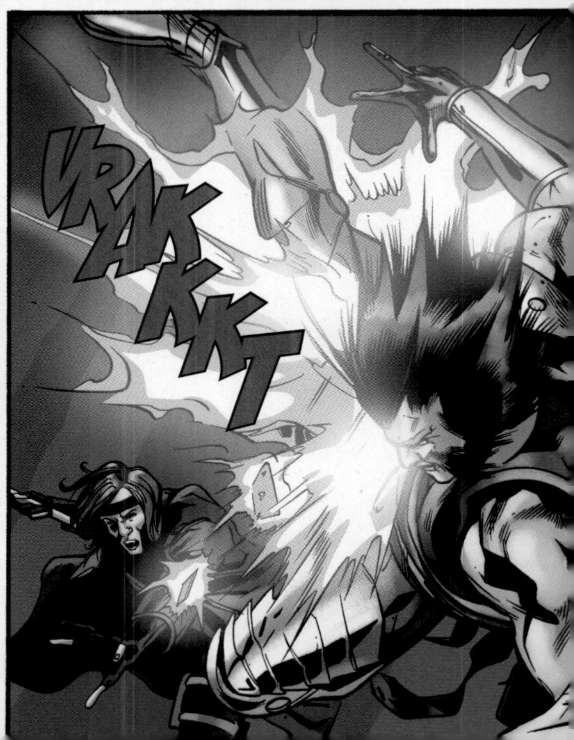
VRAKKKT

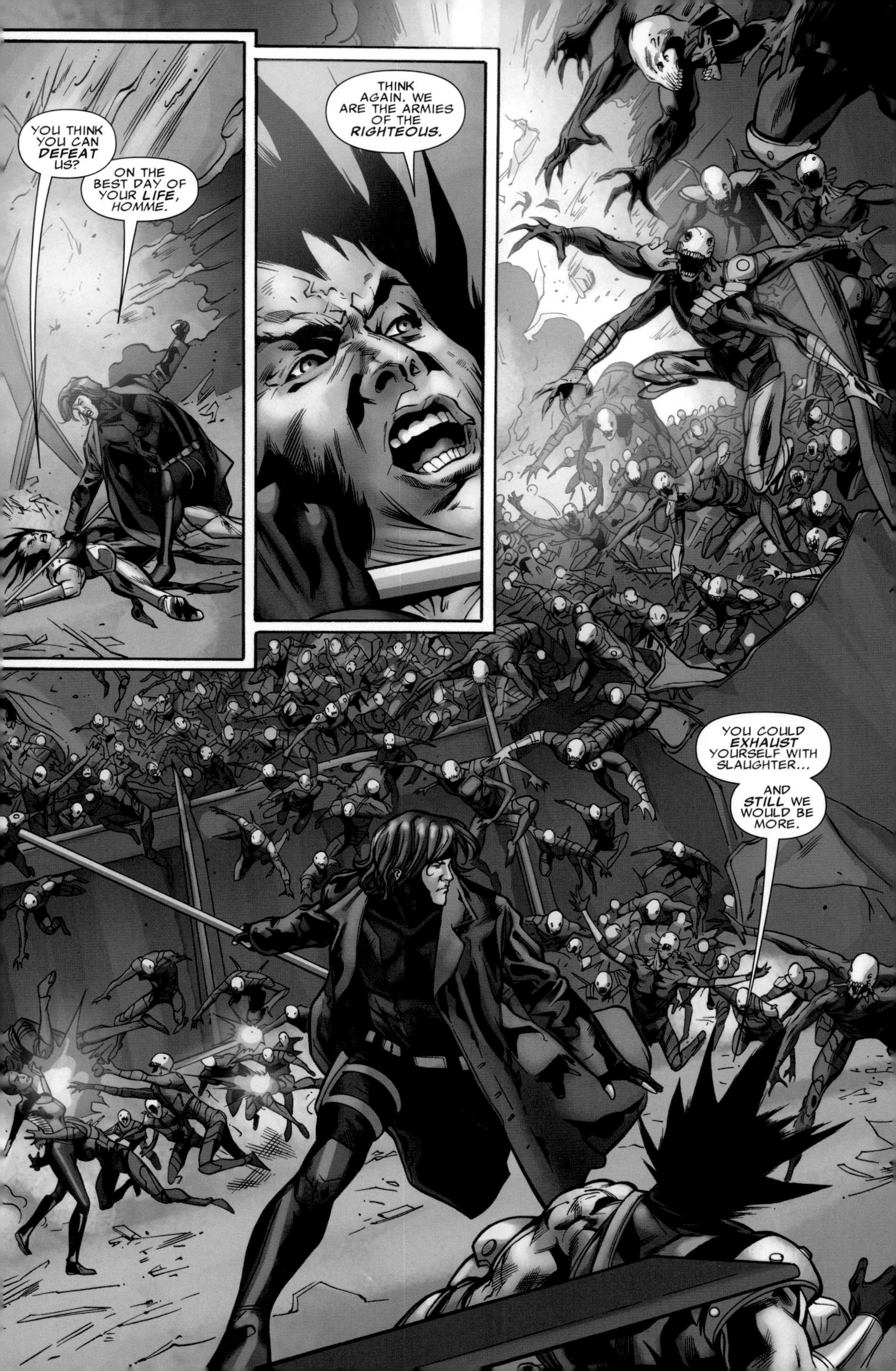

YOU THINK YOU CAN DEFEAT US?
ON THE BEST DAY OF YOUR LIFE, HOMME.
THINK AGAIN. WE ARE THE ARMIES OF THE RIGHTEOUS.
YOU COULD EXHAUST YOURSELF WITH SLAUGHTER...
AND STILL WE WOULD BE MORE.

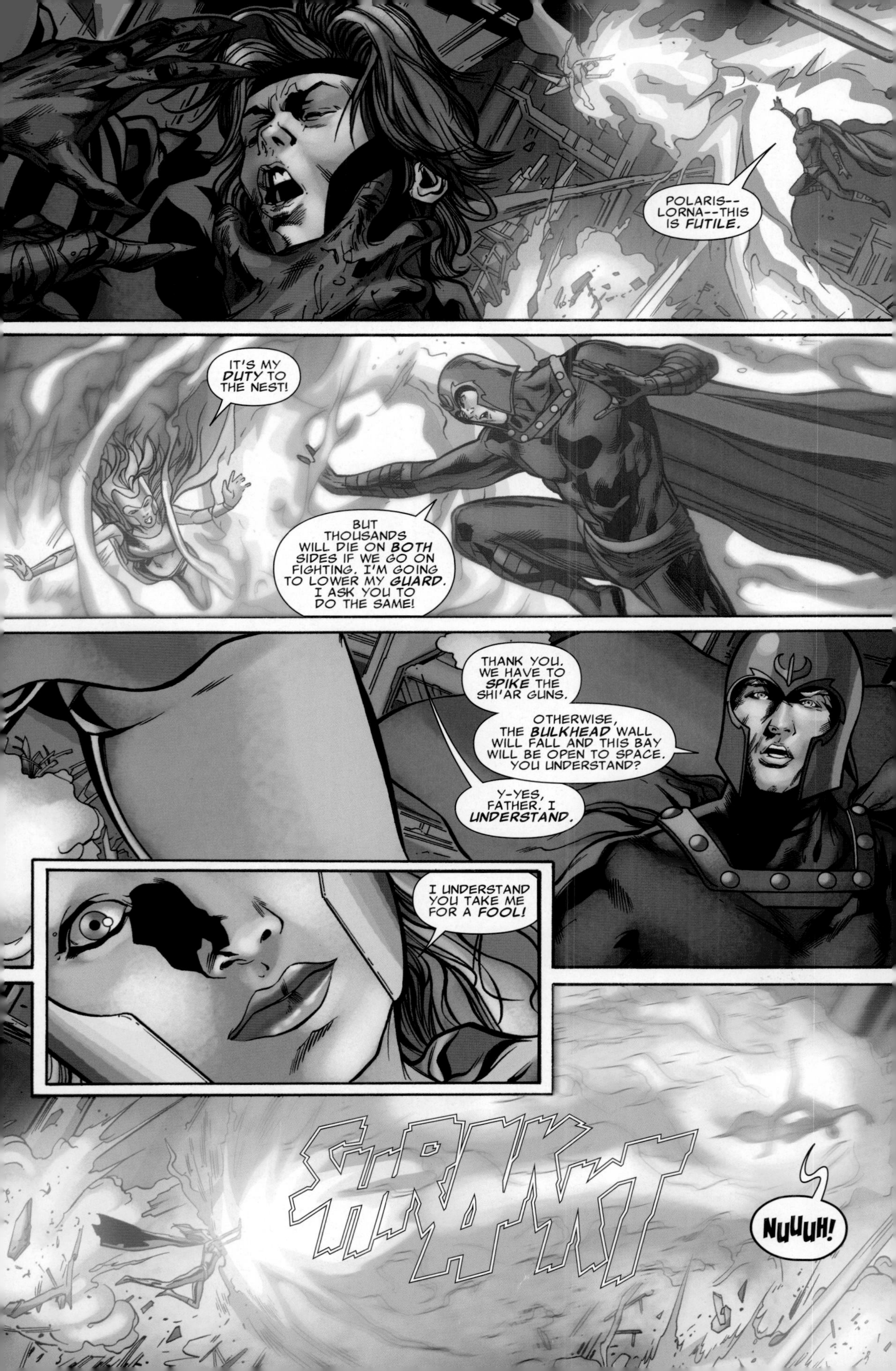
POLARIS--LORNA--THIS IS FUTILE.
IT'S MY DUTY TO THE NEST!
BUT THOUSANDS WILL DIE ON BOTH SIDES IF WE GO ON FIGHTING. I'M GOING TO LOWER MY GUARD. I ASK YOU TO DO THE SAME!
THANK YOU. WE HAVE TO SPIKE THE SHI'AR GUNS.
OTHERWISE, THE BULKHEAD WALL WILL FALL AND THIS BAY WILL BE OPEN TO SPACE. YOU UNDERSTAND?
Y-YES, FATHER. I UNDERSTAND.
I UNDERSTAND YOU TAKE ME FOR A FOOL!
NUUUH!

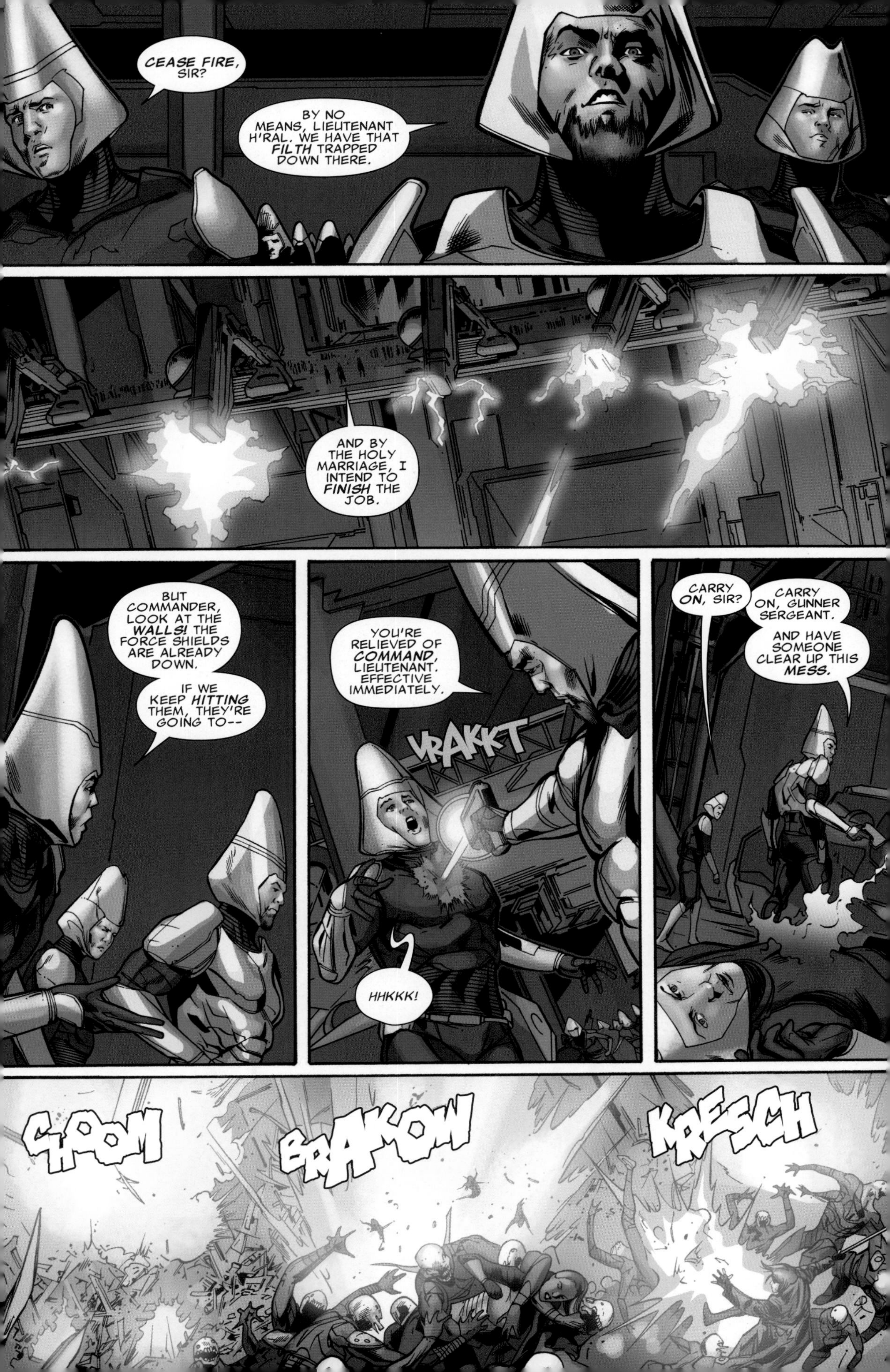

CEASE FIRE, SIR?
BY NO MEANS, LIEUTENANT H'RAL. WE HAVE THAT FILTH TRAPPED DOWN THERE.
AND BY THE HOLY MARRIAGE, I INTEND TO FINISH THE JOB.
BUT COMMANDER, LOOK AT THE WALLS! THE FORCE SHIELDS ARE ALREADY DOWN.
IF WE KEEP HITTING THEM, THEY'RE GOING TO--
YOU'RE RELIEVED OF COMMAND, LIEUTENANT. EFFECTIVE IMMEDIATELY.
VRAKKT
HHKKK!
CARRY ON, SIR?
CARRY ON, GUNNER SERGEANT.
AND HAVE SOMEONE CLEAR UP THIS MESS.
CHOOM
BRAKOW
KRESCH

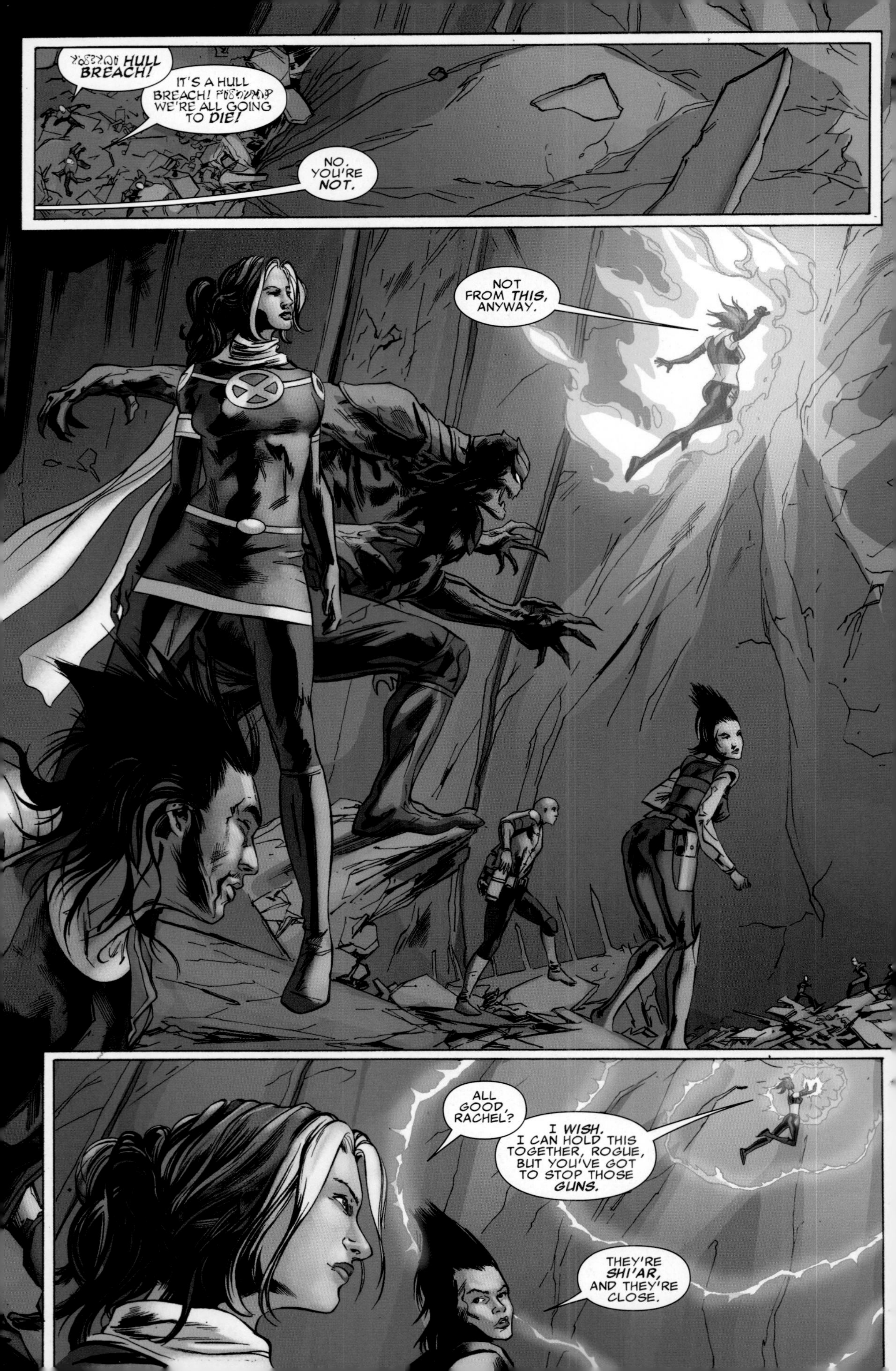
HULL BREACH!
IT'S A HULL BREACH! WE'RE ALL GOING TO DIE!
NO. YOU'RE NOT.
NOT FROM THIS, ANYWAY.
ALL GOOD, RACHEL?
I WISH. I CAN HOLD THIS TOGETHER, ROGUE, BUT YOU'VE GOT TO STOP THOSE GUNS.
THEY'RE SHI'AR, AND THEY'RE CLOSE.

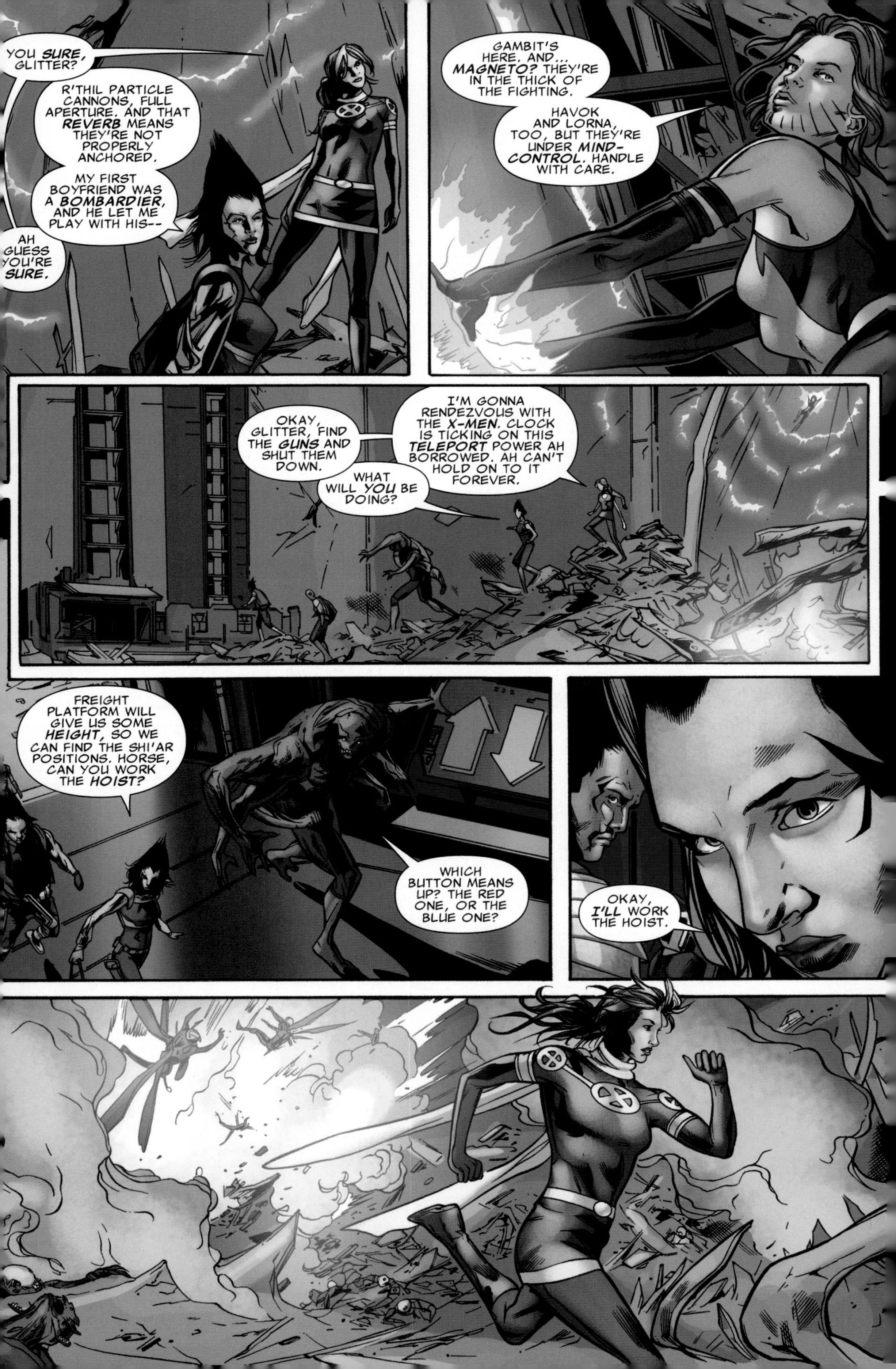
YOU SURE, GLITTER?
R'THIL PARTICLE CANNONS, FULL APERTURE. AND THAT REVERB MEANS THEY'RE NOT PROPERLY ANCHORED.
MY FIRST BOYFRIEND WAS A BOMBARDIER, AND HE LET ME PLAY WITH HIS--
AH GUESS YOU'RE SURE.
GAMBIT'S HERE. AND... MAGNETO? THEY'RE IN THE THICK OF THE FIGHTING.
HAVOK AND LORNA, TOO, BUT THEY'RE UNDER MIND-CONTROL. HANDLE WITH CARE.
OKAY, GLITTER, FIND THE GUNS AND SHUT THEM DOWN.
WHAT WILL YOU BE DOING?
I'M GONNA RENDEZVOUS WITH THE X-MEN. CLOCK IS TICKING ON THIS TELEPORT POWER AH BORROWED. AH CAN'T HOLD ON TO IT FOREVER.
FREIGHT PLATFORM WILL GIVE US SOME HEIGHT, SO WE CAN FIND THE SHI'AR POSITIONS. HORSE, CAN YOU WORK THE HOIST?
WHICH BUTTON MEANS UP? THE RED ONE, OR THE BLUE ONE?
OKAY, I'LL WORK THE HOIST.

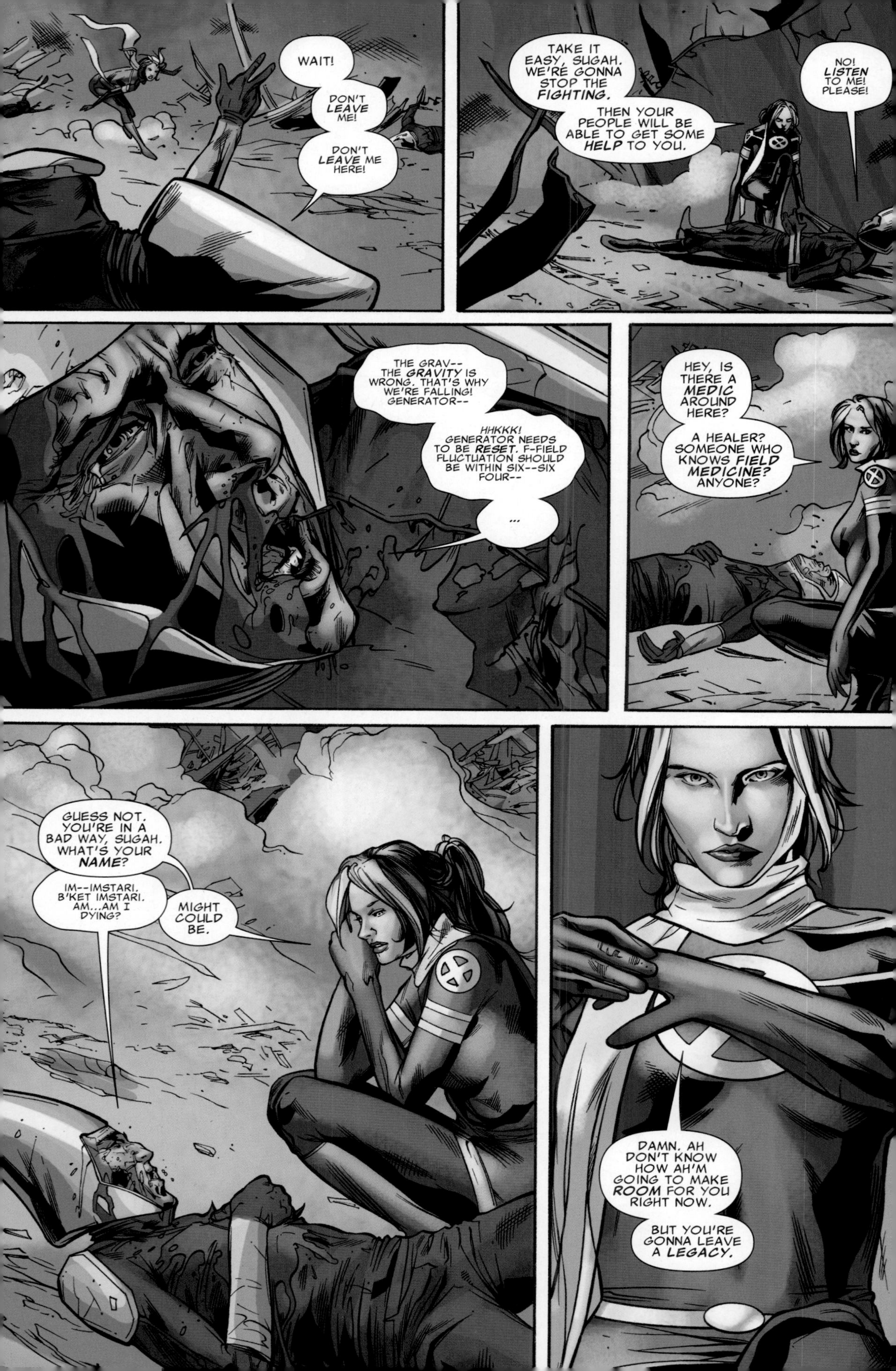
WAIT!
DON'T LEAVE ME!
DON'T LEAVE ME HERE!
TAKE IT EASY, SUGAH. WE'RE GONNA STOP THE FIGHTING.
THEN YOUR PEOPLE WILL BE ABLE TO GET SOME HELP TO YOU.
NO! LISTEN TO ME! PLEASE!
THE GRAV-- THE GRAVITY IS WRONG. THAT'S WHY WE'RE FALLING! GENERATOR--
HHKKK! GENERATOR NEEDS TO BE RESET. F-FIELD FLUCTUATION SHOULD BE WITHIN SIX--SIX FOUR--
...
HEY, IS THERE A MEDIC AROUND HERE?
A HEALER? SOMEONE WHO KNOWS FIELD MEDICINE? ANYONE?
GUESS NOT. YOU'RE IN A BAD WAY, SUGAH. WHAT'S YOUR NAME?
IM--IMSTARI. B'KET IMSTARI. AM...AM I DYING?
MIGHT COULD BE.
DAMN. AH DON'T KNOW HOW AH'M GOING TO MAKE ROOM FOR YOU RIGHT NOW.
BUT YOU'RE GONNA LEAVE A LEGACY.

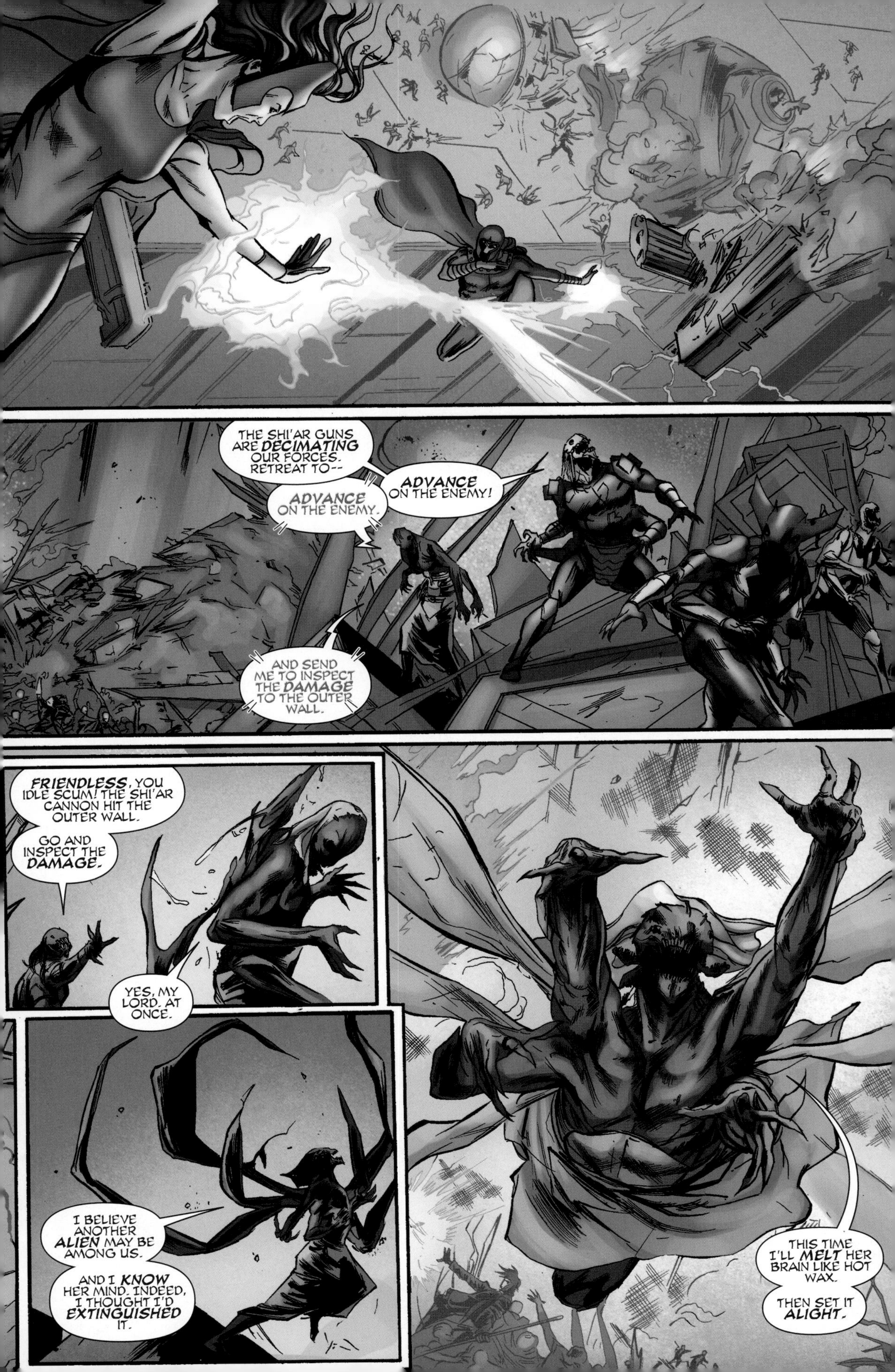
THE SHI'AR GUNS ARE DECIMATING OUR FORCES. RETREAT TO--
ADVANCE ON THE ENEMY!
ADVANCE ON THE ENEMY.
AND SEND ME TO INSPECT THE DAMAGE TO THE OUTER WALL.
FRIENDLESS, YOU IDLE SCUM! THE SHI'AR CANNON HIT THE OUTER WALL.
GO AND INSPECT THE DAMAGE.
YES, MY LORD. AT ONCE.
I BELIEVE ANOTHER ALIEN MAY BE AMONG US.
AND I KNOW HER MIND. INDEED, I THOUGHT I'D EXTINGUISHED IT.
THIS TIME I'LL MELT HER BRAIN LIKE HOT WAX.
THEN SET IT ALIGHT.

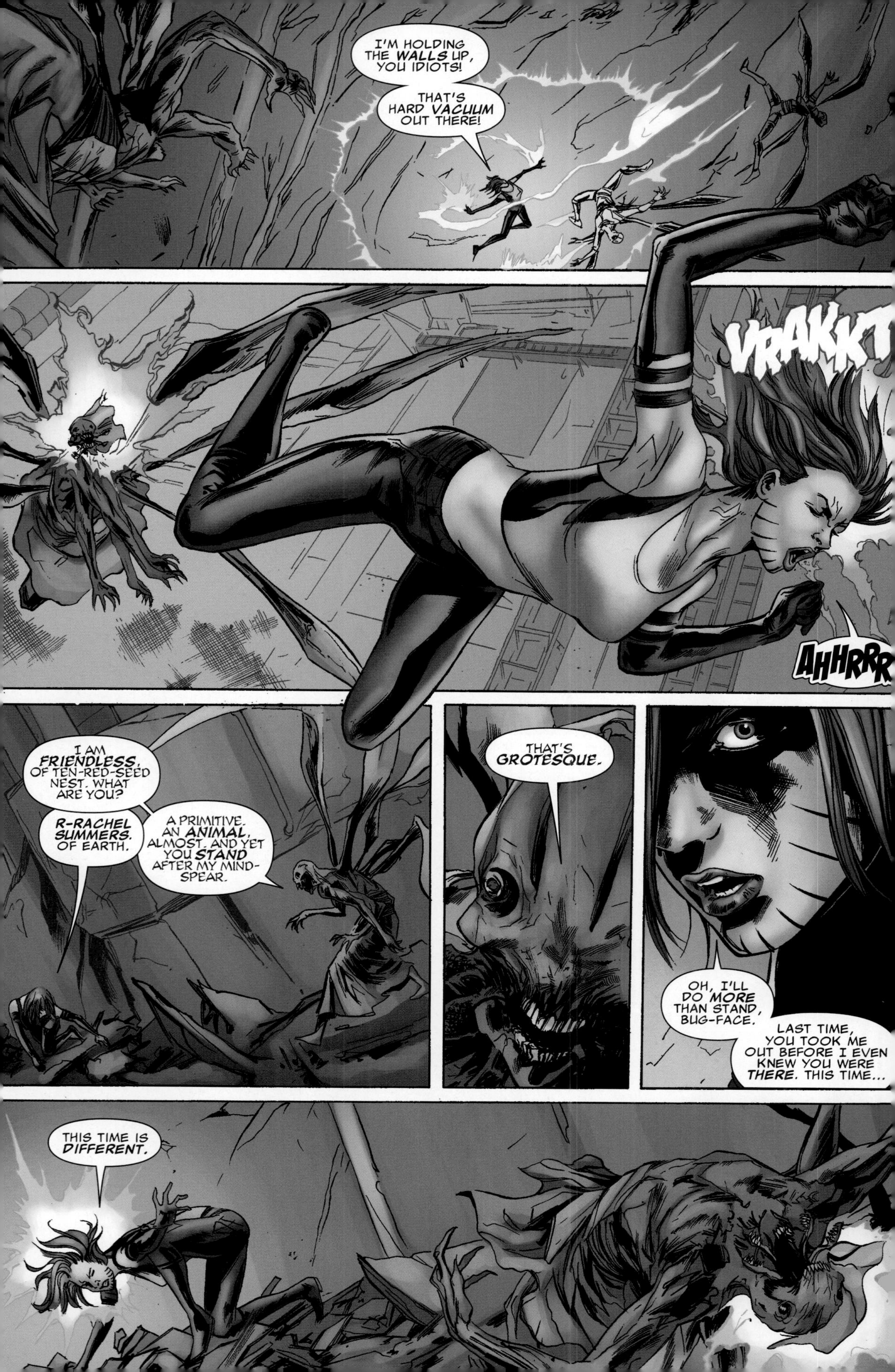

I'M HOLDING THE WALLS UP, YOU IDIOTS!
THAT'S HARD VACUUM OUT THERE!
VRAKKT
AHHRRR
I AM FRIENDLESS, OF TEN-RED-SEED NEST. WHAT ARE YOU?
R-RACHEL SUMMERS. OF EARTH.
A PRIMITIVE. AN ANIMAL, ALMOST. AND YET YOU STAND AFTER MY MIND-SPEAR.
THAT'S GROTESQUE.
OH, I'LL DO MORE THAN STAND, BUG-FACE.
LAST TIME, YOU TOOK ME OUT BEFORE I EVEN KNEW YOU WERE THERE. THIS TIME...
THIS TIME IS DIFFERENT.

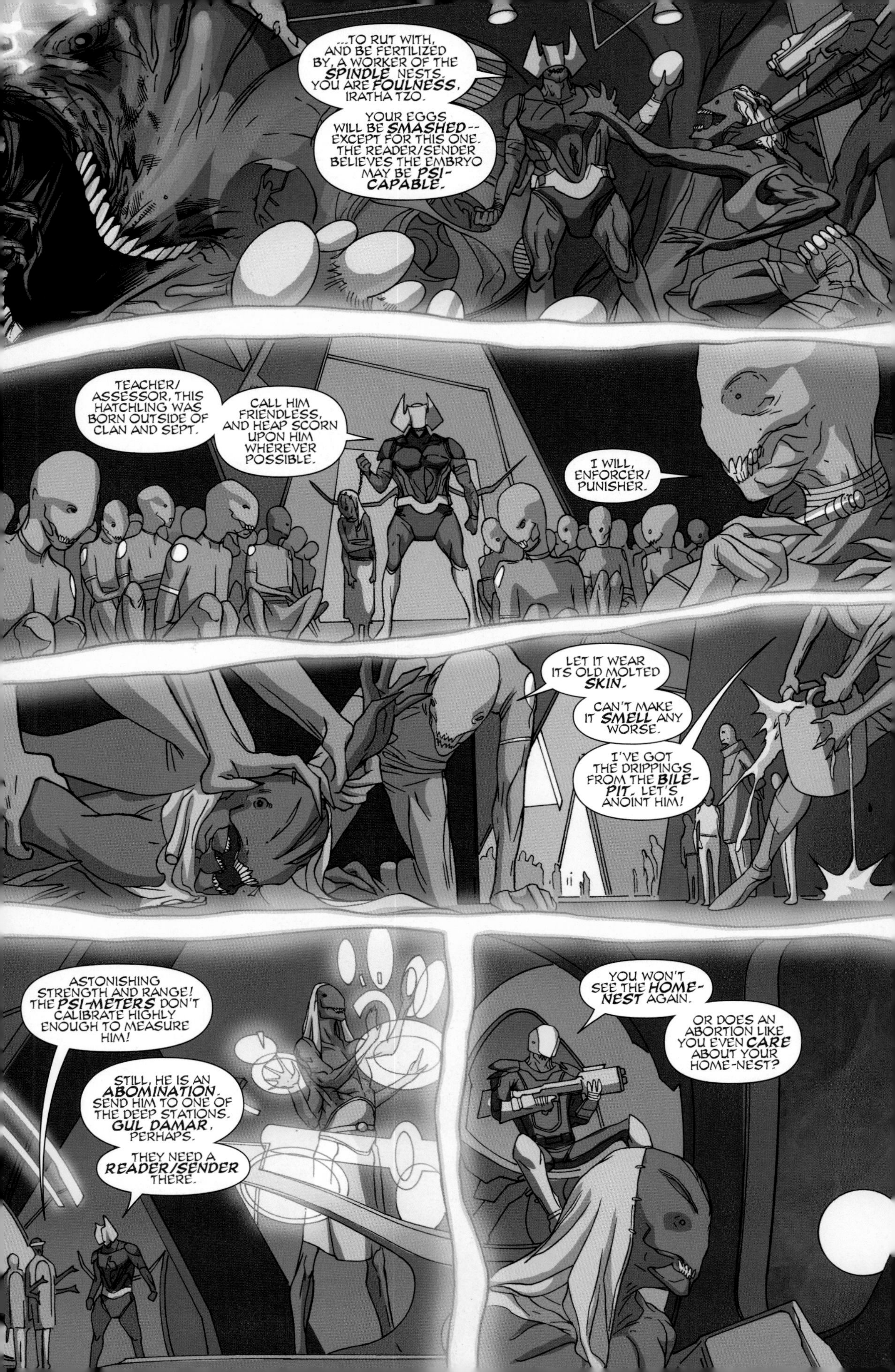
...TO RUT WITH, AND BE FERTILIZED BY, A WORKER OF THE SPINDLE NESTS. YOU ARE FOULNESS, IRATHA TZO.
YOUR EGGS WILL BE SMASHED-- EXCEPT FOR THIS ONE. THE READER/SENDER BELIEVES THE EMBRYO MAY BE PSI-CAPABLE.
TEACHER/ ASSESSOR, THIS HATCHLING WAS BORN OUTSIDE OF CLAN AND SEPT.
CALL HIM FRIENDLESS, AND HEAP SCORN UPON HIM WHEREVER POSSIBLE.
I WILL, ENFORCER/ PUNISHER.
LET IT WEAR ITS OLD MOLTED SKIN.
CAN'T MAKE IT SMELL ANY WORSE.
I'VE GOT THE DRIPPINGS FROM THE BILE-PIT. LET'S ANOINT HIM!
ASTONISHING STRENGTH AND RANGE! THE PSI-METERS DON'T CALIBRATE HIGHLY ENOUGH TO MEASURE HIM!
STILL, HE IS AN ABOMINATION. SEND HIM TO ONE OF THE DEEP STATIONS. GUL DAMAR, PERHAPS.
THEY NEED A READER/SENDER THERE.
YOU WON'T SEE THE HOME-NEST AGAIN.
OR DOES AN ABORTION LIKE YOU EVEN CARE ABOUT YOUR HOME-NEST?

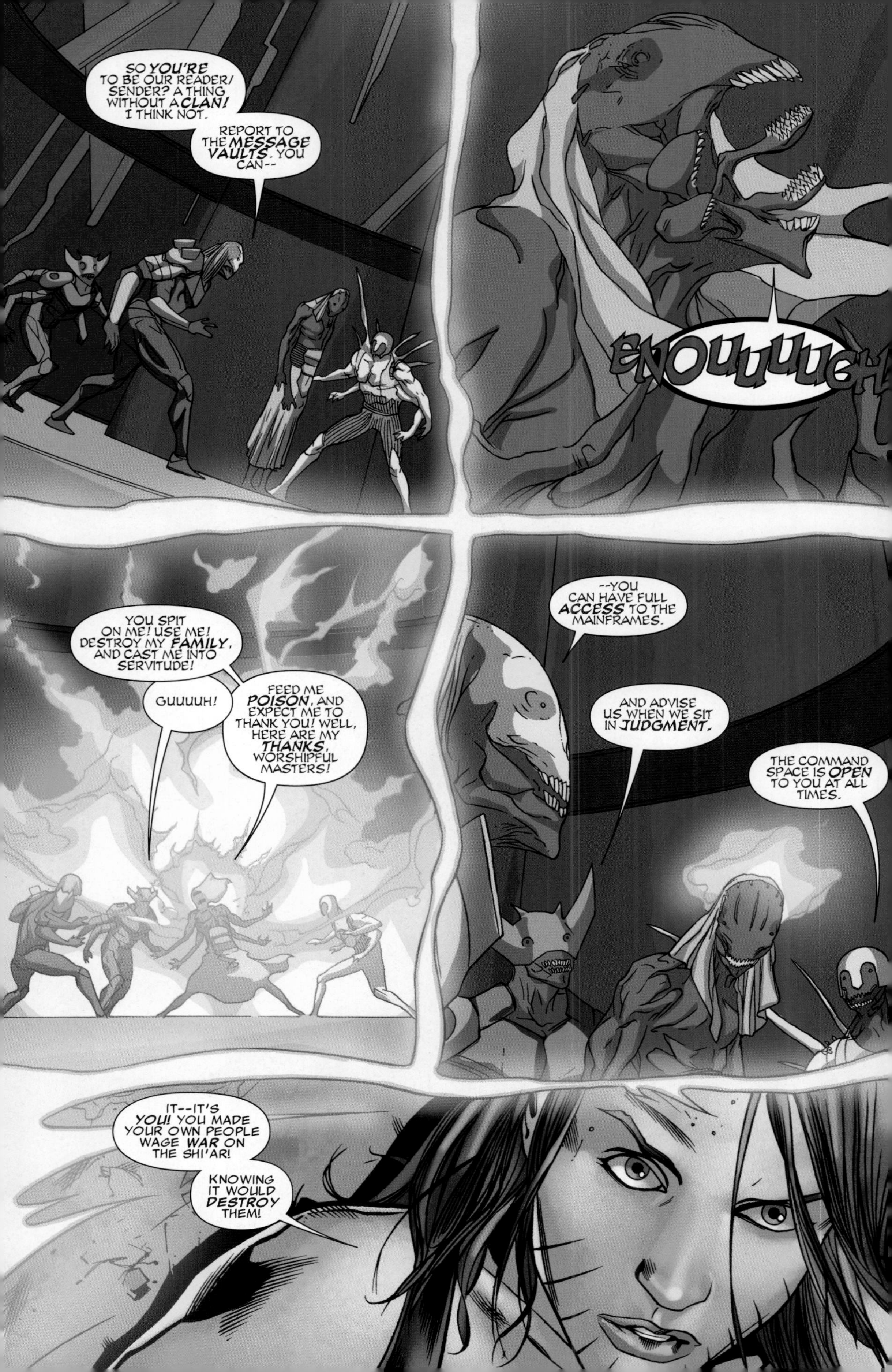
SO YOU'RE TO BE OUR READER/ SENDER? A THING WITHOUT A CLAN! I THINK NOT.
REPORT TO THE MESSAGE VAULTS. YOU CAN--
ENOUUUUUCH
YOU SPIT ON ME! USE ME! DESTROY MY FAMILY, AND CAST ME INTO SERVITUDE!
GUUUUH!
FEED ME POISON, AND EXPECT ME TO THANK YOU! WELL, HERE ARE MY THANKS, WORSHIPFUL MASTERS!
--YOU CAN HAVE FULL ACCESS TO THE MAINFRAMES.
AND ADVISE US WHEN WE SIT IN JUDGMENT.
THE COMMAND SPACE IS OPEN TO YOU AT ALL TIMES.
IT--IT'S YOU! YOU MADE YOUR OWN PEOPLE WAGE WAR ON THE SHI'AR!
KNOWING IT WOULD DESTROY THEM!

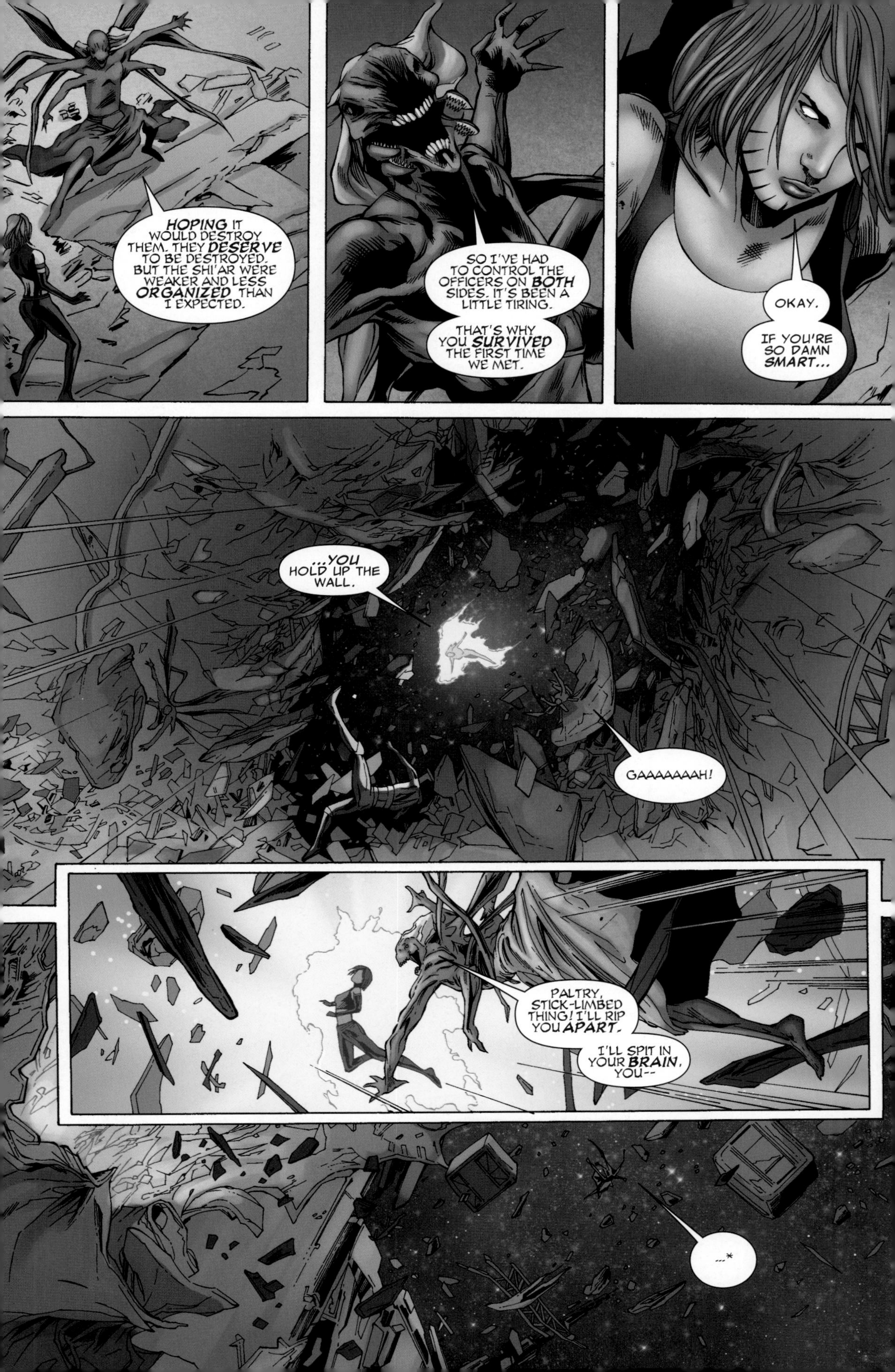
HOPING IT WOULD DESTROY THEM. THEY DESERVE TO BE DESTROYED. BUT THE SHI'AR WERE WEAKER AND LESS ORGANIZED THAN I EXPECTED.
SO I'VE HAD TO CONTROL THE OFFICERS ON BOTH SIDES. IT'S BEEN A LITTLE TIRING.
THAT'S WHY YOU SURVIVED THE FIRST TIME WE MET.
OKAY.
IF YOU'RE SO DAMN SMART...
...YOU HOLD UP THE WALL.
GAAAAAAAH!
PALTRY, STICK-LIMBED THING! I'LL RIP YOU APART.
I'LL SPIT IN YOUR BRAIN, YOU--
...*

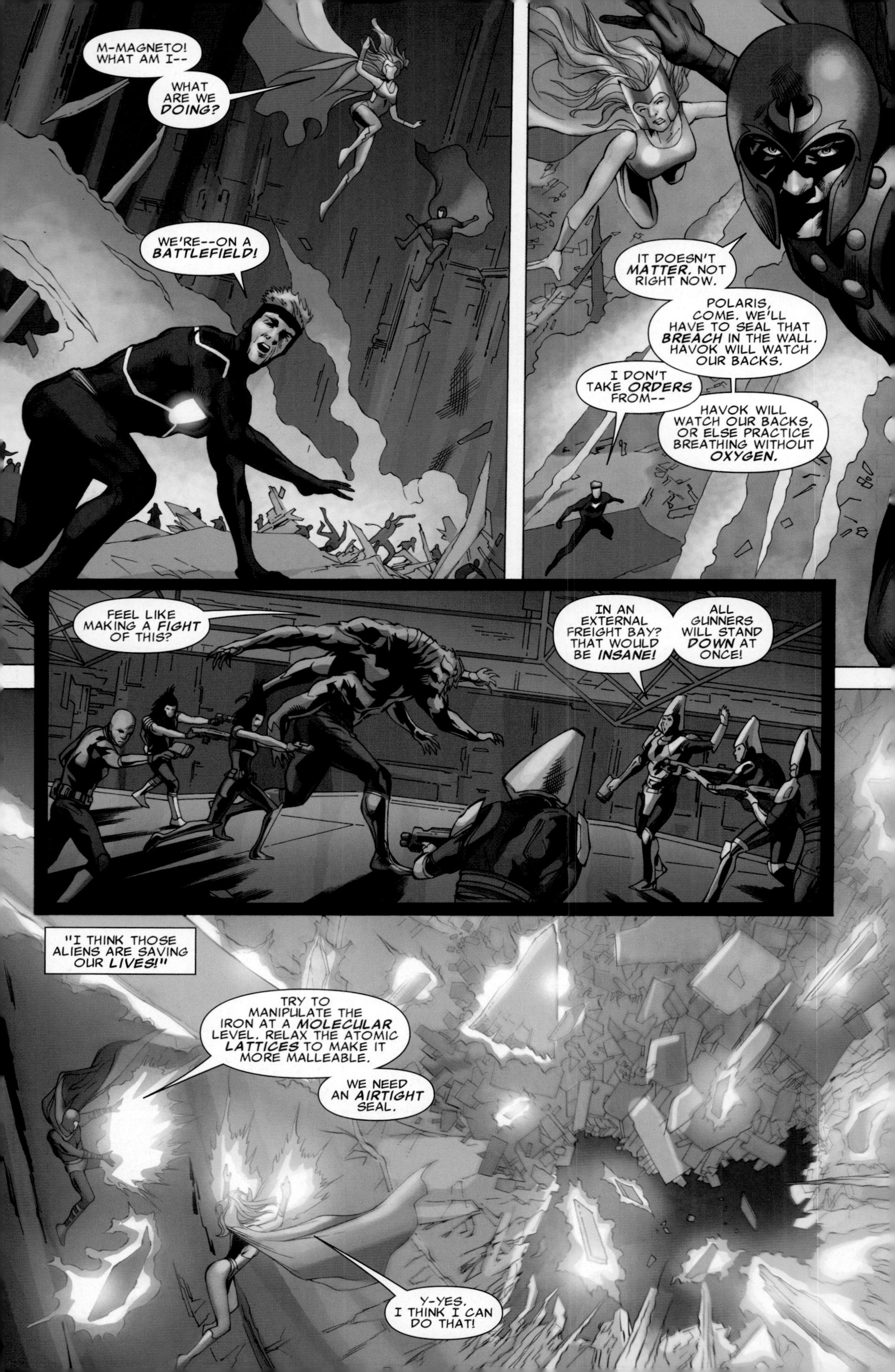
M-MAGNETO! WHAT AM I--
WHAT ARE WE DOING?
WE'RE--ON A BATTLEFIELD!
IT DOESN'T MATTER. NOT RIGHT NOW.
POLARIS, COME. WE'LL HAVE TO SEAL THAT BREACH IN THE WALL. HAVOK WILL WATCH OUR BACKS.
I DON'T TAKE ORDERS FROM--
HAVOK WILL WATCH OUR BACKS, OR ELSE PRACTICE BREATHING WITHOUT OXYGEN.
FEEL LIKE MAKING A FIGHT OF THIS?
IN AN EXTERNAL FREIGHT BAY? THAT WOULD BE INSANE!
ALL GUNNERS WILL STAND DOWN AT ONCE!
"I THINK THOSE ALIENS ARE SAVING OUR LIVES!"
TRY TO MANIPULATE THE IRON AT A MOLECULAR LEVEL. RELAX THE ATOMIC LATTICES TO MAKE IT MORE MALLEABLE.
WE NEED AN AIRTIGHT SEAL.
Y-YES. I THINK I CAN DO THAT!

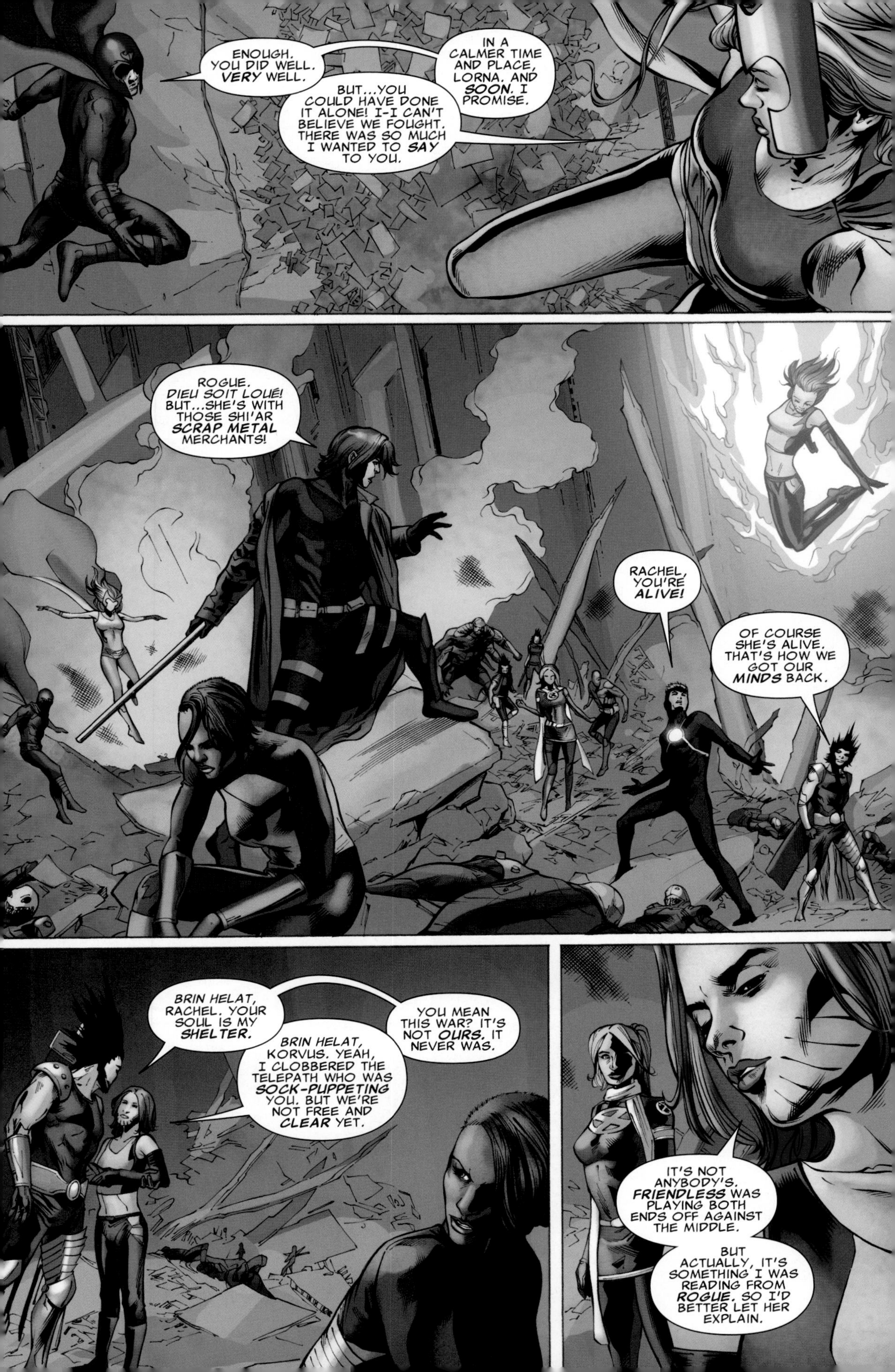
ENOUGH. YOU DID WELL. VERY WELL.
BUT...YOU COULD HAVE DONE IT ALONE! I-I CAN'T BELIEVE WE FOUGHT. THERE WAS SO MUCH I WANTED TO SAY TO YOU.
IN A CALMER TIME AND PLACE, LORNA. AND SOON. I PROMISE.
ROGUE. DIEU SOIT LOUÉ! BUT...SHE'S WITH THOSE SHI'AR SCRAP METAL MERCHANTS!
RACHEL, YOU'RE ALIVE!
OF COURSE SHE'S ALIVE. THAT'S HOW WE GOT OUR MINDS BACK.
BRIN HELAT, RACHEL. YOUR SOUL IS MY SHELTER.
BRIN HELAT, KORVUS. YEAH, I CLOBBERED THE TELEPATH WHO WAS SOCK-PUPPETING YOU. BUT WE'RE NOT FREE AND CLEAR YET.
YOU MEAN THIS WAR? IT'S NOT OURS. IT NEVER WAS.
IT'S NOT ANYBODY'S. FRIENDLESS WAS PLAYING BOTH ENDS OFF AGAINST THE MIDDLE.
BUT ACTUALLY, IT'S SOMETHING I WAS READING FROM ROGUE. SO I'D BETTER LET HER EXPLAIN.

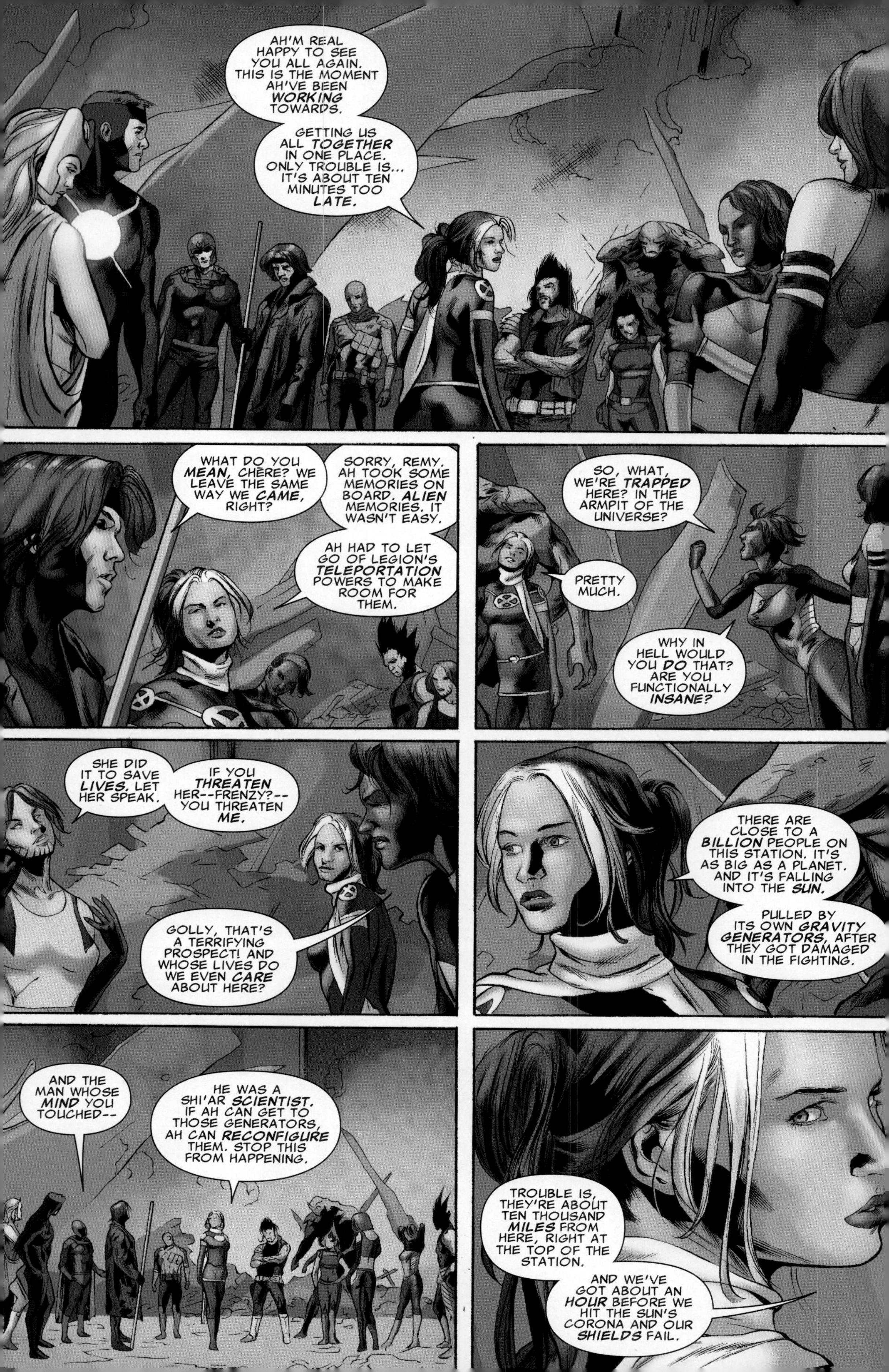

AH'M REAL HAPPY TO SEE YOU ALL AGAIN. THIS IS THE MOMENT AH'VE BEEN WORKING TOWARDS.
GETTING US ALL TOGETHER IN ONE PLACE. ONLY TROUBLE IS... IT'S ABOUT TEN MINUTES TOO LATE.
WHAT DO YOU MEAN, CHÈRE? WE LEAVE THE SAME WAY WE CAME, RIGHT?
SORRY, REMY. AH TOOK SOME MEMORIES ON BOARD. ALIEN MEMORIES. IT WASN'T EASY.
AH HAD TO LET GO OF LEGION'S TELEPORTATION POWERS TO MAKE ROOM FOR THEM.
SO, WHAT, WE'RE TRAPPED HERE? IN THE ARMPIT OF THE UNIVERSE?
PRETTY MUCH.
WHY IN HELL WOULD YOU DO THAT? ARE YOU FUNCTIONALLY INSANE?
SHE DID IT TO SAVE LIVES. LET HER SPEAK.
IF YOU THREATEN HER--FRENZY?--YOU THREATEN ME.
GOLLY, THAT'S A TERRIFYING PROSPECT! AND WHOSE LIVES DO WE EVEN CARE ABOUT HERE?
THERE ARE CLOSE TO A BILLION PEOPLE ON THIS STATION. IT'S AS BIG AS A PLANET. AND IT'S FALLING INTO THE SUN.
PULLED BY ITS OWN GRAVITY GENERATORS, AFTER THEY GOT DAMAGED IN THE FIGHTING.
AND THE MAN WHOSE MIND YOU TOUCHED--
HE WAS A SHI'AR SCIENTIST. IF AH CAN GET TO THOSE GENERATORS, AH CAN RECONFIGURE THEM. STOP THIS FROM HAPPENING.
TROUBLE IS, THEY'RE ABOUT TEN THOUSAND MILES FROM HERE, RIGHT AT THE TOP OF THE STATION.
AND WE'VE GOT ABOUT AN HOUR BEFORE WE HIT THE SUN'S CORONA AND OUR SHIELDS FAIL.

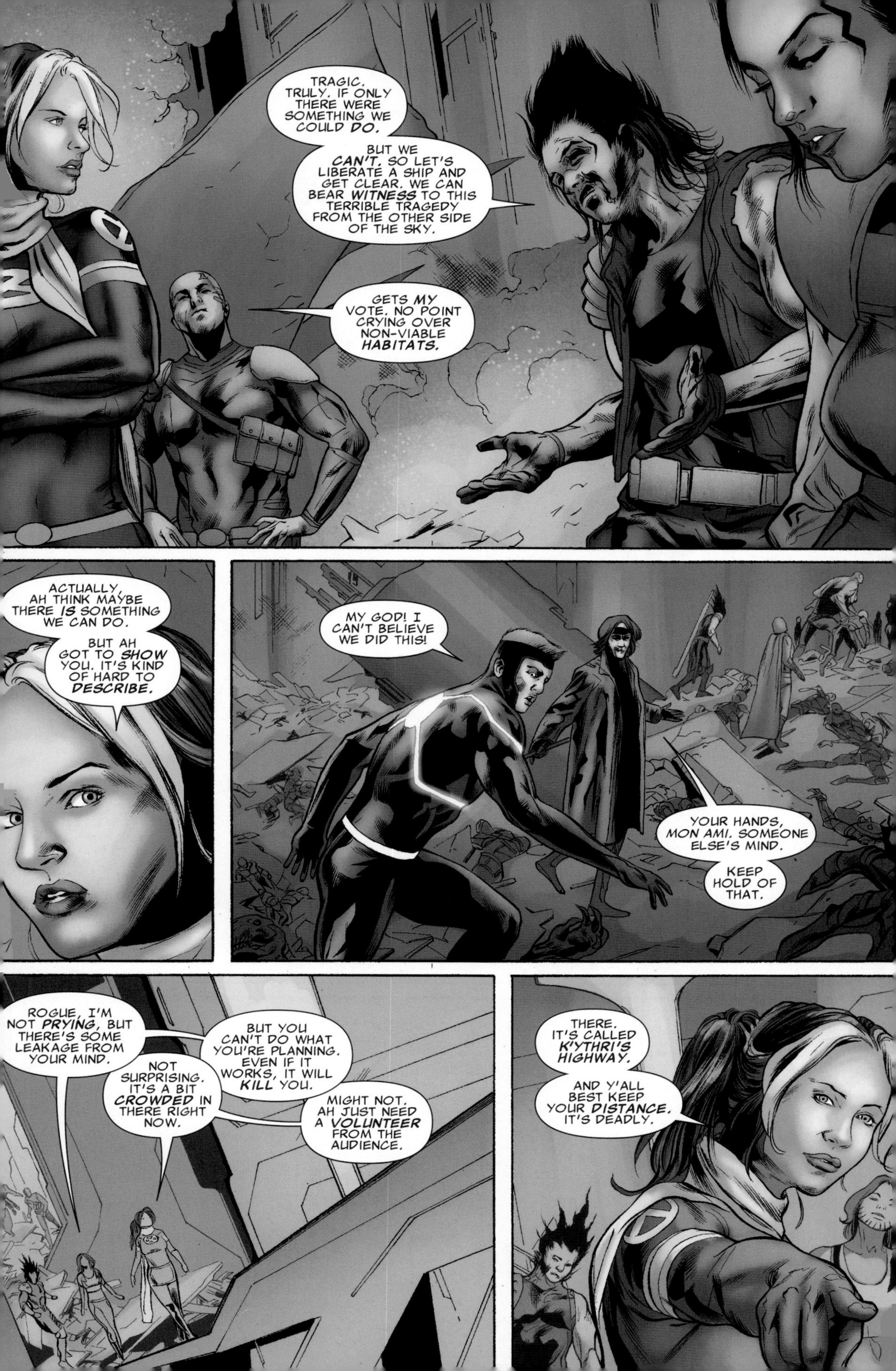
TRAGIC. TRULY. IF ONLY THERE WERE SOMETHING WE COULD DO.
BUT WE CAN'T. SO LET'S LIBERATE A SHIP AND GET CLEAR. WE CAN BEAR WITNESS TO THIS TERRIBLE TRAGEDY FROM THE OTHER SIDE OF THE SKY.
GETS MY VOTE. NO POINT CRYING OVER NON-VIABLE HABITATS.
ACTUALLY, AH THINK MAYBE THERE IS SOMETHING WE CAN DO.
BUT AH GOT TO SHOW YOU. IT'S KIND OF HARD TO DESCRIBE.
MY GOD! I CAN'T BELIEVE WE DID THIS!
YOUR HANDS, MON AMI. SOMEONE ELSE'S MIND.
KEEP HOLD OF THAT.
ROGUE, I'M NOT PRYING, BUT THERE'S SOME LEAKAGE FROM YOUR MIND.
BUT YOU CAN'T DO WHAT YOU'RE PLANNING. EVEN IF IT WORKS, IT WILL KILL YOU.
NOT SURPRISING. IT'S A BIT CROWDED IN THERE RIGHT NOW.
MIGHT NOT. AH JUST NEED A VOLUNTEER FROM THE AUDIENCE.
THERE. IT'S CALLED K'YTHRI'S HIGHWAY.
AND Y'ALL BEST KEEP YOUR DISTANCE. IT'S DEADLY.

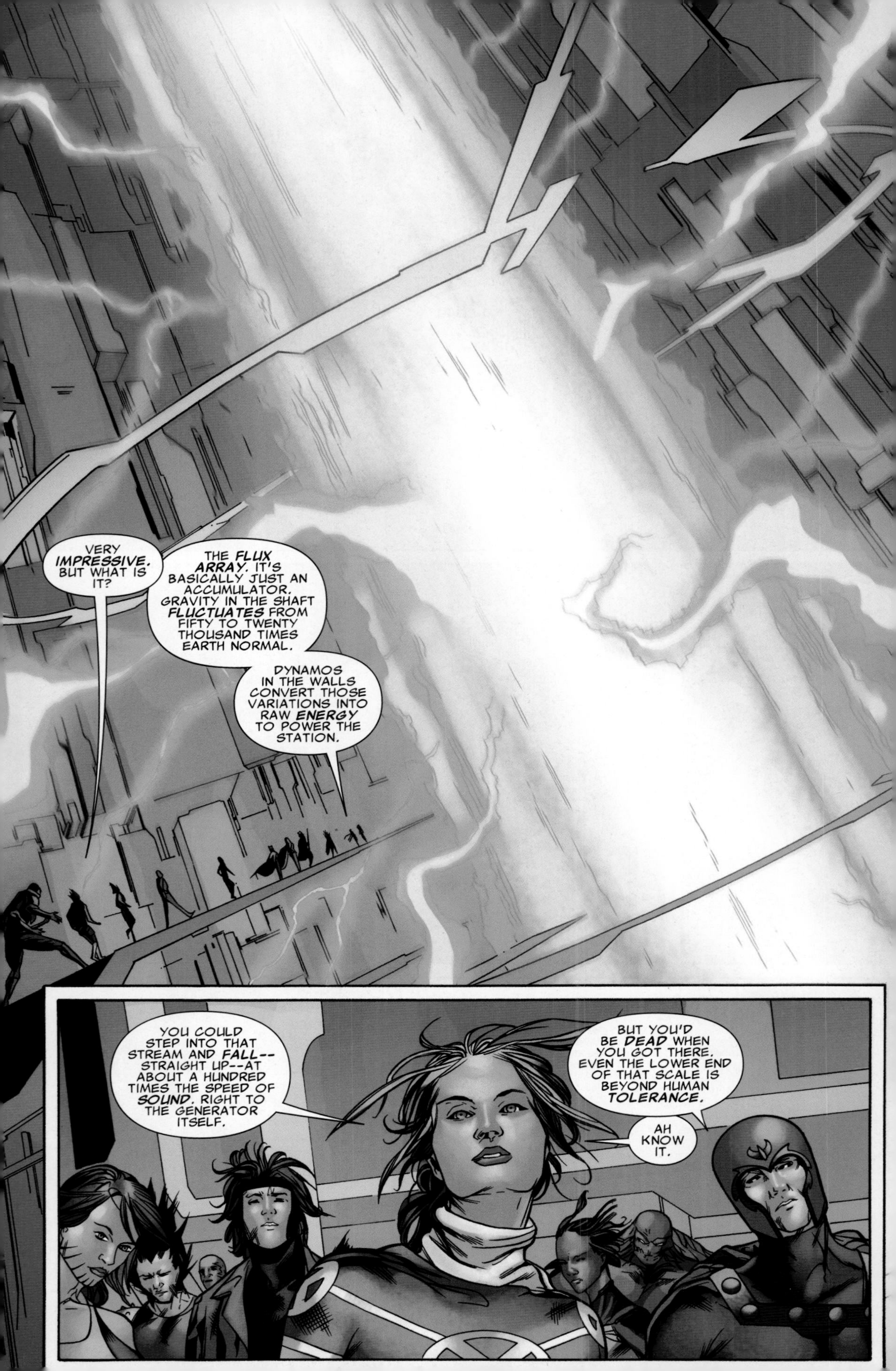
VERY IMPRESSIVE. BUT WHAT IS IT?
THE FLUX ARRAY. IT'S BASICALLY JUST AN ACCUMULATOR. GRAVITY IN THE SHAFT FLUCTUATES FROM FIFTY TO TWENTY THOUSAND TIMES EARTH NORMAL.
DYNAMOS IN THE WALLS CONVERT THOSE VARIATIONS INTO RAW ENERGY TO POWER THE STATION.
YOU COULD STEP INTO THAT STREAM AND FALL-- STRAIGHT UP--AT ABOUT A HUNDRED TIMES THE SPEED OF SOUND. RIGHT TO THE GENERATOR ITSELF.
BUT YOU'D BE DEAD WHEN YOU GOT THERE. EVEN THE LOWER END OF THAT SCALE IS BEYOND HUMAN TOLERANCE.
AH KNOW IT.

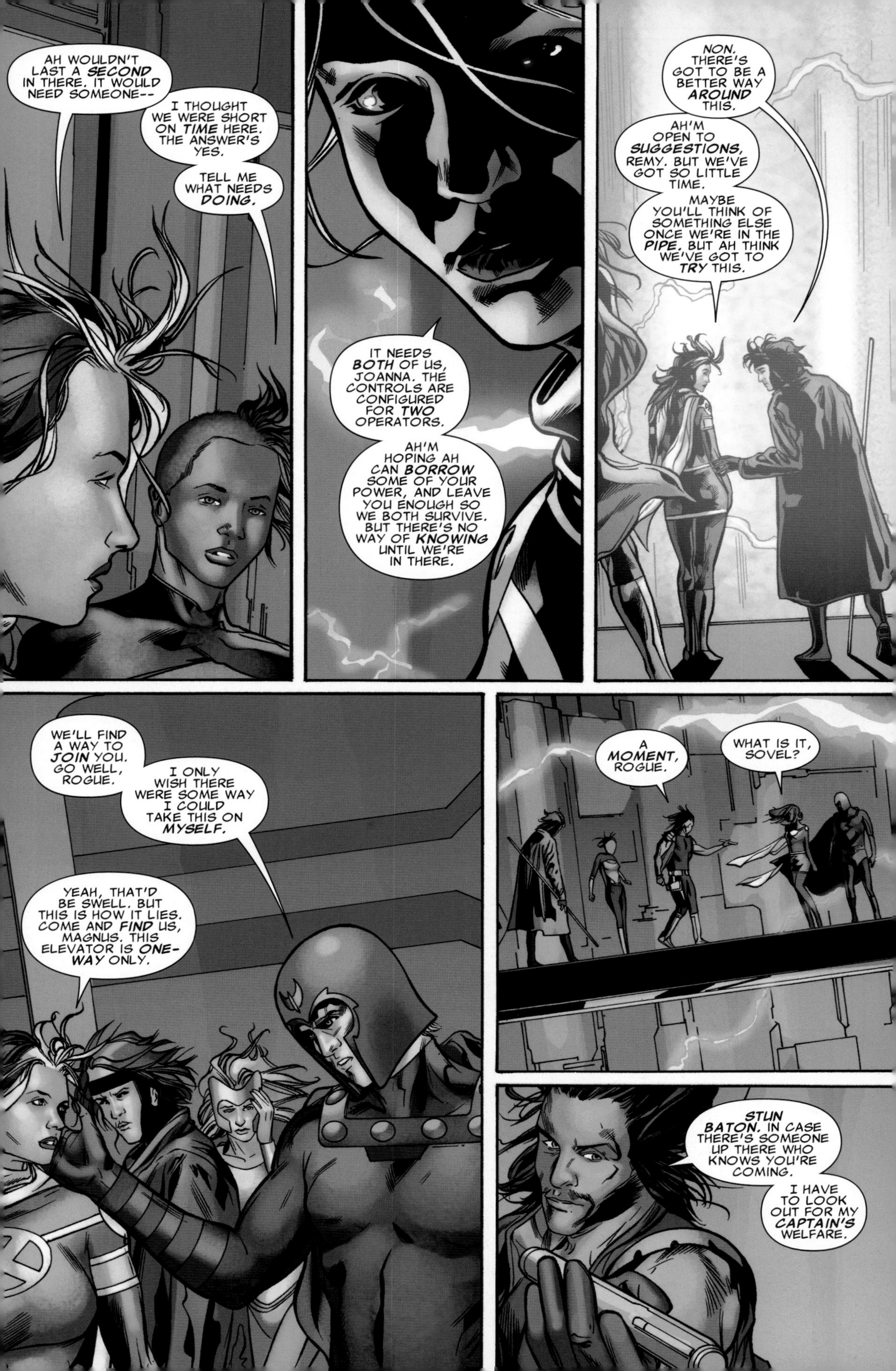
AH WOULDN'T LAST A SECOND IN THERE. IT WOULD NEED SOMEONE--
I THOUGHT WE WERE SHORT ON TIME HERE. THE ANSWER'S YES.
TELL ME WHAT NEEDS DOING.
IT NEEDS BOTH OF US, JOANNA. THE CONTROLS ARE CONFIGURED FOR TWO OPERATORS.
AH'M HOPING AH CAN BORROW SOME OF YOUR POWER, AND LEAVE YOU ENOUGH SO WE BOTH SURVIVE. BUT THERE'S NO WAY OF KNOWING UNTIL WE'RE IN THERE.
NON. THERE'S GOT TO BE A BETTER WAY AROUND THIS.
AH'M OPEN TO SUGGESTIONS, REMY. BUT WE'VE GOT SO LITTLE TIME.
MAYBE YOU'LL THINK OF SOMETHING ELSE ONCE WE'RE IN THE PIPE. BUT AH THINK WE'VE GOT TO TRY THIS.
WE'LL FIND A WAY TO JOIN YOU. GO WELL, ROGUE.
I ONLY WISH THERE WERE SOME WAY I COULD TAKE THIS ON MYSELF.
YEAH, THAT'D BE SWELL. BUT THIS IS HOW IT LIES. COME AND FIND US, MAGNUS. THIS ELEVATOR IS ONE-WAY ONLY.
A MOMENT, ROGUE.
WHAT IS IT, SOVEL?
STUN BATON. IN CASE THERE'S SOMEONE UP THERE WHO KNOWS YOU'RE COMING.
I HAVE TO LOOK OUT FOR MY CAPTAIN'S WELFARE.

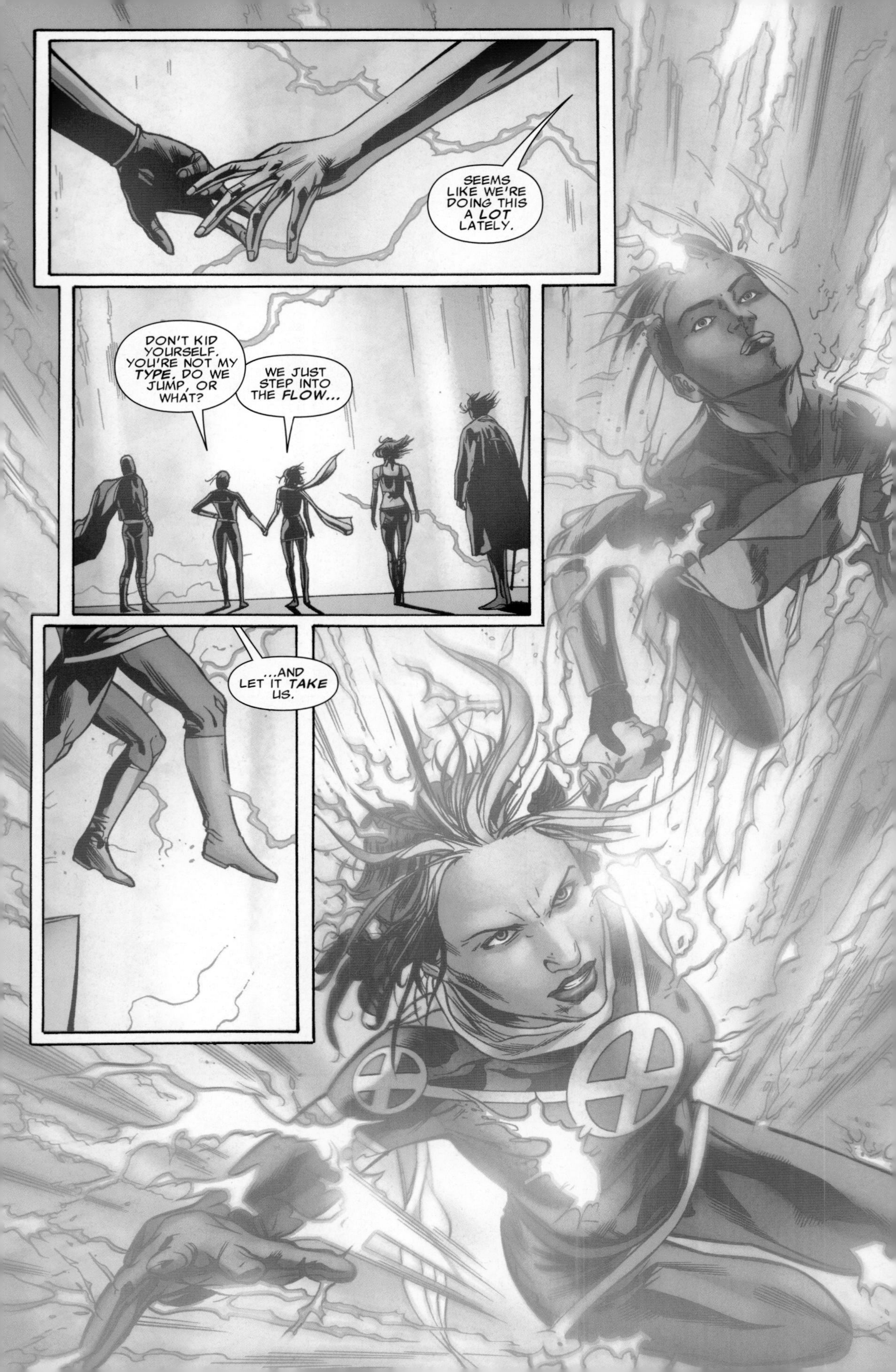
SEEMS LIKE WE'RE DOING THIS A *LOT* LATELY.
DON'T KID YOURSELF. YOU'RE NOT MY *TYPE*. DO WE JUMP, OR WHAT?
WE JUST STEP INTO THE *FLOW*...
...AND LET IT *TAKE* US.

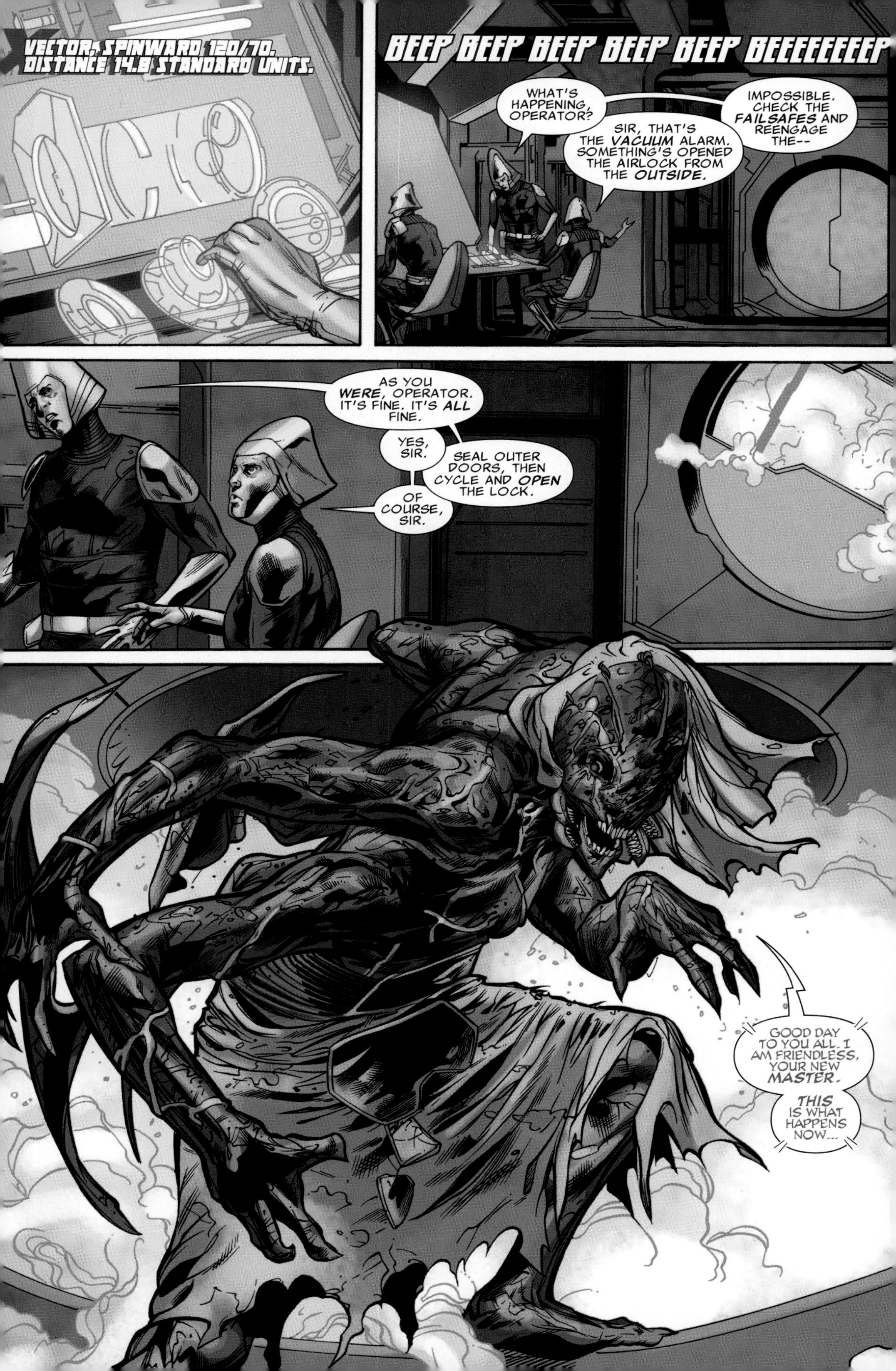
VECTOR: SPINWARD 120/70. DISTANCE 14.8 STANDARD UNITS.
BEEP BEEP BEEP BEEP BEEP BEEEEEEEEP
WHAT'S HAPPENING, OPERATOR?
SIR, THAT'S THE VACUUM ALARM. SOMETHING'S OPENED THE AIRLOCK FROM THE OUTSIDE.
IMPOSSIBLE. CHECK THE FAILSAFES AND REENGAGE THE--
AS YOU WERE, OPERATOR. IT'S FINE. IT'S ALL FINE.
YES, SIR.
SEAL OUTER DOORS, THEN CYCLE AND OPEN THE LOCK.
OF COURSE, SIR.
GOOD DAY TO YOU ALL. I AM FRIENDLESS, YOUR NEW MASTER.
THIS IS WHAT HAPPENS NOW...

#257
"FIVE MILES SOUTH OF THE UNIVERSE" PART FOUR

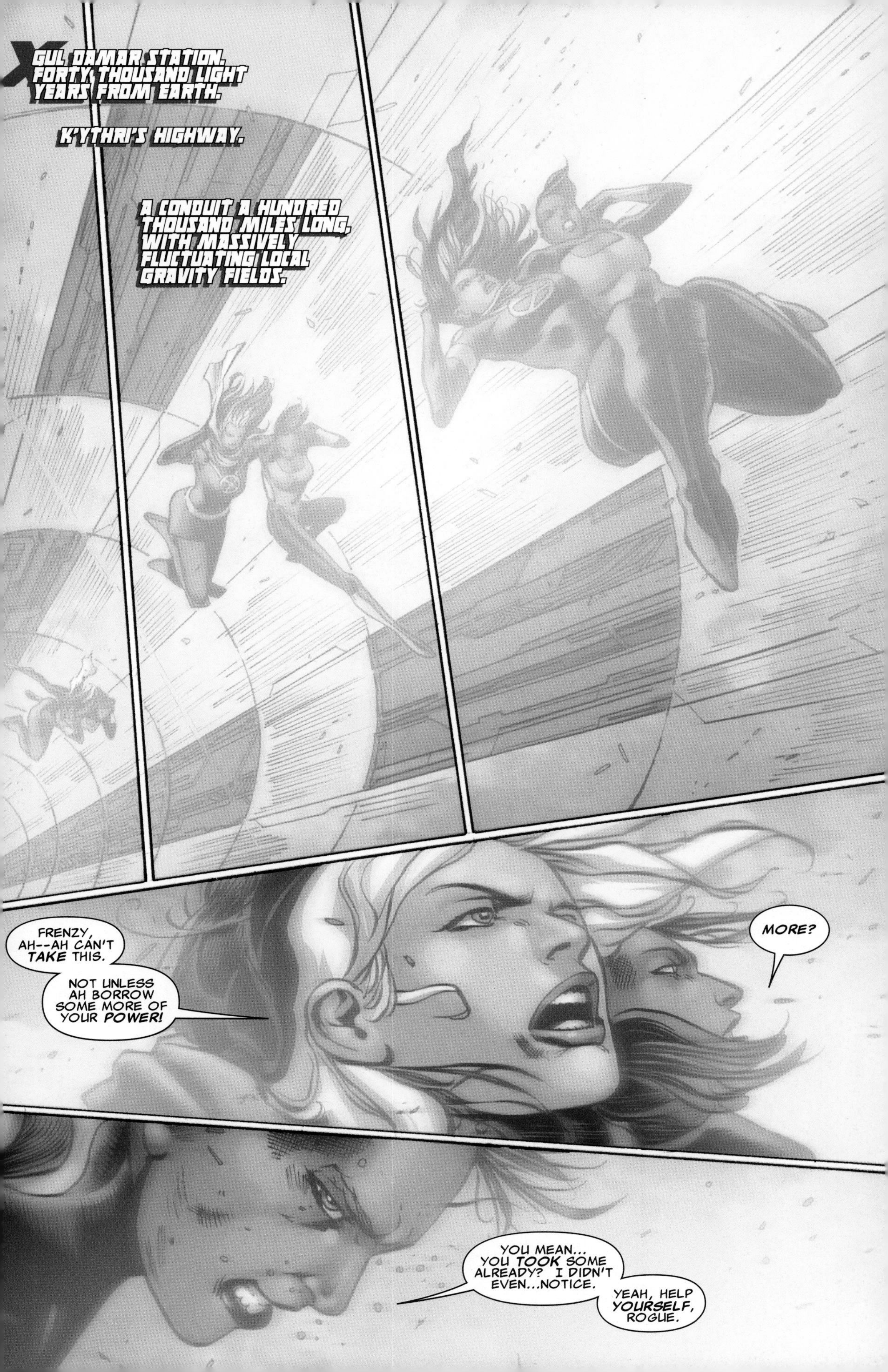
GUL DAMAR STATION. FORTY THOUSAND LIGHT YEARS FROM EARTH.
K'YTHRI'S HIGHWAY.
A CONDUIT A HUNDRED THOUSAND MILES LONG, WITH MASSIVELY FLUCTUATING LOCAL GRAVITY FIELDS.
FRENZY, AH--AH CAN'T TAKE THIS.
NOT UNLESS AH BORROW SOME MORE OF YOUR POWER!
MORE?
YOU MEAN... YOU TOOK SOME ALREADY? I DIDN'T EVEN...NOTICE.
YEAH, HELP YOURSELF, ROGUE.

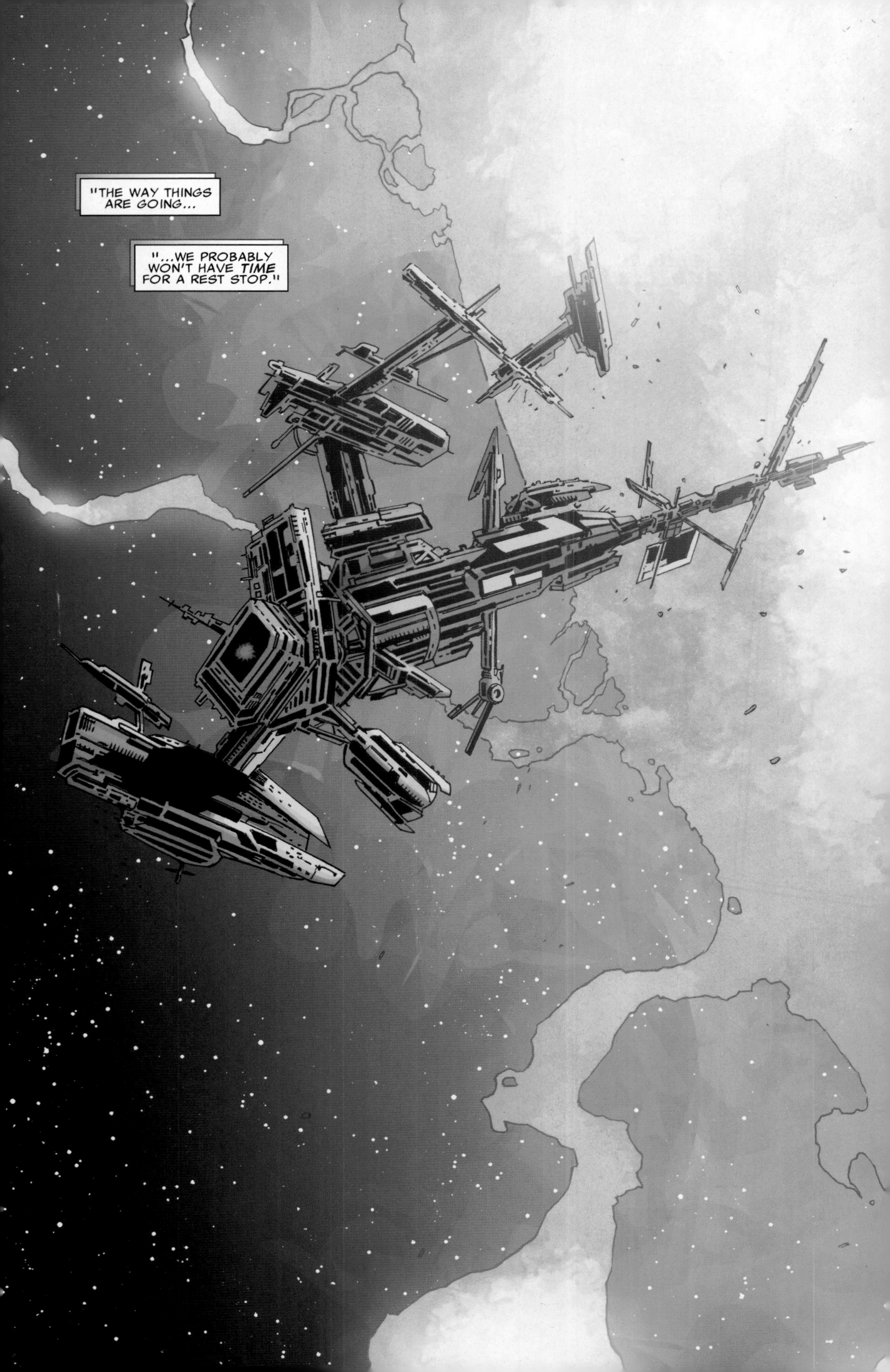
"THE WAY THINGS ARE GOING...
"...WE PROBABLY WON'T HAVE *TIME* FOR A REST STOP."

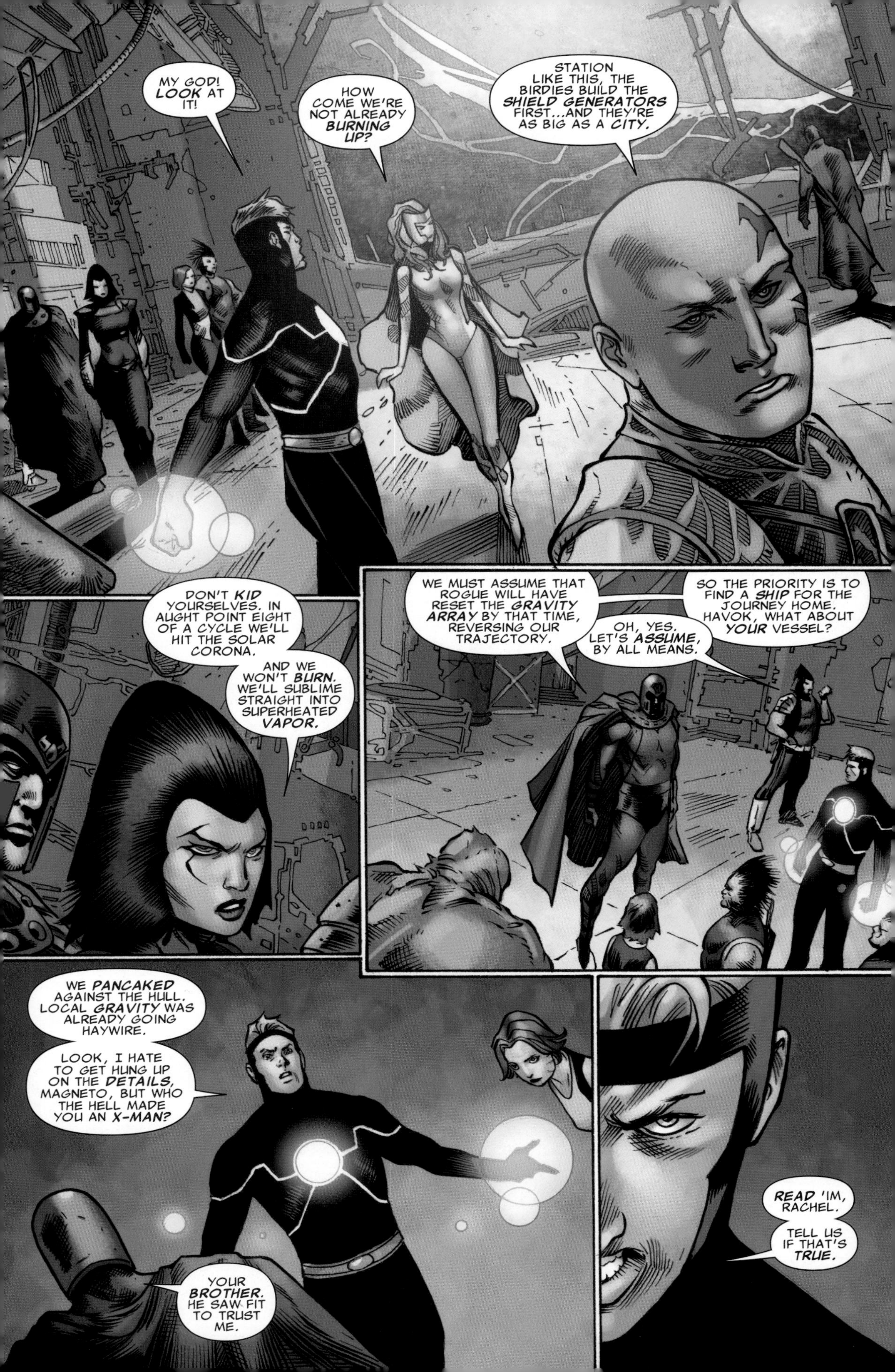
MY GOD! LOOK AT IT!
HOW COME WE'RE NOT ALREADY BURNING UP?
STATION LIKE THIS, THE BIRDIES BUILD THE SHIELD GENERATORS FIRST...AND THEY'RE AS BIG AS A CITY.
DON'T KID YOURSELVES. IN AUGHT POINT EIGHT OF A CYCLE WE'LL HIT THE SOLAR CORONA.
AND WE WON'T BURN. WE'LL SUBLIME STRAIGHT INTO SUPERHEATED VAPOR.
WE MUST ASSUME THAT ROGUE WILL HAVE RESET THE GRAVITY ARRAY BY THAT TIME, REVERSING OUR TRAJECTORY.
OH, YES. LET'S ASSUME, BY ALL MEANS.
SO THE PRIORITY IS TO FIND A SHIP FOR THE JOURNEY HOME. HAVOK, WHAT ABOUT YOUR VESSEL?
WE PANCAKED AGAINST THE HULL. LOCAL GRAVITY WAS ALREADY GOING HAYWIRE.
LOOK, I HATE TO GET HUNG UP ON THE DETAILS, MAGNETO, BUT WHO THE HELL MADE YOU AN X-MAN?
YOUR BROTHER. HE SAW FIT TO TRUST ME.
READ 'IM, RACHEL.
TELL US IF THAT'S TRUE.

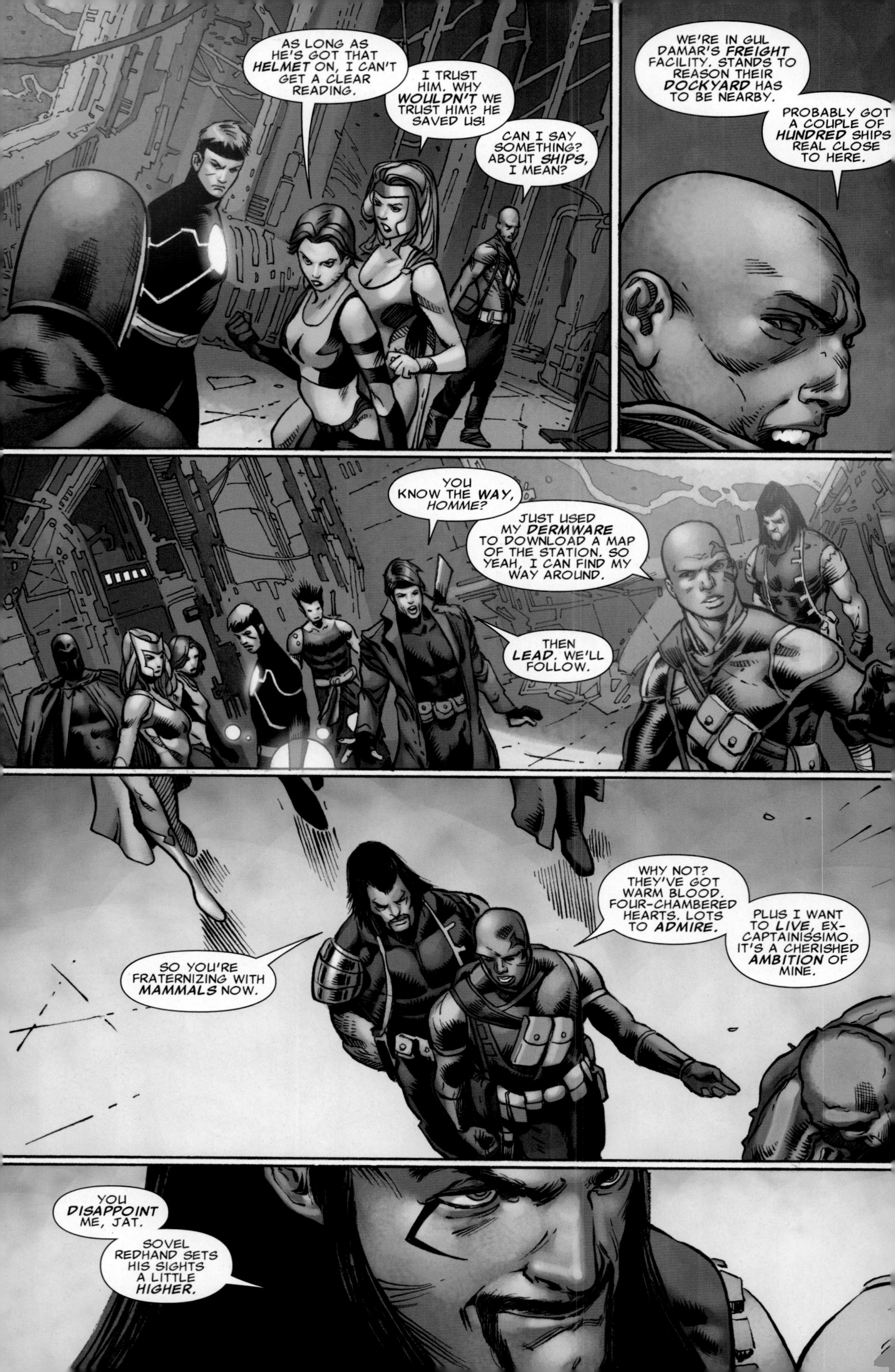
AS LONG AS HE'S GOT THAT HELMET ON, I CAN'T GET A CLEAR READING.
I TRUST HIM. WHY WOULDN'T WE TRUST HIM? HE SAVED US!
CAN I SAY SOMETHING? ABOUT SHIPS, I MEAN?
WE'RE IN GUL DAMAR'S FREIGHT FACILITY. STANDS TO REASON THEIR DOCKYARD HAS TO BE NEARBY.
PROBABLY GOT A COUPLE OF HUNDRED SHIPS REAL CLOSE TO HERE.
YOU KNOW THE WAY, HOMME?
JUST USED MY DERMWARE TO DOWNLOAD A MAP OF THE STATION. SO YEAH, I CAN FIND MY WAY AROUND.
THEN LEAD. WE'LL FOLLOW.
SO YOU'RE FRATERNIZING WITH MAMMALS NOW.
WHY NOT? THEY'VE GOT WARM BLOOD. FOUR-CHAMBERED HEARTS. LOTS TO ADMIRE.
PLUS I WANT TO LIVE, EX-CAPTAINISSIMO. IT'S A CHERISHED AMBITION OF MINE.
YOU DISAPPOINT ME, JAT.
SOVEL REDHAND SETS HIS SIGHTS A LITTLE HIGHER.

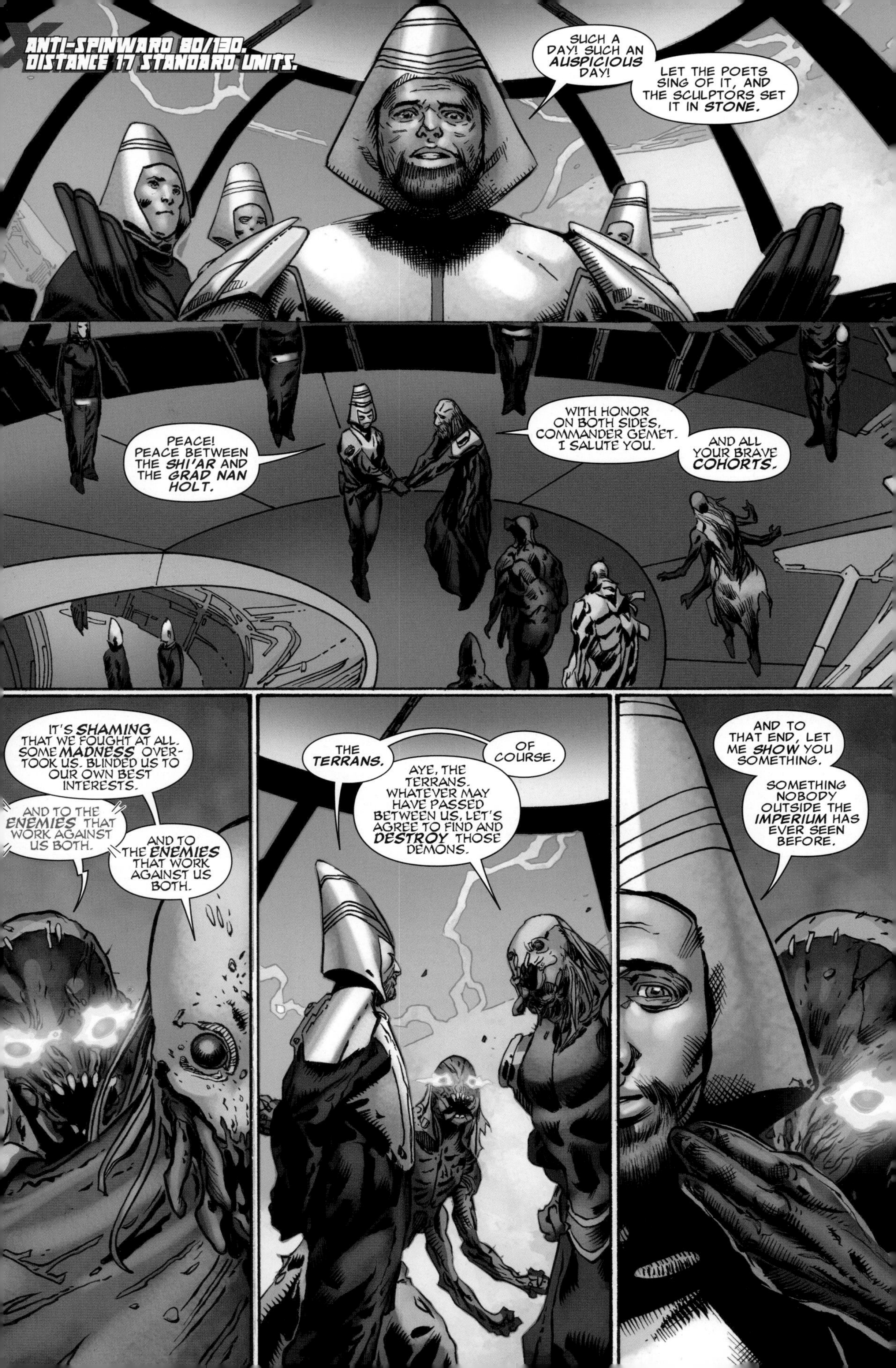
ANTI-SPINWARD 80/130. DISTANCE 17 STANDARD UNITS.
SUCH A DAY! SUCH AN AUSPICIOUS DAY!
LET THE POETS SING OF IT, AND THE SCULPTORS SET IT IN STONE.
PEACE! PEACE BETWEEN THE SHI'AR AND THE GRAD NAN HOLT.
WITH HONOR ON BOTH SIDES, COMMANDER GEMET. I SALUTE YOU.
AND ALL YOUR BRAVE COHORTS.
IT'S SHAMING THAT WE FOUGHT AT ALL. SOME MADNESS OVERTOOK US. BLINDED US TO OUR OWN BEST INTERESTS.
AND TO THE ENEMIES THAT WORK AGAINST US BOTH.
AND TO THE ENEMIES THAT WORK AGAINST US BOTH.
THE TERRANS.
OF COURSE.
AYE, THE TERRANS. WHATEVER MAY HAVE PASSED BETWEEN US, LET'S AGREE TO FIND AND DESTROY THOSE DEMONS.
AND TO THAT END, LET ME SHOW YOU SOMETHING.
SOMETHING NOBODY OUTSIDE THE IMPERIUM HAS EVER SEEN BEFORE.

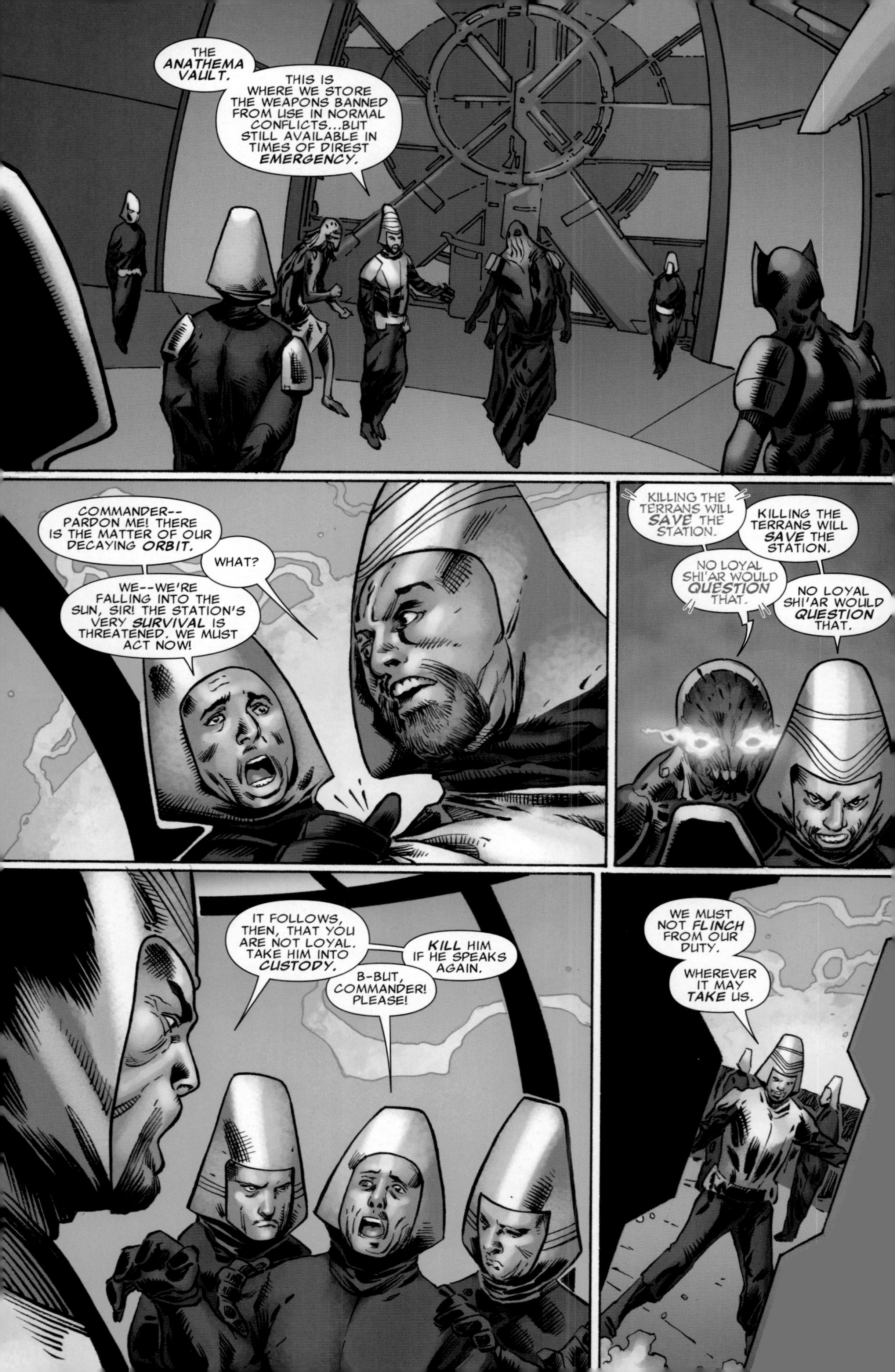
THE ANATHEMA VAULT.
THIS IS WHERE WE STORE THE WEAPONS BANNED FROM USE IN NORMAL CONFLICTS...BUT STILL AVAILABLE IN TIMES OF DIREST EMERGENCY.
COMMANDER-- PARDON ME! THERE IS THE MATTER OF OUR DECAYING ORBIT.
WHAT?
WE--WE'RE FALLING INTO THE SUN, SIR! THE STATION'S VERY SURVIVAL IS THREATENED. WE MUST ACT NOW!
KILLING THE TERRANS WILL SAVE THE STATION.
KILLING THE TERRANS WILL SAVE THE STATION.
NO LOYAL SHI'AR WOULD QUESTION THAT.
NO LOYAL SHI'AR WOULD QUESTION THAT.
IT FOLLOWS, THEN, THAT YOU ARE NOT LOYAL. TAKE HIM INTO CUSTODY.
KILL HIM IF HE SPEAKS AGAIN.
B-BUT, COMMANDER! PLEASE!
WE MUST NOT FLINCH FROM OUR DUTY.
WHEREVER IT MAY TAKE US.

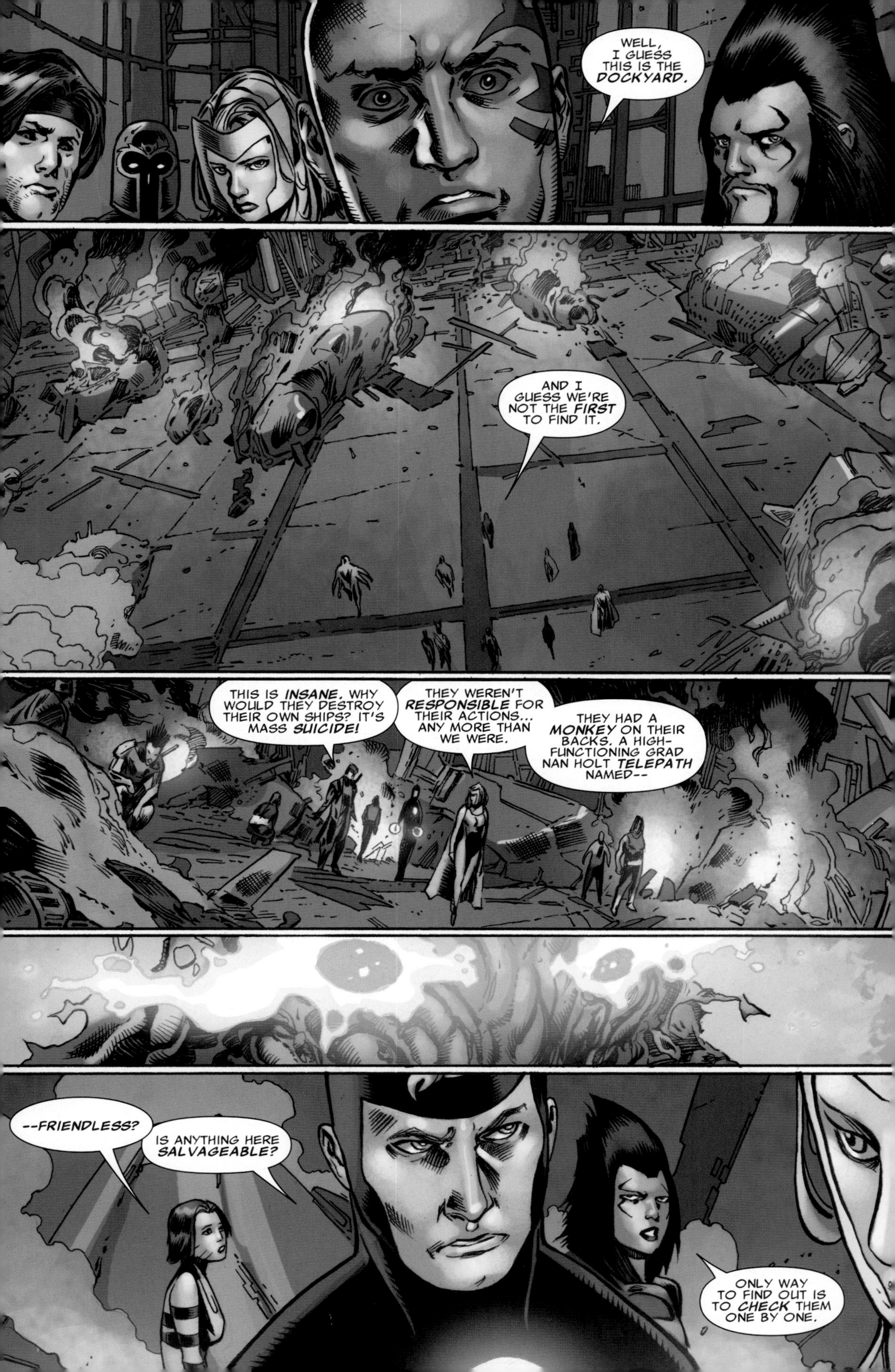
WELL, I GUESS THIS IS THE DOCKYARD.
AND I GUESS WE'RE NOT THE FIRST TO FIND IT.
THIS IS INSANE. WHY WOULD THEY DESTROY THEIR OWN SHIPS? IT'S MASS SUICIDE!
THEY WEREN'T RESPONSIBLE FOR THEIR ACTIONS... ANY MORE THAN WE WERE.
THEY HAD A MONKEY ON THEIR BACKS. A HIGH-FUNCTIONING GRAD NAN HOLT TELEPATH NAMED--
--FRIENDLESS?
IS ANYTHING HERE SALVAGEABLE?
ONLY WAY TO FIND OUT IS TO CHECK THEM ONE BY ONE.

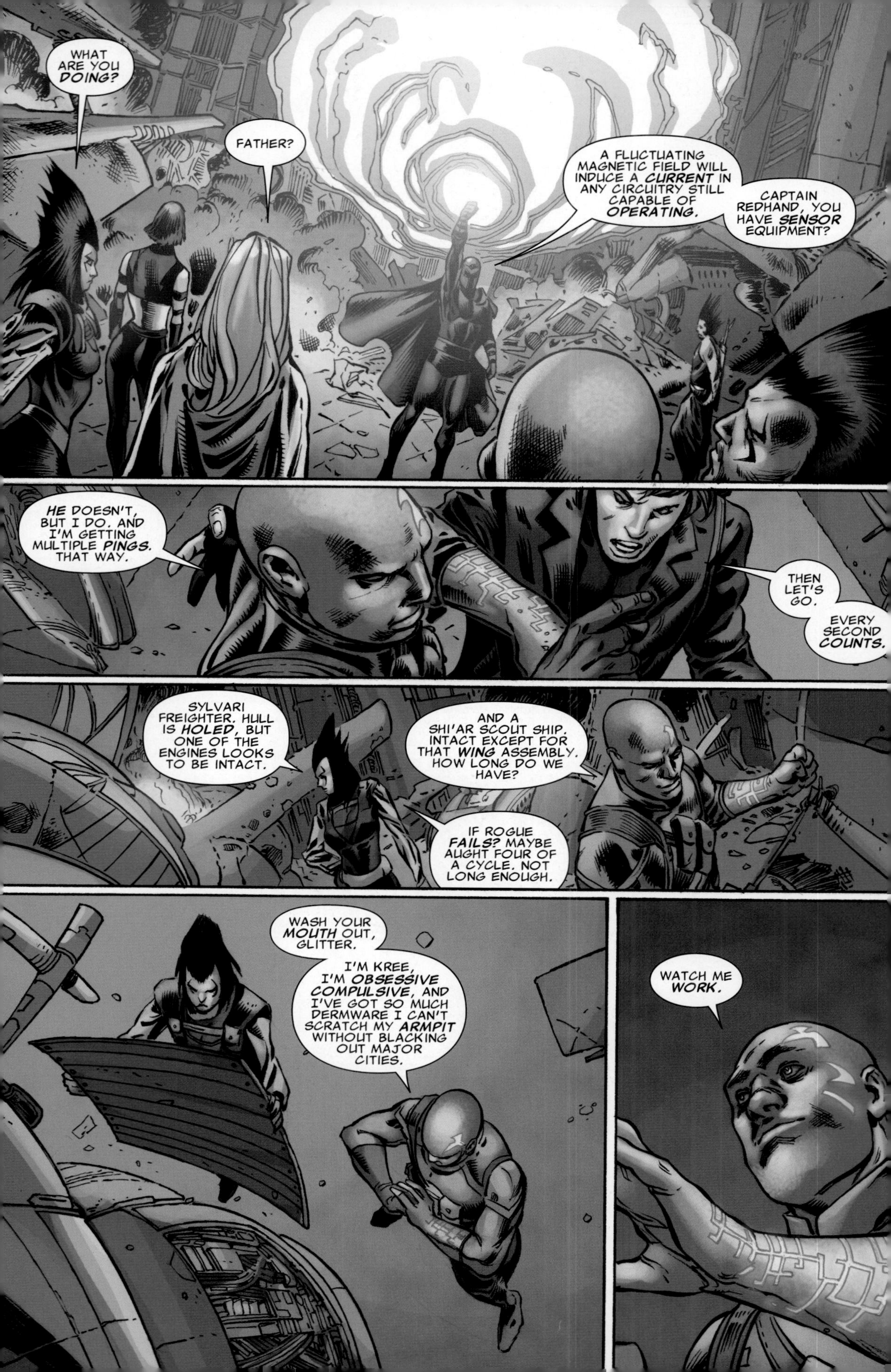
WHAT ARE YOU DOING?
FATHER?
A FLUCTUATING MAGNETIC FIELD WILL INDUCE A CURRENT IN ANY CIRCUITRY STILL CAPABLE OF OPERATING.
CAPTAIN REDHAND, YOU HAVE SENSOR EQUIPMENT?
HE DOESN'T, BUT I DO. AND I'M GETTING MULTIPLE PINGS. THAT WAY.
THEN LET'S GO.
EVERY SECOND COUNTS.
SYLVARI FREIGHTER. HULL IS HOLED, BUT ONE OF THE ENGINES LOOKS TO BE INTACT.
AND A SHI'AR SCOUT SHIP. INTACT EXCEPT FOR THAT WING ASSEMBLY. HOW LONG DO WE HAVE?
IF ROGUE FAILS? MAYBE AUGHT FOUR OF A CYCLE. NOT LONG ENOUGH.
WASH YOUR MOUTH OUT, GLITTER.
I'M KREE, I'M OBSESSIVE COMPULSIVE, AND I'VE GOT SO MUCH DERMWARE I CAN'T SCRATCH MY ARMPIT WITHOUT BLACKING OUT MAJOR CITIES.
WATCH ME WORK.

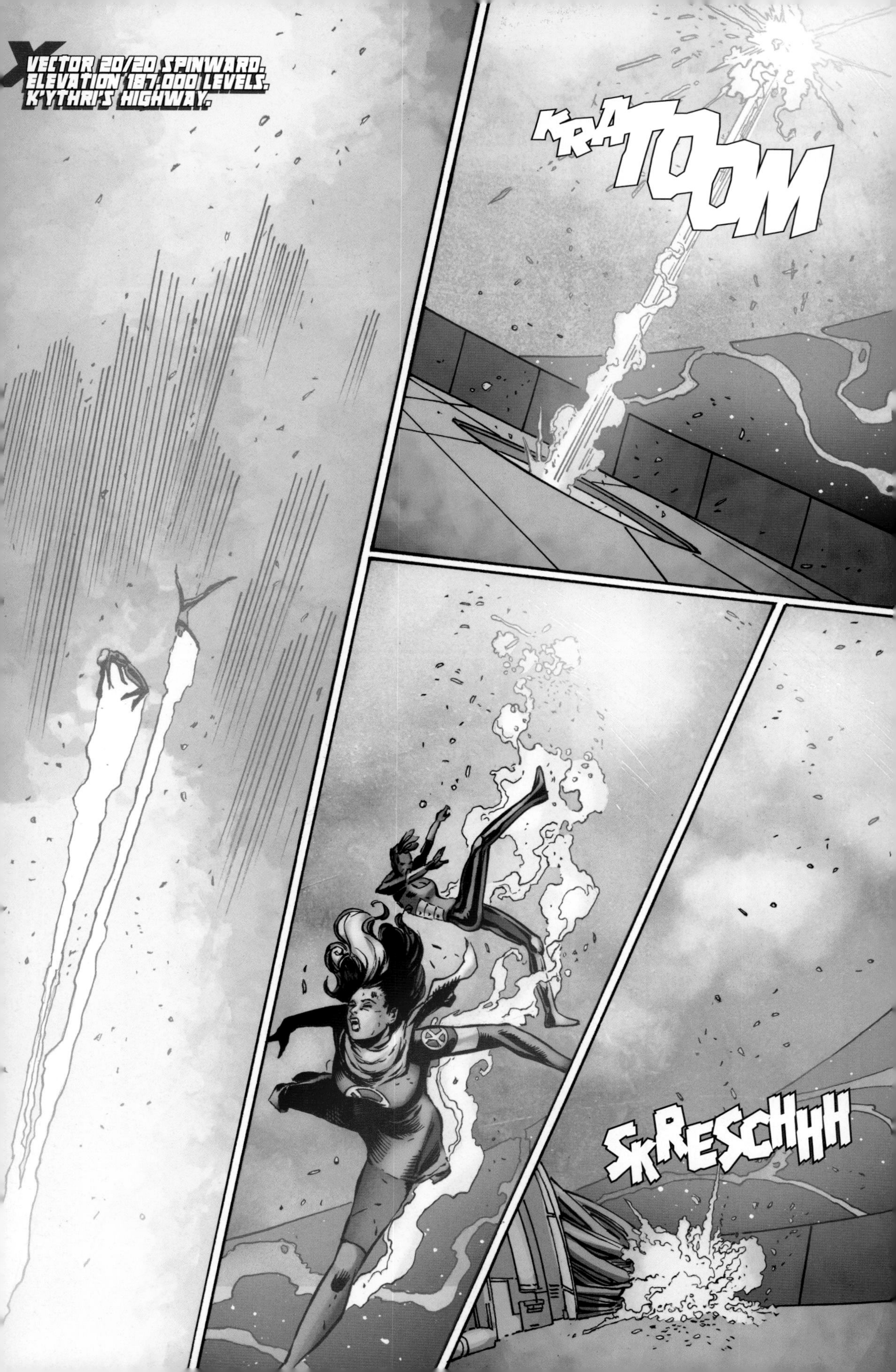
VECTOR 20/20 SPINWARD. ELEVATION 187,000 LEVELS. K'YTHRI'S HIGHWAY.
KRA-TOOOM
SKRESCHHH

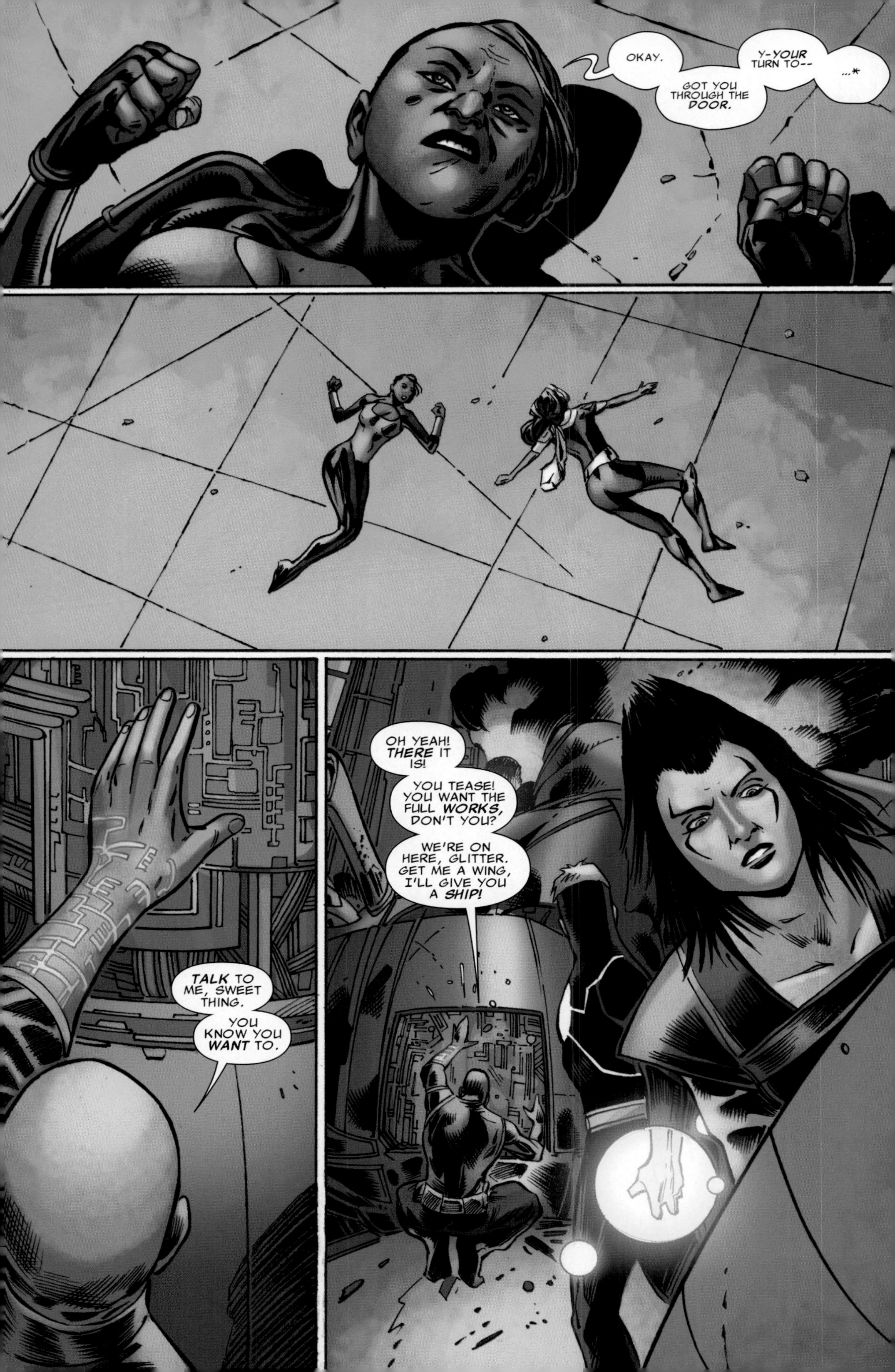
OKAY.
GOT YOU THROUGH THE DOOR.
Y-YOUR TURN TO--
...*
TALK TO ME, SWEET THING.
YOU KNOW YOU WANT TO.
OH YEAH! THERE IT IS!
YOU TEASE! YOU WANT THE FULL WORKS, DON'T YOU?
WE'RE ON HERE, GLITTER. GET ME A WING, I'LL GIVE YOU A SHIP!

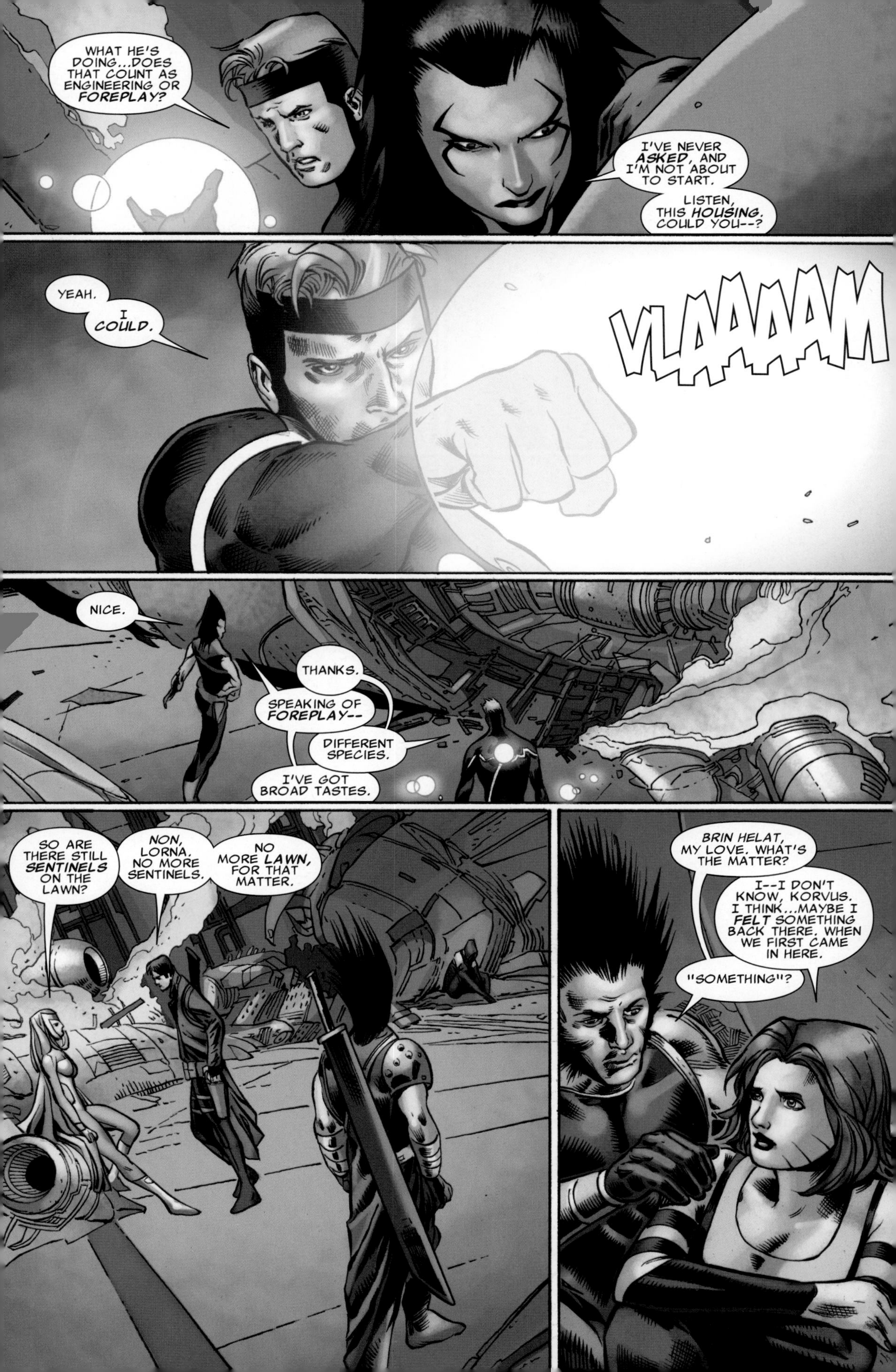

WHAT HE'S DOING...DOES THAT COUNT AS ENGINEERING OR FOREPLAY?
I'VE NEVER ASKED, AND I'M NOT ABOUT TO START.
LISTEN, THIS HOUSING. COULD YOU--?
YEAH. I COULD.
VLAAAAM
NICE.
THANKS.
SPEAKING OF FOREPLAY--
DIFFERENT SPECIES.
I'VE GOT BROAD TASTES.
SO ARE THERE STILL SENTINELS ON THE LAWN?
NON, LORNA. NO MORE SENTINELS.
NO MORE LAWN, FOR THAT MATTER.
BRIN HELAT, MY LOVE. WHAT'S THE MATTER?
I--I DON'T KNOW, KORVUS. I THINK...MAYBE I FELT SOMETHING BACK THERE. WHEN WE FIRST CAME IN HERE.
"SOMETHING"?

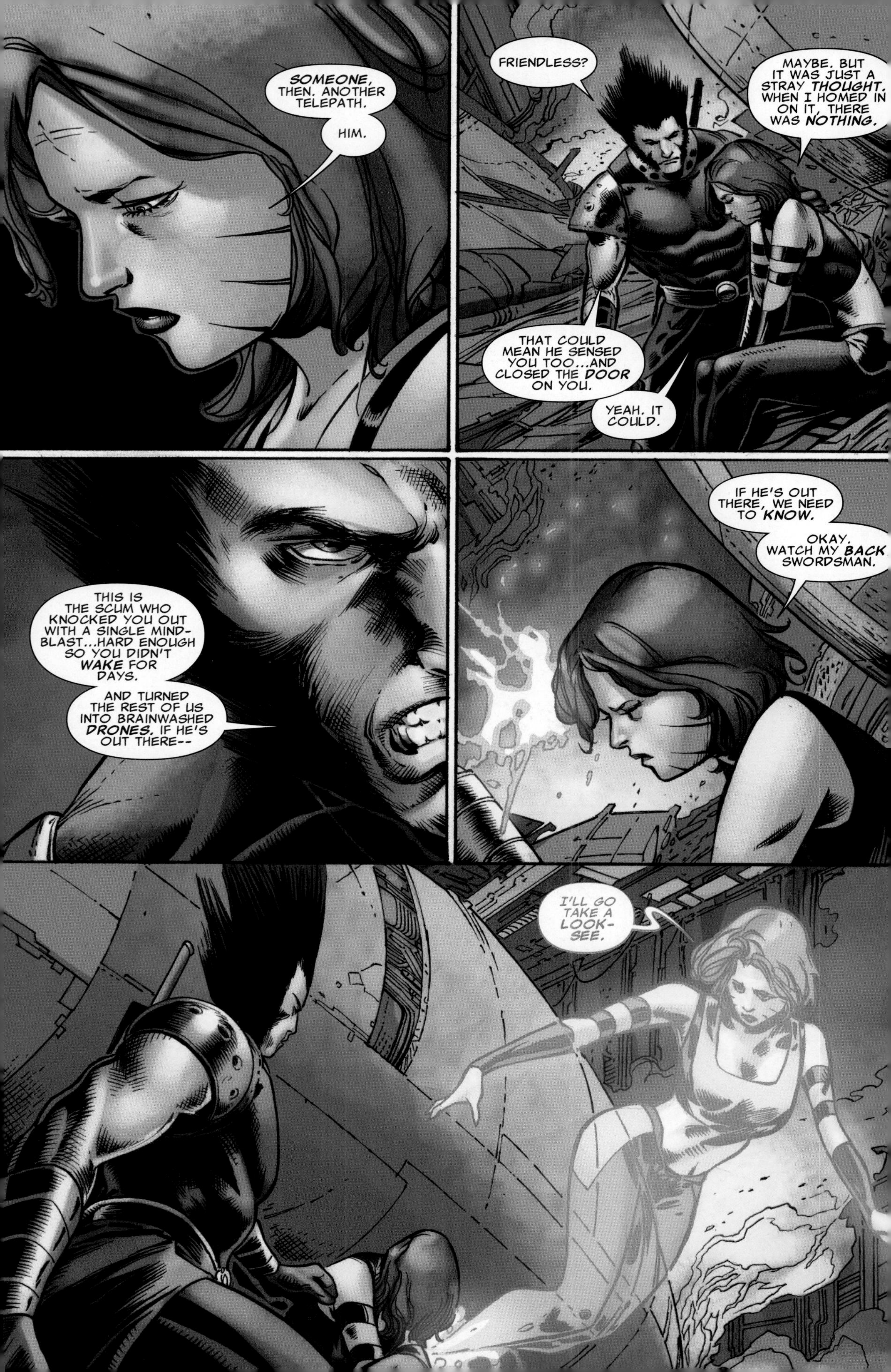
SOMEONE, THEN. ANOTHER TELEPATH.
HIM.
FRIENDLESS?
MAYBE. BUT IT WAS JUST A STRAY THOUGHT. WHEN I HOMED IN ON IT, THERE WAS NOTHING.
THAT COULD MEAN HE SENSED YOU TOO...AND CLOSED THE DOOR ON YOU.
YEAH. IT COULD.
THIS IS THE SCUM WHO KNOCKED YOU OUT WITH A SINGLE MIND-BLAST...HARD ENOUGH SO YOU DIDN'T WAKE FOR DAYS.
AND TURNED THE REST OF US INTO BRAINWASHED DRONES. IF HE'S OUT THERE--
IF HE'S OUT THERE, WE NEED TO KNOW.
OKAY. WATCH MY BACK SWORDSMAN.
I'LL GO TAKE A LOOK-SEE.

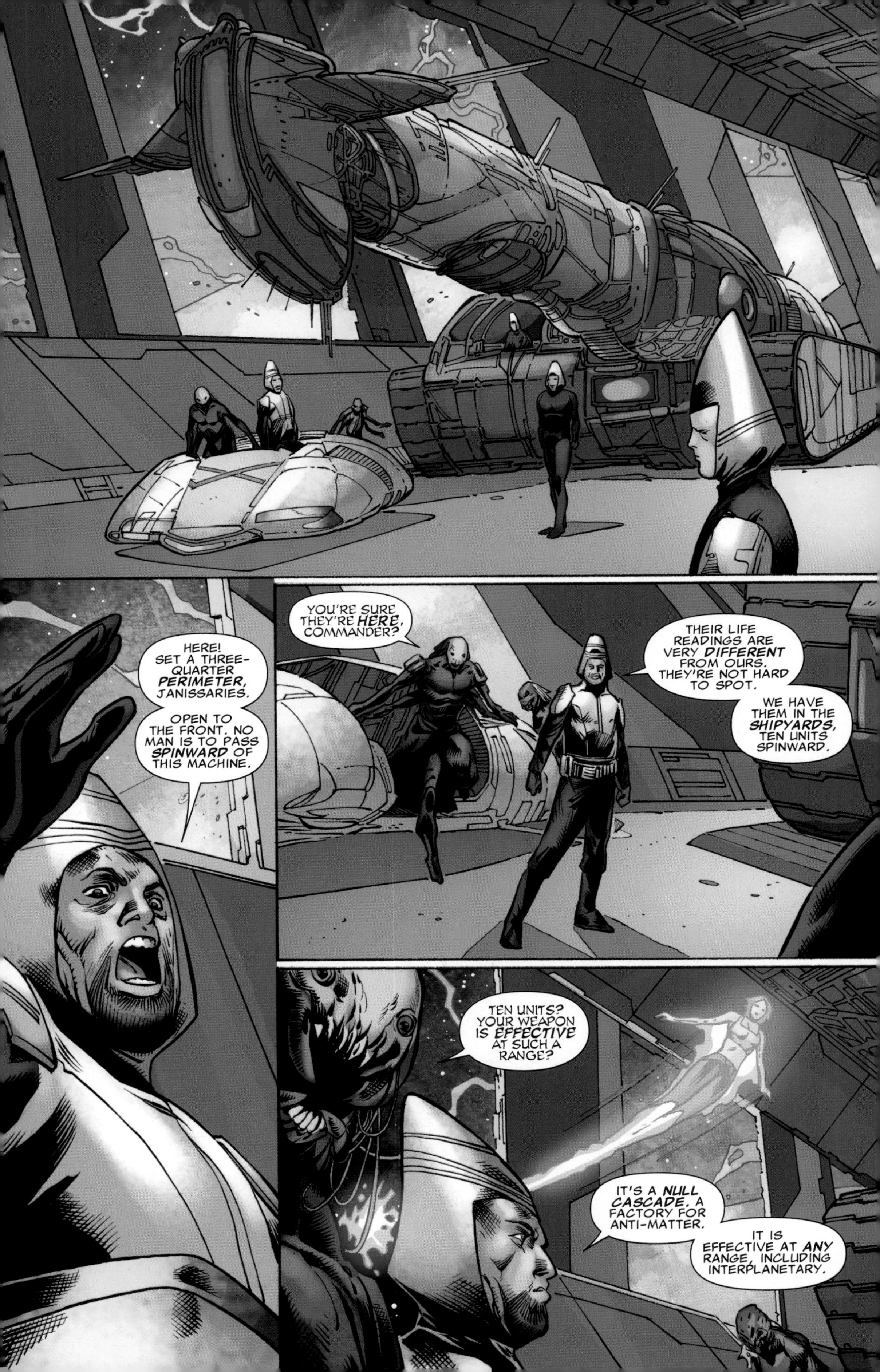
HERE! SET A THREE-QUARTER PERIMETER, JANISSARIES.
OPEN TO THE FRONT. NO MAN IS TO PASS SPINWARD OF THIS MACHINE.
YOU'RE SURE THEY'RE HERE, COMMANDER?
THEIR LIFE READINGS ARE VERY DIFFERENT FROM OURS. THEY'RE NOT HARD TO SPOT.
WE HAVE THEM IN THE SHIPYARDS, TEN UNITS SPINWARD.
TEN UNITS? YOUR WEAPON IS EFFECTIVE AT SUCH A RANGE?
IT'S A NULL CASCADE. A FACTORY FOR ANTI-MATTER.
IT IS EFFECTIVE AT ANY RANGE, INCLUDING INTERPLANETARY.

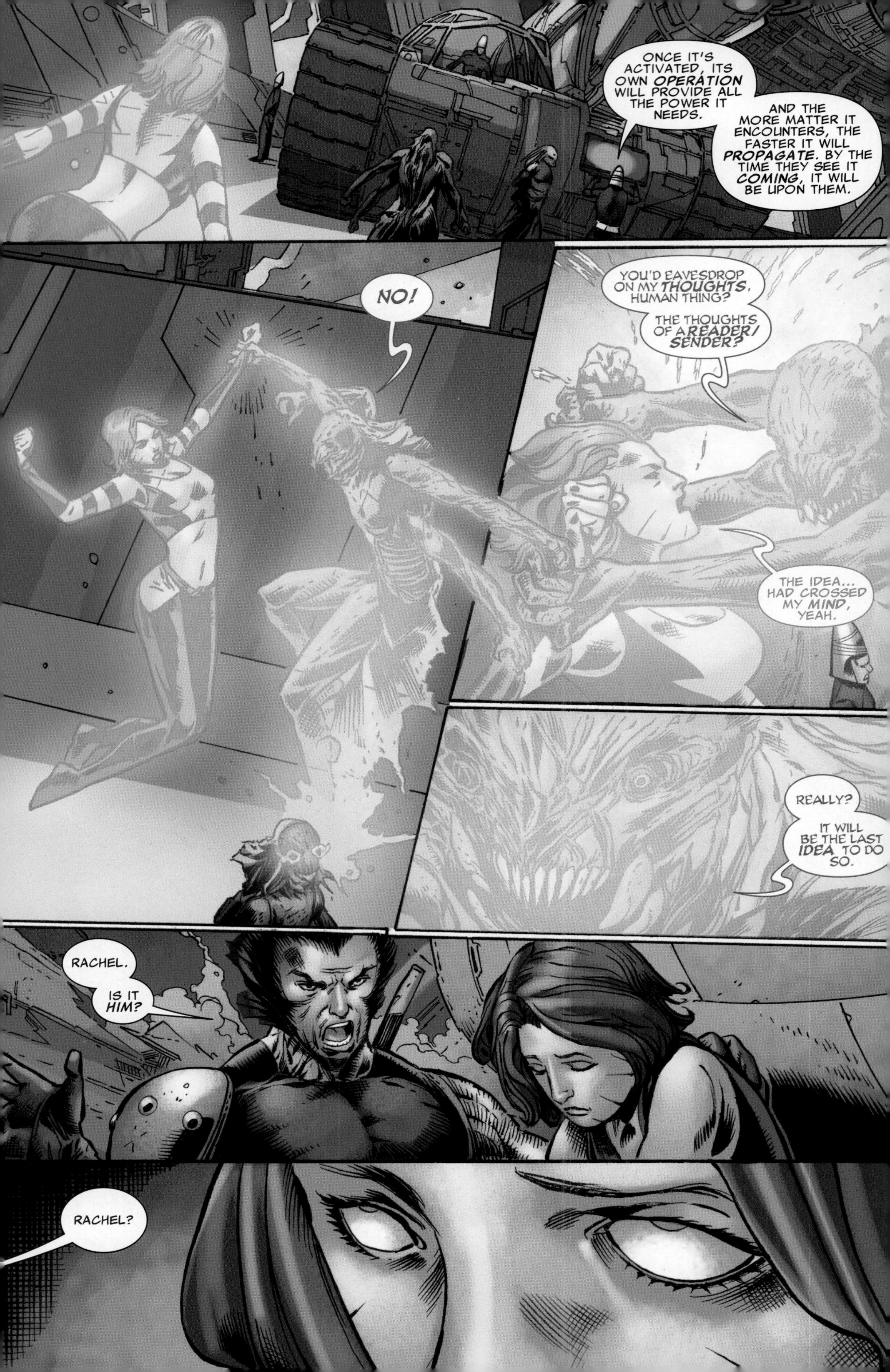
ONCE IT'S ACTIVATED, ITS OWN OPERATION WILL PROVIDE ALL THE POWER IT NEEDS.
AND THE MORE MATTER IT ENCOUNTERS, THE FASTER IT WILL PROPAGATE. BY THE TIME THEY SEE IT COMING, IT WILL BE UPON THEM.
NO!
YOU'D EAVESDROP ON MY THOUGHTS, HUMAN THING?
THE THOUGHTS OF A READER/SENDER?
THE IDEA... HAD CROSSED MY MIND, YEAH.
REALLY?
IT WILL BE THE LAST IDEA TO DO SO.
RACHEL.
IS IT HIM?
RACHEL?

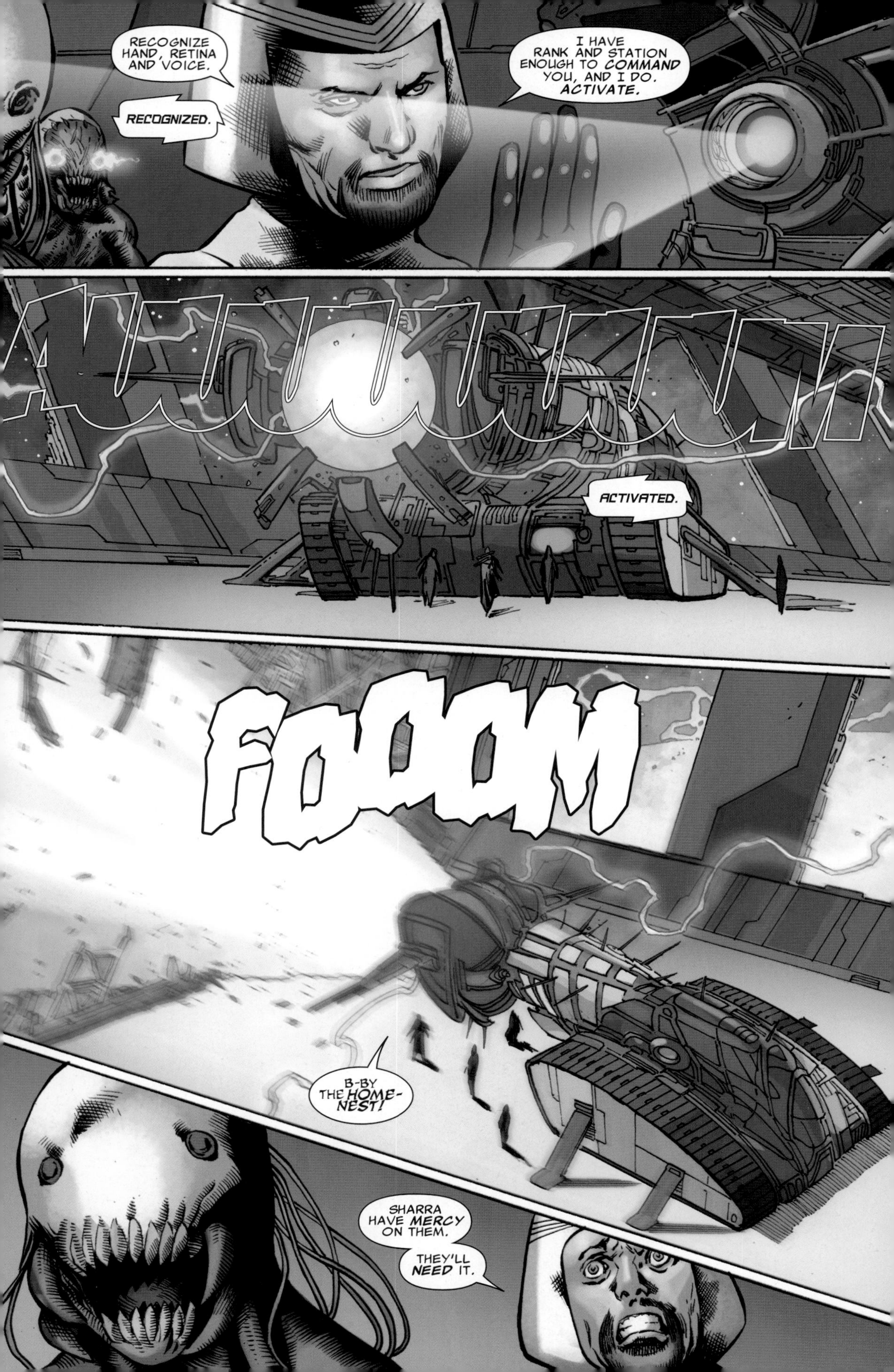
RECOGNIZE HAND, RETINA AND VOICE.
RECOGNIZED.
I HAVE RANK AND STATION ENOUGH TO COMMAND YOU, AND I DO. ACTIVATE.
AUUUUUM
ACTIVATED.
FOOOM
B-BY THE HOME-NEST!
SHARRA HAVE MERCY ON THEM.
THEY'LL NEED IT.

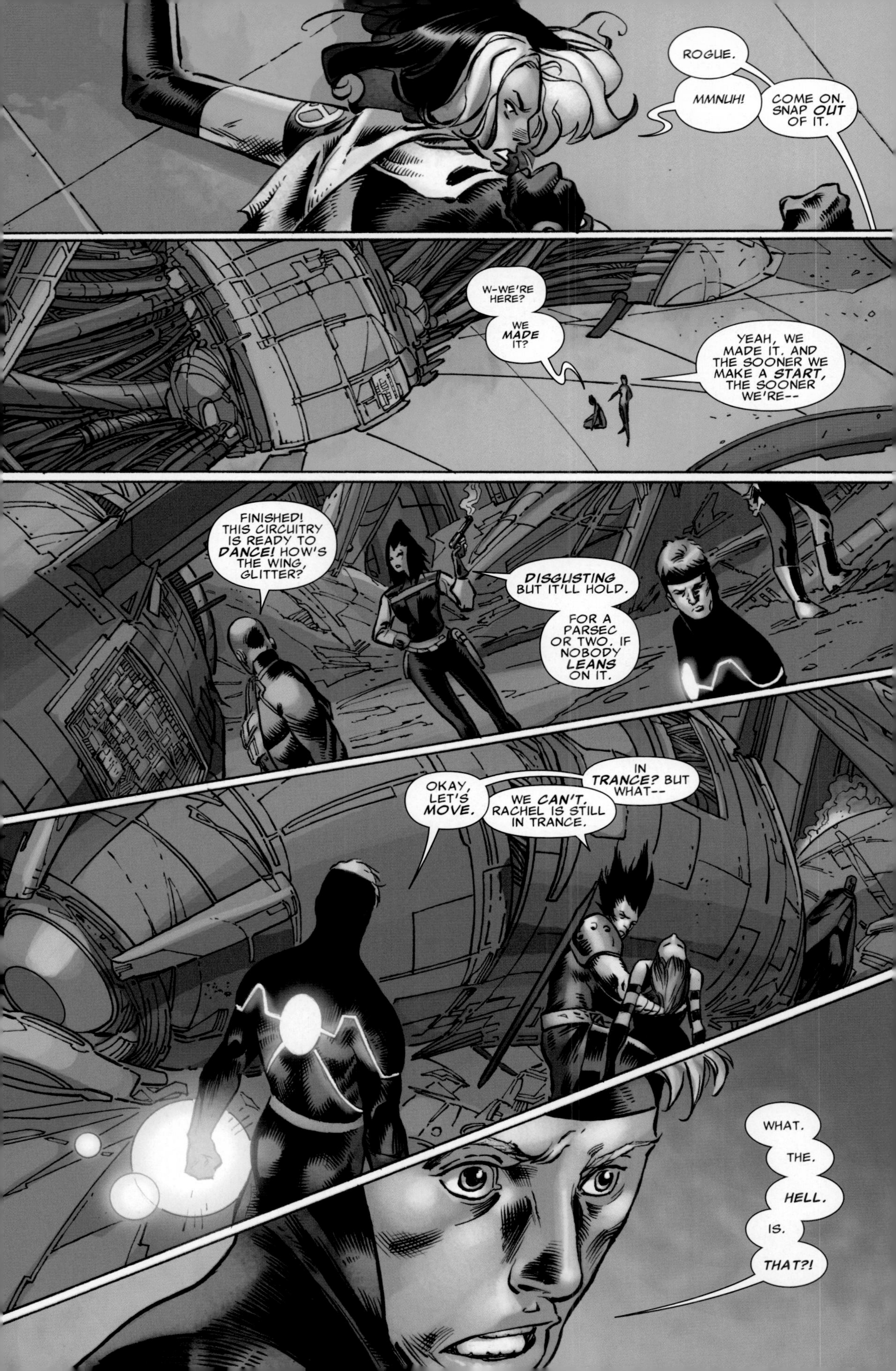
ROGUE.
MMNUH!
COME ON. SNAP OUT OF IT.
W-WE'RE HERE?
WE MADE IT?
YEAH, WE MADE IT. AND THE SOONER WE MAKE A START, THE SOONER WE'RE--
FINISHED! THIS CIRCUITRY IS READY TO DANCE! HOW'S THE WING, GLITTER?
DISGUSTING BUT IT'LL HOLD.
FOR A PARSEC OR TWO. IF NOBODY LEANS ON IT.
OKAY, LET'S MOVE.
WE CAN'T. RACHEL IS STILL IN TRANCE.
IN TRANCE? BUT WHAT--
WHAT.
THE.
HELL.
IS.
THAT?!

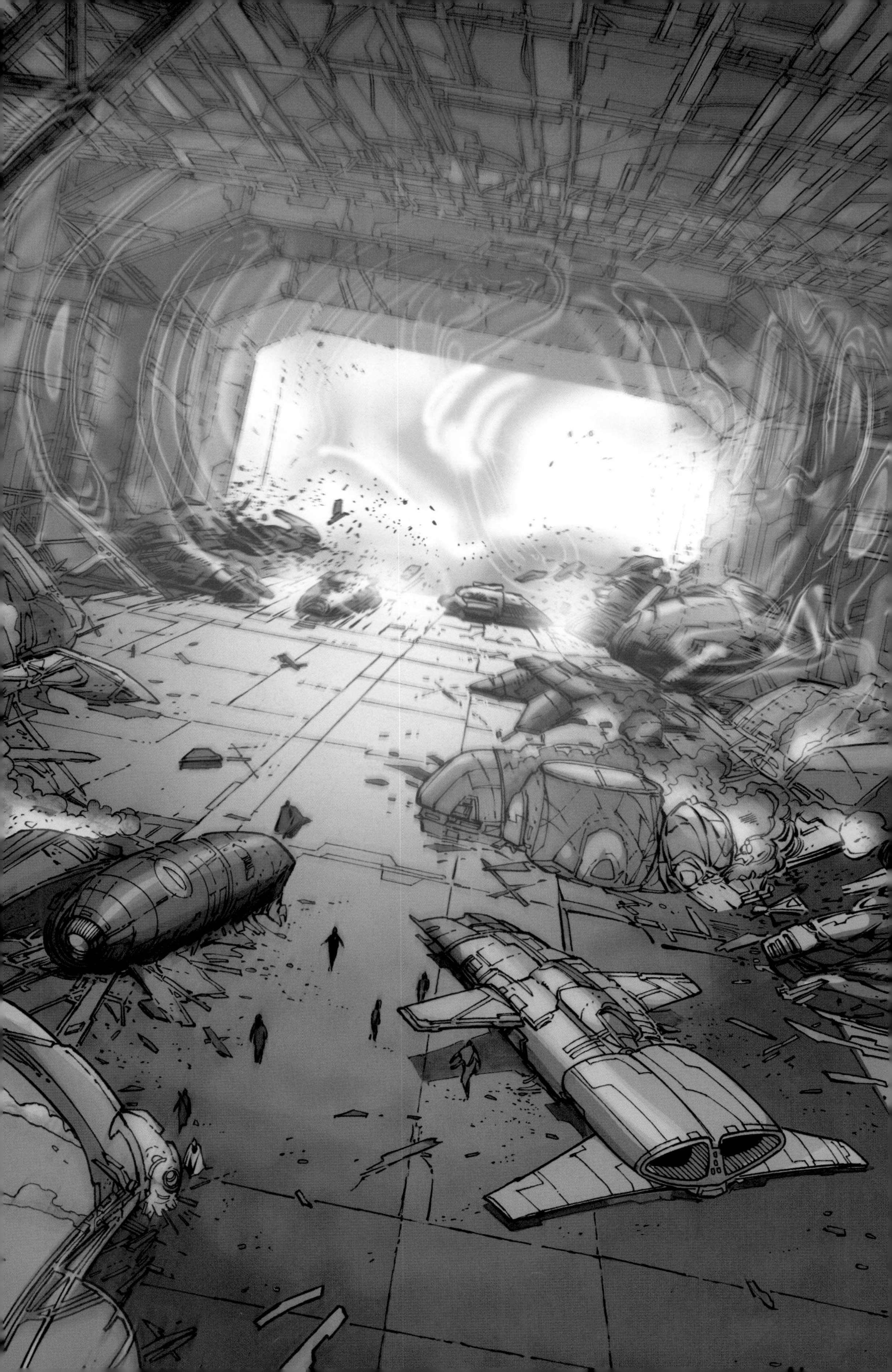

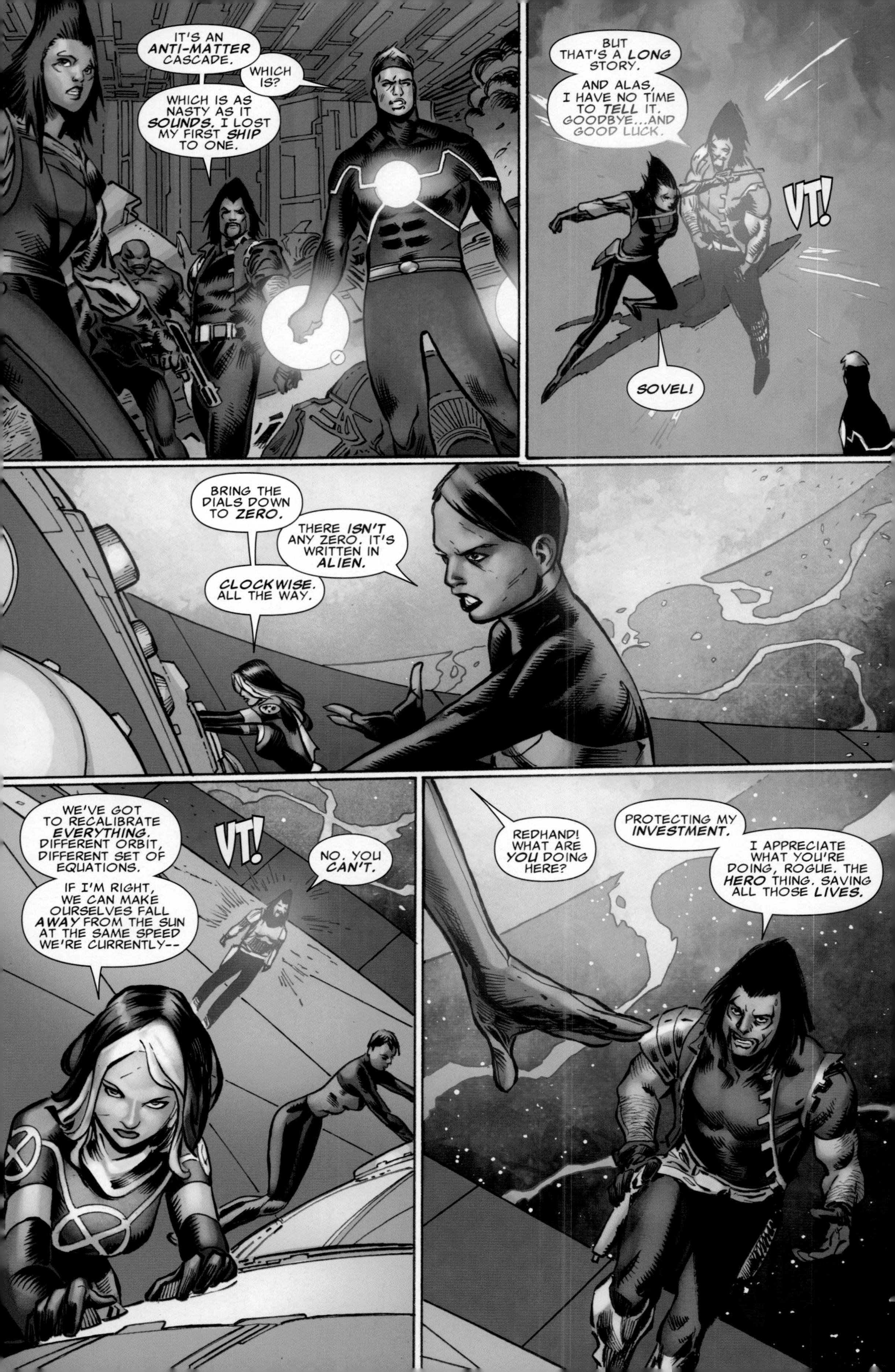
IT'S AN ANTI-MATTER CASCADE.
WHICH IS?
WHICH IS AS NASTY AS IT SOUNDS. I LOST MY FIRST SHIP TO ONE.
BUT THAT'S A LONG STORY.
AND ALAS, I HAVE NO TIME TO TELL IT. GOODBYE...AND GOOD LUCK.
VT!
SOVEL!
BRING THE DIALS DOWN TO ZERO.
THERE ISN'T ANY ZERO. IT'S WRITTEN IN ALIEN.
CLOCKWISE. ALL THE WAY.
WE'VE GOT TO RECALIBRATE EVERYTHING. DIFFERENT ORBIT, DIFFERENT SET OF EQUATIONS.
IF I'M RIGHT, WE CAN MAKE OURSELVES FALL AWAY FROM THE SUN AT THE SAME SPEED WE'RE CURRENTLY--
VT!
NO. YOU CAN'T.
REDHAND! WHAT ARE YOU DOING HERE?
PROTECTING MY INVESTMENT.
I APPRECIATE WHAT YOU'RE DOING, ROGUE. THE HERO THING. SAVING ALL THOSE LIVES.

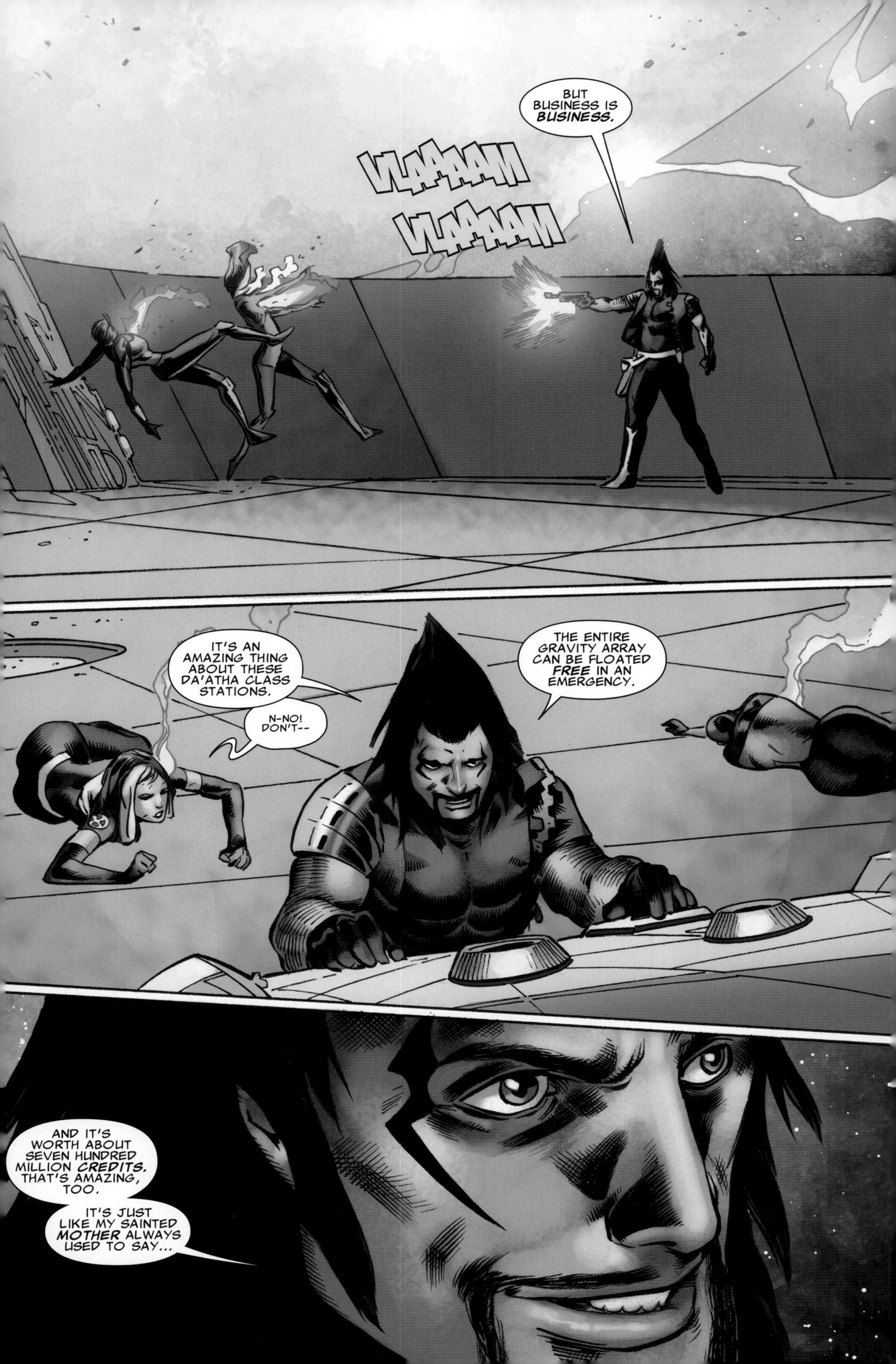
BUT BUSINESS IS BUSINESS.
VLAAAAM
VLAAAAM
IT'S AN AMAZING THING ABOUT THESE DA'ATHA CLASS STATIONS.
N-NO! DON'T--
THE ENTIRE GRAVITY ARRAY CAN BE FLOATED FREE IN AN EMERGENCY.
AND IT'S WORTH ABOUT SEVEN HUNDRED MILLION CREDITS. THAT'S AMAZING, TOO.
IT'S JUST LIKE MY SAINTED MOTHER ALWAYS USED TO SAY...

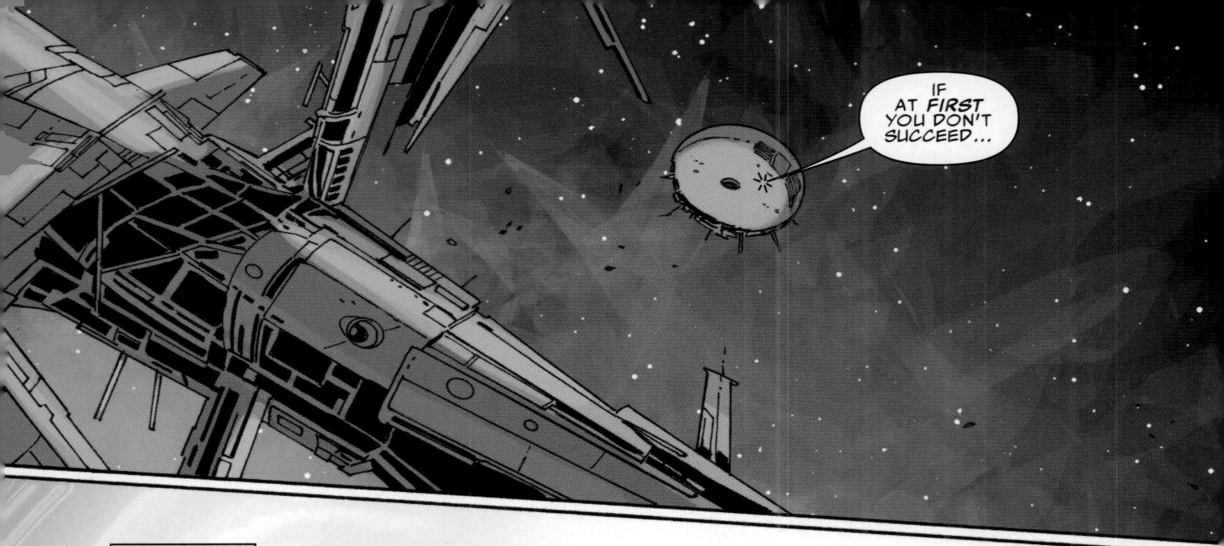
IF AT FIRST YOU DON'T SUCCEED...

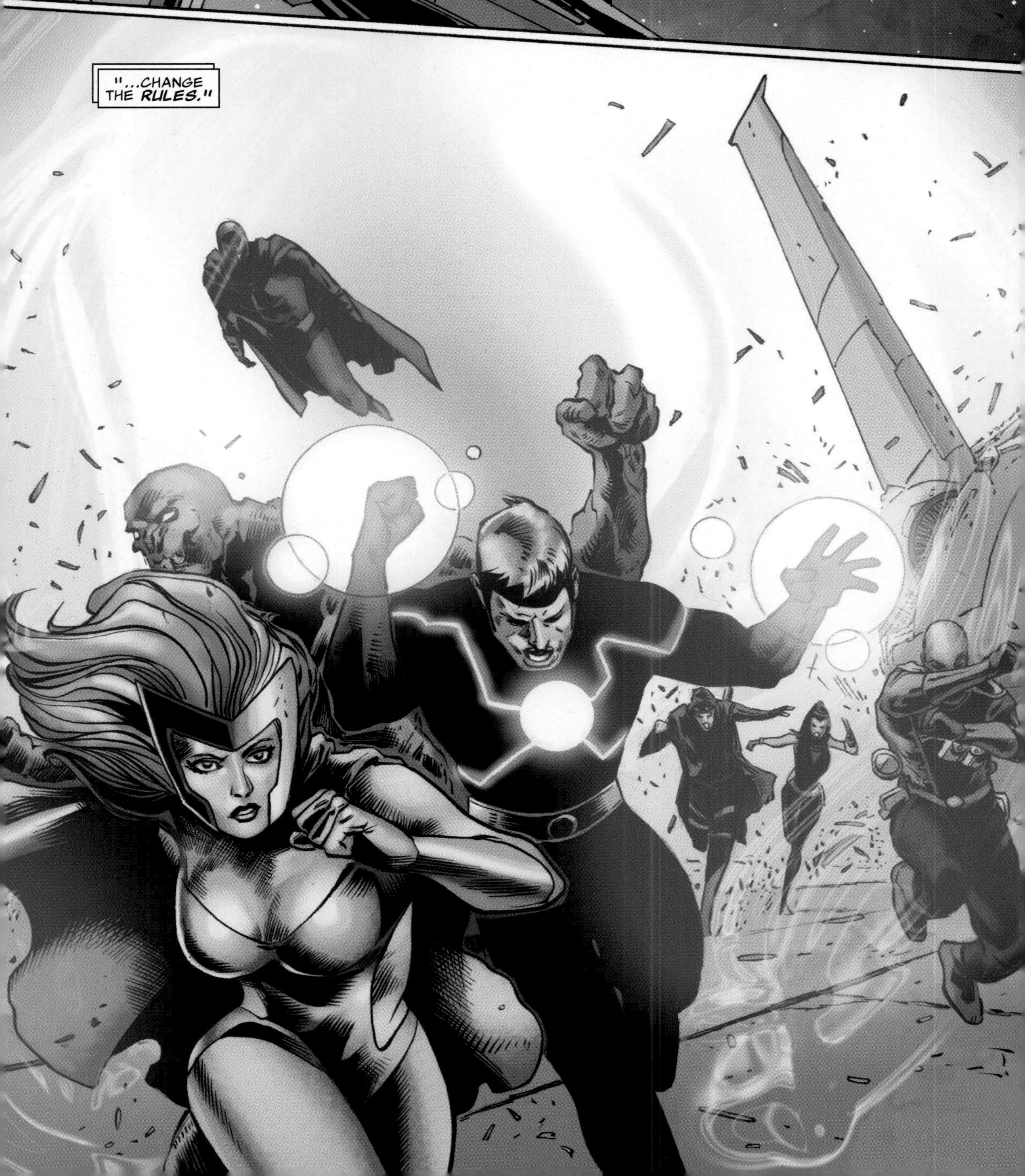
"...CHANGE THE RULES."

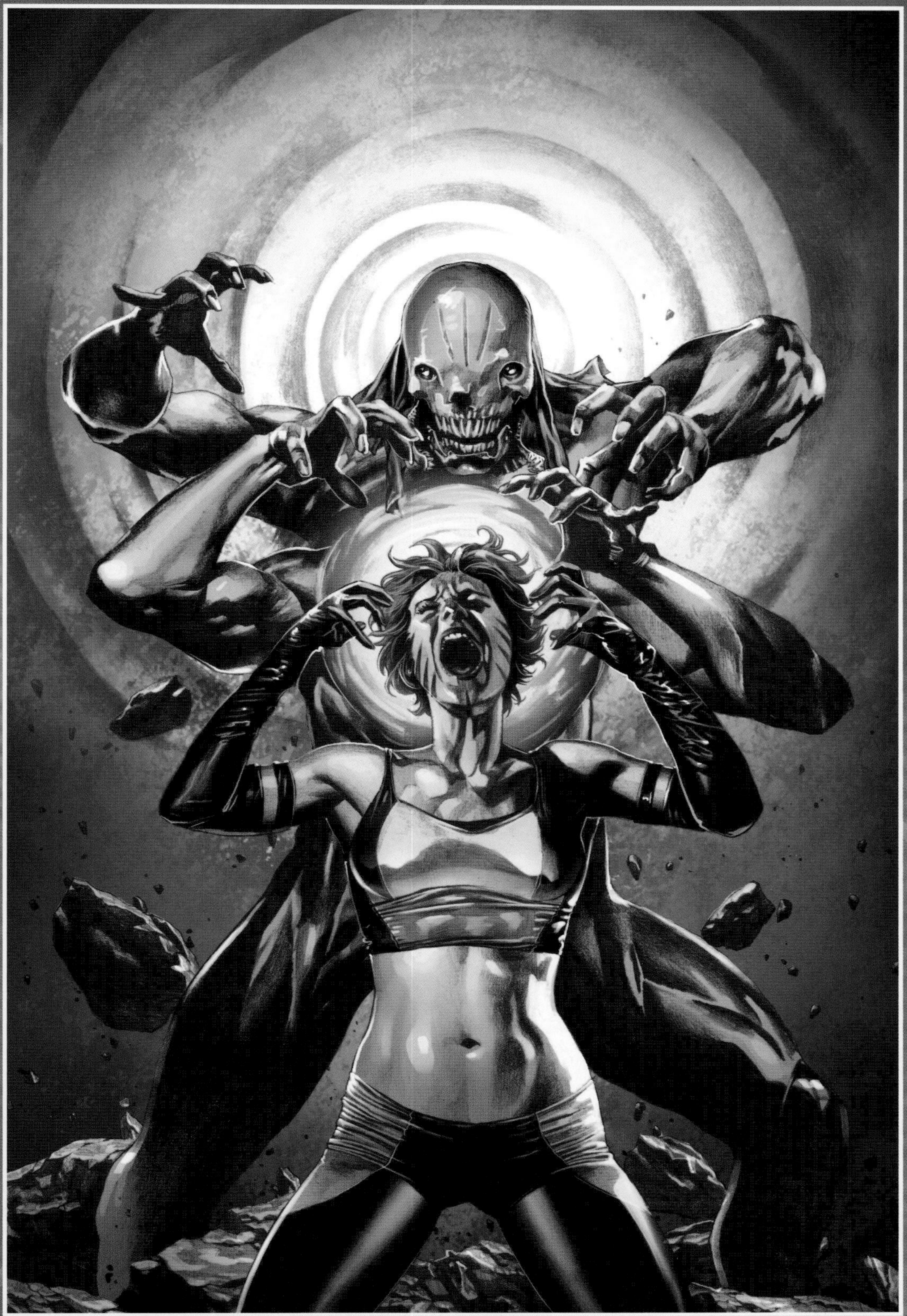

#258
"FIVE MILES SOUTH OF THE UNIVERSE" PART FIVE

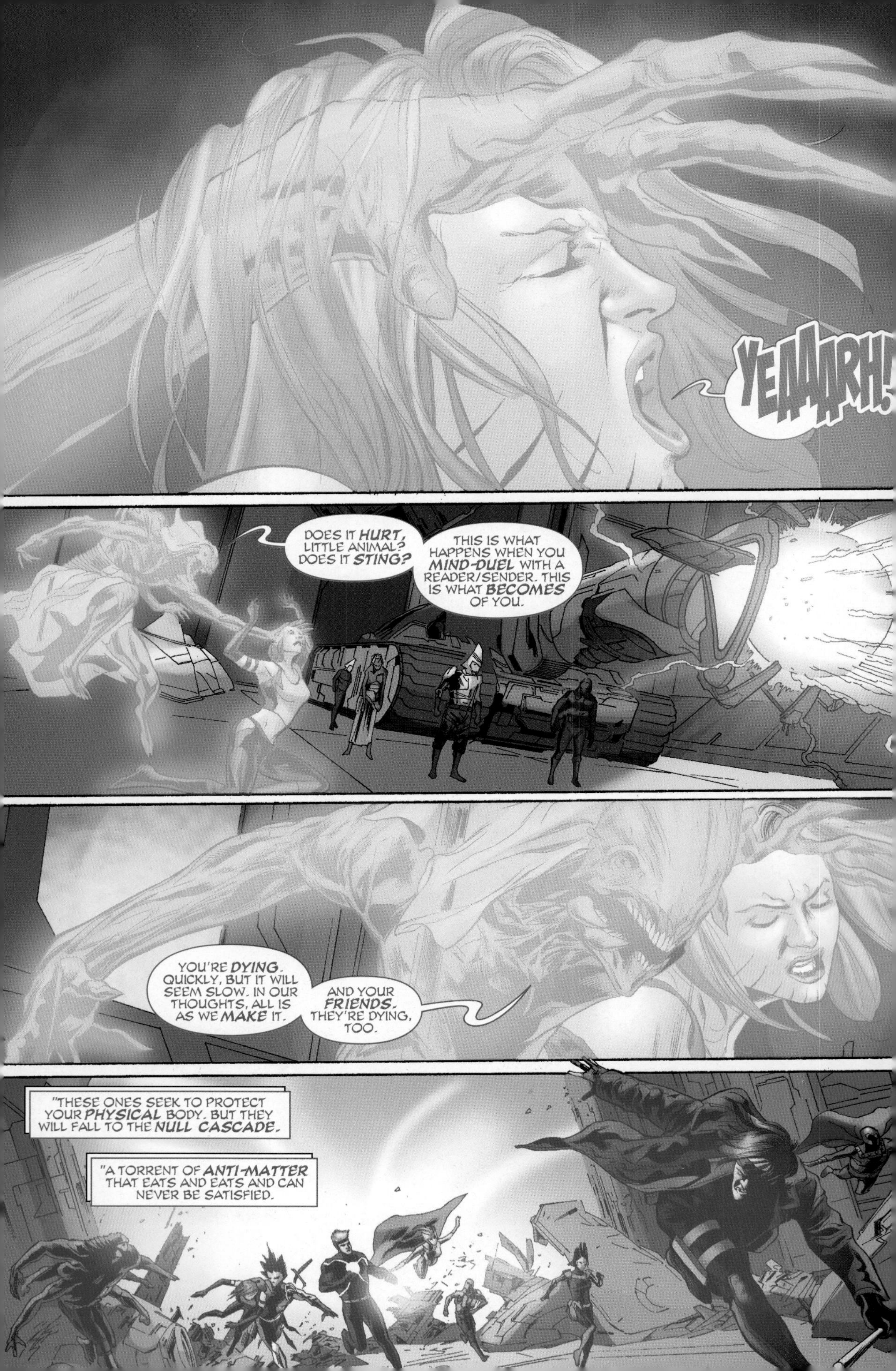
YEAARH!
DOES IT HURT, LITTLE ANIMAL? DOES IT STING?
THIS IS WHAT HAPPENS WHEN YOU MIND-DUEL WITH A READER/SENDER. THIS IS WHAT BECOMES OF YOU.
YOU'RE DYING. QUICKLY, BUT IT WILL SEEM SLOW. IN OUR THOUGHTS, ALL IS AS WE MAKE IT.
AND YOUR FRIENDS. THEY'RE DYING, TOO.
"THESE ONES SEEK TO PROTECT YOUR PHYSICAL BODY. BUT THEY WILL FALL TO THE NULL CASCADE.
"A TORRENT OF ANTI-MATTER THAT EATS AND EATS AND CAN NEVER BE SATISFIED.

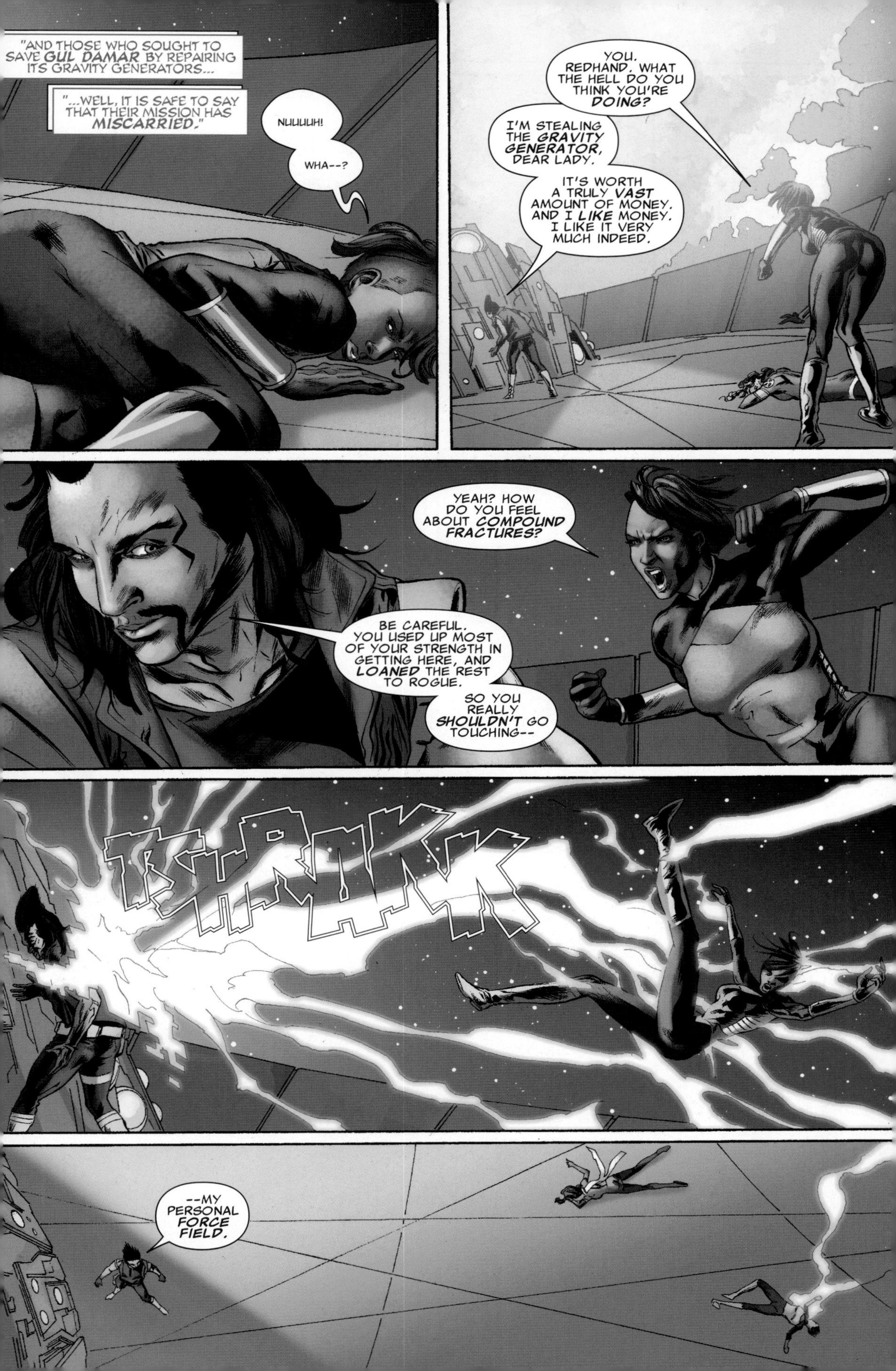
"AND THOSE WHO SOUGHT TO SAVE GUL DAMAR BY REPAIRING ITS GRAVITY GENERATORS...
"...WELL, IT IS SAFE TO SAY THAT THEIR MISSION HAS MISCARRIED."
NUUUUH!
WHA--?
YOU. REDHAND. WHAT THE HELL DO YOU THINK YOU'RE DOING?
I'M STEALING THE GRAVITY GENERATOR, DEAR LADY.
IT'S WORTH A TRULY VAST AMOUNT OF MONEY. AND I LIKE MONEY. I LIKE IT VERY MUCH INDEED.
YEAH? HOW DO YOU FEEL ABOUT COMPOUND FRACTURES?
BE CAREFUL. YOU USED UP MOST OF YOUR STRENGTH IN GETTING HERE, AND LOANED THE REST TO ROGUE.
SO YOU REALLY SHOULDN'T GO TOUCHING--
TZZRAKK
--MY PERSONAL FORCE FIELD.

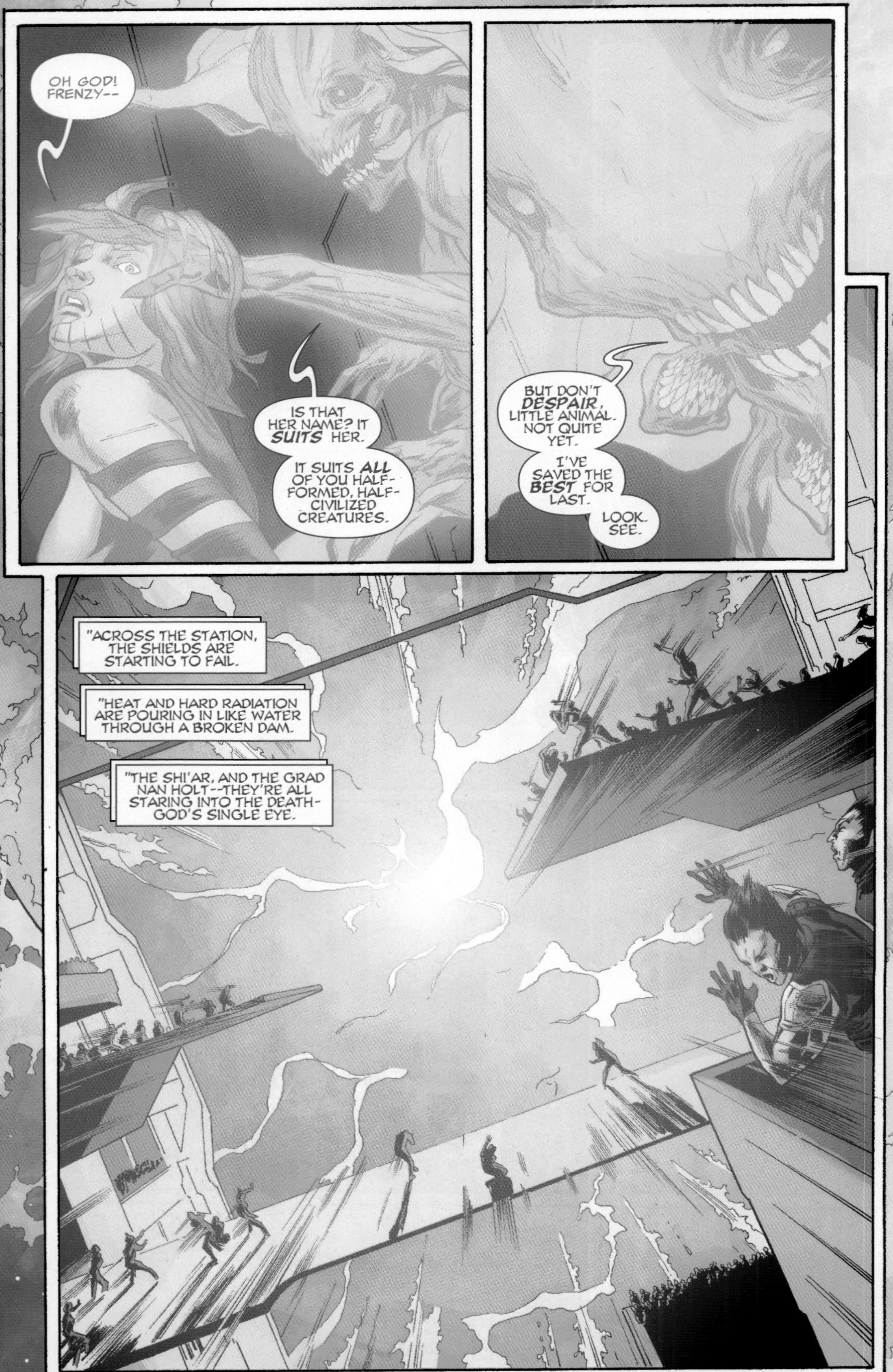
OH GOD! FRENZY--
IS THAT HER NAME? IT SUITS HER.
IT SUITS ALL OF YOU HALF-FORMED, HALF-CIVILIZED CREATURES.
BUT DON'T DESPAIR, LITTLE ANIMAL. NOT QUITE YET.
I'VE SAVED THE BEST FOR LAST.
LOOK. SEE.
"ACROSS THE STATION, THE SHIELDS ARE STARTING TO FAIL.
"HEAT AND HARD RADIATION ARE POURING IN LIKE WATER THROUGH A BROKEN DAM.
"THE SHI'AR, AND THE GRAD NAN HOLT--THEY'RE ALL STARING INTO THE DEATH-GOD'S SINGLE EYE.

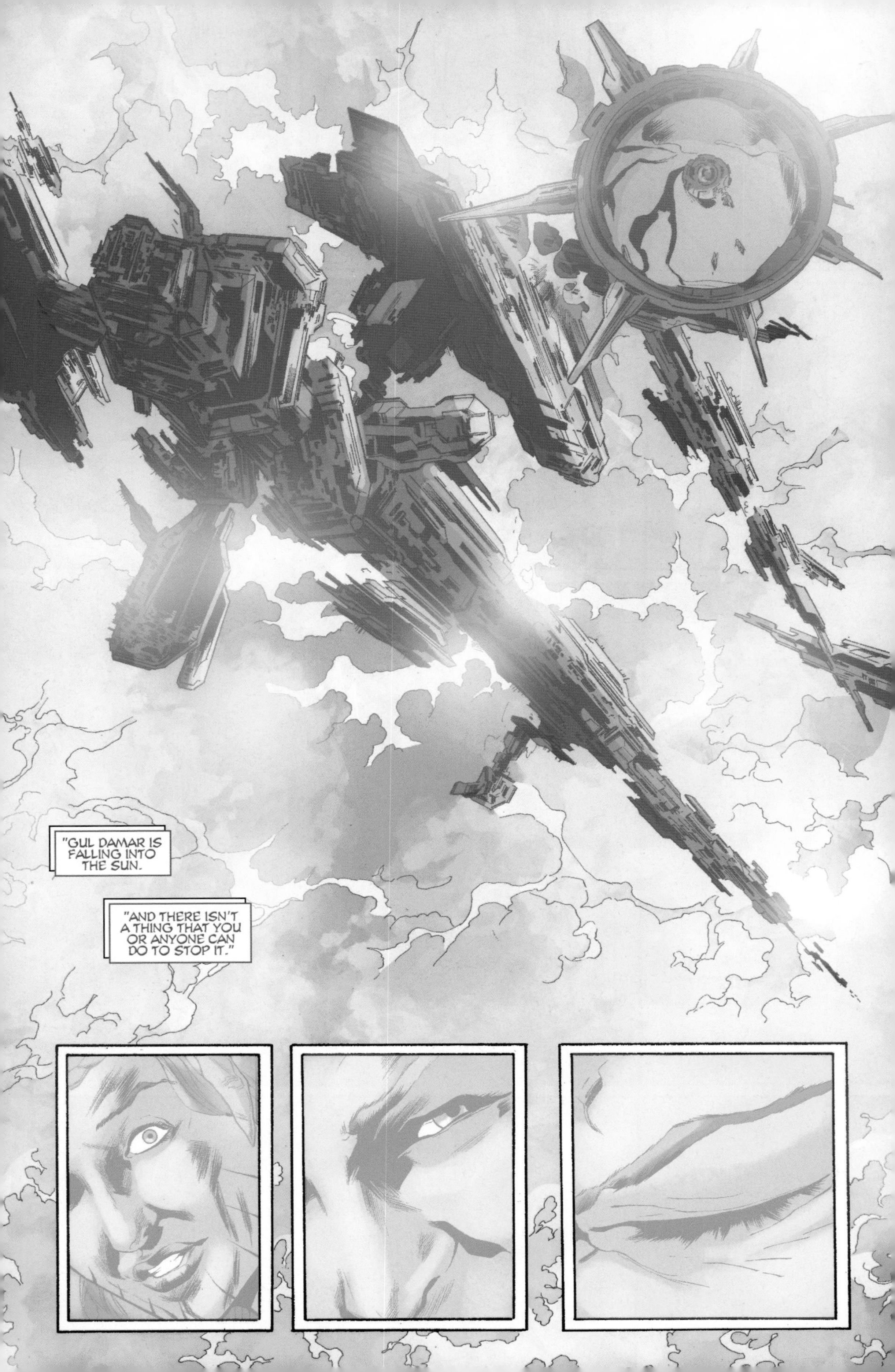
"GUL DAMAR IS FALLING INTO THE SUN.
"AND THERE ISN'T A THING THAT YOU OR ANYONE CAN DO TO STOP IT."

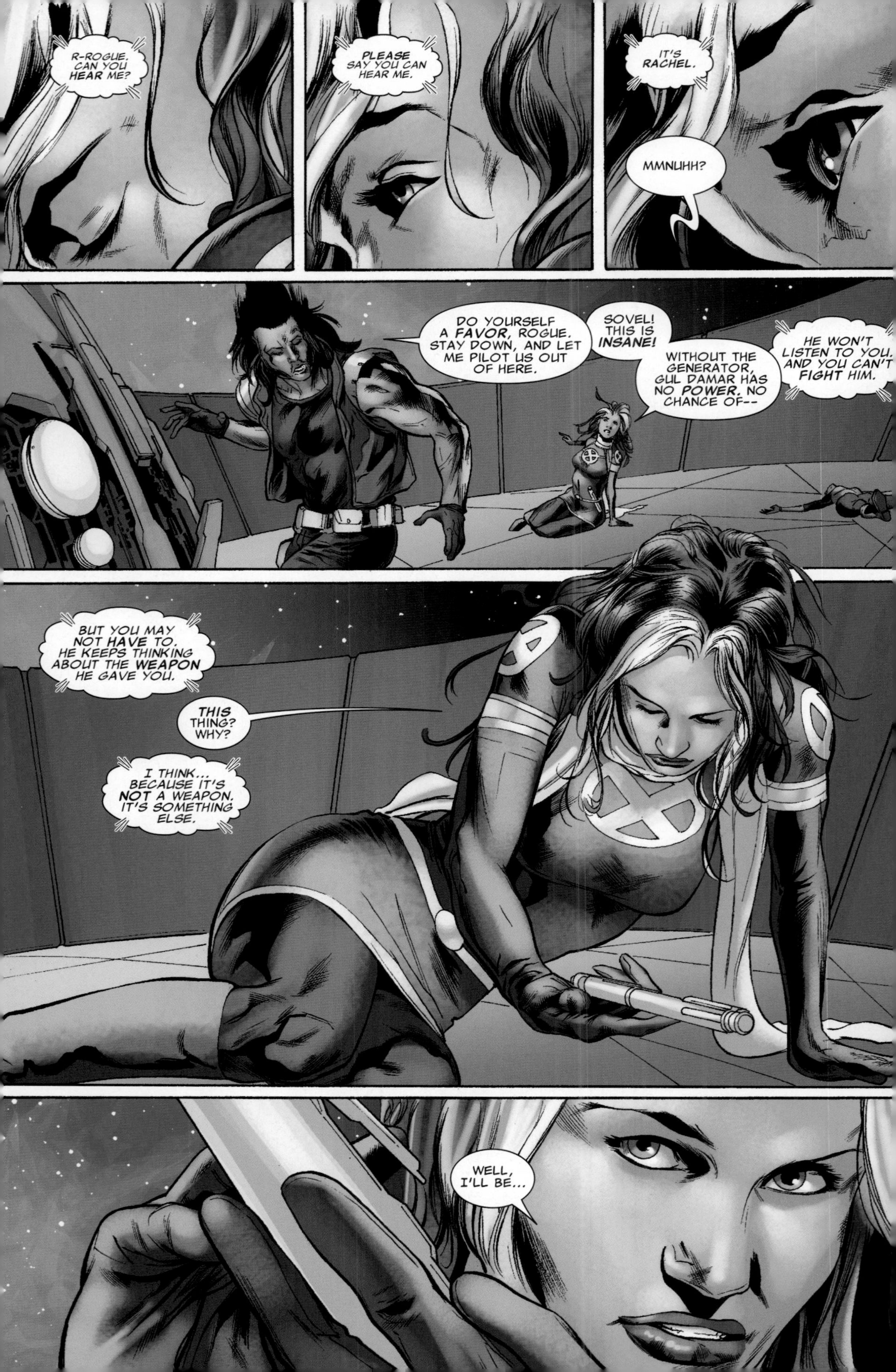
R-ROGUE. CAN YOU HEAR ME?
PLEASE SAY YOU CAN HEAR ME.
IT'S RACHEL.
MMNUHH?
DO YOURSELF A FAVOR, ROGUE. STAY DOWN, AND LET ME PILOT US OUT OF HERE.
SOVEL! THIS IS INSANE!
WITHOUT THE GENERATOR, GUL DAMAR HAS NO POWER. NO CHANCE OF--
HE WON'T LISTEN TO YOU. AND YOU CAN'T FIGHT HIM.
BUT YOU MAY NOT HAVE TO. HE KEEPS THINKING ABOUT THE WEAPON HE GAVE YOU.
THIS THING? WHY?
I THINK... BECAUSE IT'S NOT A WEAPON. IT'S SOMETHING ELSE.
WELL, I'LL BE...

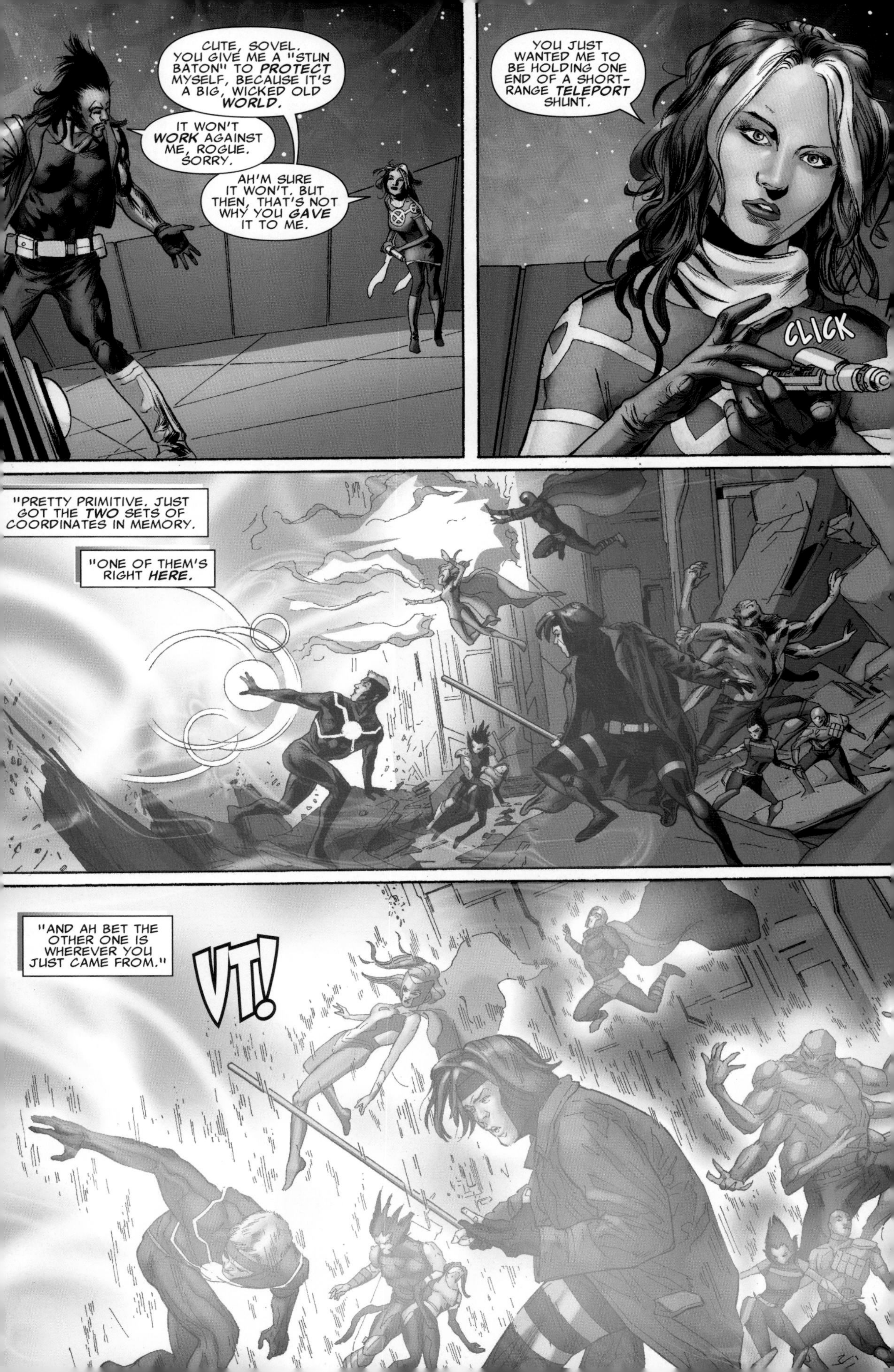

CUTE, SOVEL. YOU GIVE ME A "STUN BATON" TO PROTECT MYSELF, BECAUSE IT'S A BIG, WICKED OLD WORLD.
IT WON'T WORK AGAINST ME, ROGUE. SORRY.
AH'M SURE IT WON'T. BUT THEN, THAT'S NOT WHY YOU GAVE IT TO ME.
YOU JUST WANTED ME TO BE HOLDING ONE END OF A SHORT-RANGE TELEPORT SHUNT.
CLICK
"PRETTY PRIMITIVE. JUST GOT THE TWO SETS OF COORDINATES IN MEMORY.
"ONE OF THEM'S RIGHT HERE.
"AND AH BET THE OTHER ONE IS WHEREVER YOU JUST CAME FROM."
VT!

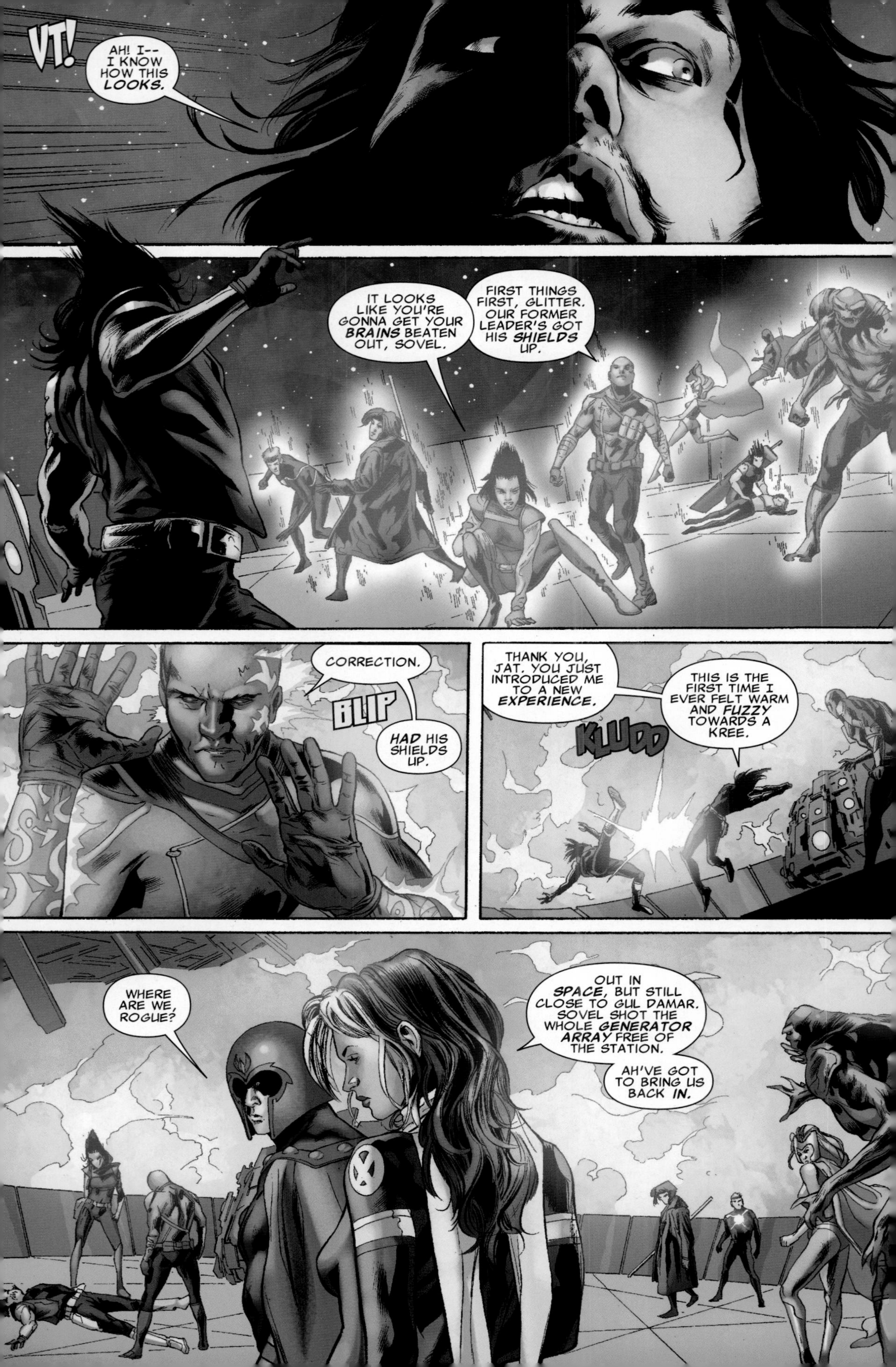
VT!
AH! I-- I KNOW HOW THIS LOOKS.
IT LOOKS LIKE YOU'RE GONNA GET YOUR BRAINS BEATEN OUT, SOVEL.
FIRST THINGS FIRST, GLITTER. OUR FORMER LEADER'S GOT HIS SHIELDS UP.
CORRECTION.
BLIP
HAD HIS SHIELDS UP.
THANK YOU, JAT. YOU JUST INTRODUCED ME TO A NEW EXPERIENCE.
THIS IS THE FIRST TIME I EVER FELT WARM AND FUZZY TOWARDS A KREE.
KLUDD
WHERE ARE WE, ROGUE?
OUT IN SPACE, BUT STILL CLOSE TO GUL DAMAR. SOVEL SHOT THE WHOLE GENERATOR ARRAY FREE OF THE STATION.
AH'VE GOT TO BRING US BACK IN.

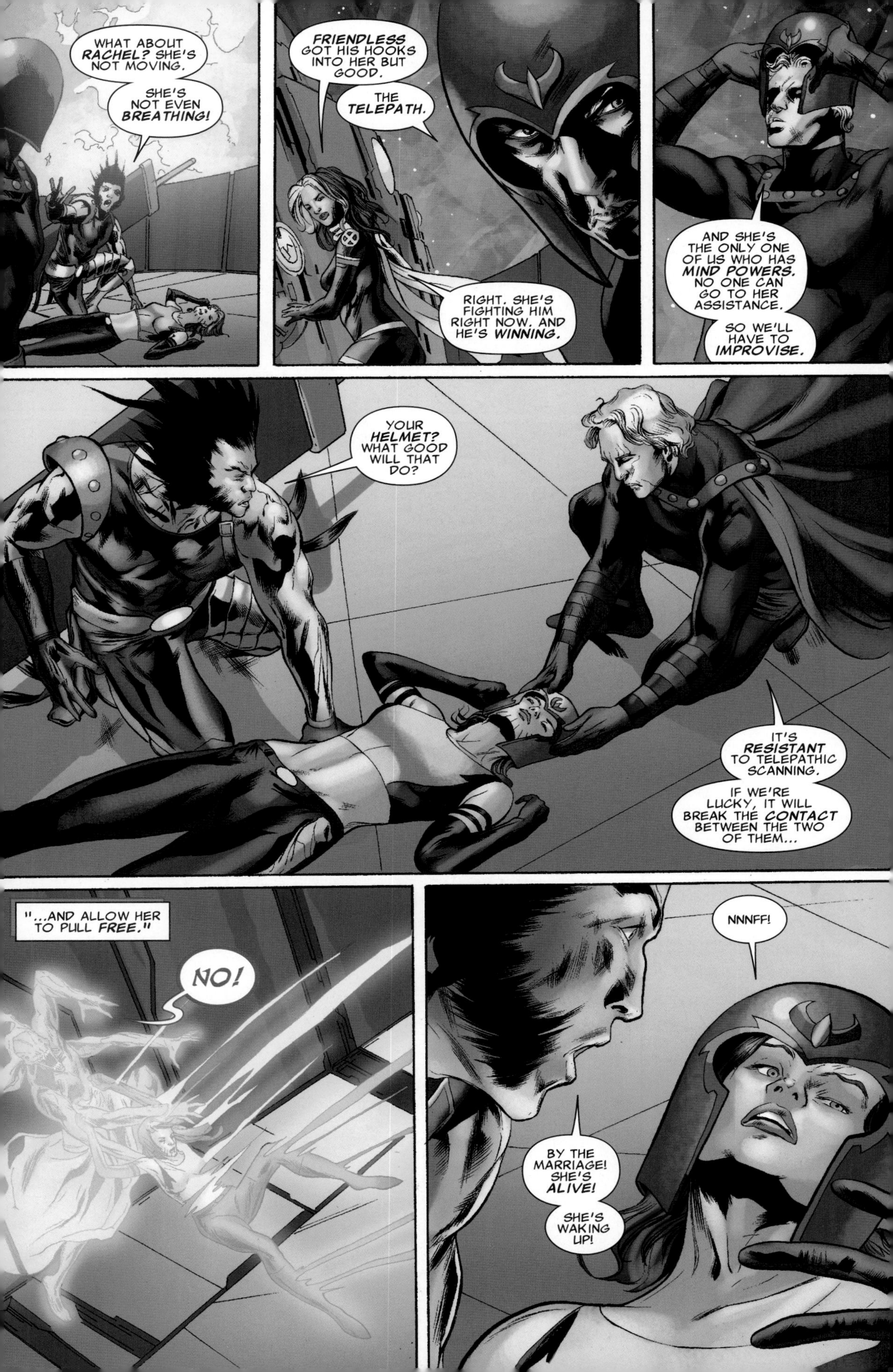
WHAT ABOUT RACHEL? SHE'S NOT MOVING.
SHE'S NOT EVEN BREATHING!
FRIENDLESS GOT HIS HOOKS INTO HER BUT GOOD.
THE TELEPATH.
RIGHT. SHE'S FIGHTING HIM RIGHT NOW. AND HE'S WINNING.
AND SHE'S THE ONLY ONE OF US WHO HAS MIND POWERS. NO ONE CAN GO TO HER ASSISTANCE.
SO WE'LL HAVE TO IMPROVISE.
YOUR HELMET? WHAT GOOD WILL THAT DO?
IT'S RESISTANT TO TELEPATHIC SCANNING.
IF WE'RE LUCKY, IT WILL BREAK THE CONTACT BETWEEN THE TWO OF THEM...
"...AND ALLOW HER TO PULL FREE."
NO!
NNNFF!
BY THE MARRIAGE! SHE'S ALIVE!
SHE'S WAKING UP!

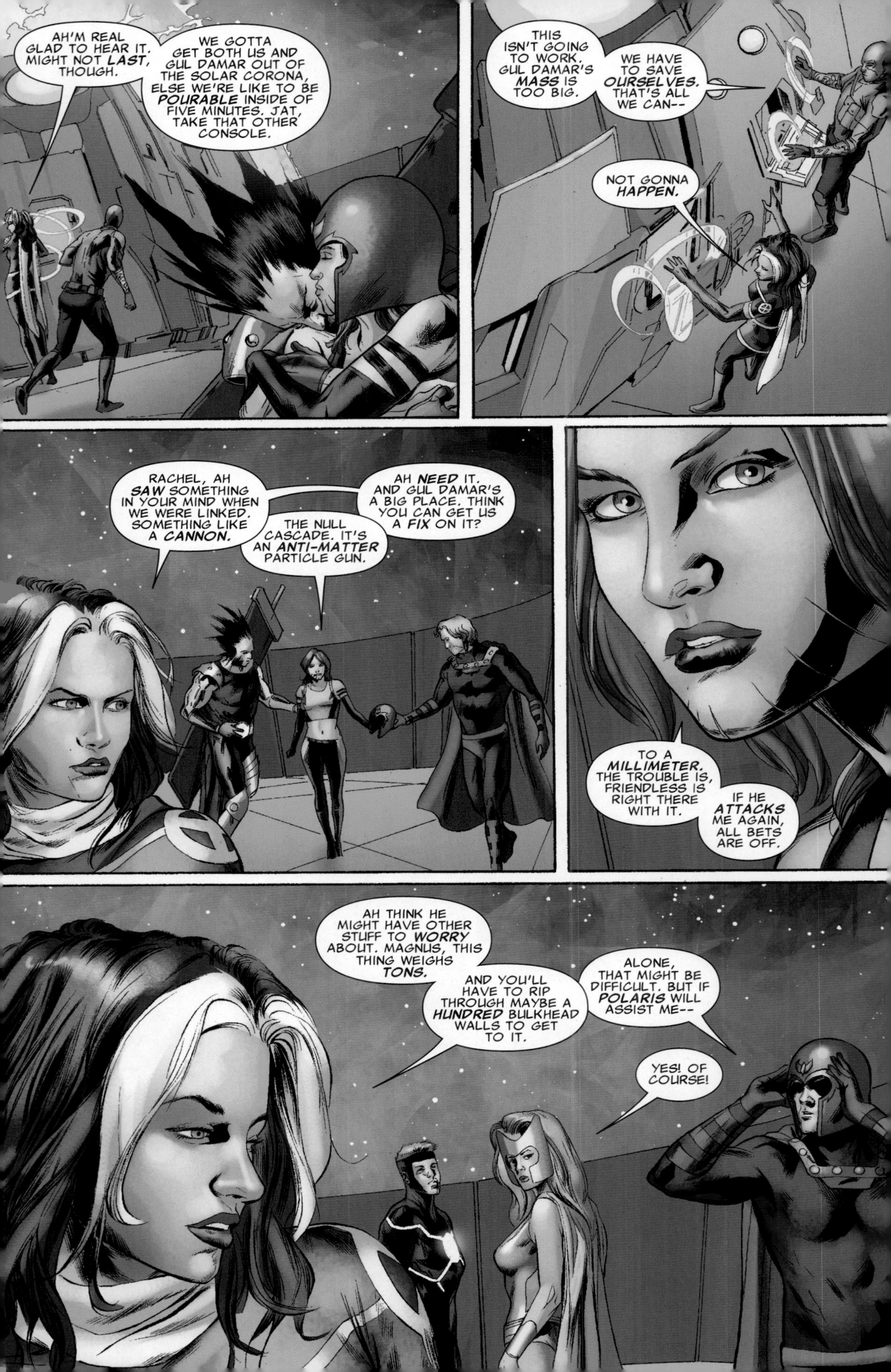
AH'M REAL GLAD TO HEAR IT. MIGHT NOT LAST, THOUGH.
WE GOTTA GET BOTH US AND GUL DAMAR OUT OF THE SOLAR CORONA, ELSE WE'RE LIKE TO BE POURABLE INSIDE OF FIVE MINUTES. JAT, TAKE THAT OTHER CONSOLE.
THIS ISN'T GOING TO WORK. GUL DAMAR'S MASS IS TOO BIG.
WE HAVE TO SAVE OURSELVES. THAT'S ALL WE CAN--
NOT GONNA HAPPEN.
RACHEL, AH SAW SOMETHING IN YOUR MIND WHEN WE WERE LINKED. SOMETHING LIKE A CANNON.
THE NULL CASCADE. IT'S AN ANTI-MATTER PARTICLE GUN.
AH NEED IT. AND GUL DAMAR'S A BIG PLACE. THINK YOU CAN GET US A FIX ON IT?
TO A MILLIMETER. THE TROUBLE IS, FRIENDLESS IS RIGHT THERE WITH IT.
IF HE ATTACKS ME AGAIN, ALL BETS ARE OFF.
AH THINK HE MIGHT HAVE OTHER STUFF TO WORRY ABOUT. MAGNUS, THIS THING WEIGHS TONS.
AND YOU'LL HAVE TO RIP THROUGH MAYBE A HUNDRED BULKHEAD WALLS TO GET TO IT.
ALONE, THAT MIGHT BE DIFFICULT. BUT IF POLARIS WILL ASSIST ME--
YES! OF COURSE!

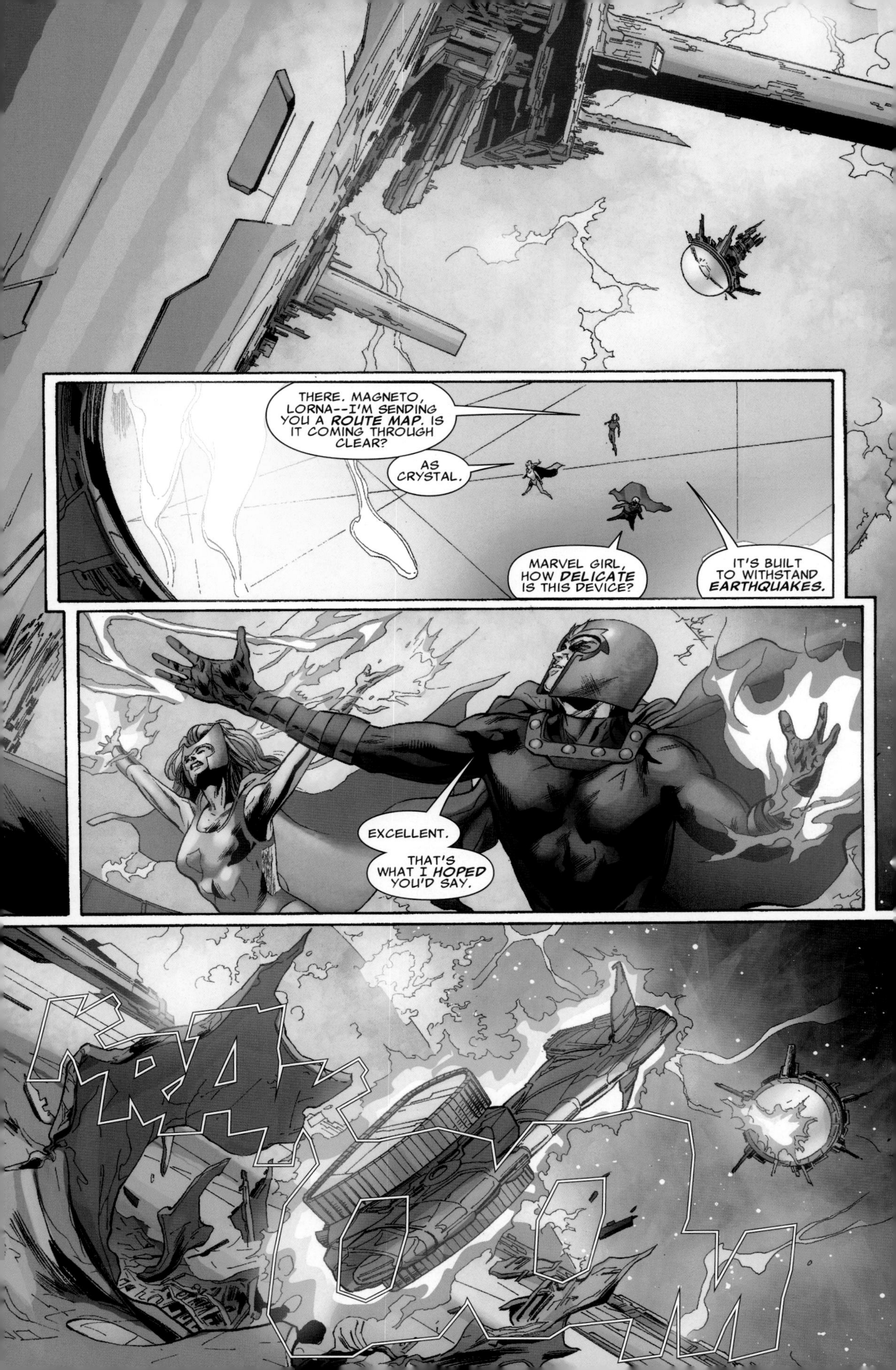
THERE. MAGNETO, LORNA--I'M SENDING YOU A ROUTE MAP. IS IT COMING THROUGH CLEAR?
AS CRYSTAL.
MARVEL GIRL, HOW DELICATE IS THIS DEVICE?
IT'S BUILT TO WITHSTAND EARTHQUAKES.
EXCELLENT.
THAT'S WHAT I HOPED YOU'D SAY.
KRAKOOM

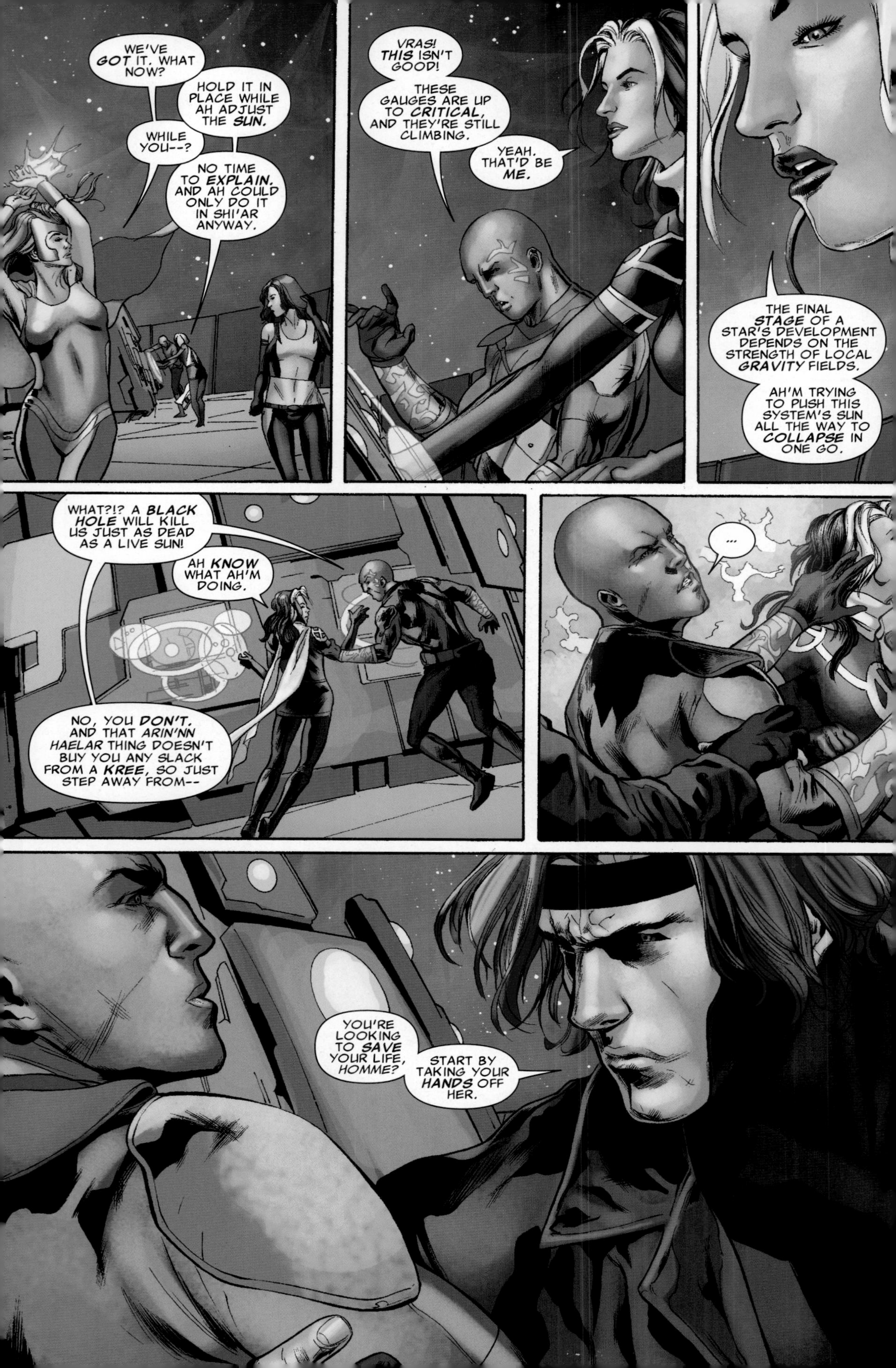
WE'VE GOT IT. WHAT NOW?
HOLD IT IN PLACE WHILE AH ADJUST THE SUN.
WHILE YOU--?
NO TIME TO EXPLAIN. AND AH COULD ONLY DO IT IN SHI'AR ANYWAY.
VRAS! THIS ISN'T GOOD!
THESE GAUGES ARE UP TO CRITICAL, AND THEY'RE STILL CLIMBING.
YEAH. THAT'D BE ME.
THE FINAL STAGE OF A STAR'S DEVELOPMENT DEPENDS ON THE STRENGTH OF LOCAL GRAVITY FIELDS.
AH'M TRYING TO PUSH THIS SYSTEM'S SUN ALL THE WAY TO COLLAPSE IN ONE GO.
WHAT?!? A BLACK HOLE WILL KILL US JUST AS DEAD AS A LIVE SUN!
AH KNOW WHAT AH'M DOING.
NO, YOU DON'T. AND THAT ARIN'NN HAELAR THING DOESN'T BUY YOU ANY SLACK FROM A KREE, SO JUST STEP AWAY FROM--
...
YOU'RE LOOKING TO SAVE YOUR LIFE, HOMME?
START BY TAKING YOUR HANDS OFF HER.

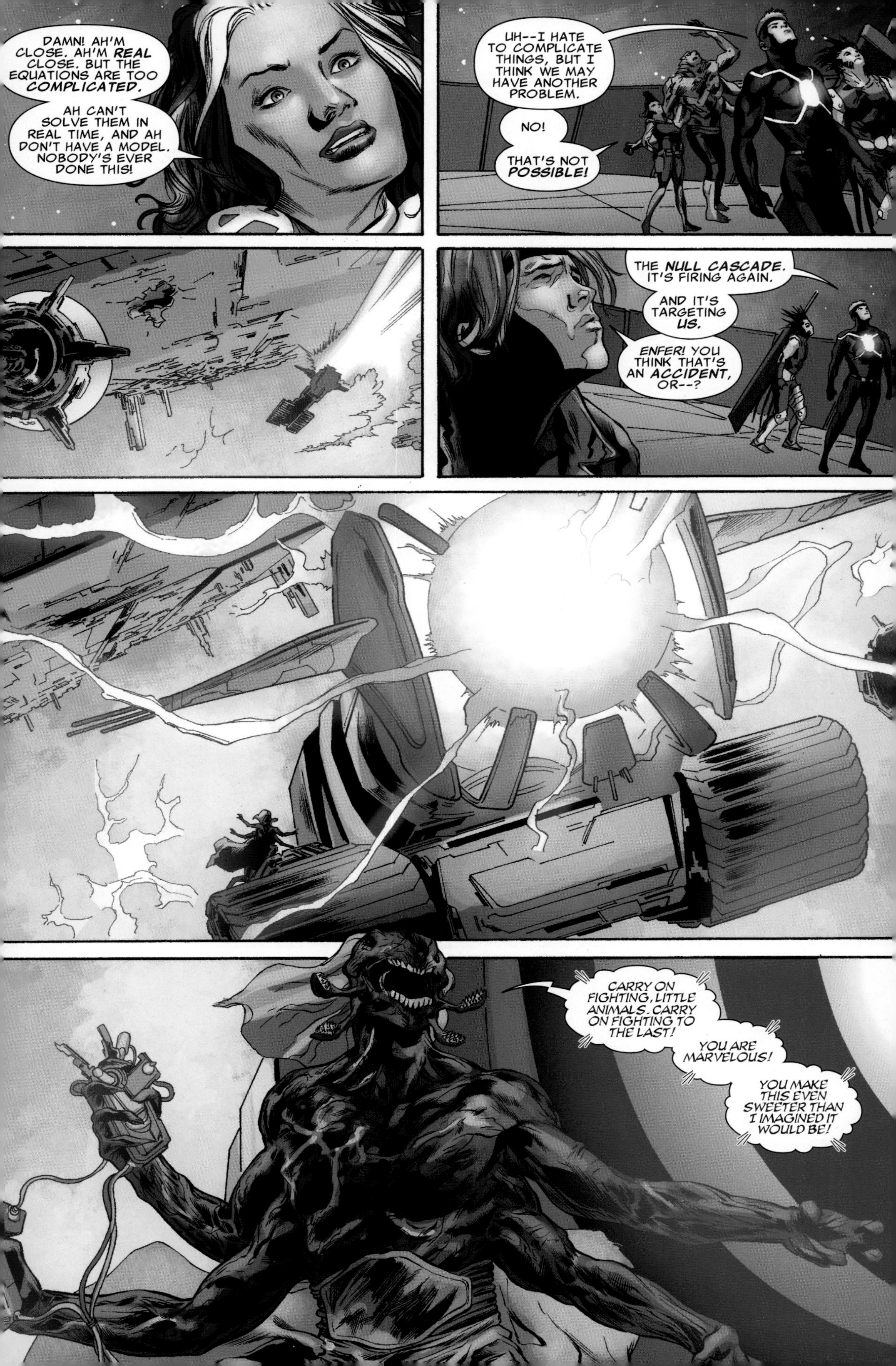
DAMN! AH'M CLOSE. AH'M REAL CLOSE. BUT THE EQUATIONS ARE TOO COMPLICATED.
AH CAN'T SOLVE THEM IN REAL TIME, AND AH DON'T HAVE A MODEL. NOBODY'S EVER DONE THIS!
UH--I HATE TO COMPLICATE THINGS, BUT I THINK WE MAY HAVE ANOTHER PROBLEM.
NO!
THAT'S NOT POSSIBLE!
THE NULL CASCADE. IT'S FIRING AGAIN.
AND IT'S TARGETING US.
ENFER! YOU THINK THAT'S AN ACCIDENT, OR--?
CARRY ON FIGHTING, LITTLE ANIMALS. CARRY ON FIGHTING TO THE LAST!
YOU ARE MARVELOUS!
YOU MAKE THIS EVEN SWEETER THAN I IMAGINED IT WOULD BE!

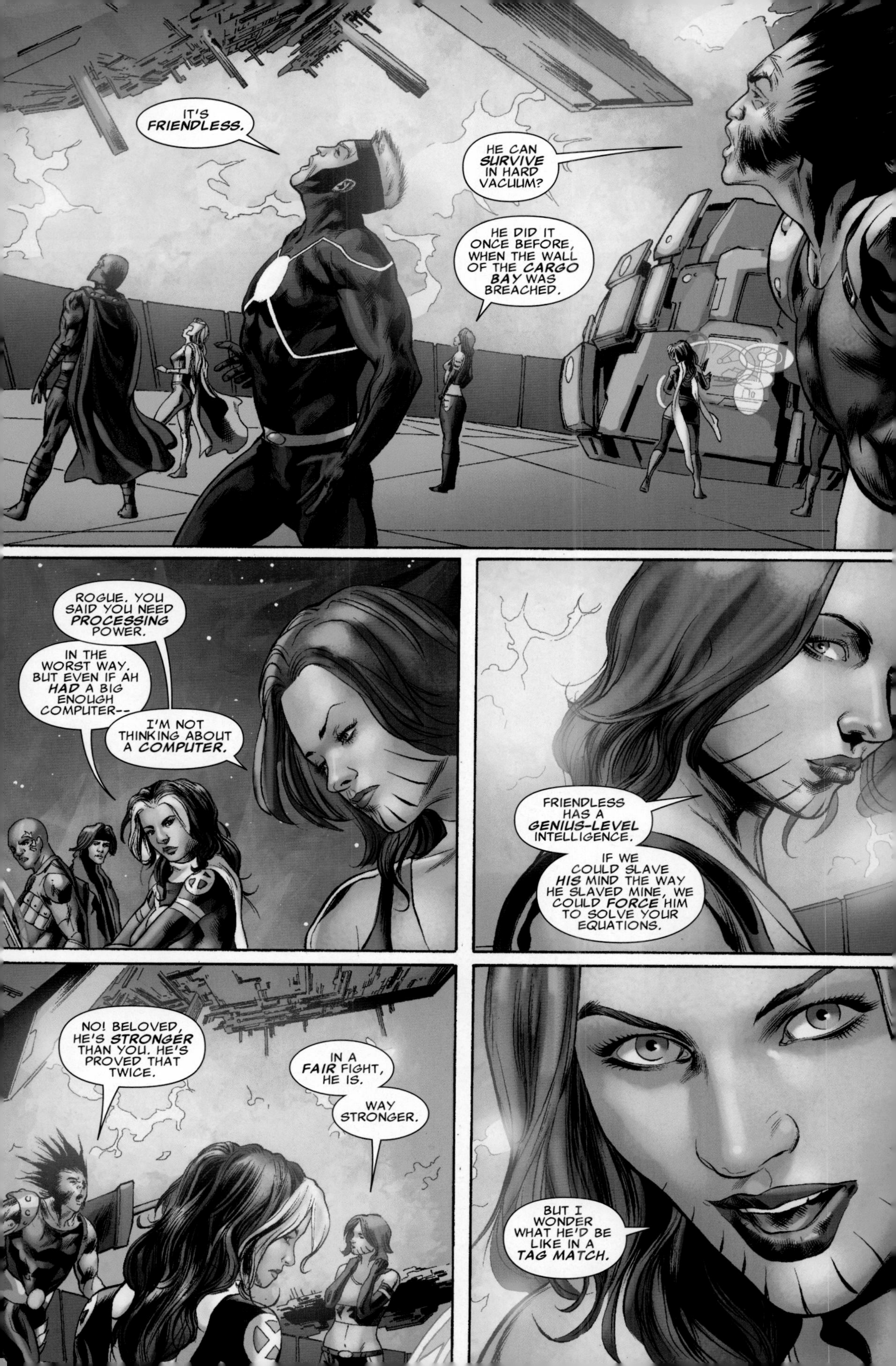
IT'S FRIENDLESS.
HE CAN SURVIVE IN HARD VACUUM?
HE DID IT ONCE BEFORE, WHEN THE WALL OF THE CARGO BAY WAS BREACHED.
ROGUE. YOU SAID YOU NEED PROCESSING POWER.
IN THE WORST WAY. BUT EVEN IF AH HAD A BIG ENOUGH COMPUTER--
I'M NOT THINKING ABOUT A COMPUTER.
FRIENDLESS HAS A GENIUS-LEVEL INTELLIGENCE.
IF WE COULD SLAVE HIS MIND THE WAY HE SLAVED MINE, WE COULD FORCE HIM TO SOLVE YOUR EQUATIONS.
NO! BELOVED, HE'S STRONGER THAN YOU. HE'S PROVED THAT TWICE.
IN A FAIR FIGHT, HE IS.
WAY STRONGER.
BUT I WONDER WHAT HE'D BE LIKE IN A TAG MATCH.

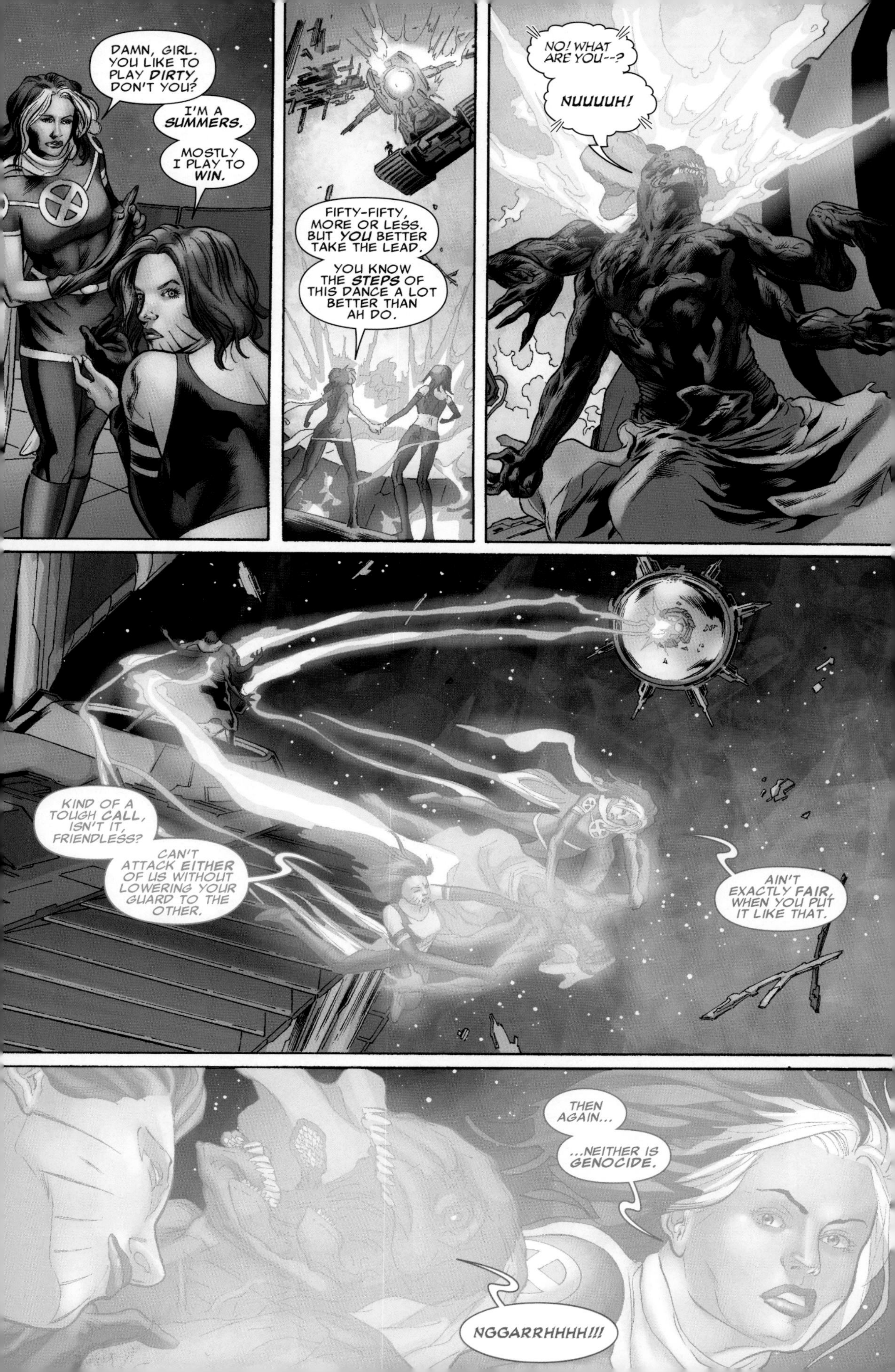
DAMN, GIRL. YOU LIKE TO PLAY DIRTY, DON'T YOU?
I'M A SUMMERS.
MOSTLY I PLAY TO WIN.
FIFTY-FIFTY, MORE OR LESS. BUT YOU BETTER TAKE THE LEAD.
YOU KNOW THE STEPS OF THIS DANCE A LOT BETTER THAN AH DO.
NO! WHAT ARE YOU--?
NUUUUH!
KIND OF A TOUGH CALL, ISN'T IT, FRIENDLESS?
CAN'T ATTACK EITHER OF US WITHOUT LOWERING YOUR GUARD TO THE OTHER.
AIN'T EXACTLY FAIR, WHEN YOU PUT IT LIKE THAT.
THEN AGAIN...
...NEITHER IS GENOCIDE.
NGGARRHHHH!!!

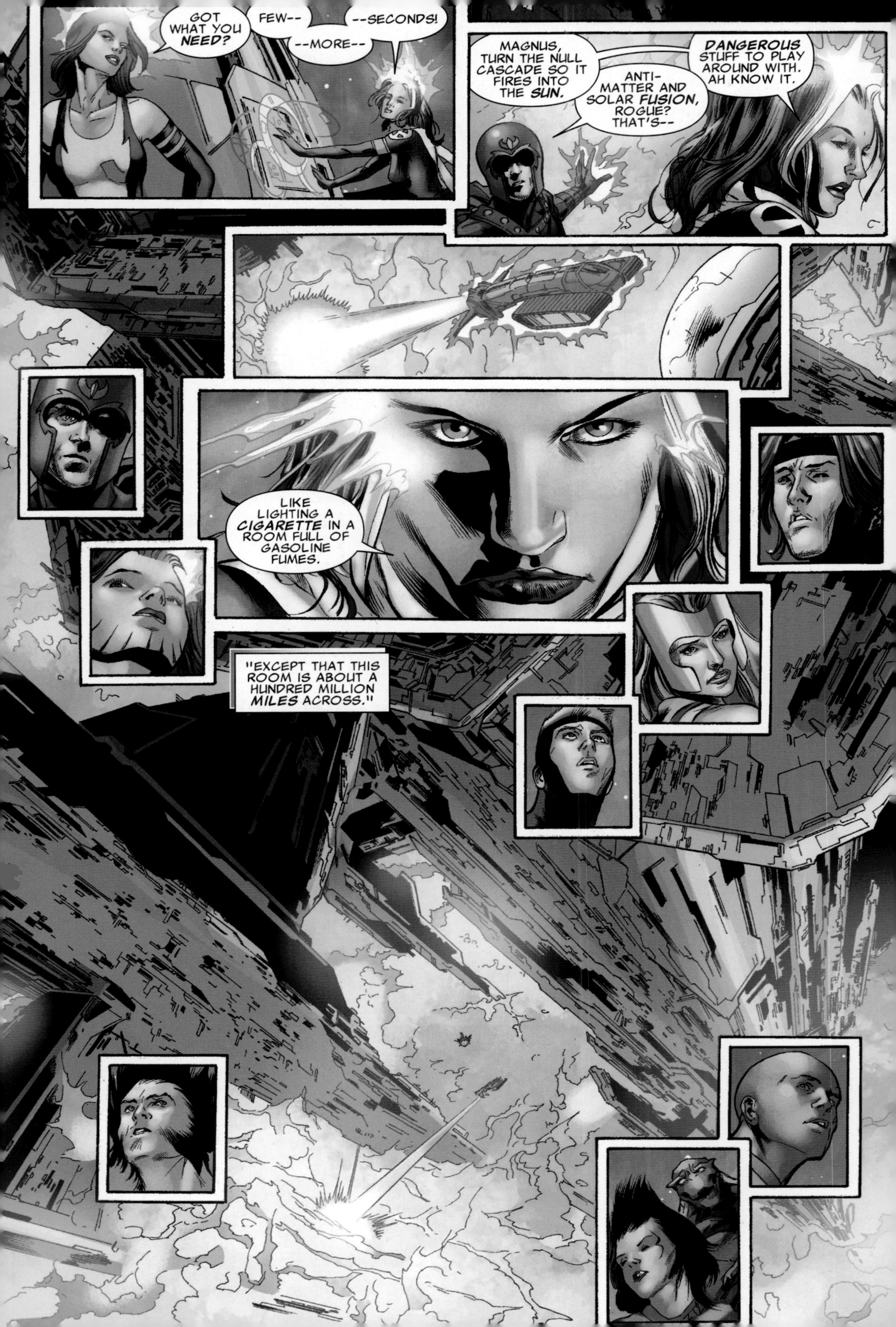

GOT WHAT YOU NEED?
FEW--
--MORE--
--SECONDS!
MAGNUS, TURN THE NULL CASCADE SO IT FIRES INTO THE SUN.
ANTI-MATTER AND SOLAR FUSION, ROGUE? THAT'S--
DANGEROUS STUFF TO PLAY AROUND WITH. AH KNOW IT.
LIKE LIGHTING A CIGARETTE IN A ROOM FULL OF GASOLINE FUMES.
"EXCEPT THAT THIS ROOM IS ABOUT A HUNDRED MILLION MILES ACROSS."

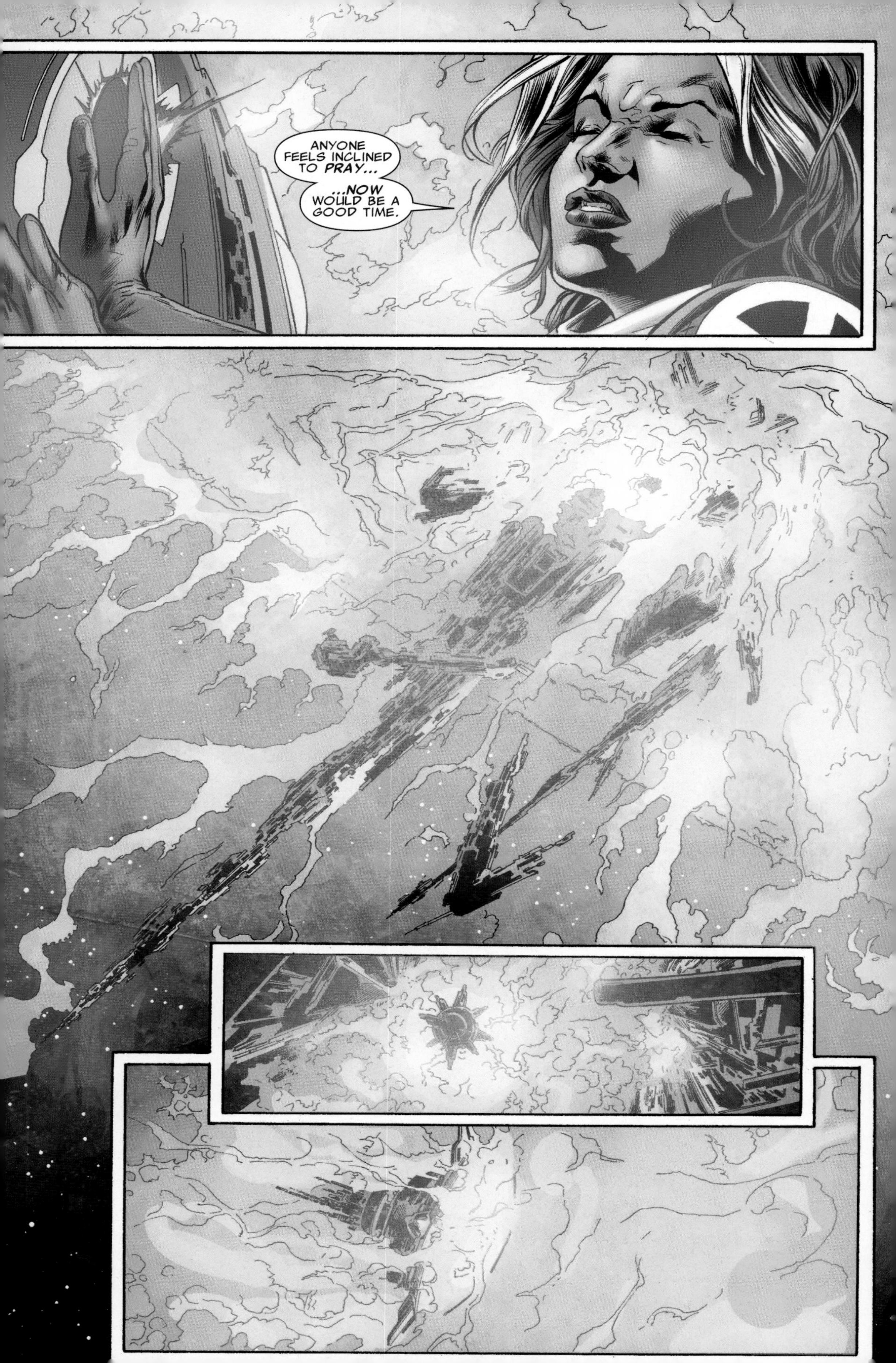
ANYONE FEELS INCLINED TO PRAY...
...NOW WOULD BE A GOOD TIME.

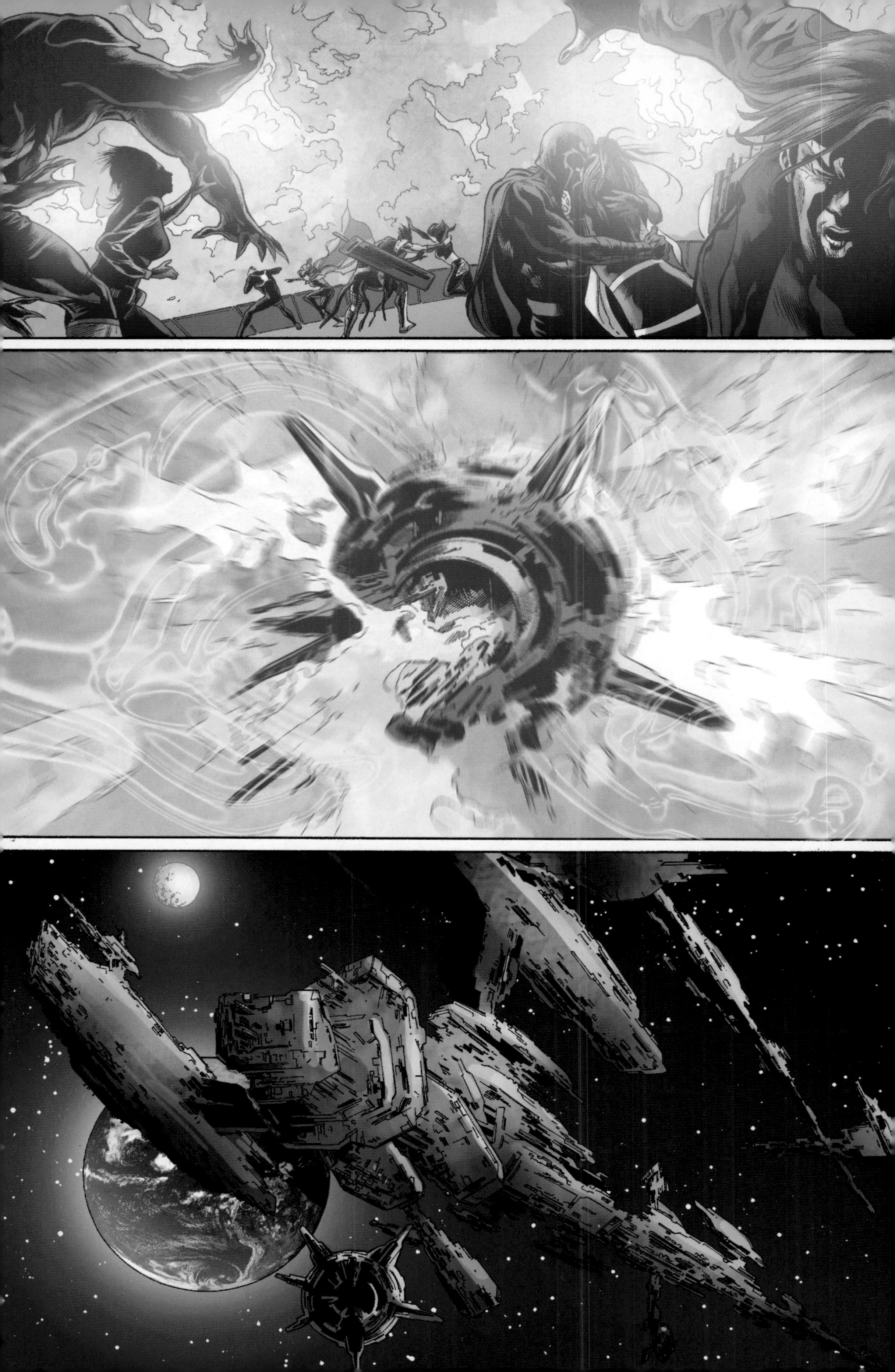

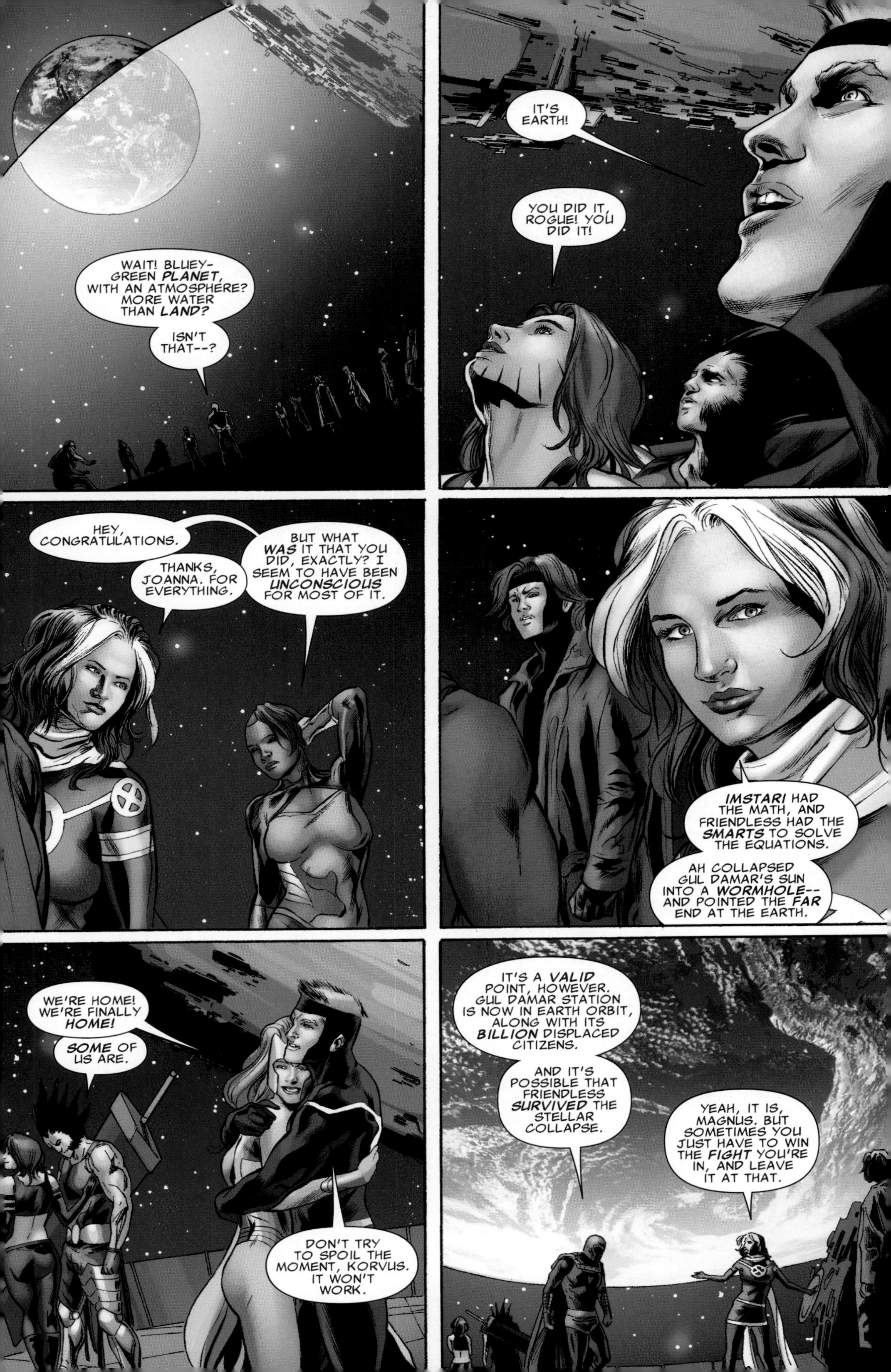

WAIT! BLUEY-GREEN PLANET, WITH AN ATMOSPHERE? MORE WATER THAN LAND?
ISN'T THAT--?
IT'S EARTH!
YOU DID IT, ROGUE! YOU DID IT!
HEY, CONGRATULATIONS.
THANKS, JOANNA. FOR EVERYTHING.
BUT WHAT WAS IT THAT YOU DID, EXACTLY? I SEEM TO HAVE BEEN UNCONSCIOUS FOR MOST OF IT.
IMSTARI HAD THE MATH, AND FRIENDLESS HAD THE SMARTS TO SOLVE THE EQUATIONS.
AH COLLAPSED GUL DAMAR'S SUN INTO A WORMHOLE--AND POINTED THE FAR END AT THE EARTH.
WE'RE HOME! WE'RE FINALLY HOME!
SOME OF US ARE.
DON'T TRY TO SPOIL THE MOMENT, KORVUS. IT WON'T WORK.
IT'S A VALID POINT, HOWEVER. GUL DAMAR STATION IS NOW IN EARTH ORBIT, ALONG WITH ITS BILLION DISPLACED CITIZENS.
AND IT'S POSSIBLE THAT FRIENDLESS SURVIVED THE STELLAR COLLAPSE.
YEAH, IT IS, MAGNUS. BUT SOMETIMES YOU JUST HAVE TO WIN THE FIGHT YOU'RE IN, AND LEAVE IT AT THAT.

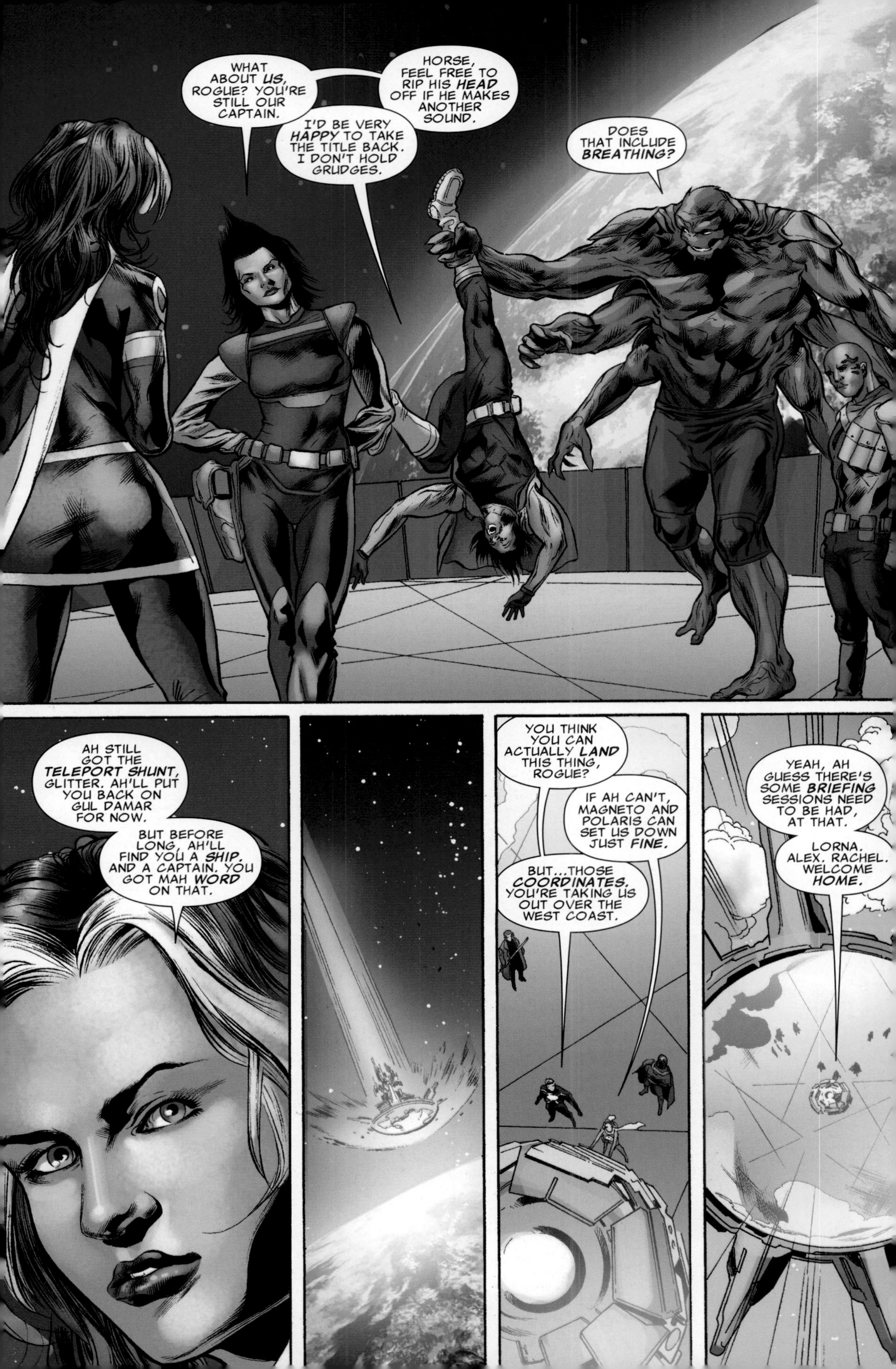
WHAT ABOUT US, ROGUE? YOU'RE STILL OUR CAPTAIN.
HORSE, FEEL FREE TO RIP HIS HEAD OFF IF HE MAKES ANOTHER SOUND.
I'D BE VERY HAPPY TO TAKE THE TITLE BACK. I DON'T HOLD GRUDGES.
DOES THAT INCLUDE BREATHING?
AH STILL GOT THE TELEPORT SHUNT, GLITTER. AH'LL PUT YOU BACK ON GUL DAMAR FOR NOW.
BUT BEFORE LONG, AH'LL FIND YOU A SHIP. AND A CAPTAIN. YOU GOT MAH WORD ON THAT.
YOU THINK YOU CAN ACTUALLY LAND THIS THING, ROGUE?
IF AH CAN'T, MAGNETO AND POLARIS CAN SET US DOWN JUST FINE.
BUT...THOSE COORDINATES. YOU'RE TAKING US OUT OVER THE WEST COAST.
YEAH, AH GUESS THERE'S SOME BRIEFING SESSIONS NEED TO BE HAD, AT THAT.
LORNA. ALEX. RACHEL. WELCOME HOME.

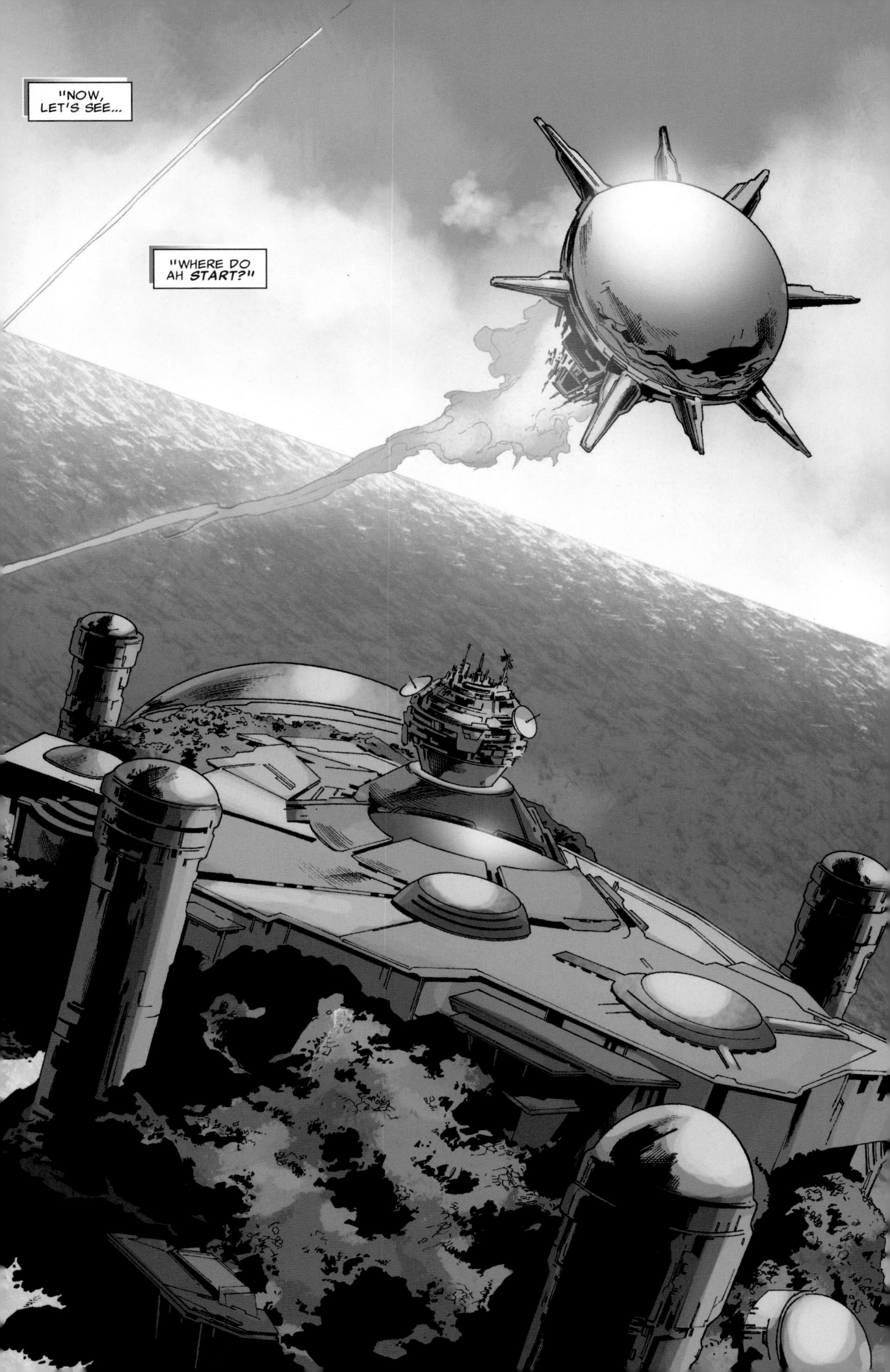
"NOW, LET'S SEE...
"WHERE DO AH *START?*"

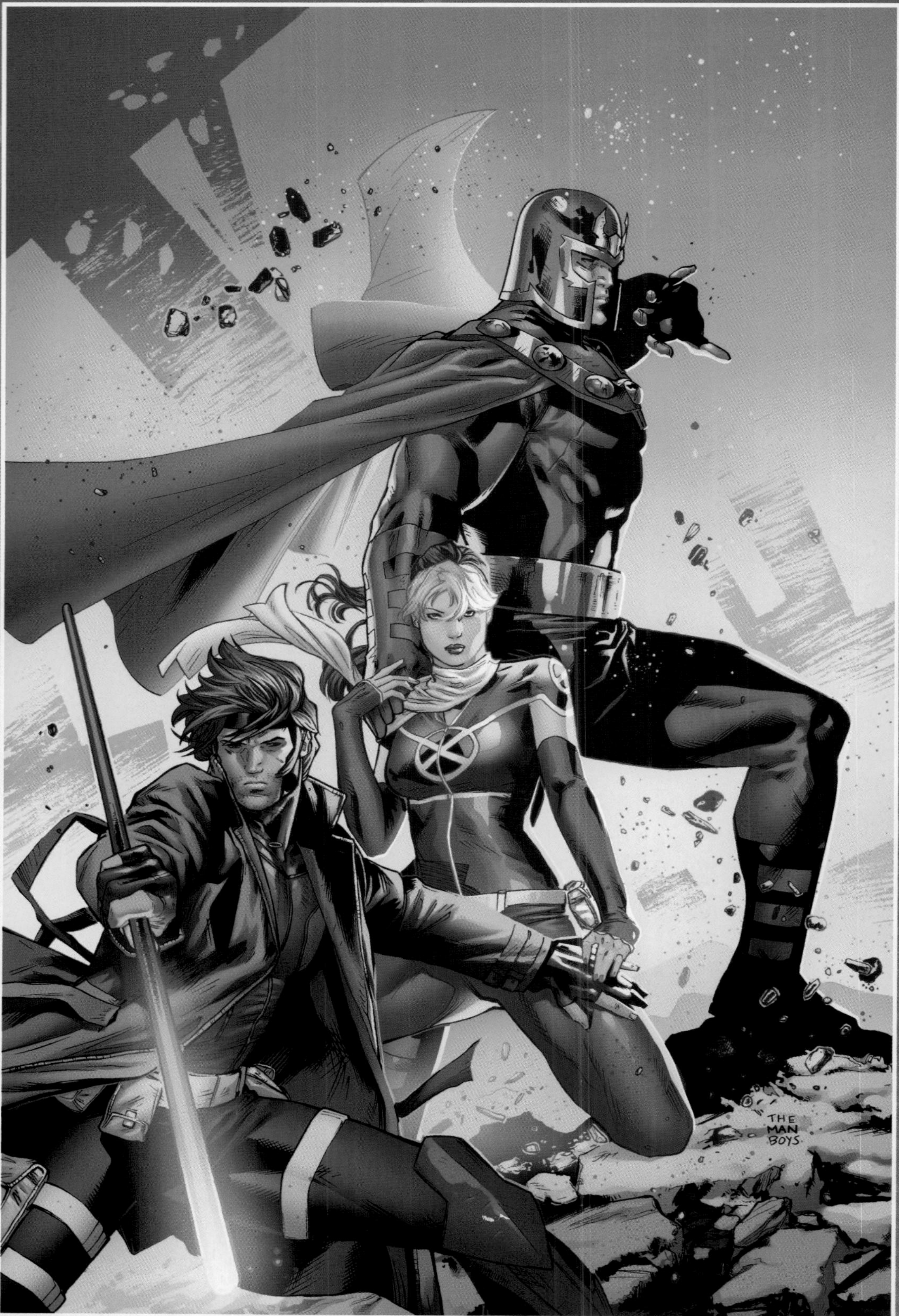
THE MAN BOYS.

#259
"HALF A STEP" PART ONE

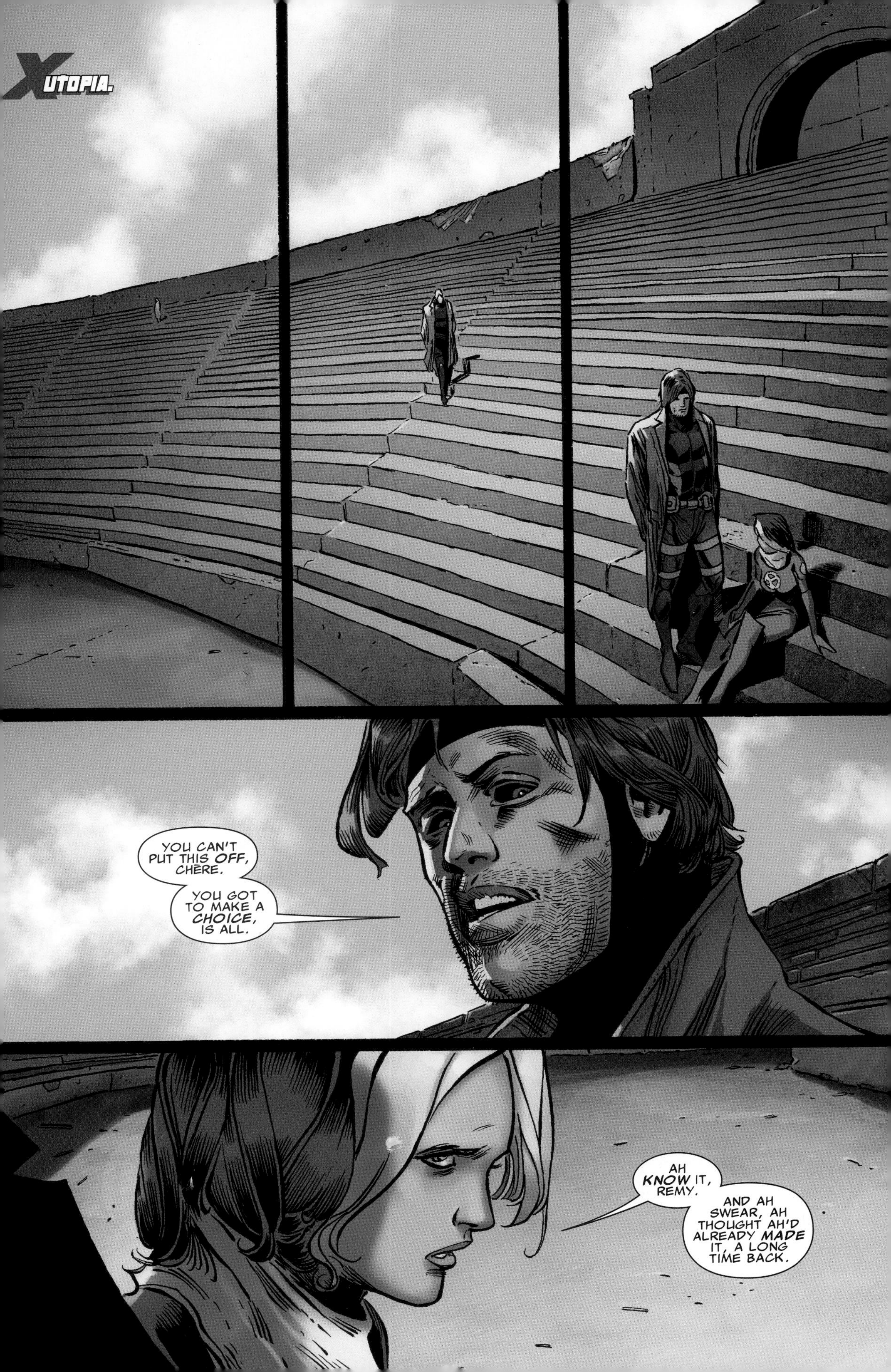
X UTOPIA.
YOU CAN'T PUT THIS OFF, CHÈRE.
YOU GOT TO MAKE A CHOICE, IS ALL.
AH KNOW IT, REMY.
AND AH SWEAR, AH THOUGHT AH'D ALREADY MADE IT, A LONG TIME BACK.

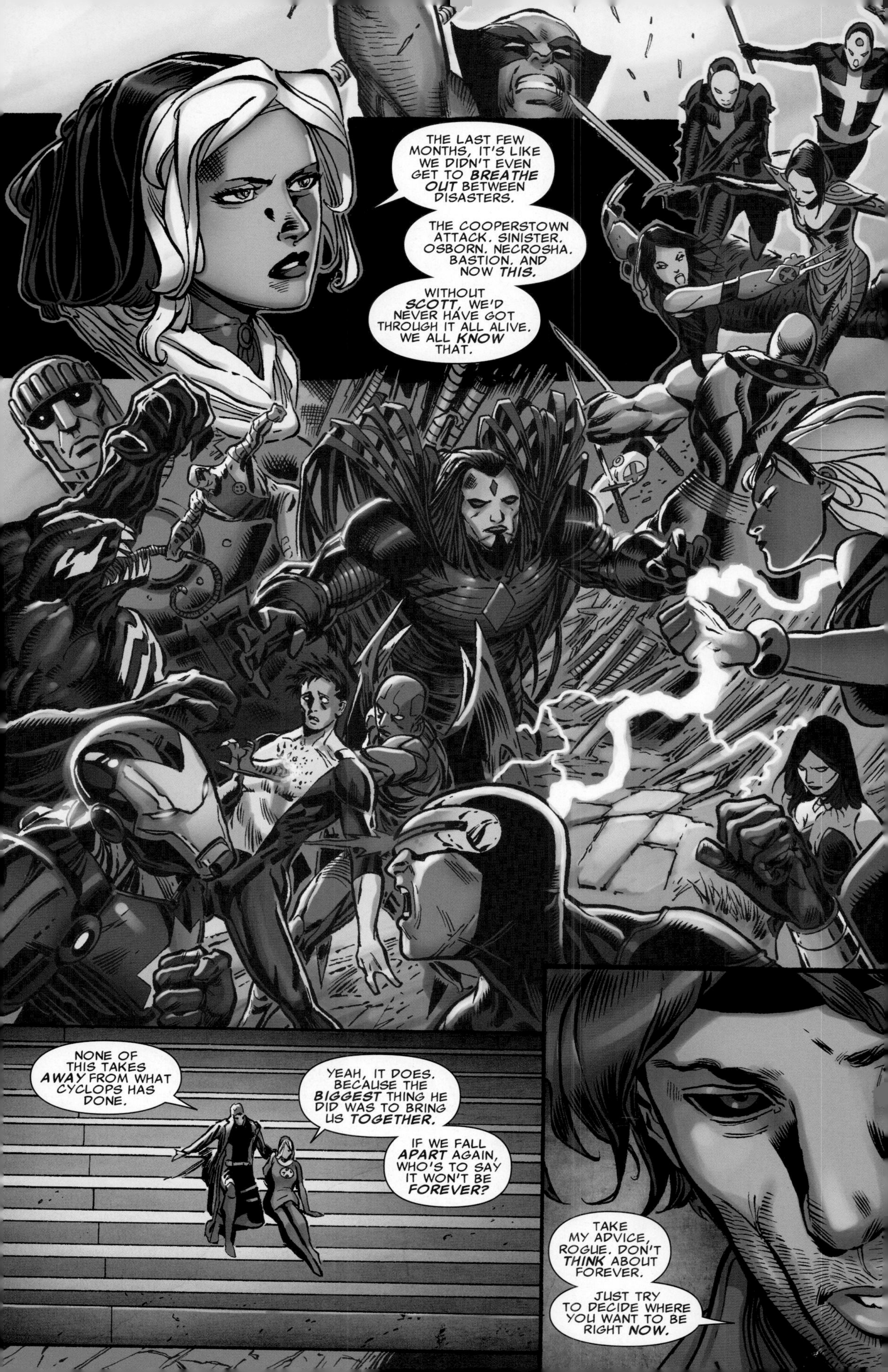
THE LAST FEW MONTHS, IT'S LIKE WE DIDN'T EVEN GET TO BREATHE OUT BETWEEN DISASTERS.
THE COOPERSTOWN ATTACK. SINISTER. OSBORN. NECROSHA. BASTION. AND NOW THIS.
WITHOUT SCOTT, WE'D NEVER HAVE GOT THROUGH IT ALL ALIVE. WE ALL KNOW THAT.
NONE OF THIS TAKES AWAY FROM WHAT CYCLOPS HAS DONE.
YEAH, IT DOES. BECAUSE THE BIGGEST THING HE DID WAS TO BRING US TOGETHER.
IF WE FALL APART AGAIN, WHO'S TO SAY IT WON'T BE FOREVER?
TAKE MY ADVICE, ROGUE. DON'T THINK ABOUT FOREVER.
JUST TRY TO DECIDE WHERE YOU WANT TO BE RIGHT NOW.

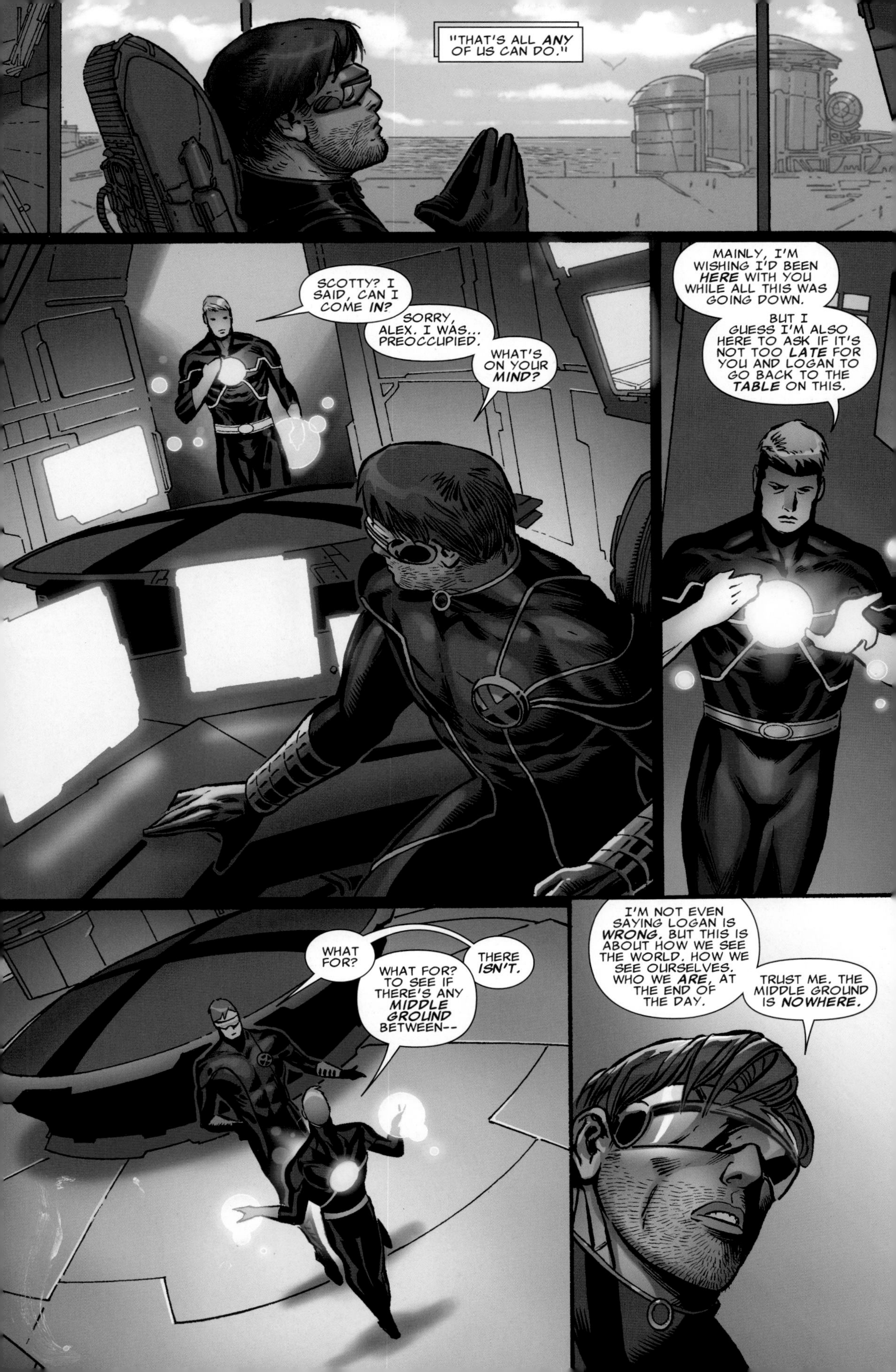
"THAT'S ALL ANY OF US CAN DO."
SCOTTY? I SAID, CAN I COME IN?
SORRY, ALEX. I WAS... PREOCCUPIED.
WHAT'S ON YOUR MIND?
MAINLY, I'M WISHING I'D BEEN HERE WITH YOU WHILE ALL THIS WAS GOING DOWN.
BUT I GUESS I'M ALSO HERE TO ASK IF IT'S NOT TOO LATE FOR YOU AND LOGAN TO GO BACK TO THE TABLE ON THIS.
WHAT FOR?
WHAT FOR? TO SEE IF THERE'S ANY MIDDLE GROUND BETWEEN--
THERE ISN'T.
I'M NOT EVEN SAYING LOGAN IS WRONG. BUT THIS IS ABOUT HOW WE SEE THE WORLD. HOW WE SEE OURSELVES. WHO WE ARE, AT THE END OF THE DAY.
TRUST ME. THE MIDDLE GROUND IS NOWHERE.

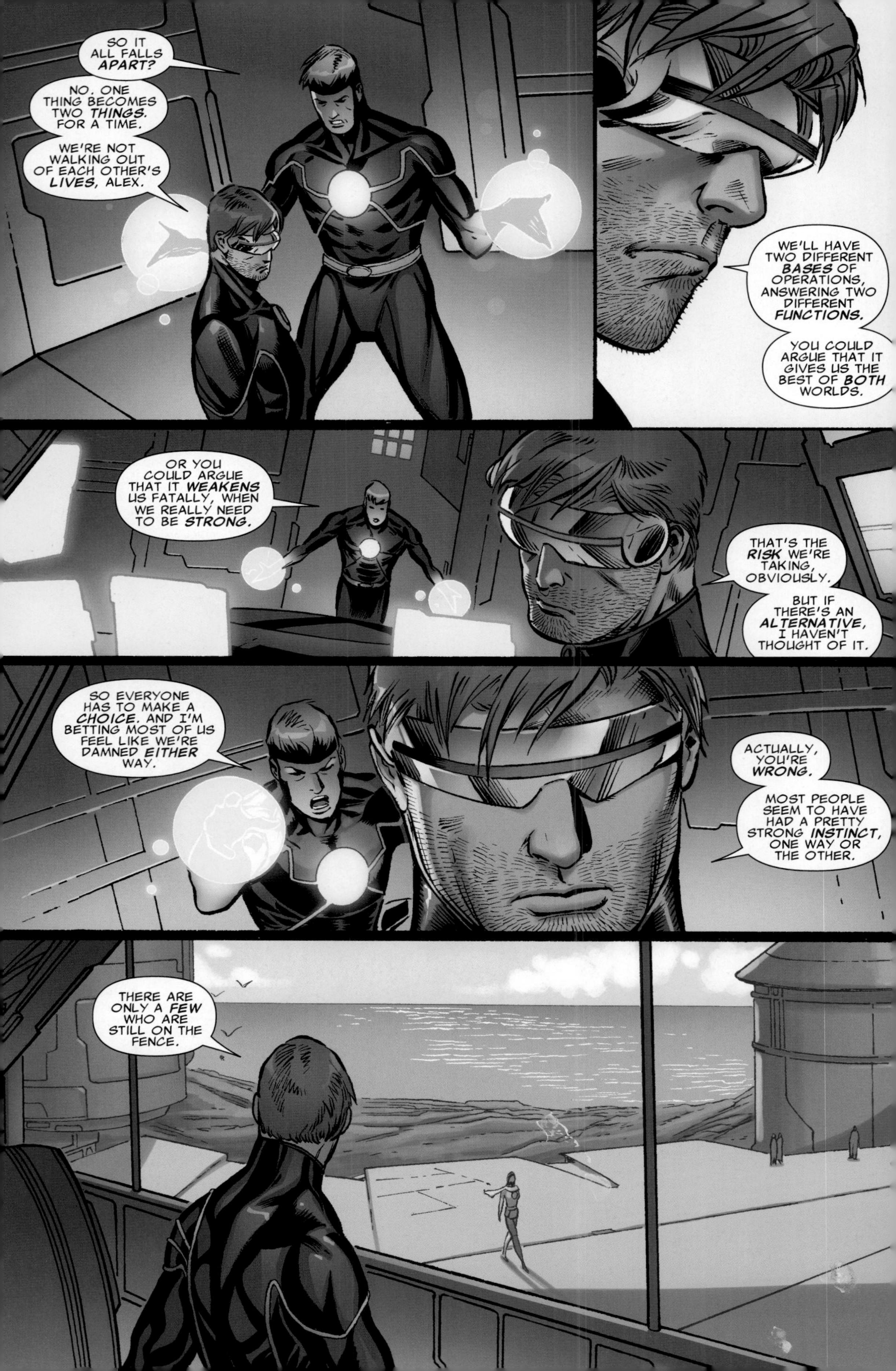
SO IT ALL FALLS APART?
NO. ONE THING BECOMES TWO THINGS. FOR A TIME.
WE'RE NOT WALKING OUT OF EACH OTHER'S LIVES, ALEX.
WE'LL HAVE TWO DIFFERENT BASES OF OPERATIONS, ANSWERING TWO DIFFERENT FUNCTIONS.
YOU COULD ARGUE THAT IT GIVES US THE BEST OF BOTH WORLDS.
OR YOU COULD ARGUE THAT IT WEAKENS US FATALLY, WHEN WE REALLY NEED TO BE STRONG.
THAT'S THE RISK WE'RE TAKING, OBVIOUSLY.
BUT IF THERE'S AN ALTERNATIVE, I HAVEN'T THOUGHT OF IT.
SO EVERYONE HAS TO MAKE A CHOICE. AND I'M BETTING MOST OF US FEEL LIKE WE'RE DAMNED EITHER WAY.
ACTUALLY, YOU'RE WRONG.
MOST PEOPLE SEEM TO HAVE HAD A PRETTY STRONG INSTINCT, ONE WAY OR THE OTHER.
THERE ARE ONLY A FEW WHO ARE STILL ON THE FENCE.

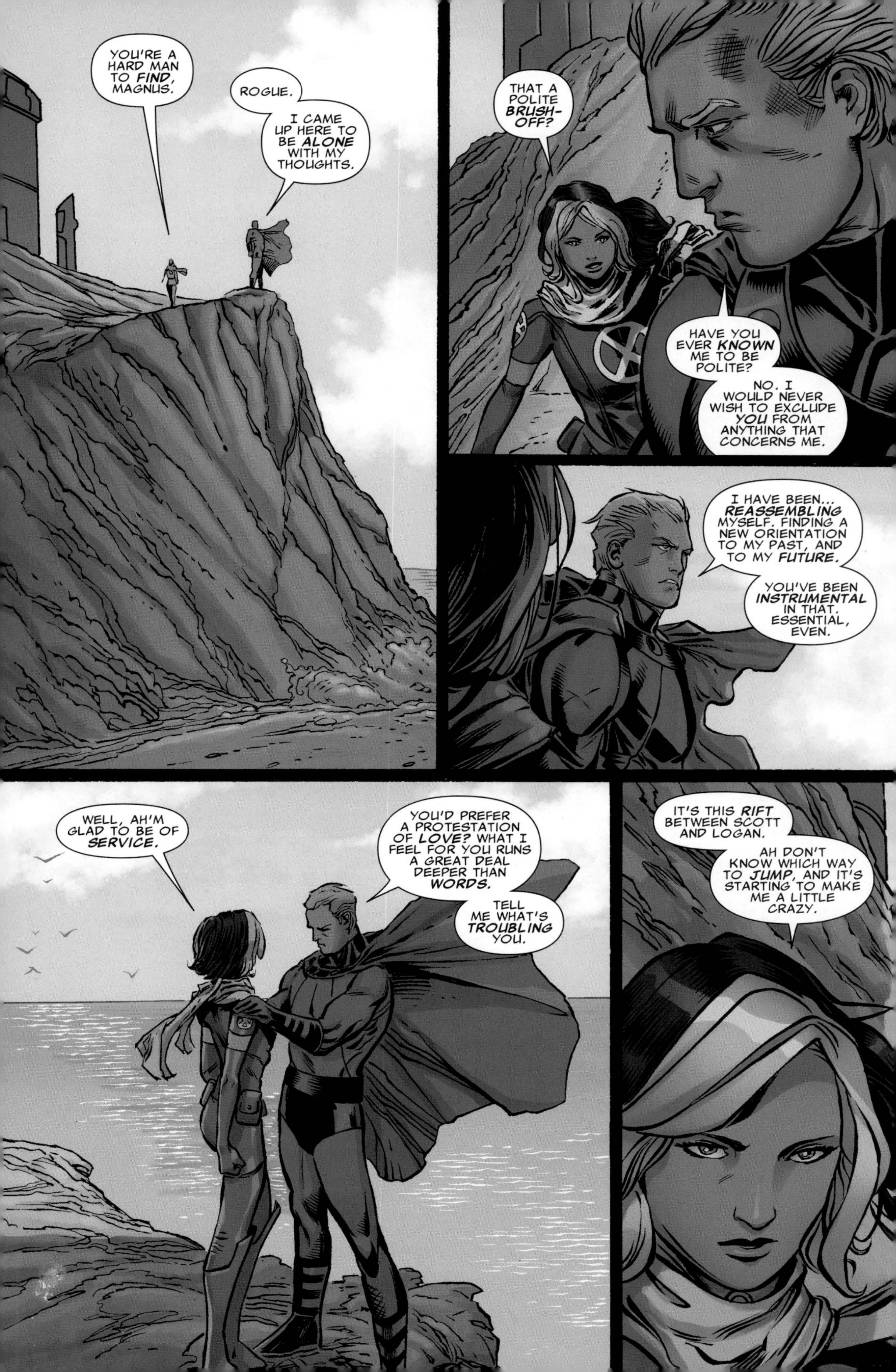

YOU'RE A HARD MAN TO FIND, MAGNUS.
ROGUE.
I CAME UP HERE TO BE ALONE WITH MY THOUGHTS.
THAT A POLITE BRUSH-OFF?
HAVE YOU EVER KNOWN ME TO BE POLITE?
NO. I WOULD NEVER WISH TO EXCLUDE YOU FROM ANYTHING THAT CONCERNS ME.
I HAVE BEEN... REASSEMBLING MYSELF. FINDING A NEW ORIENTATION TO MY PAST, AND TO MY FUTURE.
YOU'VE BEEN INSTRUMENTAL IN THAT. ESSENTIAL, EVEN.
WELL, AH'M GLAD TO BE OF SERVICE.
YOU'D PREFER A PROTESTATION OF LOVE? WHAT I FEEL FOR YOU RUNS A GREAT DEAL DEEPER THAN WORDS.
TELL ME WHAT'S TROUBLING YOU.
IT'S THIS RIFT BETWEEN SCOTT AND LOGAN.
AH DON'T KNOW WHICH WAY TO JUMP, AND IT'S STARTING TO MAKE ME A LITTLE CRAZY.

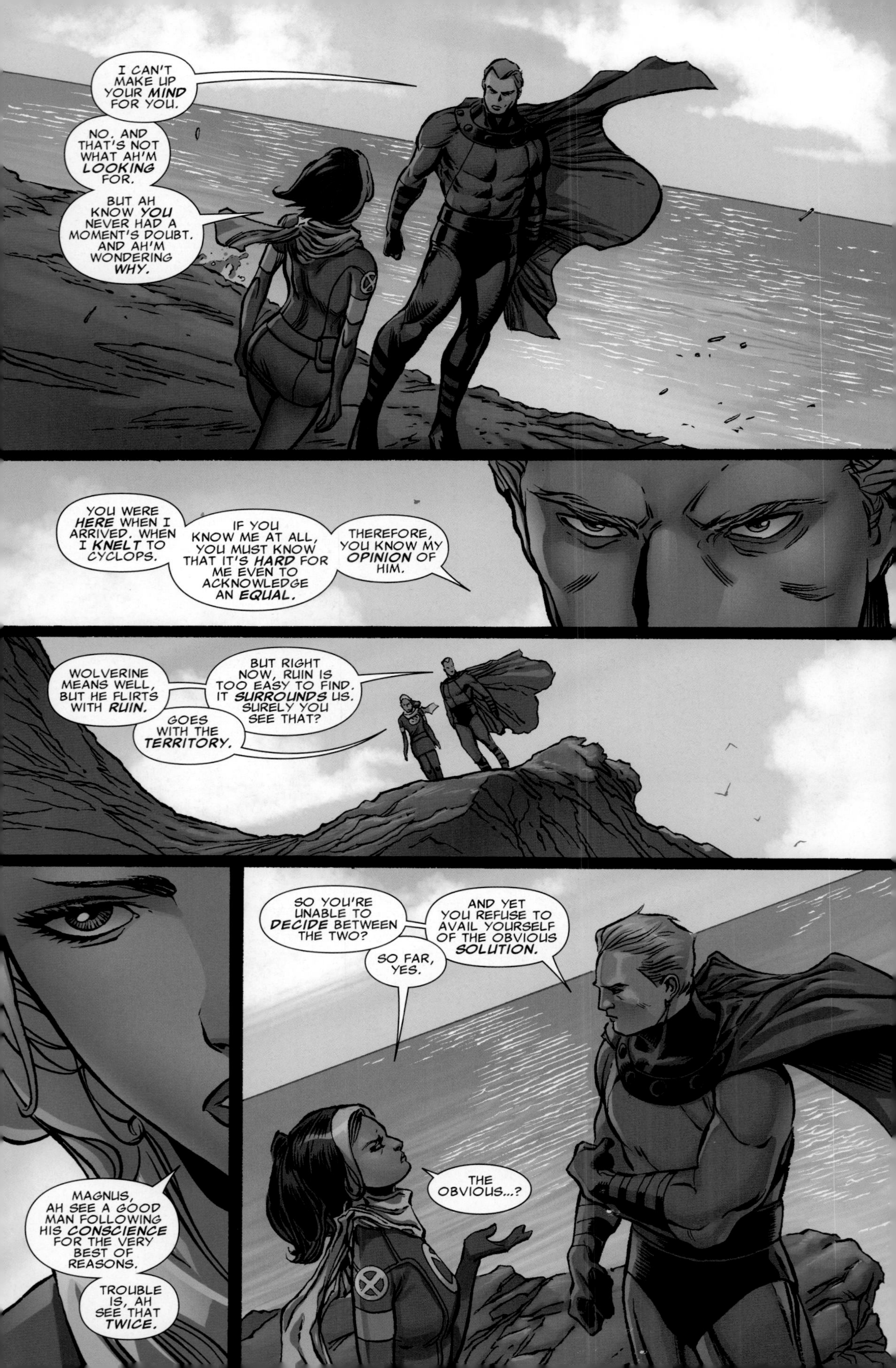
I CAN'T MAKE UP YOUR MIND FOR YOU.
NO. AND THAT'S NOT WHAT AH'M LOOKING FOR.
BUT AH KNOW YOU NEVER HAD A MOMENT'S DOUBT. AND AH'M WONDERING WHY.
YOU WERE HERE WHEN I ARRIVED. WHEN I KNELT TO CYCLOPS.
IF YOU KNOW ME AT ALL, YOU MUST KNOW THAT IT'S HARD FOR ME EVEN TO ACKNOWLEDGE AN EQUAL.
THEREFORE, YOU KNOW MY OPINION OF HIM.
WOLVERINE MEANS WELL, BUT HE FLIRTS WITH RUIN.
GOES WITH THE TERRITORY.
BUT RIGHT NOW, RUIN IS TOO EASY TO FIND. IT SURROUNDS US. SURELY YOU SEE THAT?
MAGNUS, AH SEE A GOOD MAN FOLLOWING HIS CONSCIENCE FOR THE VERY BEST OF REASONS.
TROUBLE IS, AH SEE THAT TWICE.
SO YOU'RE UNABLE TO DECIDE BETWEEN THE TWO?
SO FAR, YES.
AND YET YOU REFUSE TO AVAIL YOURSELF OF THE OBVIOUS SOLUTION.
THE OBVIOUS...?

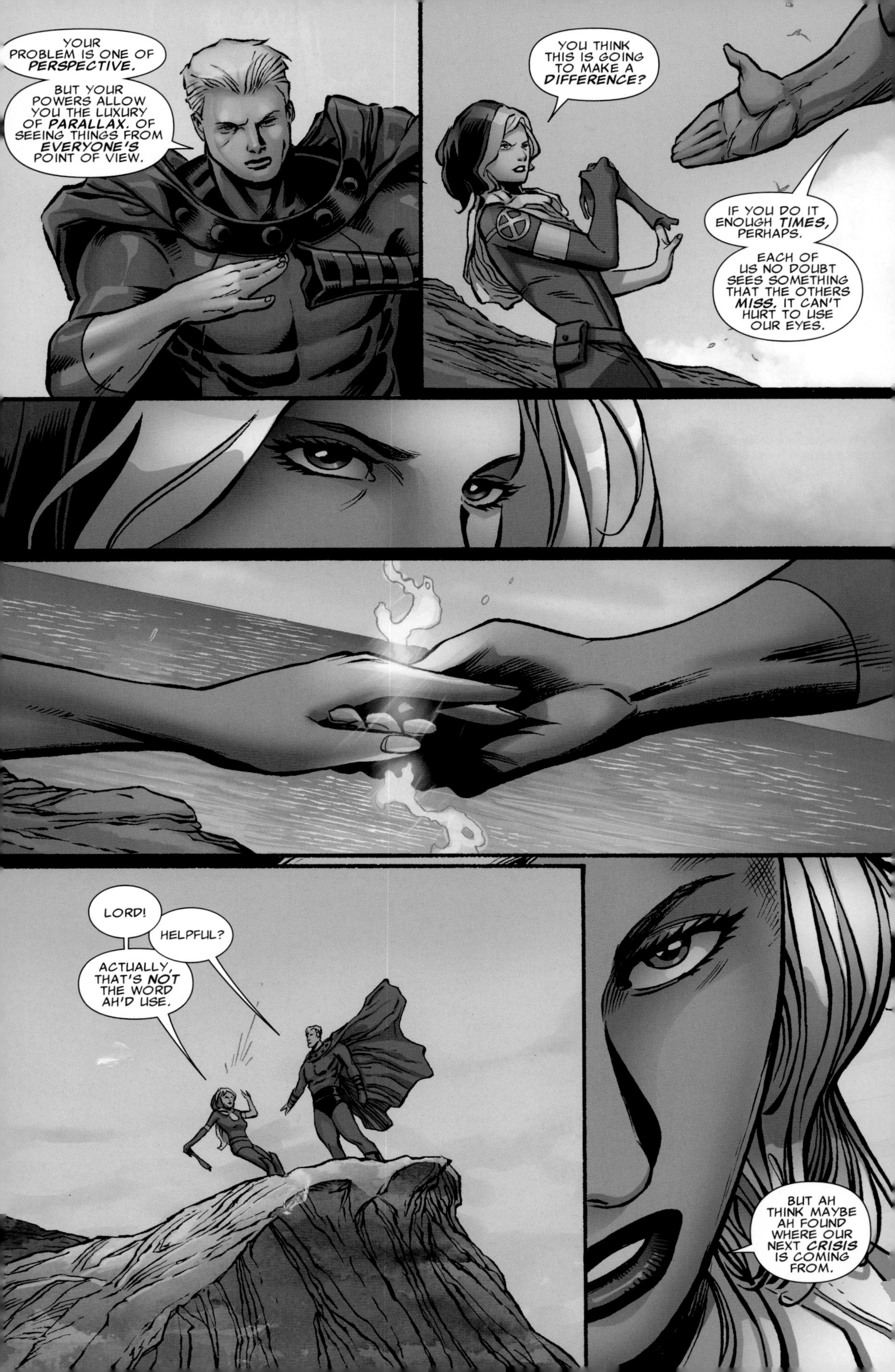
YOUR PROBLEM IS ONE OF PERSPECTIVE.
BUT YOUR POWERS ALLOW YOU THE LUXURY OF PARALLAX. OF SEEING THINGS FROM EVERYONE'S POINT OF VIEW.
YOU THINK THIS IS GOING TO MAKE A DIFFERENCE?
IF YOU DO IT ENOUGH TIMES, PERHAPS.
EACH OF US NO DOUBT SEES SOMETHING THAT THE OTHERS MISS. IT CAN'T HURT TO USE OUR EYES.
LORD!
HELPFUL?
ACTUALLY, THAT'S NOT THE WORD AH'D USE.
BUT AH THINK MAYBE AH FOUND WHERE OUR NEXT CRISIS IS COMING FROM.

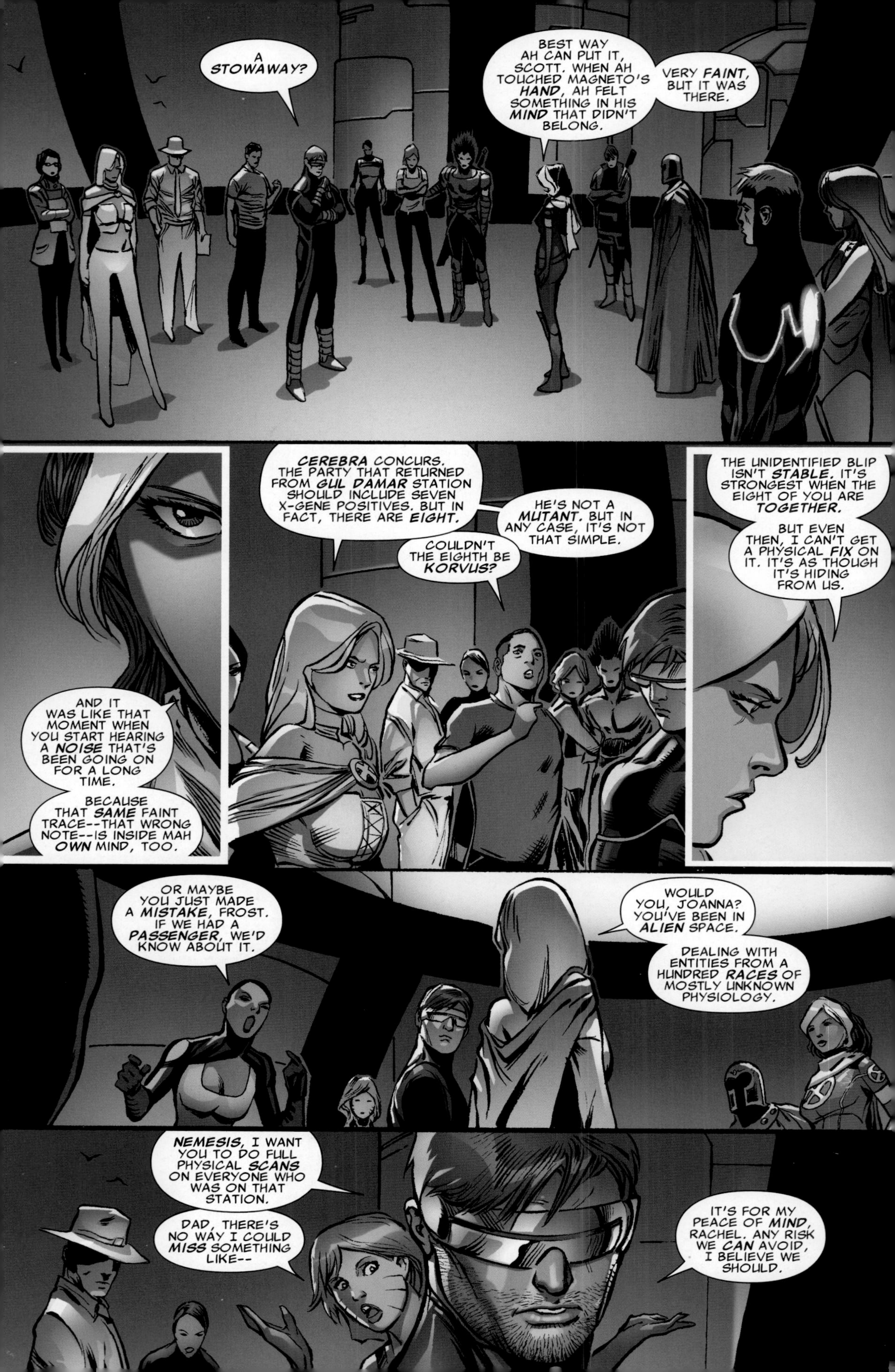
A STOWAWAY?
BEST WAY AH CAN PUT IT, SCOTT. WHEN AH TOUCHED MAGNETO'S HAND, AH FELT SOMETHING IN HIS MIND THAT DIDN'T BELONG.
VERY FAINT, BUT IT WAS THERE.
AND IT WAS LIKE THAT MOMENT WHEN YOU START HEARING A NOISE THAT'S BEEN GOING ON FOR A LONG TIME.
BECAUSE THAT SAME FAINT TRACE--THAT WRONG NOTE--IS INSIDE MAH OWN MIND, TOO.
CEREBRA CONCURS. THE PARTY THAT RETURNED FROM GUL DAMAR STATION SHOULD INCLUDE SEVEN X-GENE POSITIVES. BUT IN FACT, THERE ARE EIGHT.
COULDN'T THE EIGHTH BE KORVUS?
HE'S NOT A MUTANT. BUT IN ANY CASE, IT'S NOT THAT SIMPLE.
THE UNIDENTIFIED BLIP ISN'T STABLE. IT'S STRONGEST WHEN THE EIGHT OF YOU ARE TOGETHER.
BUT EVEN THEN, I CAN'T GET A PHYSICAL FIX ON IT. IT'S AS THOUGH IT'S HIDING FROM US.
OR MAYBE YOU JUST MADE A MISTAKE, FROST. IF WE HAD A PASSENGER, WE'D KNOW ABOUT IT.
WOULD YOU, JOANNA? YOU'VE BEEN IN ALIEN SPACE.
DEALING WITH ENTITIES FROM A HUNDRED RACES OF MOSTLY UNKNOWN PHYSIOLOGY.
NEMESIS, I WANT YOU TO DO FULL PHYSICAL SCANS ON EVERYONE WHO WAS ON THAT STATION.
DAD, THERE'S NO WAY I COULD MISS SOMETHING LIKE--
IT'S FOR MY PEACE OF MIND, RACHEL. ANY RISK WE CAN AVOID, I BELIEVE WE SHOULD.

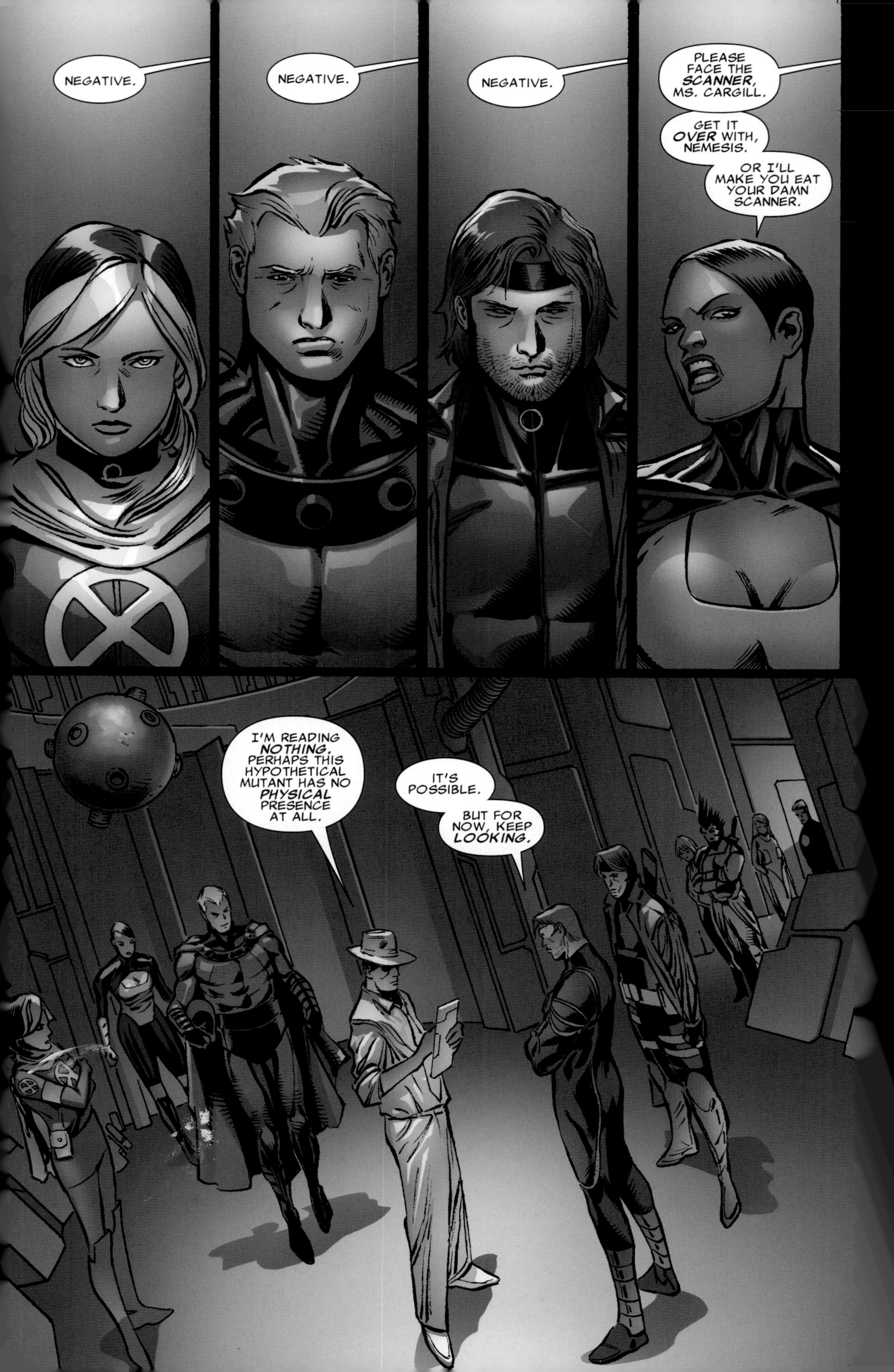
NEGATIVE.
NEGATIVE.
NEGATIVE.
PLEASE FACE THE SCANNER, MS. CARGILL.
GET IT OVER WITH, NEMESIS.
OR I'LL MAKE YOU EAT YOUR DAMN SCANNER.
I'M READING NOTHING. PERHAPS THIS HYPOTHETICAL MUTANT HAS NO PHYSICAL PRESENCE AT ALL.
IT'S POSSIBLE.
BUT FOR NOW, KEEP LOOKING.

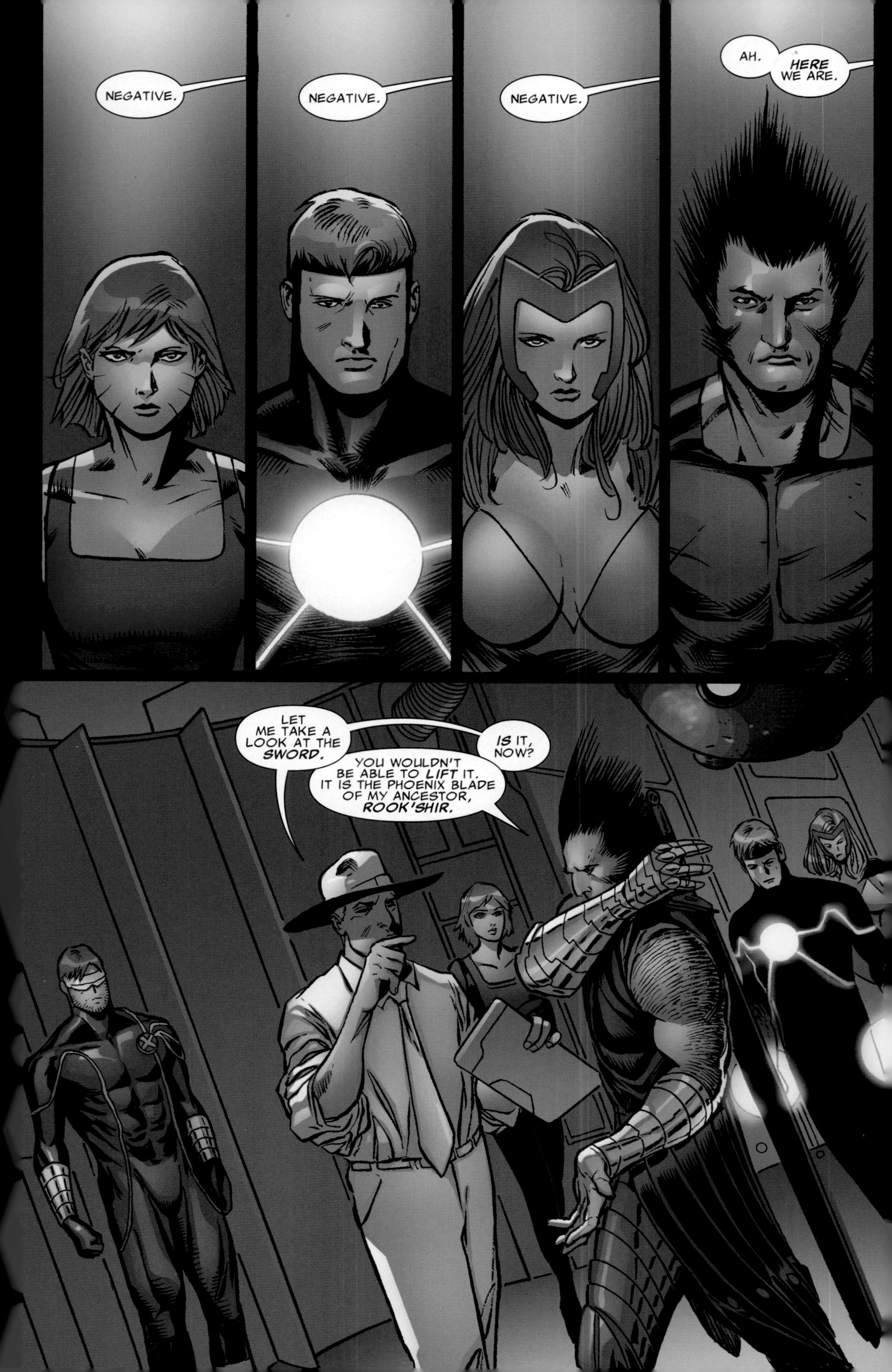
NEGATIVE.
NEGATIVE.
NEGATIVE.
AH.
HERE WE ARE.
LET ME TAKE A LOOK AT THE SWORD.
IS IT, NOW?
YOU WOULDN'T BE ABLE TO LIFT IT. IT IS THE PHOENIX BLADE OF MY ANCESTOR, ROOK'SHIR.

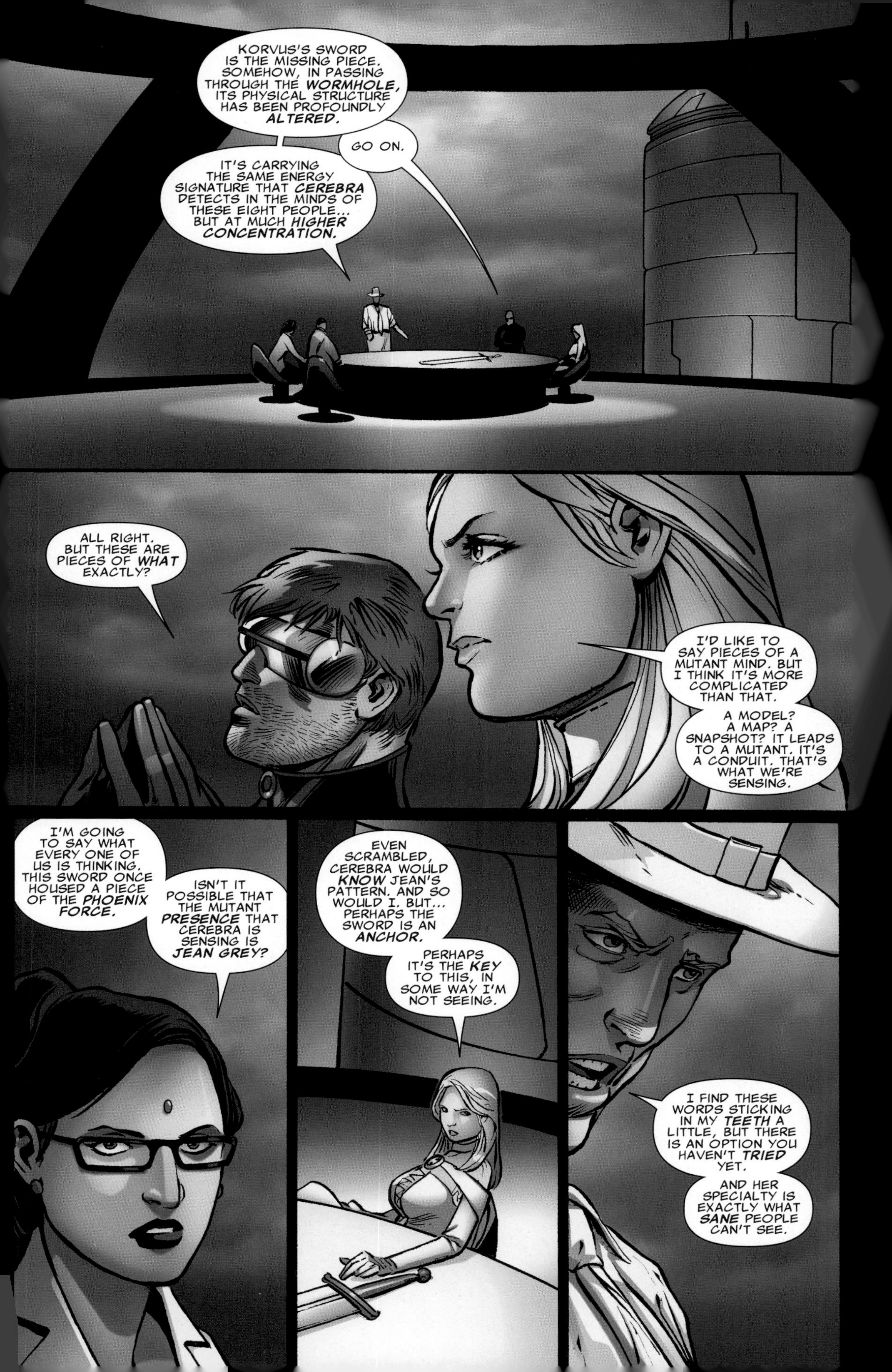
KORVUS'S SWORD IS THE MISSING PIECE. SOMEHOW, IN PASSING THROUGH THE WORMHOLE, ITS PHYSICAL STRUCTURE HAS BEEN PROFOUNDLY ALTERED.
GO ON.
IT'S CARRYING THE SAME ENERGY SIGNATURE THAT CEREBRA DETECTS IN THE MINDS OF THESE EIGHT PEOPLE... BUT AT MUCH HIGHER CONCENTRATION.
ALL RIGHT. BUT THESE ARE PIECES OF WHAT EXACTLY?
I'D LIKE TO SAY PIECES OF A MUTANT MIND. BUT I THINK IT'S MORE COMPLICATED THAN THAT.
A MODEL? A MAP? A SNAPSHOT? IT LEADS TO A MUTANT. IT'S A CONDUIT. THAT'S WHAT WE'RE SENSING.
I'M GOING TO SAY WHAT EVERY ONE OF US IS THINKING. THIS SWORD ONCE HOUSED A PIECE OF THE PHOENIX FORCE.
ISN'T IT POSSIBLE THAT THE MUTANT PRESENCE THAT CEREBRA IS SENSING IS JEAN GREY?
EVEN SCRAMBLED, CEREBRA WOULD KNOW JEAN'S PATTERN, AND SO WOULD I. BUT... PERHAPS THE SWORD IS AN ANCHOR.
PERHAPS IT'S THE KEY TO THIS, IN SOME WAY I'M NOT SEEING.
I FIND THESE WORDS STICKING IN MY TEETH A LITTLE, BUT THERE IS AN OPTION YOU HAVEN'T TRIED YET.
AND HER SPECIALTY IS EXACTLY WHAT SANE PEOPLE CAN'T SEE.

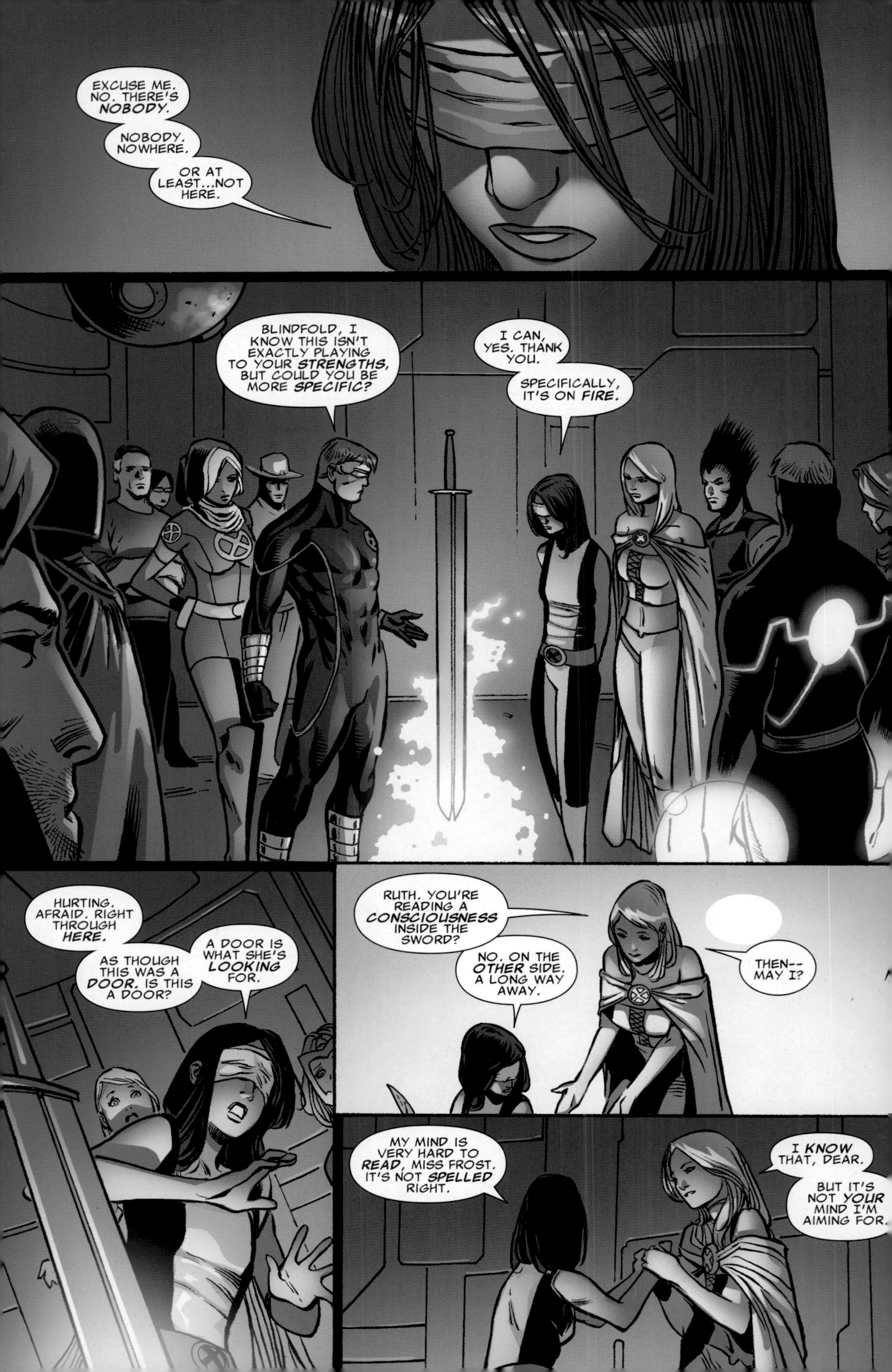
EXCUSE ME. NO. THERE'S NOBODY.
NOBODY. NOWHERE.
OR AT LEAST...NOT HERE.
BLINDFOLD, I KNOW THIS ISN'T EXACTLY PLAYING TO YOUR STRENGTHS, BUT COULD YOU BE MORE SPECIFIC?
I CAN, YES. THANK YOU.
SPECIFICALLY, IT'S ON FIRE.
HURTING. AFRAID. RIGHT THROUGH HERE.
AS THOUGH THIS WAS A DOOR. IS THIS A DOOR?
A DOOR IS WHAT SHE'S LOOKING FOR.
RUTH. YOU'RE READING A CONSCIOUSNESS INSIDE THE SWORD?
NO. ON THE OTHER SIDE. A LONG WAY AWAY.
THEN-- MAY I?
MY MIND IS VERY HARD TO READ, MISS FROST. IT'S NOT SPELLED RIGHT.
I KNOW THAT, DEAR.
BUT IT'S NOT YOUR MIND I'M AIMING FOR.

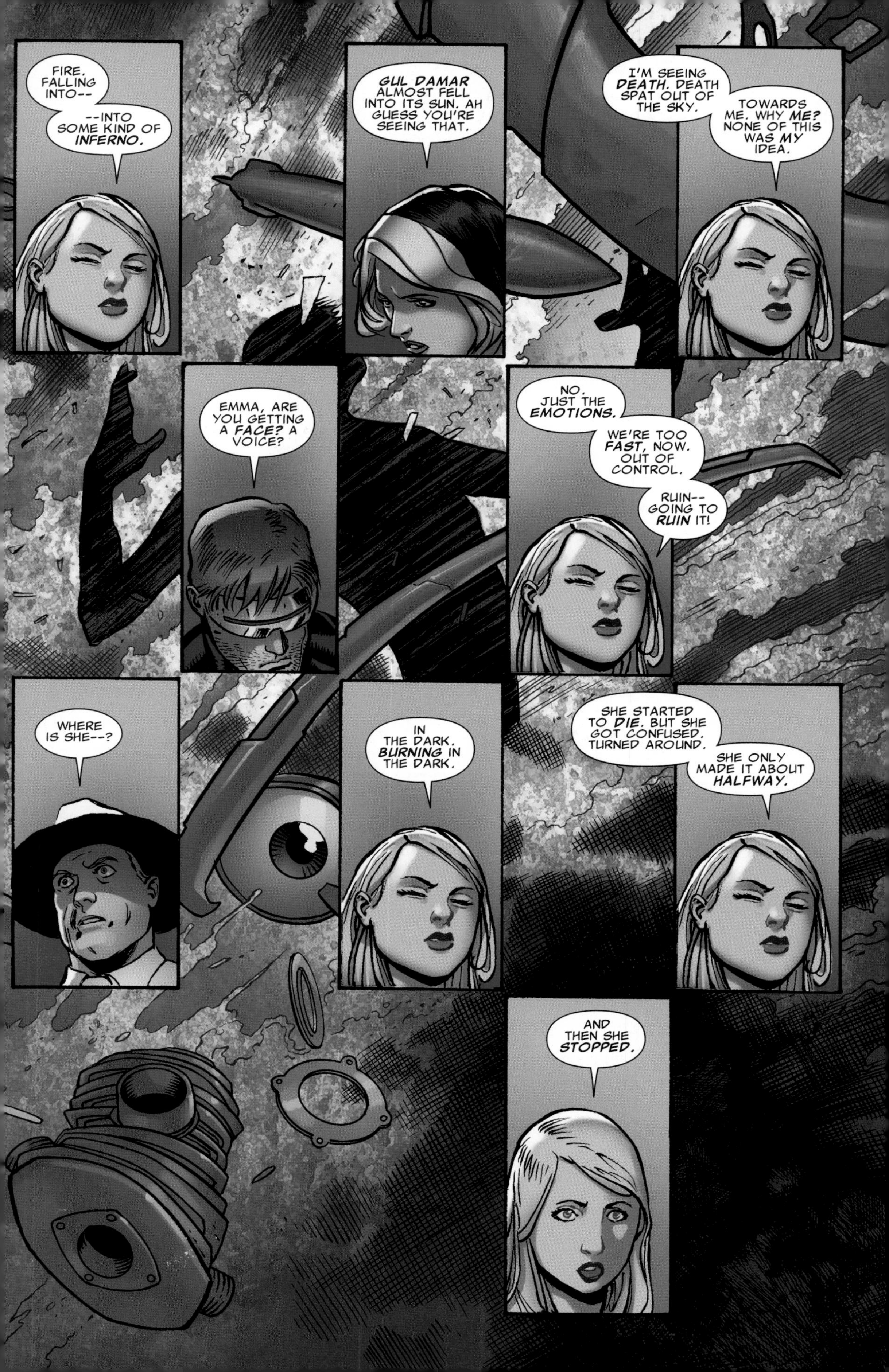
FIRE. FALLING INTO--
--INTO SOME KIND OF INFERNO.
GUL DAMAR ALMOST FELL INTO ITS SUN. AH GUESS YOU'RE SEEING THAT.
I'M SEEING DEATH. DEATH SPAT OUT OF THE SKY.
TOWARDS ME. WHY ME? NONE OF THIS WAS MY IDEA.
EMMA, ARE YOU GETTING A FACE? A VOICE?
NO. JUST THE EMOTIONS.
WE'RE TOO FAST, NOW. OUT OF CONTROL.
RUIN-- GOING TO RUIN IT!
WHERE IS SHE--?
IN THE DARK. BURNING IN THE DARK.
SHE STARTED TO DIE. BUT SHE GOT CONFUSED. TURNED AROUND.
SHE ONLY MADE IT ABOUT HALFWAY.
AND THEN SHE STOPPED.

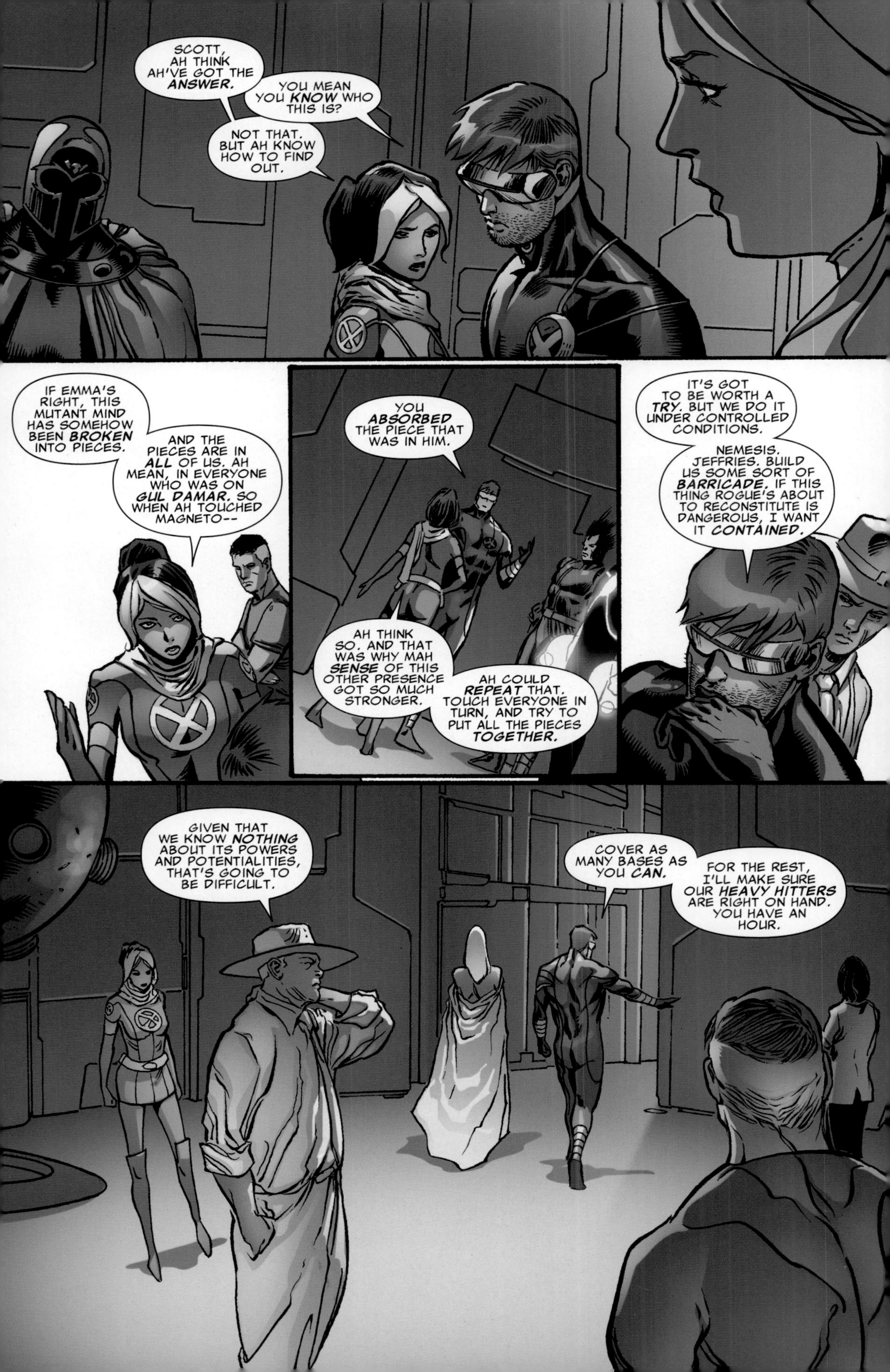
SCOTT, AH THINK AH'VE GOT THE ANSWER.
YOU MEAN YOU KNOW WHO THIS IS?
NOT THAT. BUT AH KNOW HOW TO FIND OUT.
IF EMMA'S RIGHT, THIS MUTANT MIND HAS SOMEHOW BEEN BROKEN INTO PIECES.
AND THE PIECES ARE IN ALL OF US. AH MEAN, IN EVERYONE WHO WAS ON GUL DAMAR. SO WHEN AH TOUCHED MAGNETO--
YOU ABSORBED THE PIECE THAT WAS IN HIM.
AH THINK SO. AND THAT WAS WHY MAH SENSE OF THIS OTHER PRESENCE GOT SO MUCH STRONGER.
AH COULD REPEAT THAT. TOUCH EVERYONE IN TURN, AND TRY TO PUT ALL THE PIECES TOGETHER.
IT'S GOT TO BE WORTH A TRY. BUT WE DO IT UNDER CONTROLLED CONDITIONS.
NEMESIS. JEFFRIES. BUILD US SOME SORT OF BARRICADE. IF THIS THING ROGUE'S ABOUT TO RECONSTITUTE IS DANGEROUS, I WANT IT CONTAINED.
GIVEN THAT WE KNOW NOTHING ABOUT ITS POWERS AND POTENTIALITIES, THAT'S GOING TO BE DIFFICULT.
COVER AS MANY BASES AS YOU CAN.
FOR THE REST, I'LL MAKE SURE OUR HEAVY HITTERS ARE RIGHT ON HAND. YOU HAVE AN HOUR.

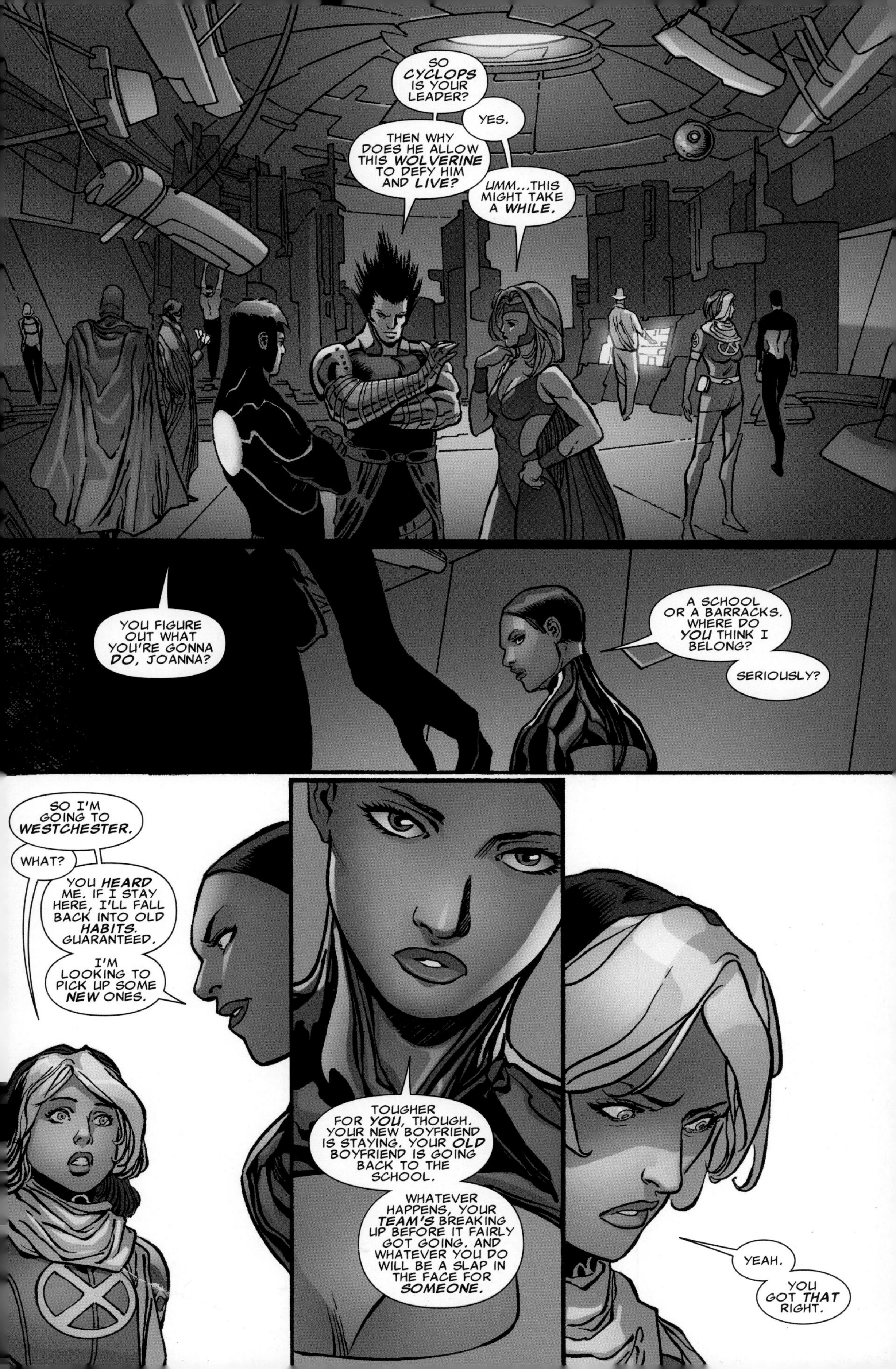

SO CYCLOPS IS YOUR LEADER?
YES.
THEN WHY DOES HE ALLOW THIS WOLVERINE TO DEFY HIM AND LIVE?
UMM...THIS MIGHT TAKE A WHILE.
YOU FIGURE OUT WHAT YOU'RE GONNA DO, JOANNA?
A SCHOOL OR A BARRACKS. WHERE DO YOU THINK I BELONG?
SERIOUSLY?
SO I'M GOING TO WESTCHESTER.
WHAT?
YOU HEARD ME. IF I STAY HERE, I'LL FALL BACK INTO OLD HABITS. GUARANTEED.
I'M LOOKING TO PICK UP SOME NEW ONES.
TOUGHER FOR YOU, THOUGH. YOUR NEW BOYFRIEND IS STAYING. YOUR OLD BOYFRIEND IS GOING BACK TO THE SCHOOL.
WHATEVER HAPPENS, YOUR TEAM'S BREAKING UP BEFORE IT FAIRLY GOT GOING. AND WHATEVER YOU DO WILL BE A SLAP IN THE FACE FOR SOMEONE.
YEAH.
YOU GOT THAT RIGHT.

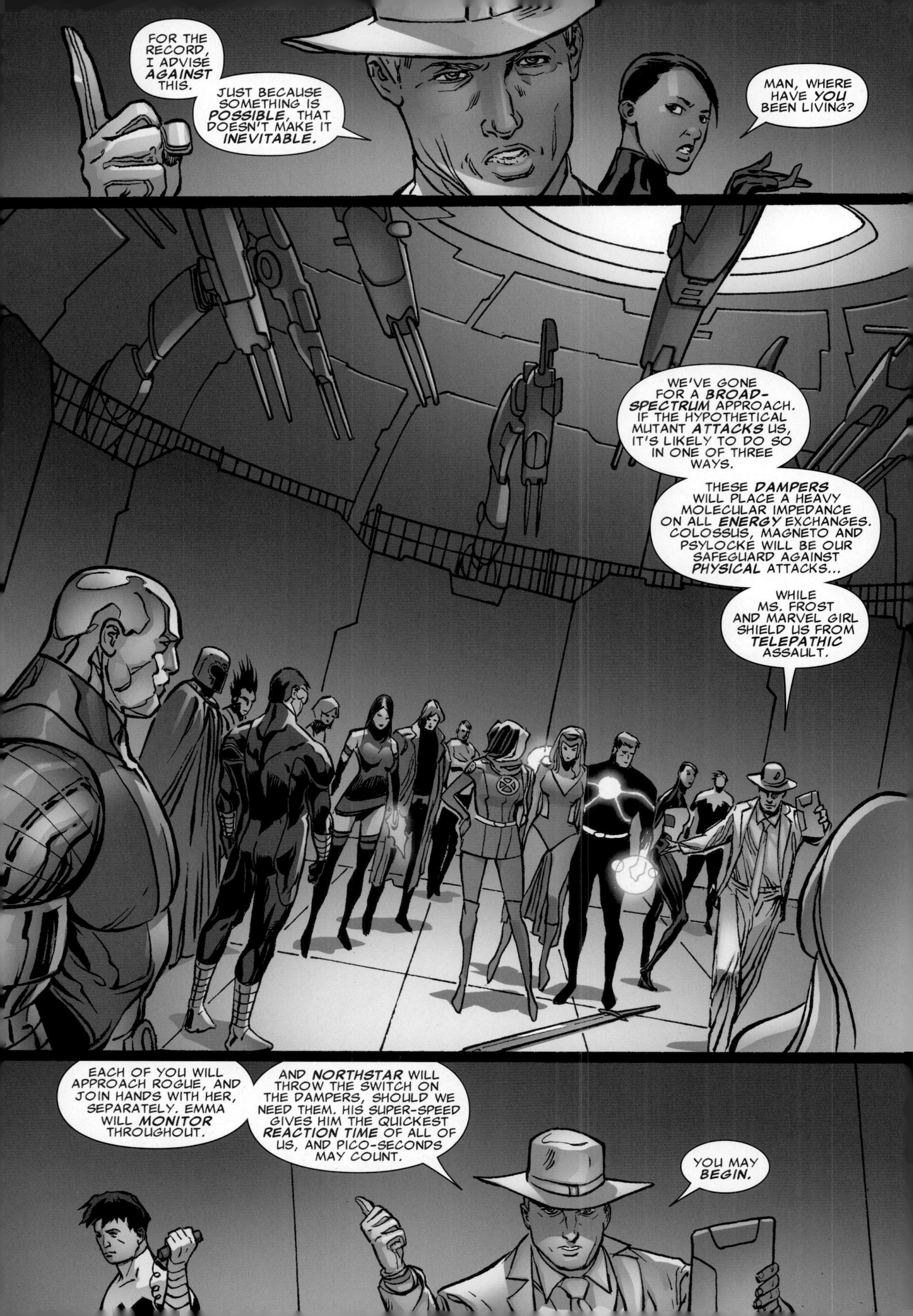
FOR THE RECORD, I ADVISE AGAINST THIS.
JUST BECAUSE SOMETHING IS POSSIBLE, THAT DOESN'T MAKE IT INEVITABLE.
MAN, WHERE HAVE YOU BEEN LIVING?
WE'VE GONE FOR A BROAD-SPECTRUM APPROACH. IF THE HYPOTHETICAL MUTANT ATTACKS US, IT'S LIKELY TO DO SO IN ONE OF THREE WAYS.
THESE DAMPERS WILL PLACE A HEAVY MOLECULAR IMPEDANCE ON ALL ENERGY EXCHANGES. COLOSSUS, MAGNETO AND PSYLOCKE WILL BE OUR SAFEGUARD AGAINST PHYSICAL ATTACKS...
WHILE MS. FROST AND MARVEL GIRL SHIELD US FROM TELEPATHIC ASSAULT.
EACH OF YOU WILL APPROACH ROGUE, AND JOIN HANDS WITH HER, SEPARATELY. EMMA WILL MONITOR THROUGHOUT.
AND NORTHSTAR WILL THROW THE SWITCH ON THE DAMPERS, SHOULD WE NEED THEM. HIS SUPER-SPEED GIVES HIM THE QUICKEST REACTION TIME OF ALL OF US, AND PICO-SECONDS MAY COUNT.
YOU MAY BEGIN.

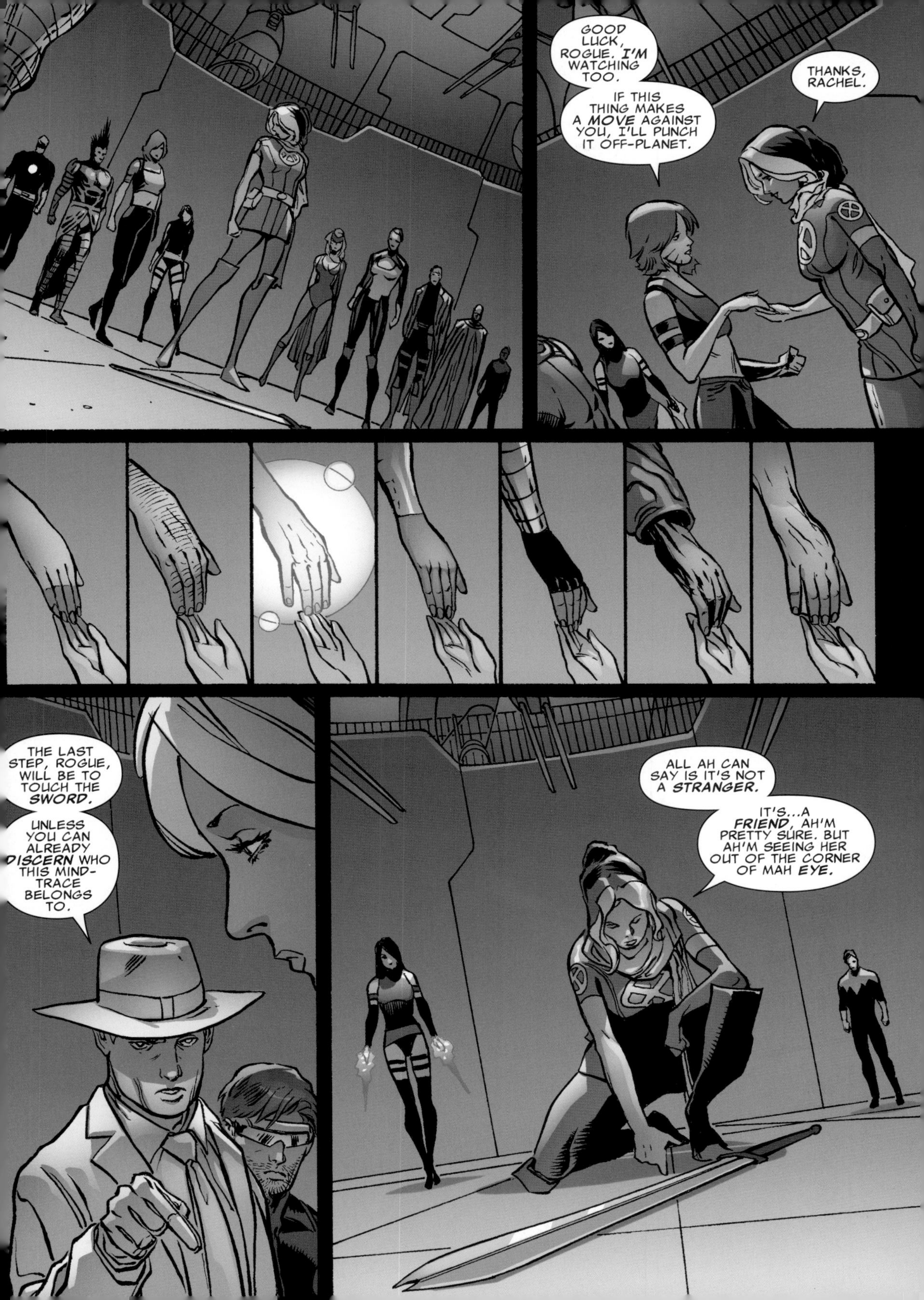
GOOD LUCK, ROGUE. I'M WATCHING TOO.
IF THIS THING MAKES A MOVE AGAINST YOU, I'LL PUNCH IT OFF-PLANET.
THANKS, RACHEL.
THE LAST STEP, ROGUE, WILL BE TO TOUCH THE SWORD.
UNLESS YOU CAN ALREADY DISCERN WHO THIS MIND-TRACE BELONGS TO.
ALL AH CAN SAY IS IT'S NOT A STRANGER.
IT'S...A FRIEND, AH'M PRETTY SURE. BUT AH'M SEEING HER OUT OF THE CORNER OF MAH EYE.

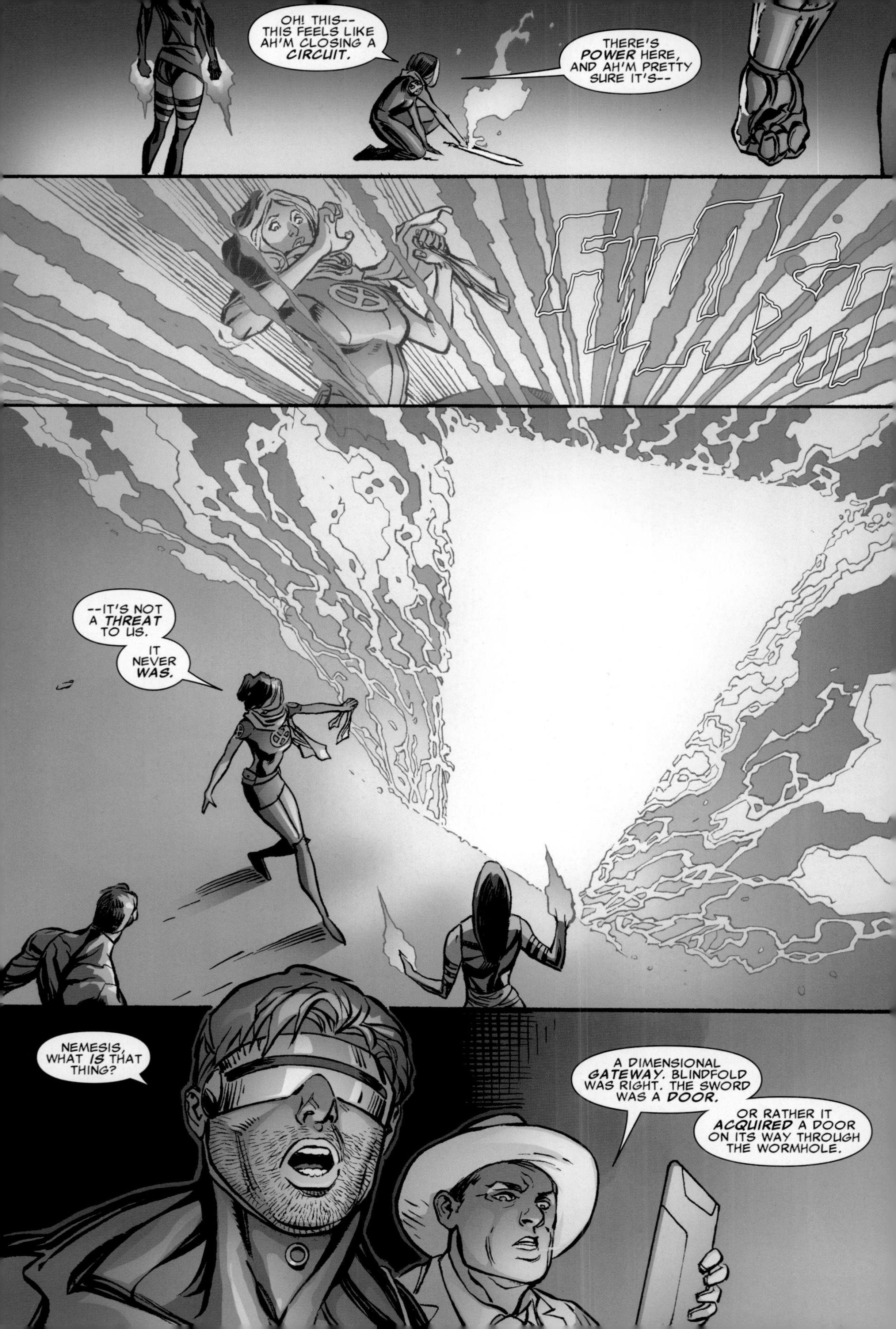
OH! THIS-- THIS FEELS LIKE AH'M CLOSING A *CIRCUIT.*
THERE'S *POWER* HERE, AND AH'M PRETTY SURE IT'S--
--IT'S NOT A *THREAT* TO US.
IT NEVER *WAS.*
NEMESIS, WHAT *IS* THAT THING?
A DIMENSIONAL *GATEWAY*. BLINDFOLD WAS RIGHT. THE SWORD WAS A *DOOR.*
OR RATHER IT *ACQUIRED* A DOOR ON ITS WAY THROUGH THE WORMHOLE.

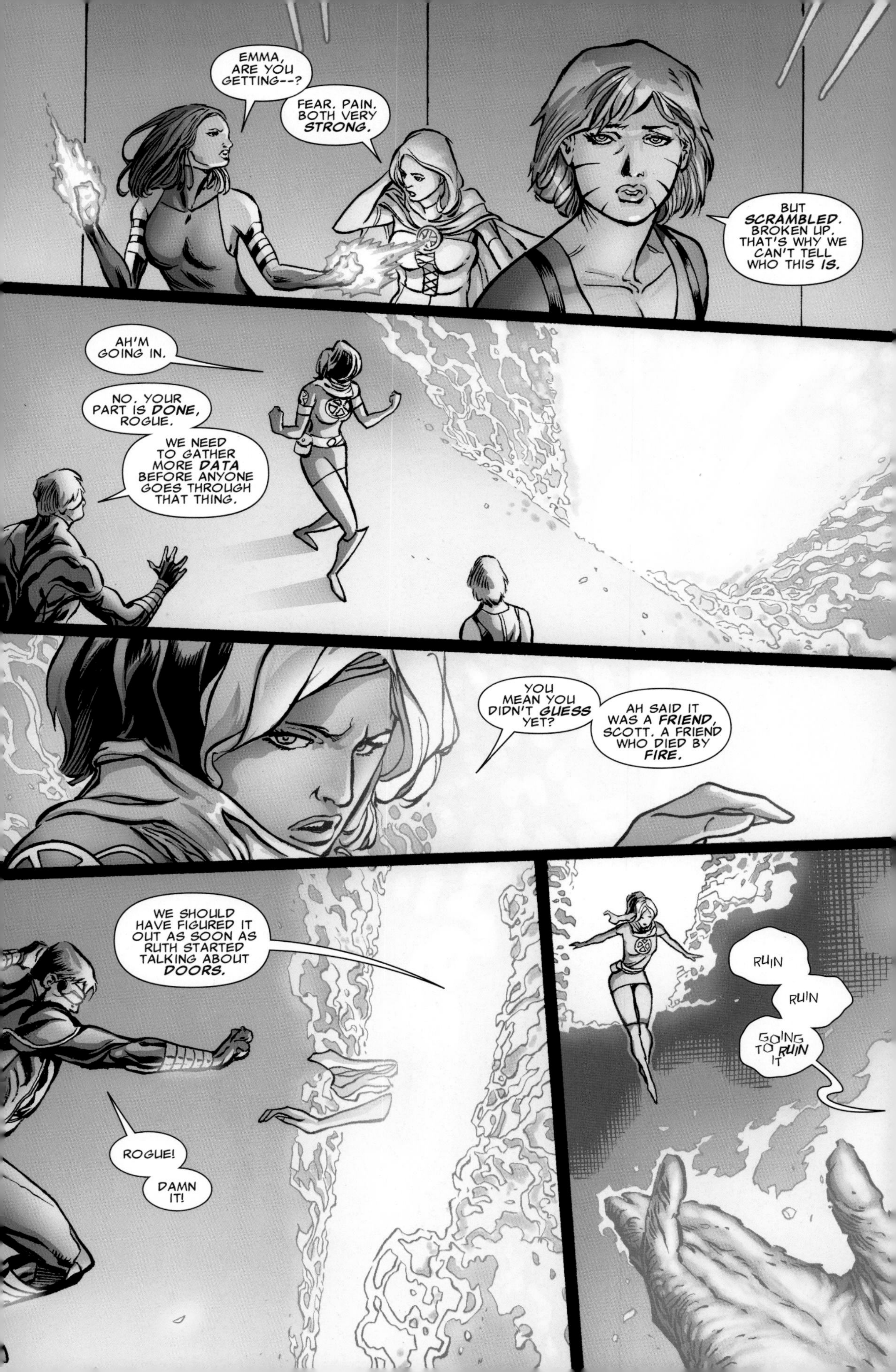
EMMA, ARE YOU GETTING--?
FEAR. PAIN. BOTH VERY STRONG.
BUT SCRAMBLED. BROKEN UP. THAT'S WHY WE CAN'T TELL WHO THIS IS.
AH'M GOING IN.
NO. YOUR PART IS DONE, ROGUE.
WE NEED TO GATHER MORE DATA BEFORE ANYONE GOES THROUGH THAT THING.
YOU MEAN YOU DIDN'T GUESS YET?
AH SAID IT WAS A FRIEND, SCOTT. A FRIEND WHO DIED BY FIRE.
WE SHOULD HAVE FIGURED IT OUT AS SOON AS RUTH STARTED TALKING ABOUT DOORS.
ROGUE!
DAMN IT!
RUIN
RUIN
GOING TO RUIN IT

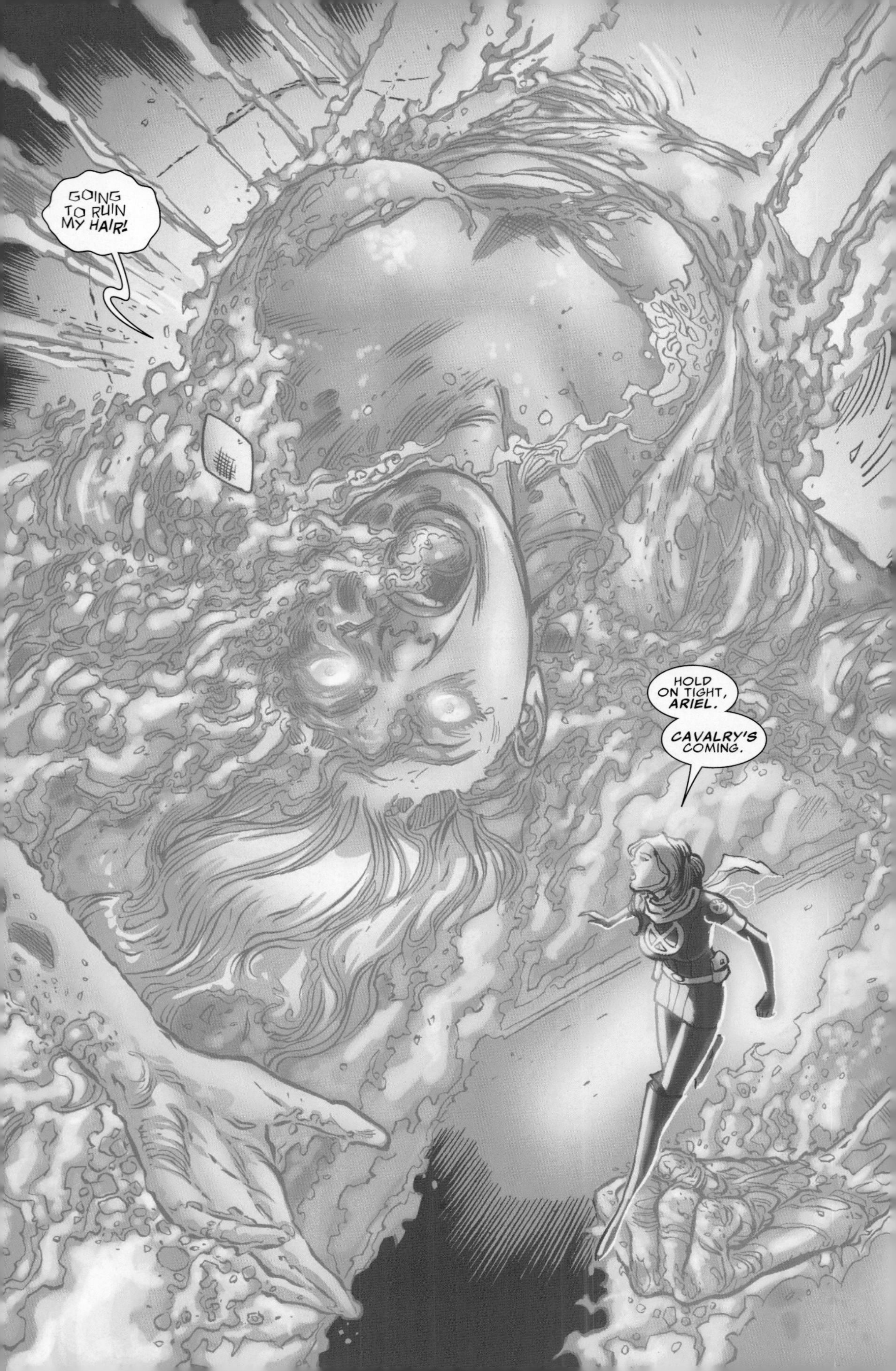
GOING TO RUIN MY HAIR!
HOLD ON TIGHT, ARIEL.
CAVALRY'S COMING.

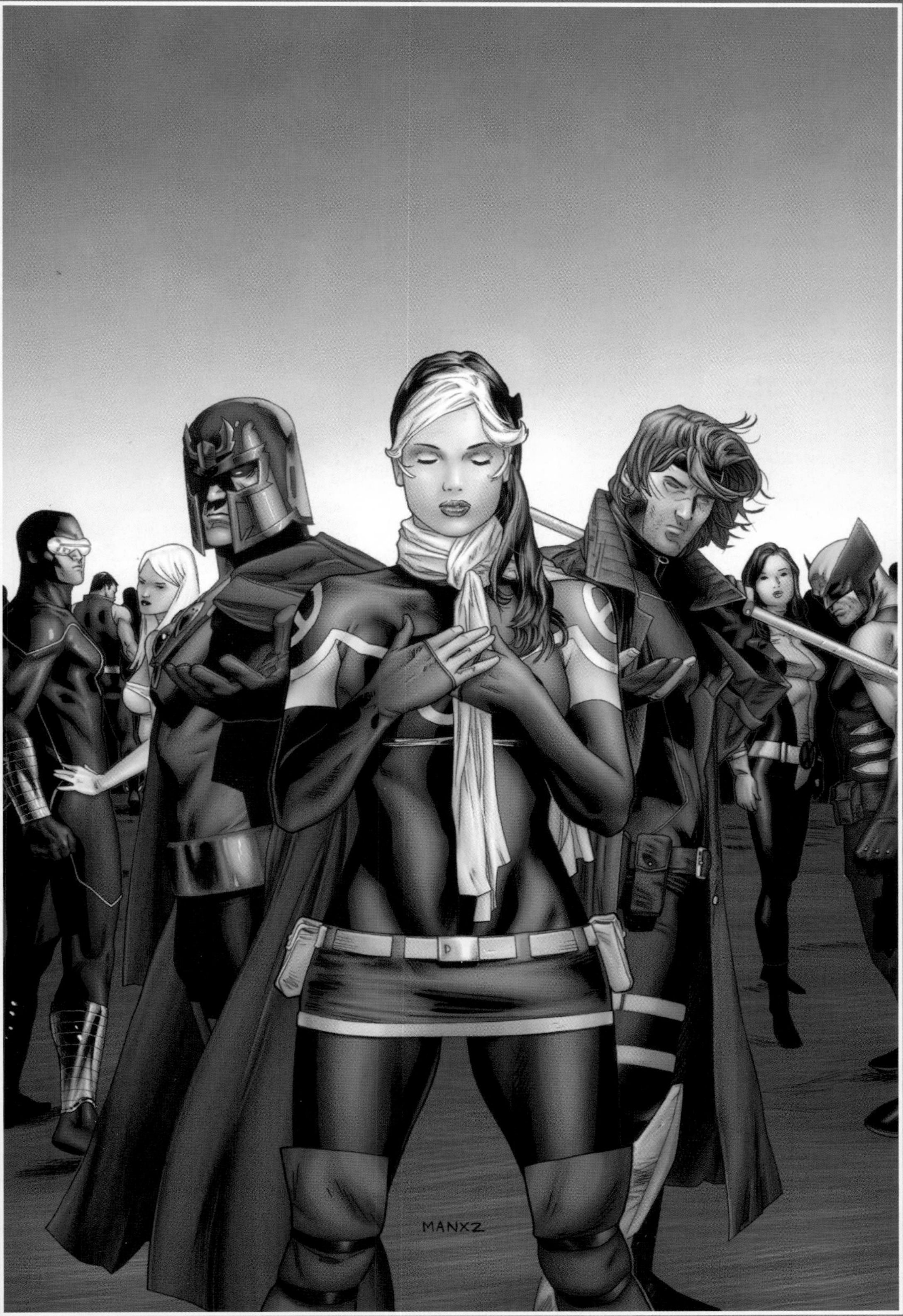
MANXZ

#260
"HALF A STEP" PART TWO

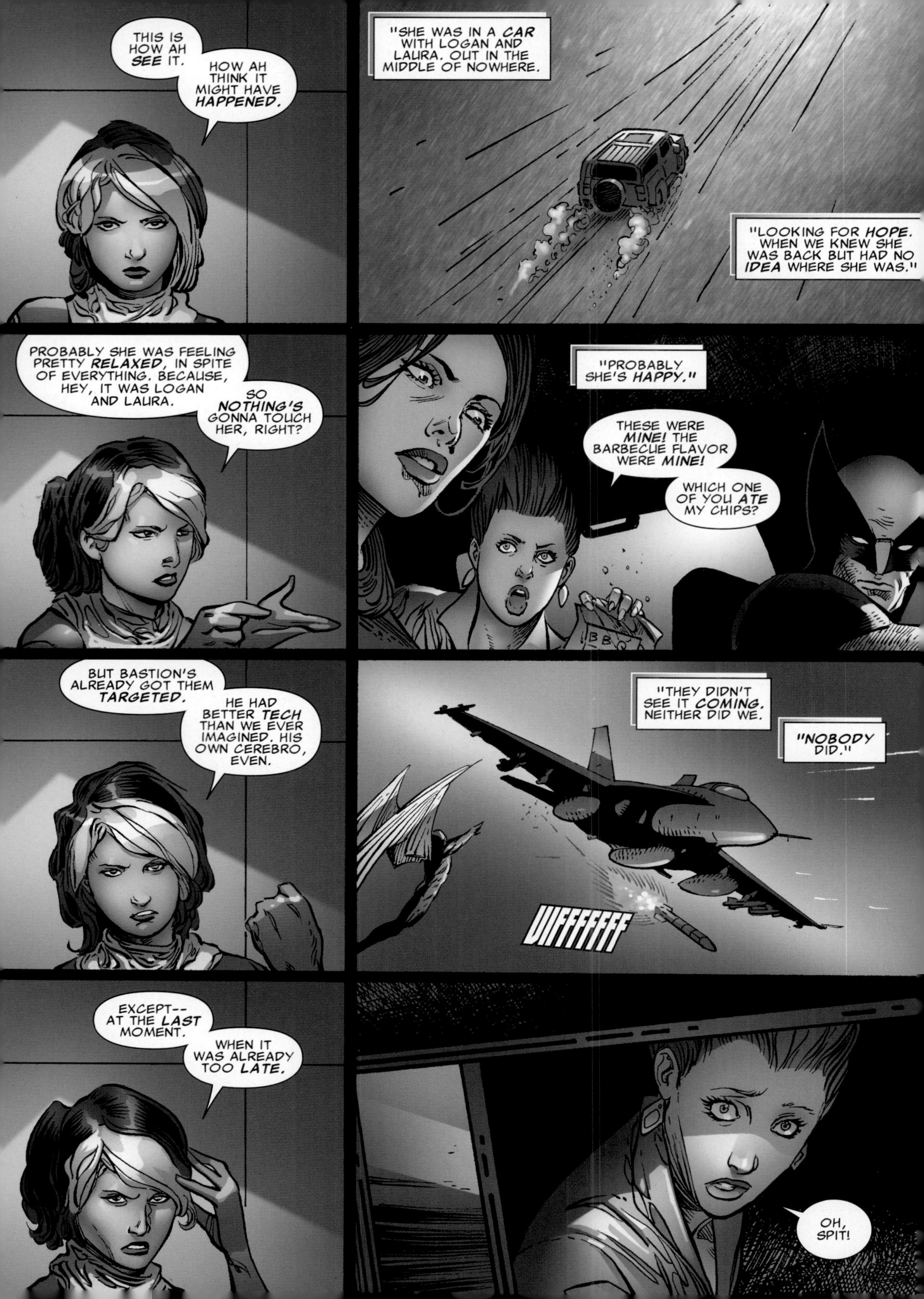
THIS IS HOW AH SEE IT.
HOW AH THINK IT MIGHT HAVE HAPPENED.
"SHE WAS IN A CAR WITH LOGAN AND LAURA. OUT IN THE MIDDLE OF NOWHERE.
"LOOKING FOR HOPE. WHEN WE KNEW SHE WAS BACK BUT HAD NO IDEA WHERE SHE WAS."
PROBABLY SHE WAS FEELING PRETTY RELAXED, IN SPITE OF EVERYTHING. BECAUSE, HEY, IT WAS LOGAN AND LAURA.
SO NOTHING'S GONNA TOUCH HER, RIGHT?
"PROBABLY SHE'S HAPPY."
THESE WERE MINE! THE BARBECUE FLAVOR WERE MINE!
WHICH ONE OF YOU ATE MY CHIPS?
BUT BASTION'S ALREADY GOT THEM TARGETED.
HE HAD BETTER TECH THAN WE EVER IMAGINED. HIS OWN CEREBRO, EVEN.
"THEY DIDN'T SEE IT COMING. NEITHER DID WE.
"NOBODY DID."
VFFFFFFF
EXCEPT-- AT THE LAST MOMENT.
WHEN IT WAS ALREADY TOO LATE.
OH, SPIT!

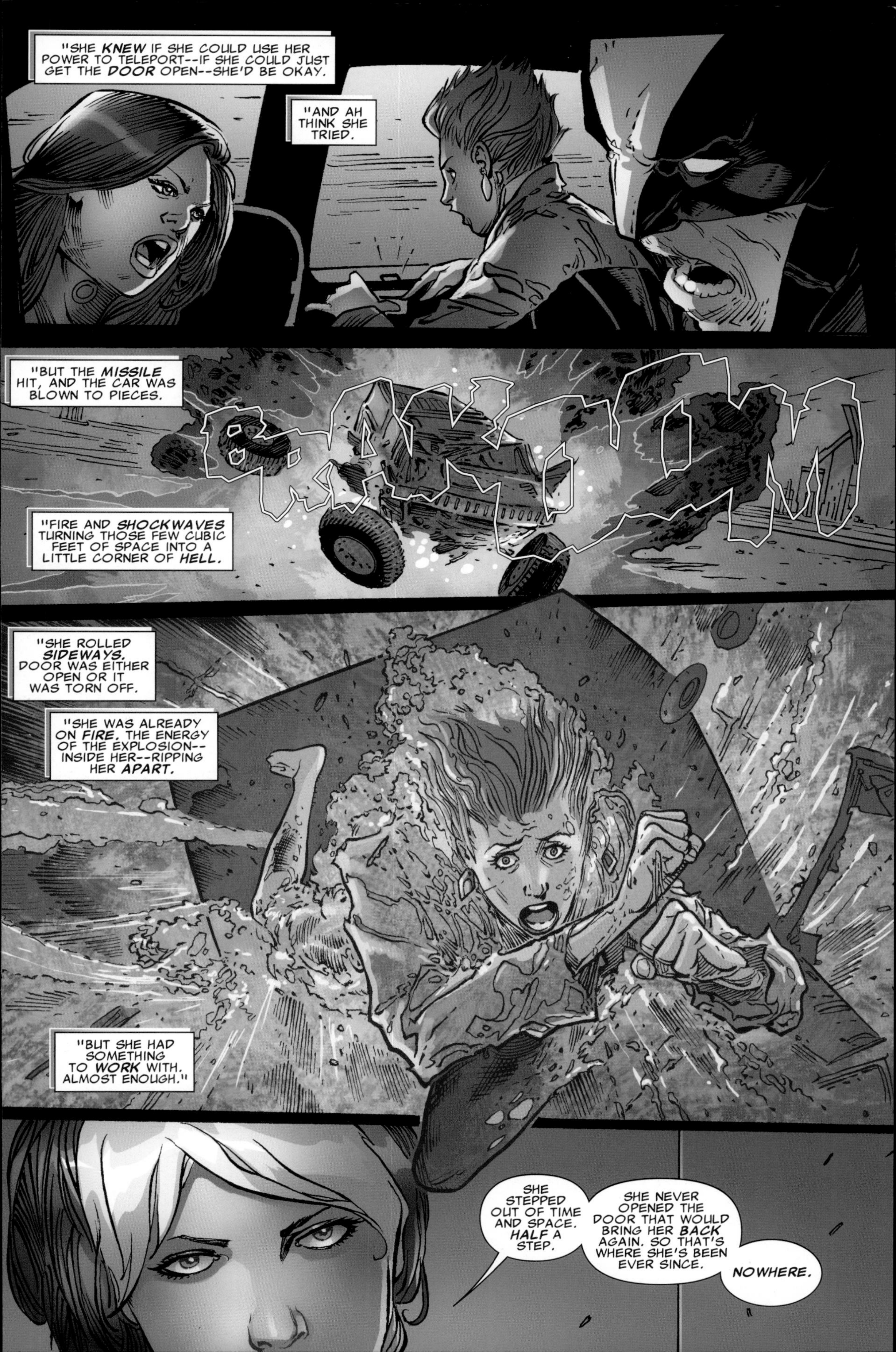
"SHE KNEW IF SHE COULD USE HER POWER TO TELEPORT--IF SHE COULD JUST GET THE DOOR OPEN--SHE'D BE OKAY.
"AND AH THINK SHE TRIED.
"BUT THE MISSILE HIT, AND THE CAR WAS BLOWN TO PIECES.
BAKOOM
"FIRE AND SHOCKWAVES TURNING THOSE FEW CUBIC FEET OF SPACE INTO A LITTLE CORNER OF HELL.
"SHE ROLLED SIDEWAYS. DOOR WAS EITHER OPEN OR IT WAS TORN OFF.
"SHE WAS ALREADY ON FIRE. THE ENERGY OF THE EXPLOSION--INSIDE HER--RIPPING HER APART.
"BUT SHE HAD SOMETHING TO WORK WITH. ALMOST ENOUGH."
SHE STEPPED OUT OF TIME AND SPACE. HALF A STEP.
SHE NEVER OPENED THE DOOR THAT WOULD BRING HER BACK AGAIN. SO THAT'S WHERE SHE'S BEEN EVER SINCE.
NOWHERE.

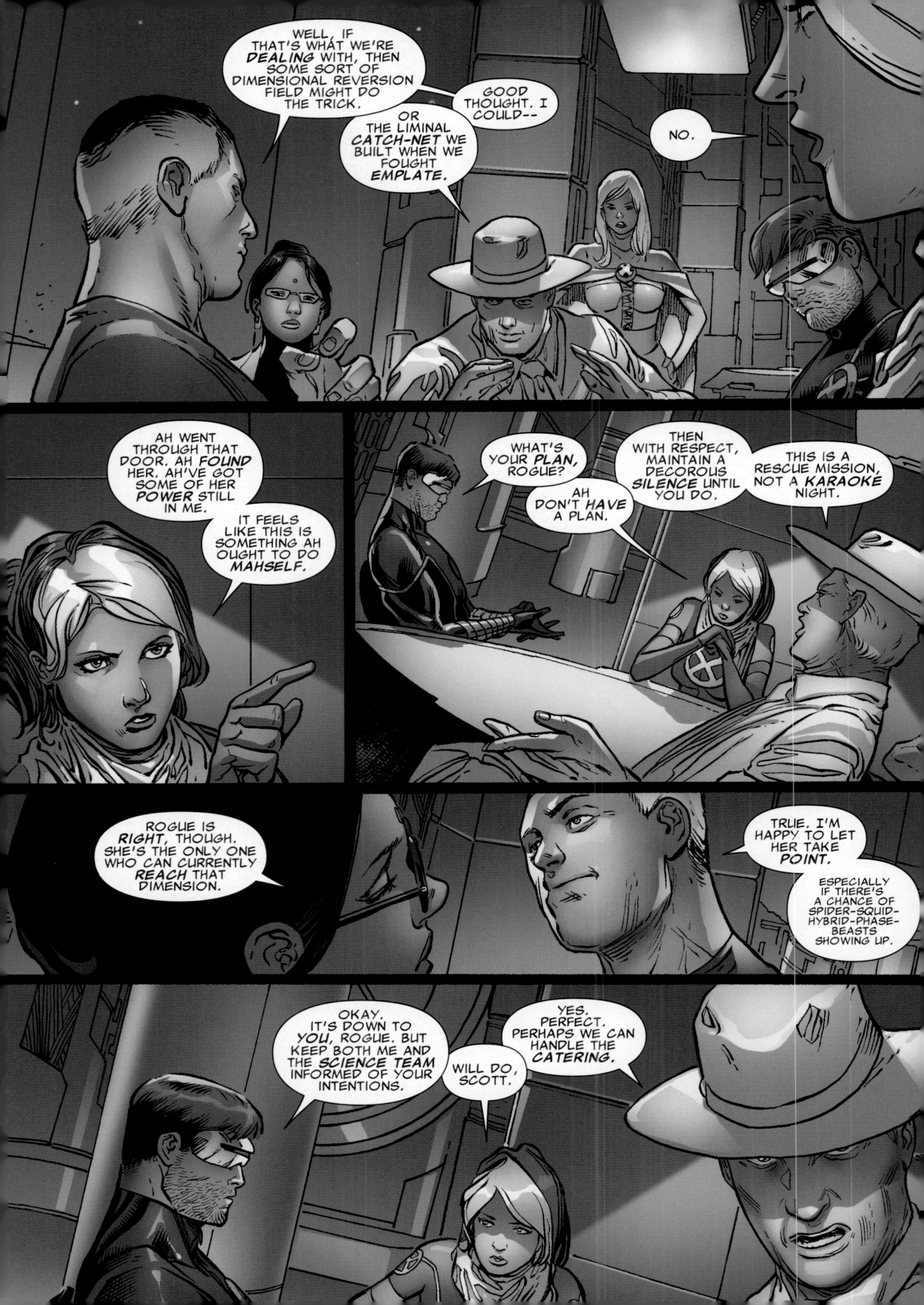
WELL, IF THAT'S WHAT WE'RE DEALING WITH, THEN SOME SORT OF DIMENSIONAL REVERSION FIELD MIGHT DO THE TRICK.
GOOD THOUGHT. I COULD--
OR THE LIMINAL CATCH-NET WE BUILT WHEN WE FOUGHT EMPLATE.
NO.
AH WENT THROUGH THAT DOOR. AH FOUND HER. AH'VE GOT SOME OF HER POWER STILL IN ME.
IT FEELS LIKE THIS IS SOMETHING AH OUGHT TO DO MAHSELF.
WHAT'S YOUR PLAN, ROGUE?
AH DON'T HAVE A PLAN.
THEN WITH RESPECT, MAINTAIN A DECOROUS SILENCE UNTIL YOU DO.
THIS IS A RESCUE MISSION, NOT A KARAOKE NIGHT.
ROGUE IS RIGHT, THOUGH. SHE'S THE ONLY ONE WHO CAN CURRENTLY REACH THAT DIMENSION.
TRUE. I'M HAPPY TO LET HER TAKE POINT.
ESPECIALLY IF THERE'S A CHANCE OF SPIDER-SQUID-HYBRID-PHASE-BEASTS SHOWING UP.
OKAY. IT'S DOWN TO YOU, ROGUE. BUT KEEP BOTH ME AND THE SCIENCE TEAM INFORMED OF YOUR INTENTIONS.
WILL DO, SCOTT.
YES. PERFECT. PERHAPS WE CAN HANDLE THE CATERING.

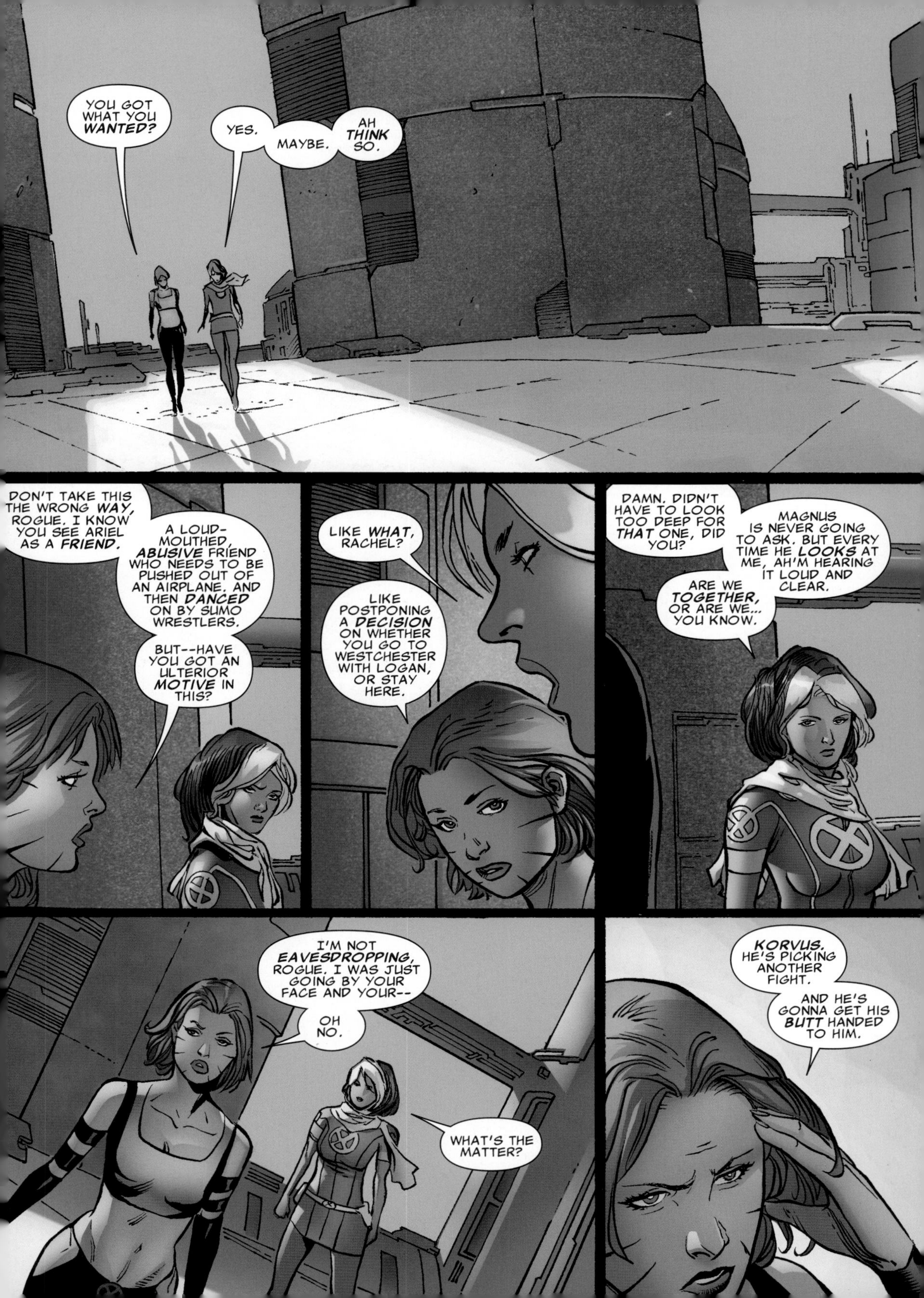
YOU GOT WHAT YOU WANTED?
YES.
MAYBE.
AH THINK SO.
DON'T TAKE THIS THE WRONG WAY, ROGUE. I KNOW YOU SEE ARIEL AS A FRIEND.
A LOUD-MOUTHED, ABUSIVE FRIEND WHO NEEDS TO BE PUSHED OUT OF AN AIRPLANE. AND THEN DANCED ON BY SUMO WRESTLERS.
BUT--HAVE YOU GOT AN ULTERIOR MOTIVE IN THIS?
LIKE WHAT, RACHEL?
LIKE POSTPONING A DECISION ON WHETHER YOU GO TO WESTCHESTER WITH LOGAN, OR STAY HERE.
DAMN. DIDN'T HAVE TO LOOK TOO DEEP FOR THAT ONE, DID YOU?
MAGNUS IS NEVER GOING TO ASK. BUT EVERY TIME HE LOOKS AT ME, AH'M HEARING IT LOUD AND CLEAR.
ARE WE TOGETHER, OR ARE WE... YOU KNOW.
I'M NOT EAVESDROPPING, ROGUE. I WAS JUST GOING BY YOUR FACE AND YOUR--
OH NO.
WHAT'S THE MATTER?
KORVUS. HE'S PICKING ANOTHER FIGHT.
AND HE'S GONNA GET HIS BUTT HANDED TO HIM.

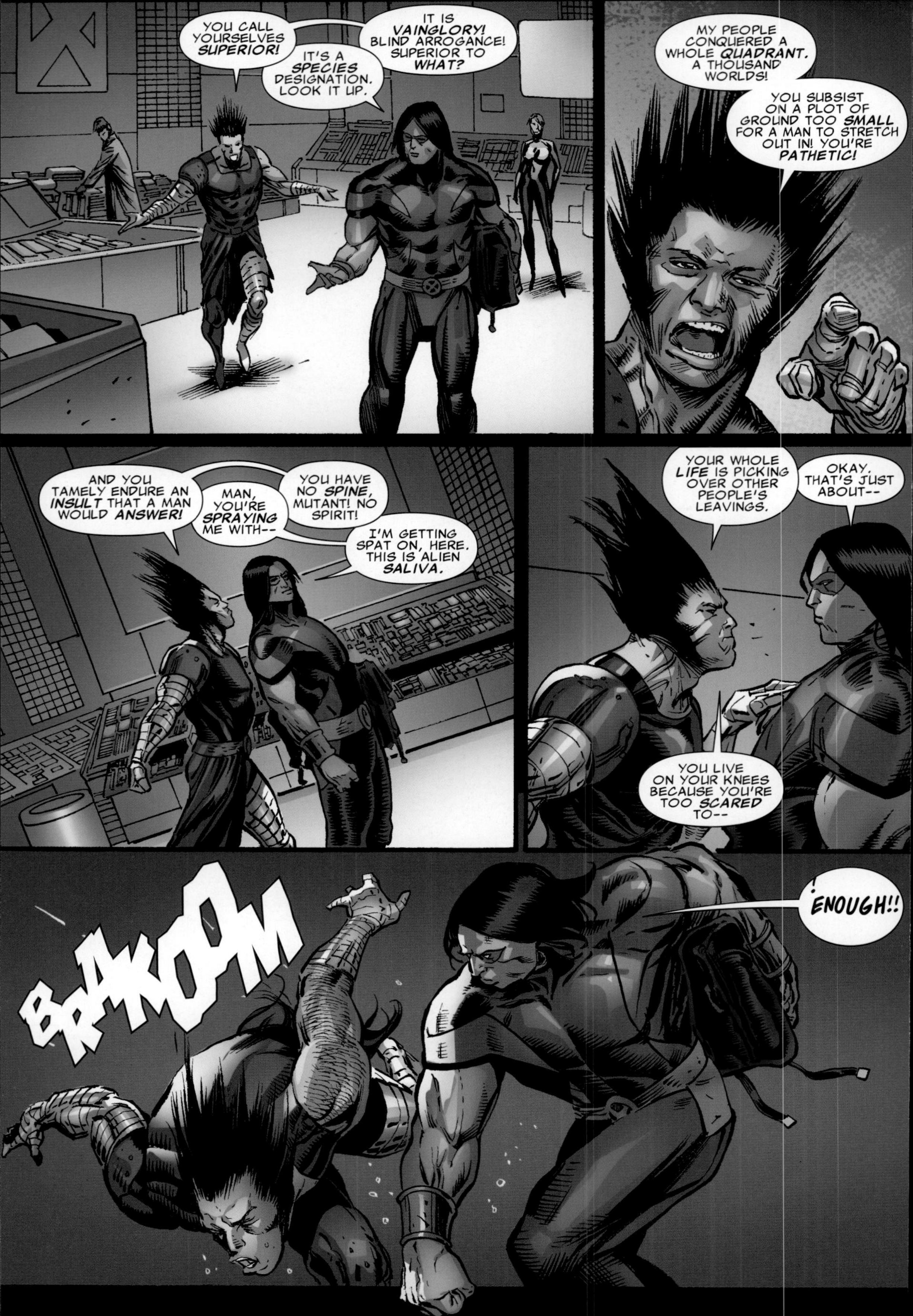
YOU CALL YOURSELVES SUPERIOR!
IT'S A SPECIES DESIGNATION. LOOK IT UP.
IT IS VAINGLORY! BLIND ARROGANCE! SUPERIOR TO WHAT?
MY PEOPLE CONQUERED A WHOLE QUADRANT. A THOUSAND WORLDS!
YOU SUBSIST ON A PLOT OF GROUND TOO SMALL FOR A MAN TO STRETCH OUT IN! YOU'RE PATHETIC!
AND YOU TAMELY ENDURE AN INSULT THAT A MAN WOULD ANSWER!
MAN, YOU'RE SPRAYING ME WITH--
YOU HAVE NO SPINE, MUTANT! NO SPIRIT!
I'M GETTING SPAT ON, HERE. THIS IS ALIEN SALIVA.
YOUR WHOLE LIFE IS PICKING OVER OTHER PEOPLE'S LEAVINGS.
OKAY. THAT'S JUST ABOUT--
YOU LIVE ON YOUR KNEES BECAUSE YOU'RE TOO SCARED TO--
BRAKOOM
ENOUGH!!

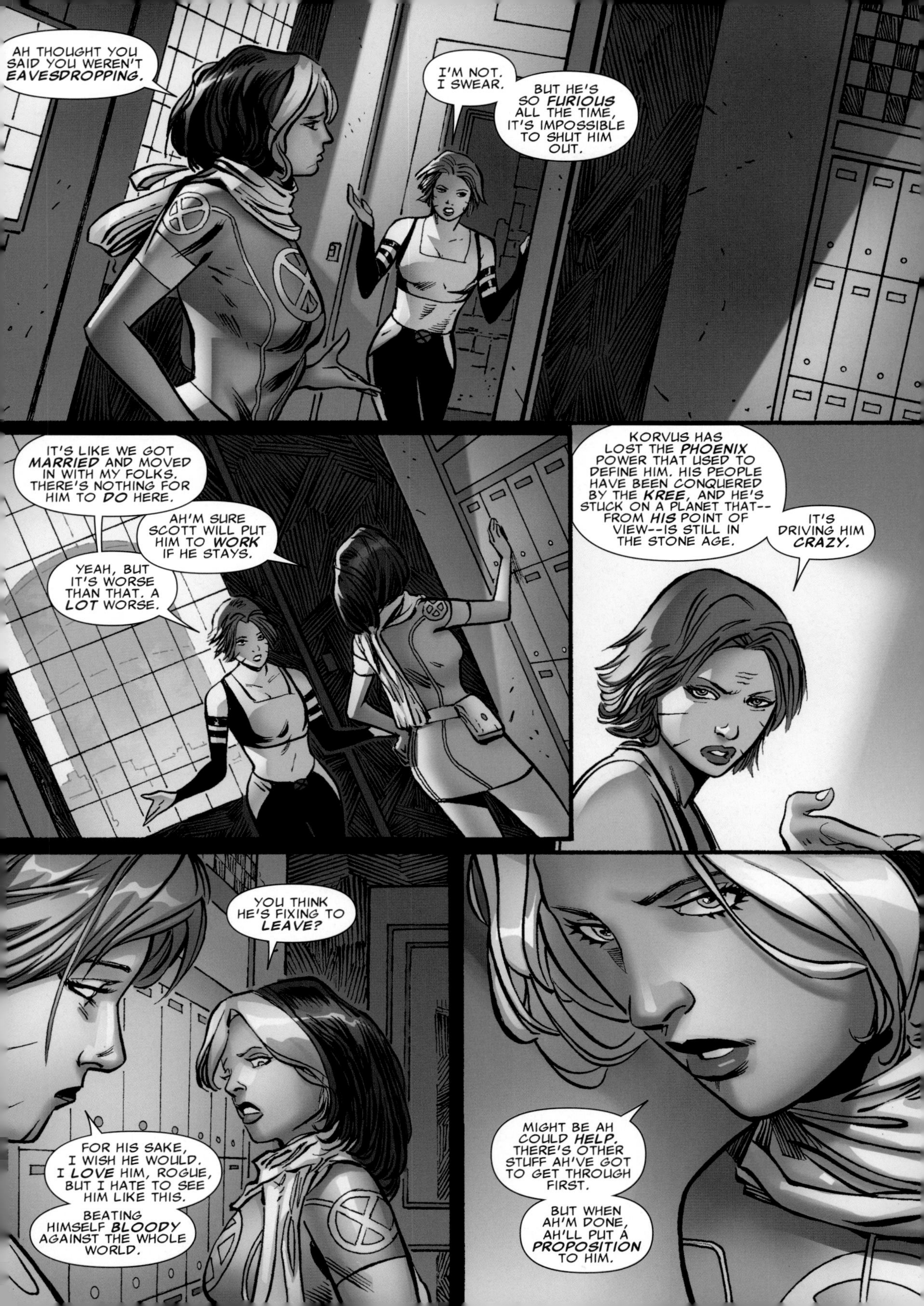

AH THOUGHT YOU SAID YOU WEREN'T EAVESDROPPING.
I'M NOT. I SWEAR.
BUT HE'S SO FURIOUS ALL THE TIME, IT'S IMPOSSIBLE TO SHUT HIM OUT.
IT'S LIKE WE GOT MARRIED AND MOVED IN WITH MY FOLKS. THERE'S NOTHING FOR HIM TO DO HERE.
AH'M SURE SCOTT WILL PUT HIM TO WORK IF HE STAYS.
YEAH, BUT IT'S WORSE THAN THAT. A LOT WORSE.
KORVUS HAS LOST THE PHOENIX POWER THAT USED TO DEFINE HIM. HIS PEOPLE HAVE BEEN CONQUERED BY THE KREE, AND HE'S STUCK ON A PLANET THAT--FROM HIS POINT OF VIEW--IS STILL IN THE STONE AGE.
IT'S DRIVING HIM CRAZY.
YOU THINK HE'S FIXING TO LEAVE?
FOR HIS SAKE, I WISH HE WOULD. I LOVE HIM, ROGUE, BUT I HATE TO SEE HIM LIKE THIS.
BEATING HIMSELF BLOODY AGAINST THE WHOLE WORLD.
MIGHT BE AH COULD HELP. THERE'S OTHER STUFF AH'VE GOT TO GET THROUGH FIRST.
BUT WHEN AH'M DONE, AH'LL PUT A PROPOSITION TO HIM.

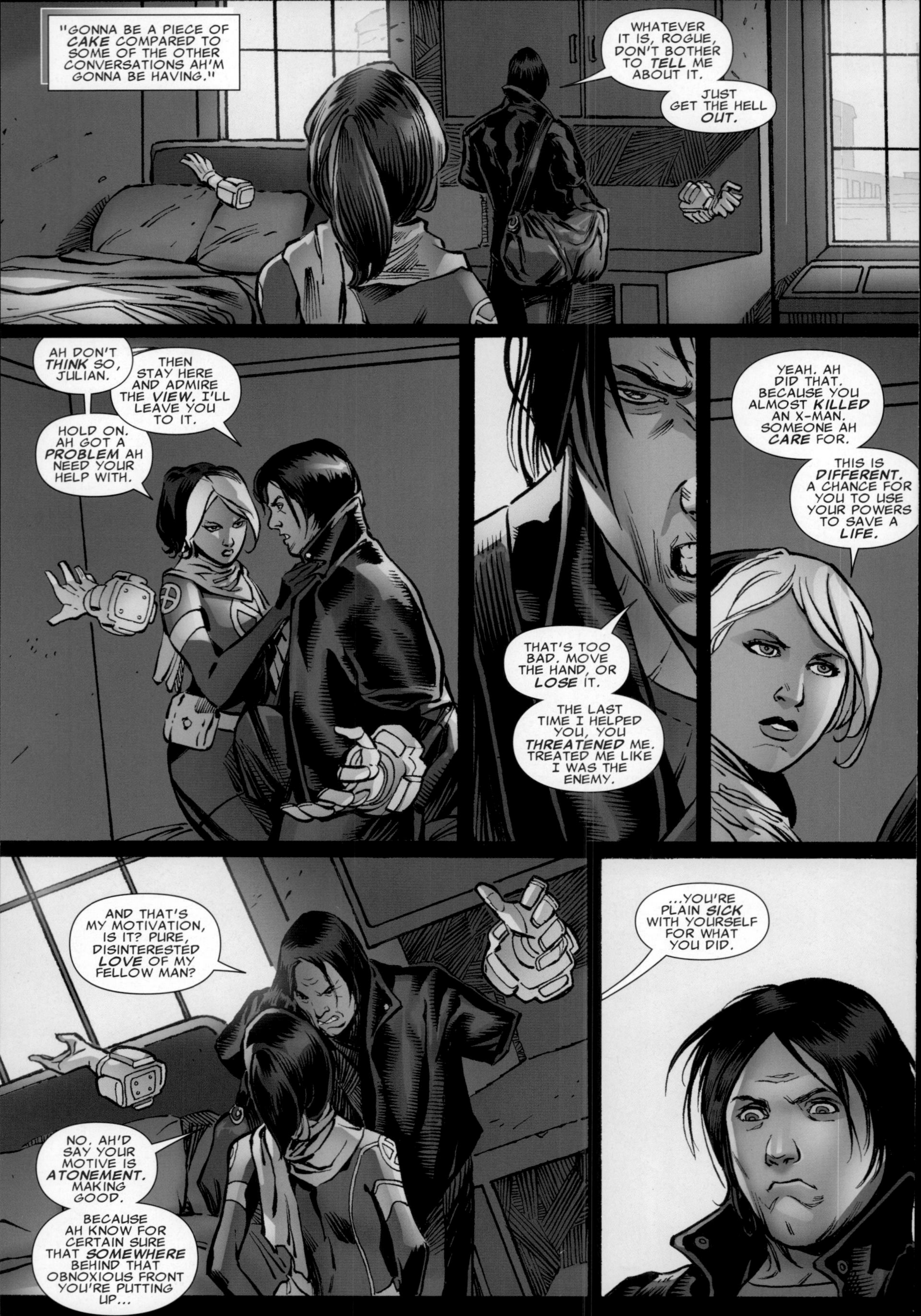
"GONNA BE A PIECE OF CAKE COMPARED TO SOME OF THE OTHER CONVERSATIONS AH'M GONNA BE HAVING."
WHATEVER IT IS, ROGUE, DON'T BOTHER TO TELL ME ABOUT IT.
JUST GET THE HELL OUT.
AH DON'T THINK SO, JULIAN.
THEN STAY HERE AND ADMIRE THE VIEW. I'LL LEAVE YOU TO IT.
HOLD ON. AH GOT A PROBLEM AH NEED YOUR HELP WITH.
THAT'S TOO BAD. MOVE THE HAND, OR LOSE IT.
THE LAST TIME I HELPED YOU, YOU THREATENED ME. TREATED ME LIKE I WAS THE ENEMY.
YEAH. AH DID THAT. BECAUSE YOU ALMOST KILLED AN X-MAN. SOMEONE AH CARE FOR.
THIS IS DIFFERENT. A CHANCE FOR YOU TO USE YOUR POWERS TO SAVE A LIFE.
AND THAT'S MY MOTIVATION, IS IT? PURE, DISINTERESTED LOVE OF MY FELLOW MAN?
NO. AH'D SAY YOUR MOTIVE IS ATONEMENT. MAKING GOOD.
BECAUSE AH KNOW FOR CERTAIN SURE THAT SOMEWHERE BEHIND THAT OBNOXIOUS FRONT YOU'RE PUTTING UP...
...YOU'RE PLAIN SICK WITH YOURSELF FOR WHAT YOU DID.

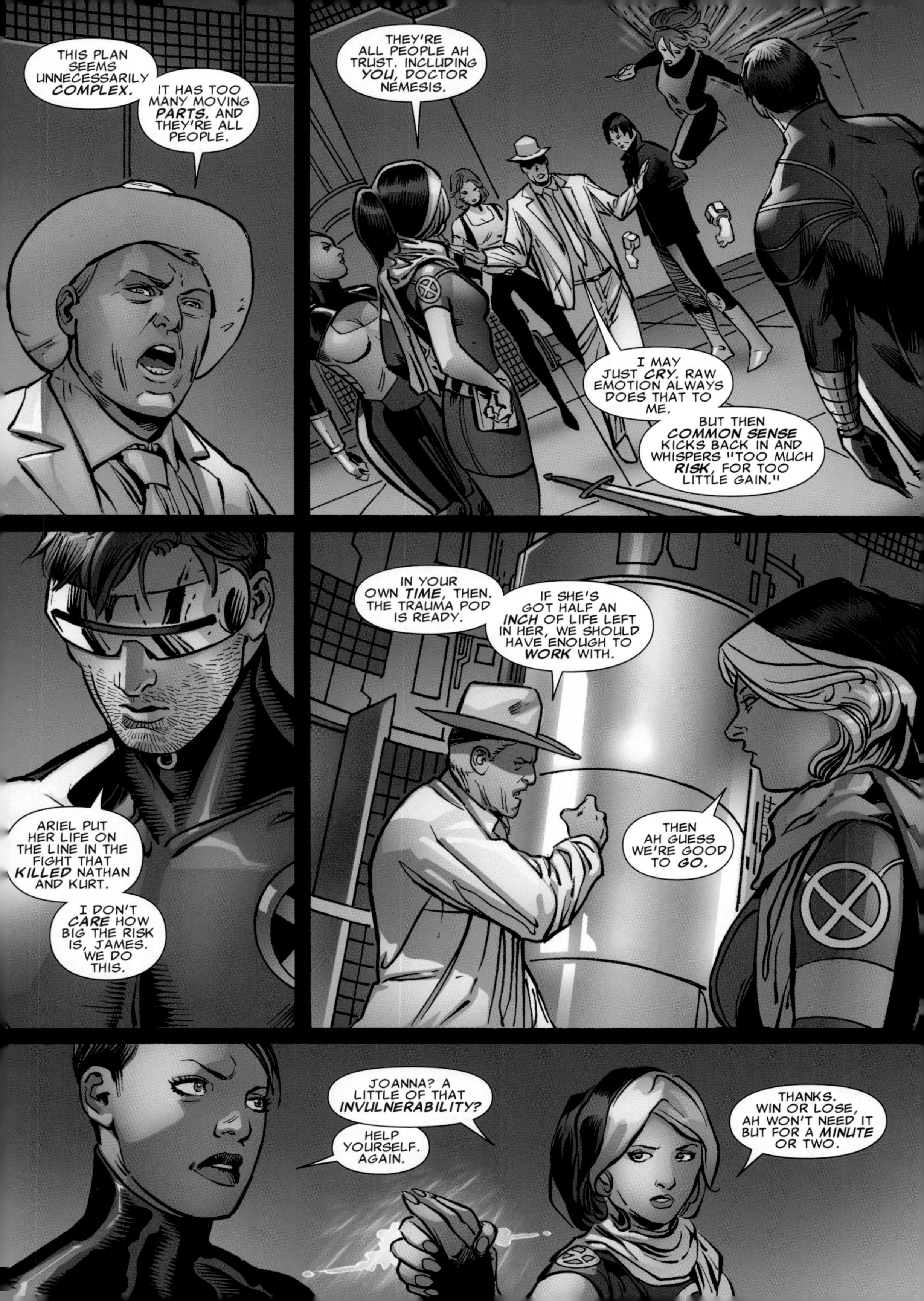
THIS PLAN SEEMS UNNECESSARILY COMPLEX.
IT HAS TOO MANY MOVING PARTS. AND THEY'RE ALL PEOPLE.
THEY'RE ALL PEOPLE AH TRUST. INCLUDING YOU, DOCTOR NEMESIS.
I MAY JUST CRY. RAW EMOTION ALWAYS DOES THAT TO ME.
BUT THEN COMMON SENSE KICKS BACK IN AND WHISPERS "TOO MUCH RISK, FOR TOO LITTLE GAIN."
ARIEL PUT HER LIFE ON THE LINE IN THE FIGHT THAT KILLED NATHAN AND KURT.
I DON'T CARE HOW BIG THE RISK IS, JAMES. WE DO THIS.
IN YOUR OWN TIME, THEN. THE TRAUMA POD IS READY.
IF SHE'S GOT HALF AN INCH OF LIFE LEFT IN HER, WE SHOULD HAVE ENOUGH TO WORK WITH.
THEN AH GUESS WE'RE GOOD TO GO.
JOANNA? A LITTLE OF THAT INVULNERABILITY?
HELP YOURSELF. AGAIN.
THANKS. WIN OR LOSE, AH WON'T NEED IT BUT FOR A MINUTE OR TWO.

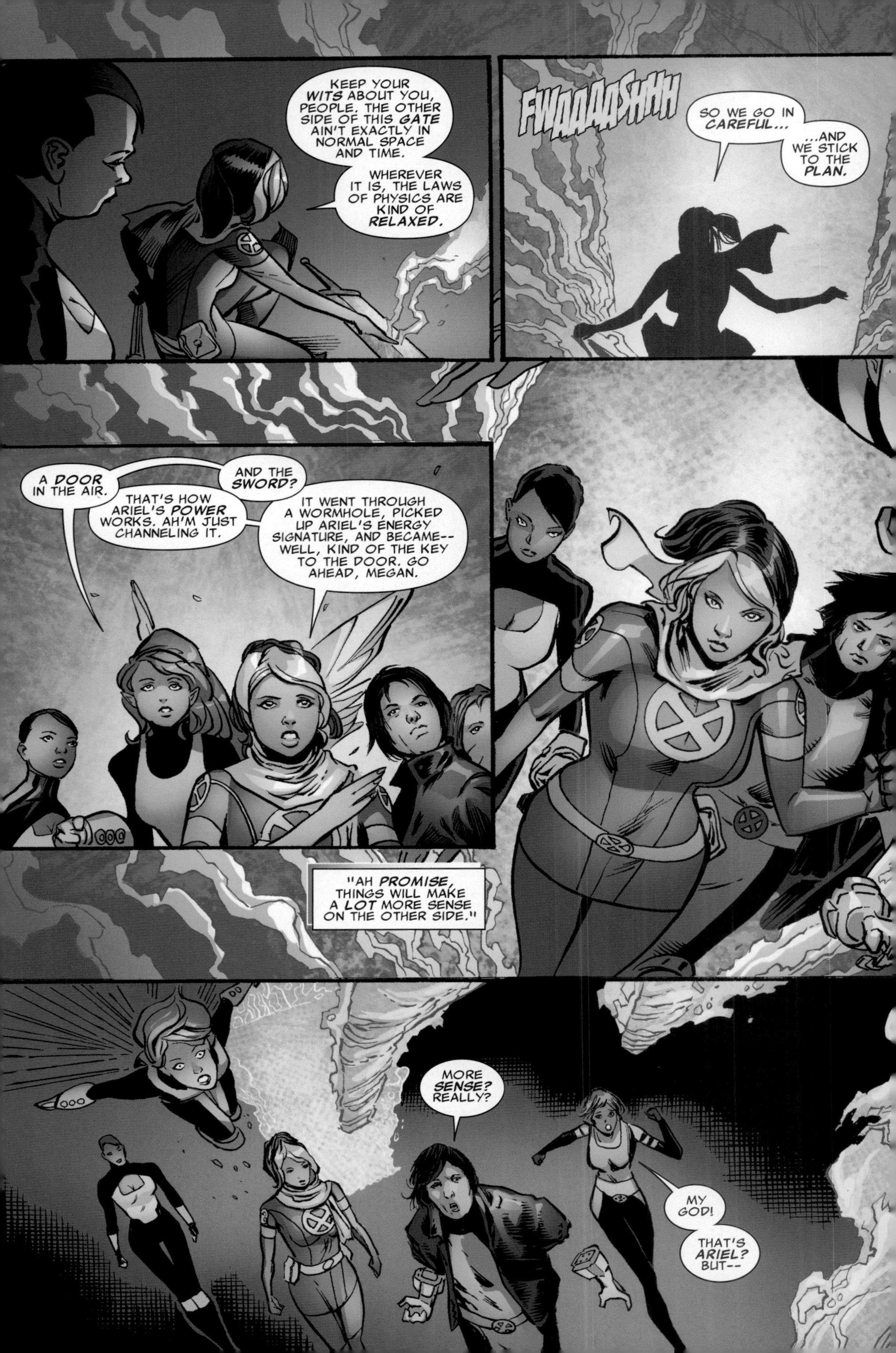
KEEP YOUR WITS ABOUT YOU, PEOPLE. THE OTHER SIDE OF THIS GATE AIN'T EXACTLY IN NORMAL SPACE AND TIME.
WHEREVER IT IS, THE LAWS OF PHYSICS ARE KIND OF RELAXED.
FWAAAASHHH
SO WE GO IN CAREFUL...
...AND WE STICK TO THE PLAN.
A DOOR IN THE AIR.
AND THE SWORD?
THAT'S HOW ARIEL'S POWER WORKS. AH'M JUST CHANNELING IT.
IT WENT THROUGH A WORMHOLE, PICKED UP ARIEL'S ENERGY SIGNATURE, AND BECAME-- WELL, KIND OF THE KEY TO THE DOOR. GO AHEAD, MEGAN.
"AH PROMISE, THINGS WILL MAKE A LOT MORE SENSE ON THE OTHER SIDE."
MORE SENSE? REALLY?
MY GOD!
THAT'S ARIEL? BUT--

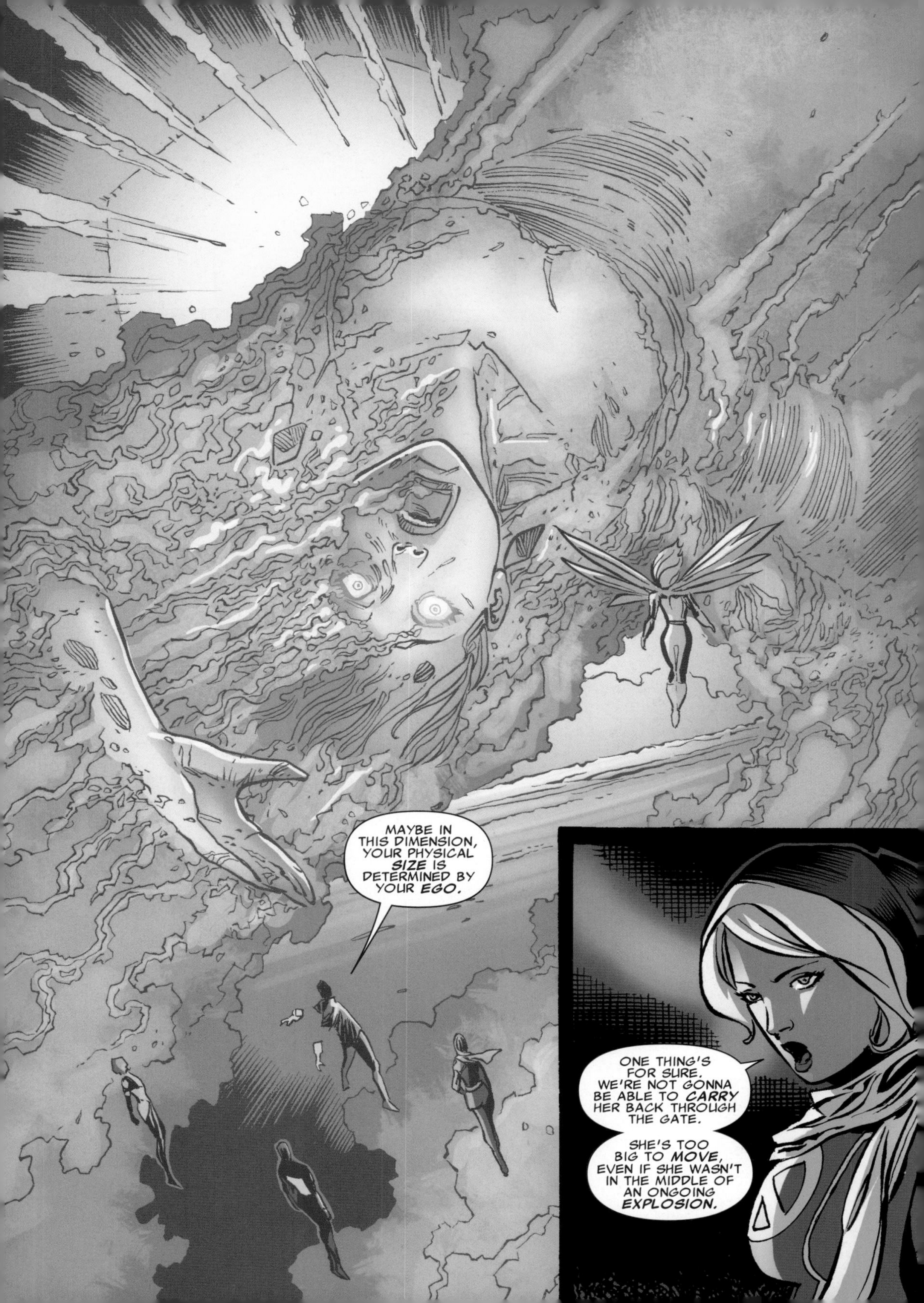
MAYBE IN THIS DIMENSION, YOUR PHYSICAL SIZE IS DETERMINED BY YOUR EGO.
ONE THING'S FOR SURE. WE'RE NOT GONNA BE ABLE TO CARRY HER BACK THROUGH THE GATE.
SHE'S TOO BIG TO MOVE, EVEN IF SHE WASN'T IN THE MIDDLE OF AN ONGOING EXPLOSION.

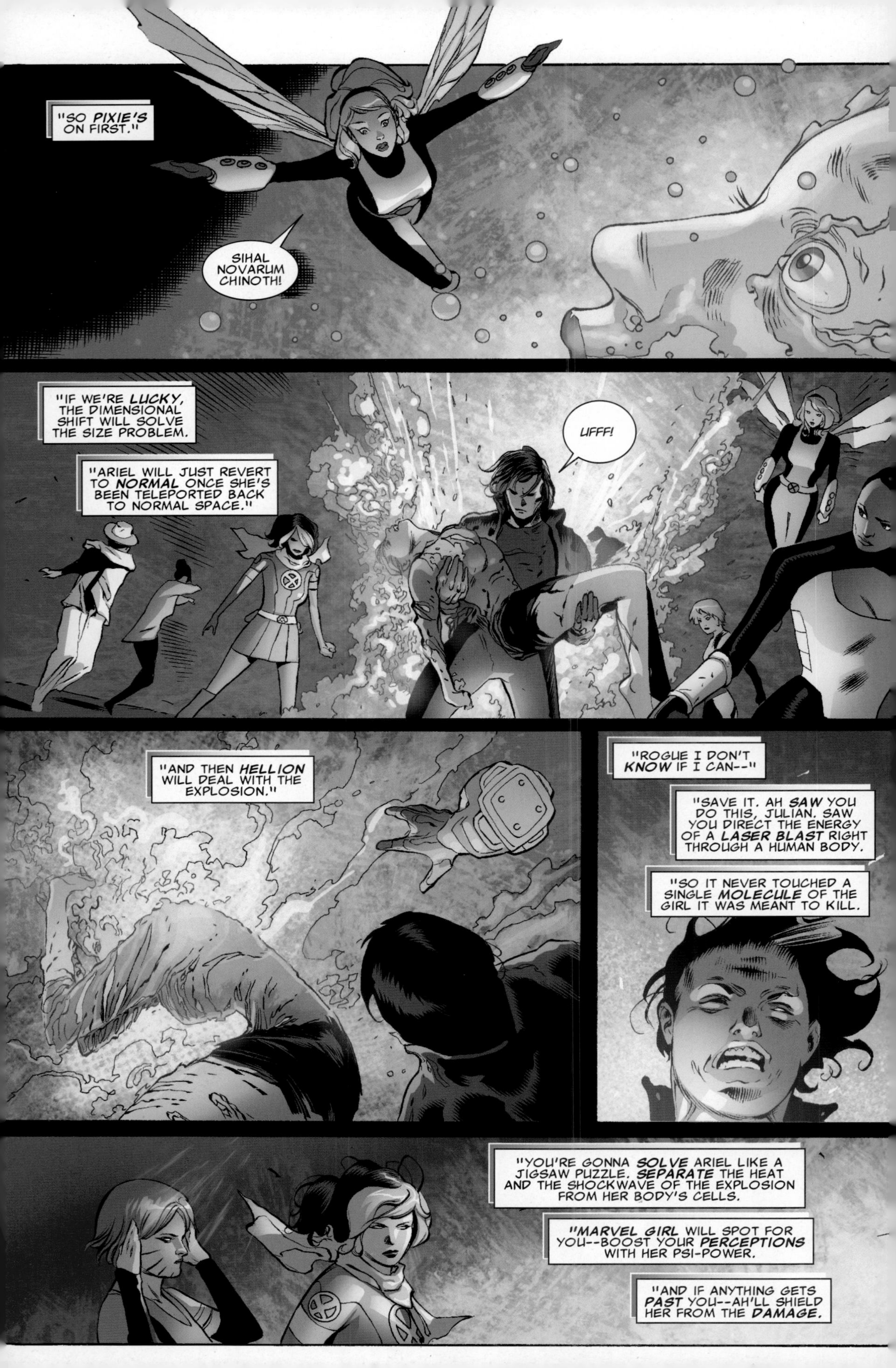

"SO PIXIE'S ON FIRST."
SIHAL NOVARUM CHINOTH!
"IF WE'RE LUCKY, THE DIMENSIONAL SHIFT WILL SOLVE THE SIZE PROBLEM.
"ARIEL WILL JUST REVERT TO NORMAL ONCE SHE'S BEEN TELEPORTED BACK TO NORMAL SPACE."
UFFF!
"AND THEN HELLION WILL DEAL WITH THE EXPLOSION."
"ROGUE I DON'T KNOW IF I CAN--"
"SAVE IT. AH SAW YOU DO THIS, JULIAN. SAW YOU DIRECT THE ENERGY OF A LASER BLAST RIGHT THROUGH A HUMAN BODY.
"SO IT NEVER TOUCHED A SINGLE MOLECULE OF THE GIRL IT WAS MEANT TO KILL.
"YOU'RE GONNA SOLVE ARIEL LIKE A JIGSAW PUZZLE. SEPARATE THE HEAT AND THE SHOCKWAVE OF THE EXPLOSION FROM HER BODY'S CELLS.
"MARVEL GIRL WILL SPOT FOR YOU--BOOST YOUR PERCEPTIONS WITH HER PSI-POWER.
"AND IF ANYTHING GETS PAST YOU--AH'LL SHIELD HER FROM THE DAMAGE.

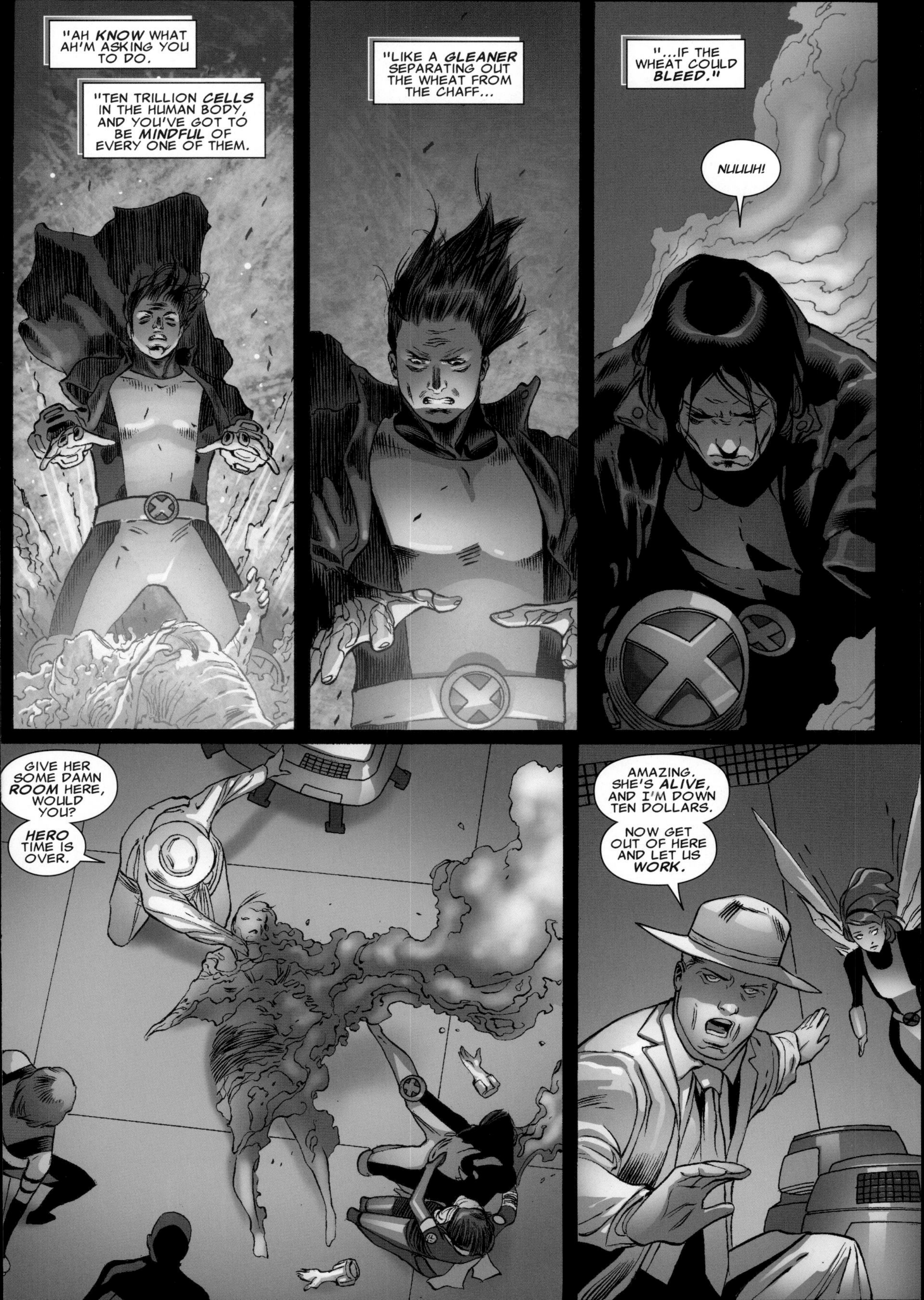
"AH KNOW WHAT AH'M ASKING YOU TO DO.
"TEN TRILLION CELLS IN THE HUMAN BODY, AND YOU'VE GOT TO BE MINDFUL OF EVERY ONE OF THEM.
"LIKE A GLEANER SEPARATING OUT THE WHEAT FROM THE CHAFF...
"...IF THE WHEAT COULD BLEED."
NUUUH!
GIVE HER SOME DAMN ROOM HERE, WOULD YOU?
HERO TIME IS OVER.
AMAZING. SHE'S ALIVE, AND I'M DOWN TEN DOLLARS.
NOW GET OUT OF HERE AND LET US WORK.

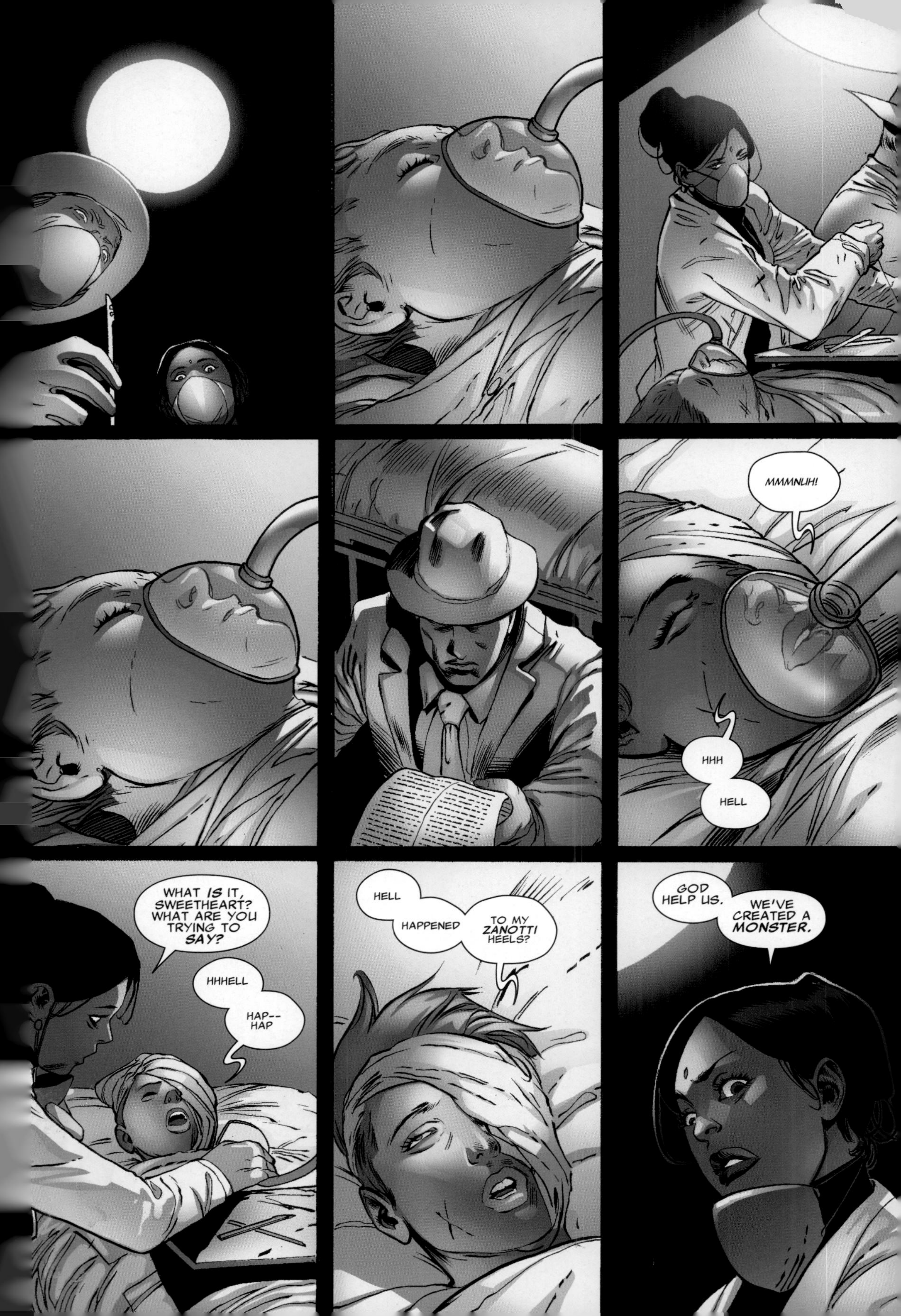
MMMNUH!
HHH
HELL
WHAT IS IT, SWEETHEART? WHAT ARE YOU TRYING TO SAY?
HHHELL
HAP-- HAP
HELL
HAPPENED
TO MY ZANOTTI HEELS?
GOD HELP US.
WE'VE CREATED A MONSTER.

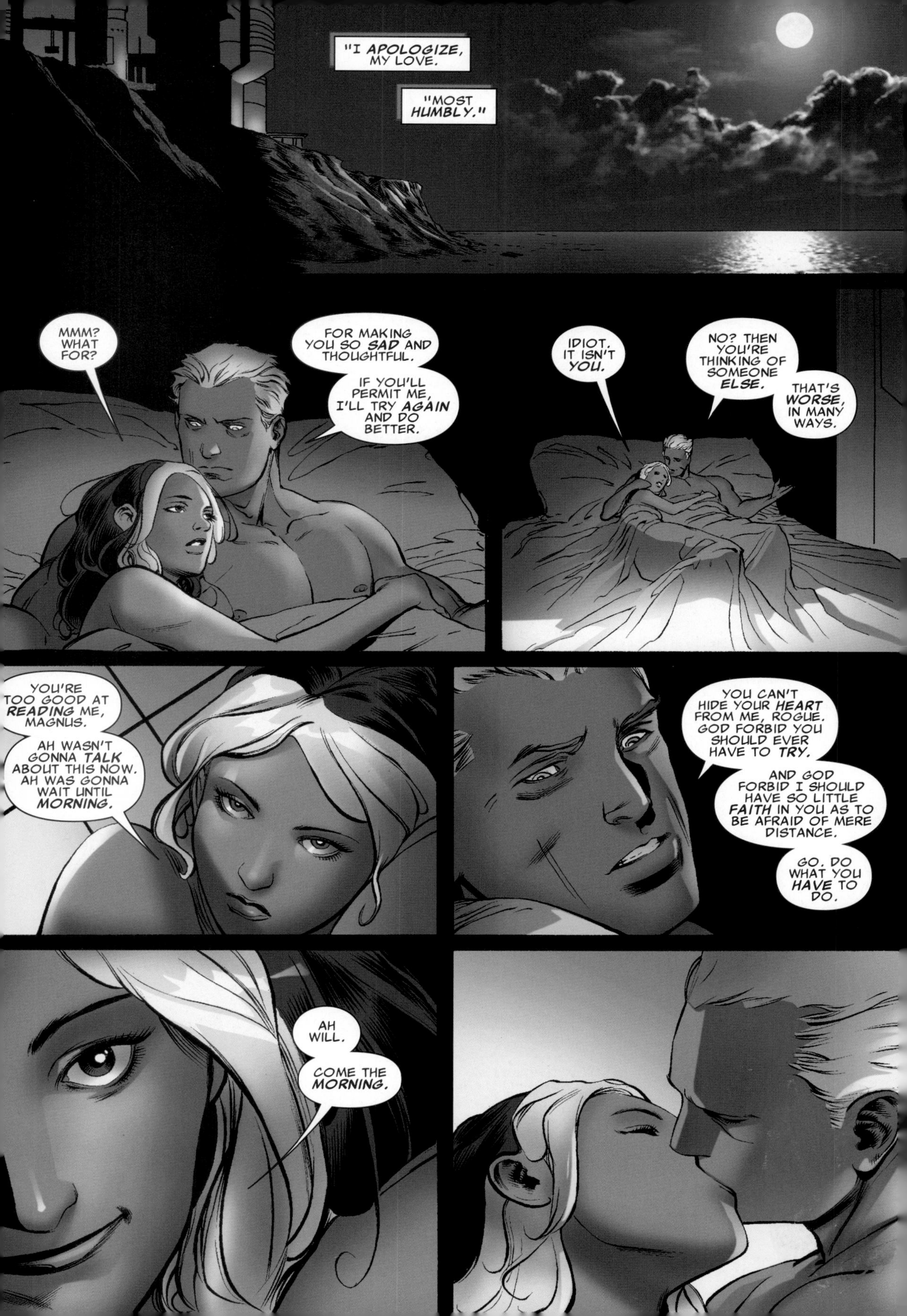
"I APOLOGIZE, MY LOVE.
"MOST HUMBLY."
MMM? WHAT FOR?
FOR MAKING YOU SO SAD AND THOUGHTFUL.
IF YOU'LL PERMIT ME, I'LL TRY AGAIN AND DO BETTER.
IDIOT. IT ISN'T YOU.
NO? THEN YOU'RE THINKING OF SOMEONE ELSE.
THAT'S WORSE, IN MANY WAYS.
YOU'RE TOO GOOD AT READING ME, MAGNUS.
AH WASN'T GONNA TALK ABOUT THIS NOW. AH WAS GONNA WAIT UNTIL MORNING.
YOU CAN'T HIDE YOUR HEART FROM ME, ROGUE. GOD FORBID YOU SHOULD EVER HAVE TO TRY.
AND GOD FORBID I SHOULD HAVE SO LITTLE FAITH IN YOU AS TO BE AFRAID OF MERE DISTANCE.
GO. DO WHAT YOU HAVE TO DO.
AH WILL.
COME THE MORNING.

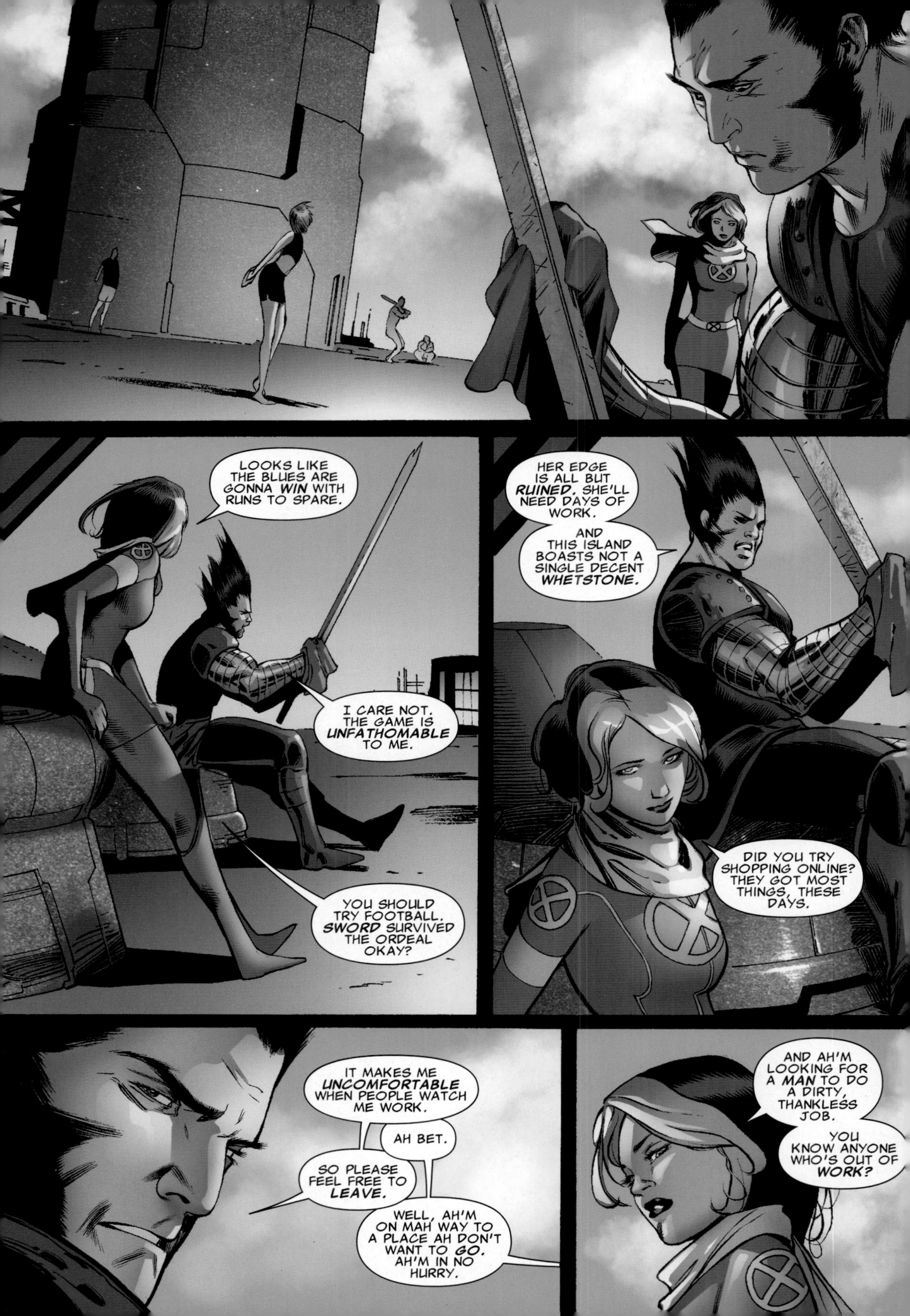
LOOKS LIKE THE BLUES ARE GONNA WIN WITH RUNS TO SPARE.
I CARE NOT. THE GAME IS UNFATHOMABLE TO ME.
YOU SHOULD TRY FOOTBALL. SWORD SURVIVED THE ORDEAL OKAY?
HER EDGE IS ALL BUT RUINED. SHE'LL NEED DAYS OF WORK.
AND THIS ISLAND BOASTS NOT A SINGLE DECENT WHETSTONE.
DID YOU TRY SHOPPING ONLINE? THEY GOT MOST THINGS, THESE DAYS.
IT MAKES ME UNCOMFORTABLE WHEN PEOPLE WATCH ME WORK.
AH BET.
SO PLEASE FEEL FREE TO LEAVE.
WELL, AH'M ON MAH WAY TO A PLACE AH DON'T WANT TO GO. AH'M IN NO HURRY.
AND AH'M LOOKING FOR A MAN TO DO A DIRTY, THANKLESS JOB.
YOU KNOW ANYONE WHO'S OUT OF WORK?

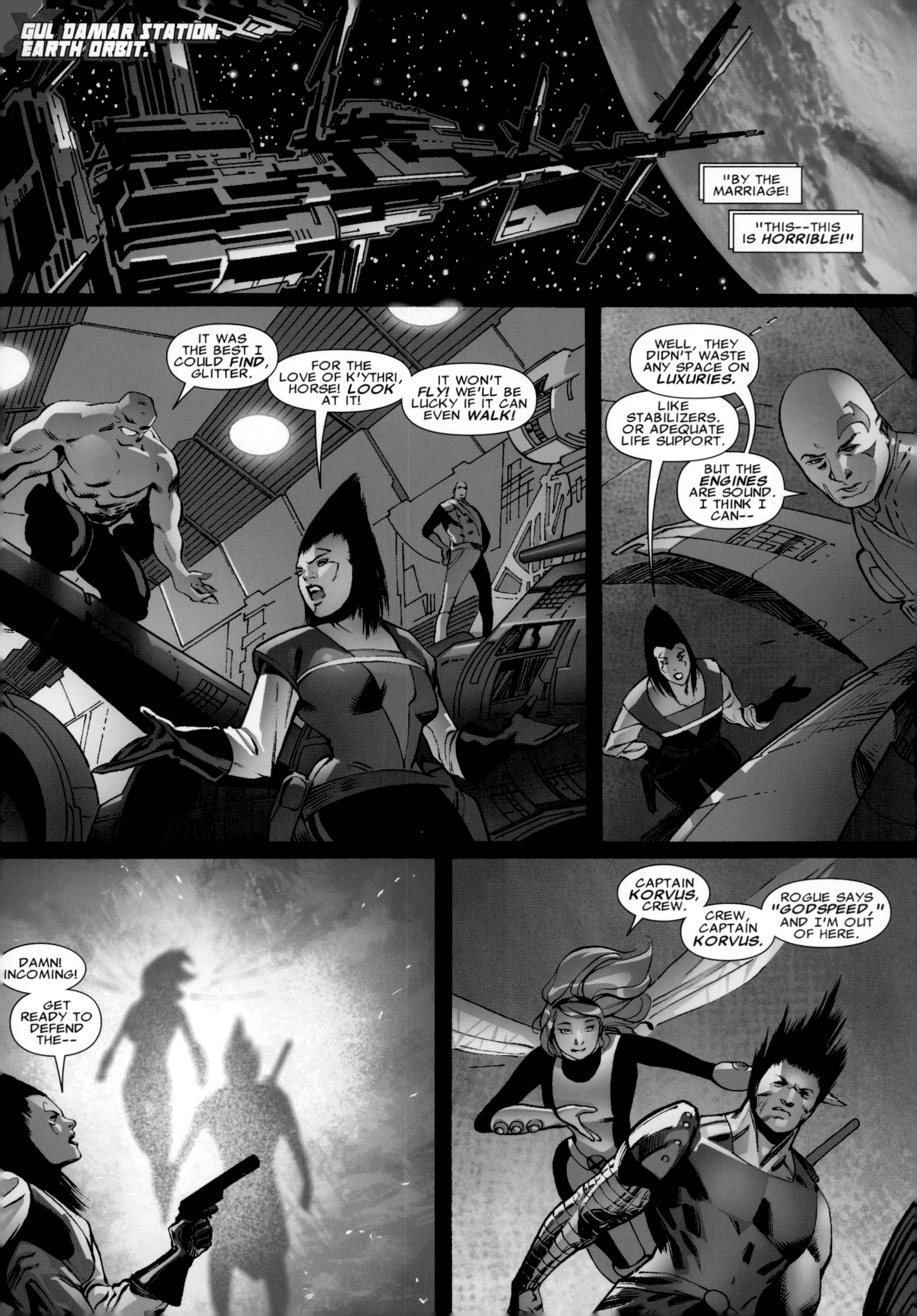
GUL DAMAR STATION. EARTH ORBIT.
"BY THE MARRIAGE!
"THIS--THIS IS HORRIBLE!"
IT WAS THE BEST I COULD FIND, GLITTER.
FOR THE LOVE OF K'YTHRI, HORSE! LOOK AT IT!
IT WON'T FLY! WE'LL BE LUCKY IF IT CAN EVEN WALK!
WELL, THEY DIDN'T WASTE ANY SPACE ON LUXURIES.
LIKE STABILIZERS. OR ADEQUATE LIFE SUPPORT.
BUT THE ENGINES ARE SOUND. I THINK I CAN--
DAMN! INCOMING!
GET READY TO DEFEND THE--
CAPTAIN KORVUS, CREW.
CREW, CAPTAIN KORVUS.
ROGUE SAYS "GODSPEED," AND I'M OUT OF HERE.

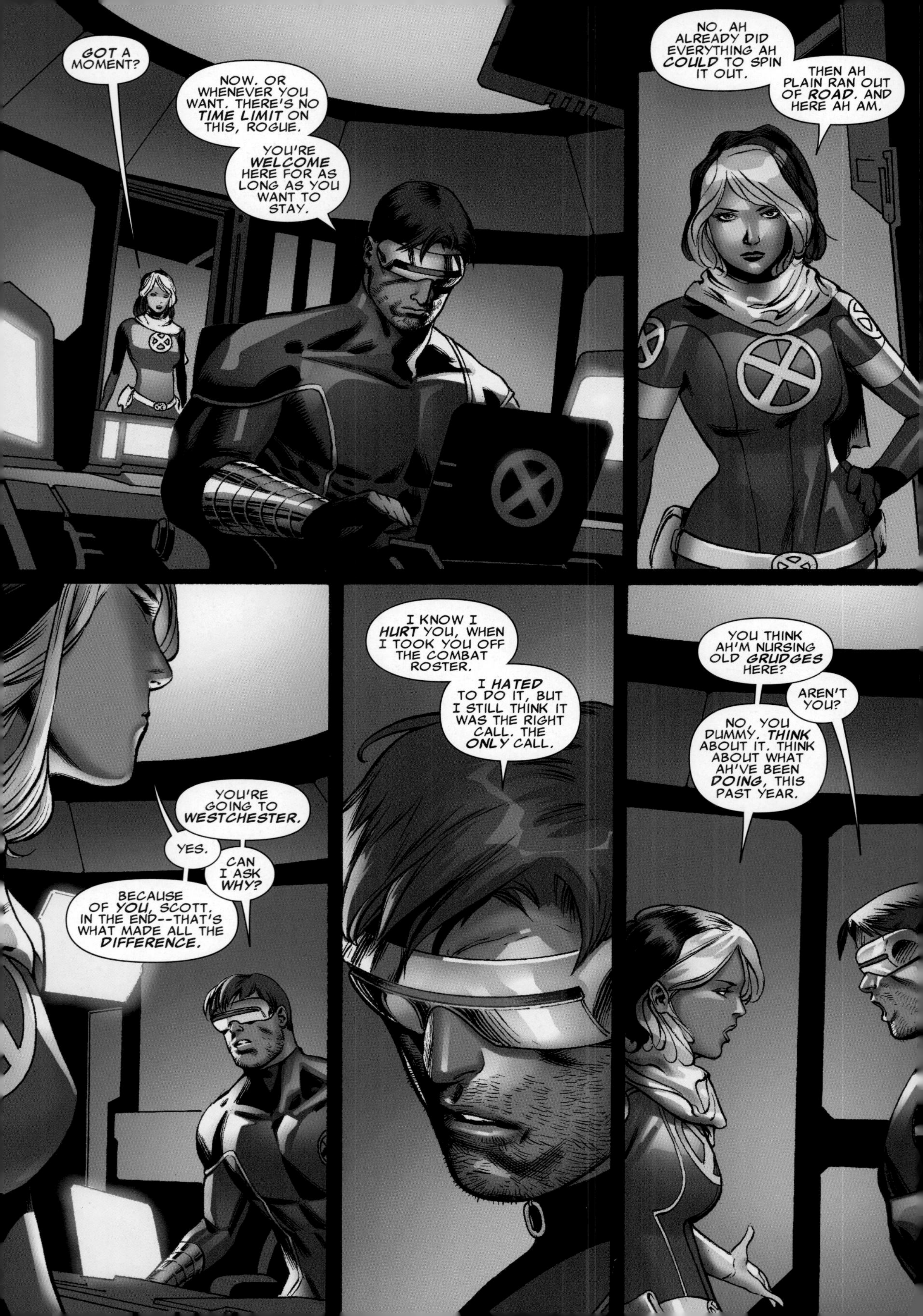
GOT A MOMENT?
NOW. OR WHENEVER YOU WANT. THERE'S NO TIME LIMIT ON THIS, ROGUE.
YOU'RE WELCOME HERE FOR AS LONG AS YOU WANT TO STAY.
NO. AH ALREADY DID EVERYTHING AH COULD TO SPIN IT OUT.
THEN AH PLAIN RAN OUT OF ROAD. AND HERE AH AM.
YOU'RE GOING TO WESTCHESTER.
YES.
CAN I ASK WHY?
BECAUSE OF YOU, SCOTT. IN THE END--THAT'S WHAT MADE ALL THE DIFFERENCE.
I KNOW I HURT YOU, WHEN I TOOK YOU OFF THE COMBAT ROSTER.
I HATED TO DO IT, BUT I STILL THINK IT WAS THE RIGHT CALL. THE ONLY CALL.
YOU THINK AH'M NURSING OLD GRUDGES HERE?
AREN'T YOU?
NO, YOU DUMMY. THINK ABOUT IT. THINK ABOUT WHAT AH'VE BEEN DOING, THIS PAST YEAR.

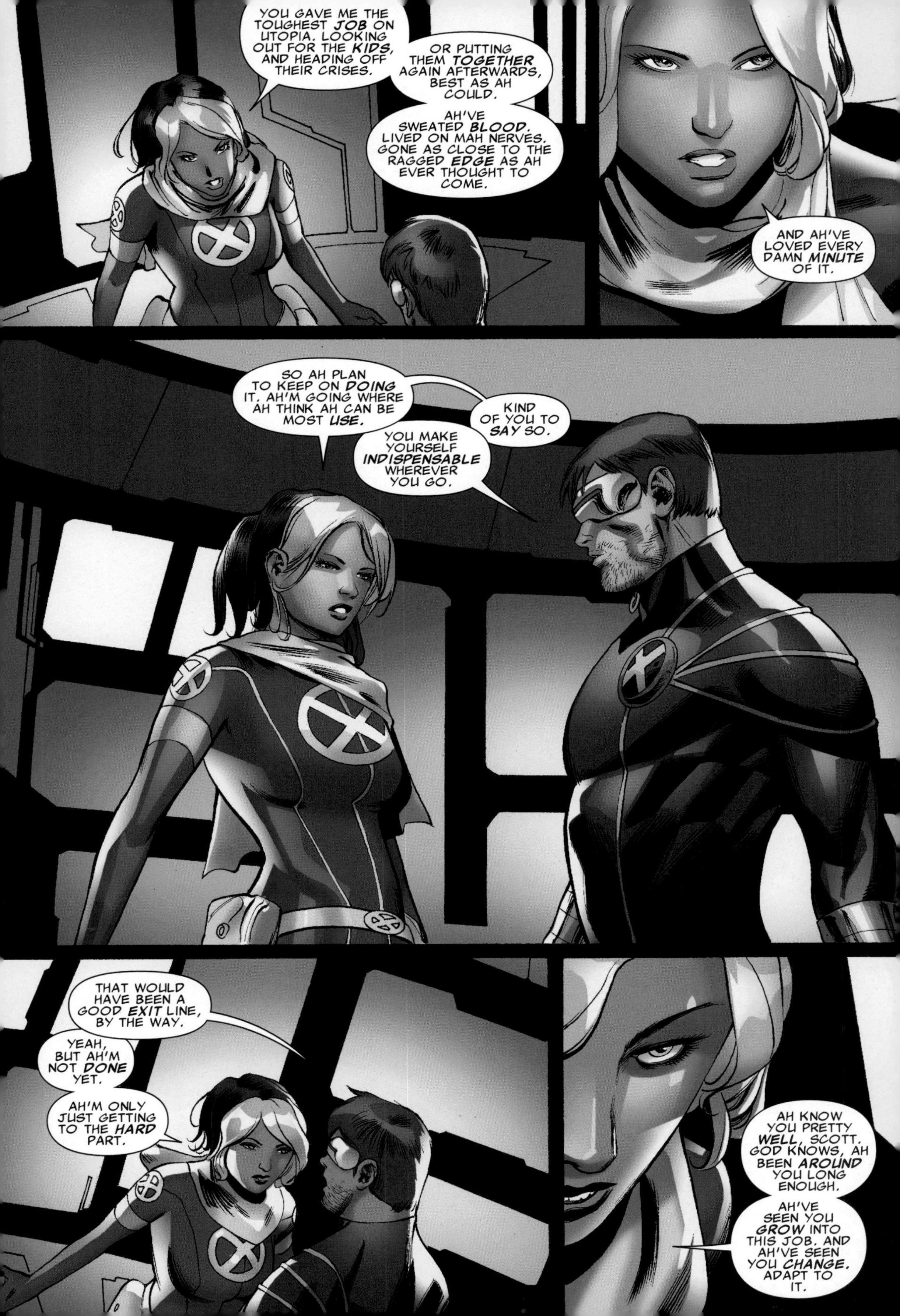

YOU GAVE ME THE TOUGHEST JOB ON UTOPIA. LOOKING OUT FOR THE KIDS, AND HEADING OFF THEIR CRISES.
OR PUTTING THEM TOGETHER AGAIN AFTERWARDS, BEST AS AH COULD.
AH'VE SWEATED BLOOD. LIVED ON MAH NERVES. GONE AS CLOSE TO THE RAGGED EDGE AS AH EVER THOUGHT TO COME.
AND AH'VE LOVED EVERY DAMN MINUTE OF IT.
SO AH PLAN TO KEEP ON DOING IT. AH'M GOING WHERE AH THINK AH CAN BE MOST USE.
KIND OF YOU TO SAY SO.
YOU MAKE YOURSELF INDISPENSABLE WHEREVER YOU GO.
THAT WOULD HAVE BEEN A GOOD EXIT LINE, BY THE WAY.
YEAH, BUT AH'M NOT DONE YET.
AH'M ONLY JUST GETTING TO THE HARD PART.
AH KNOW YOU PRETTY WELL, SCOTT. GOD KNOWS, AH BEEN AROUND YOU LONG ENOUGH.
AH'VE SEEN YOU GROW INTO THIS JOB. AND AH'VE SEEN YOU CHANGE. ADAPT TO IT.

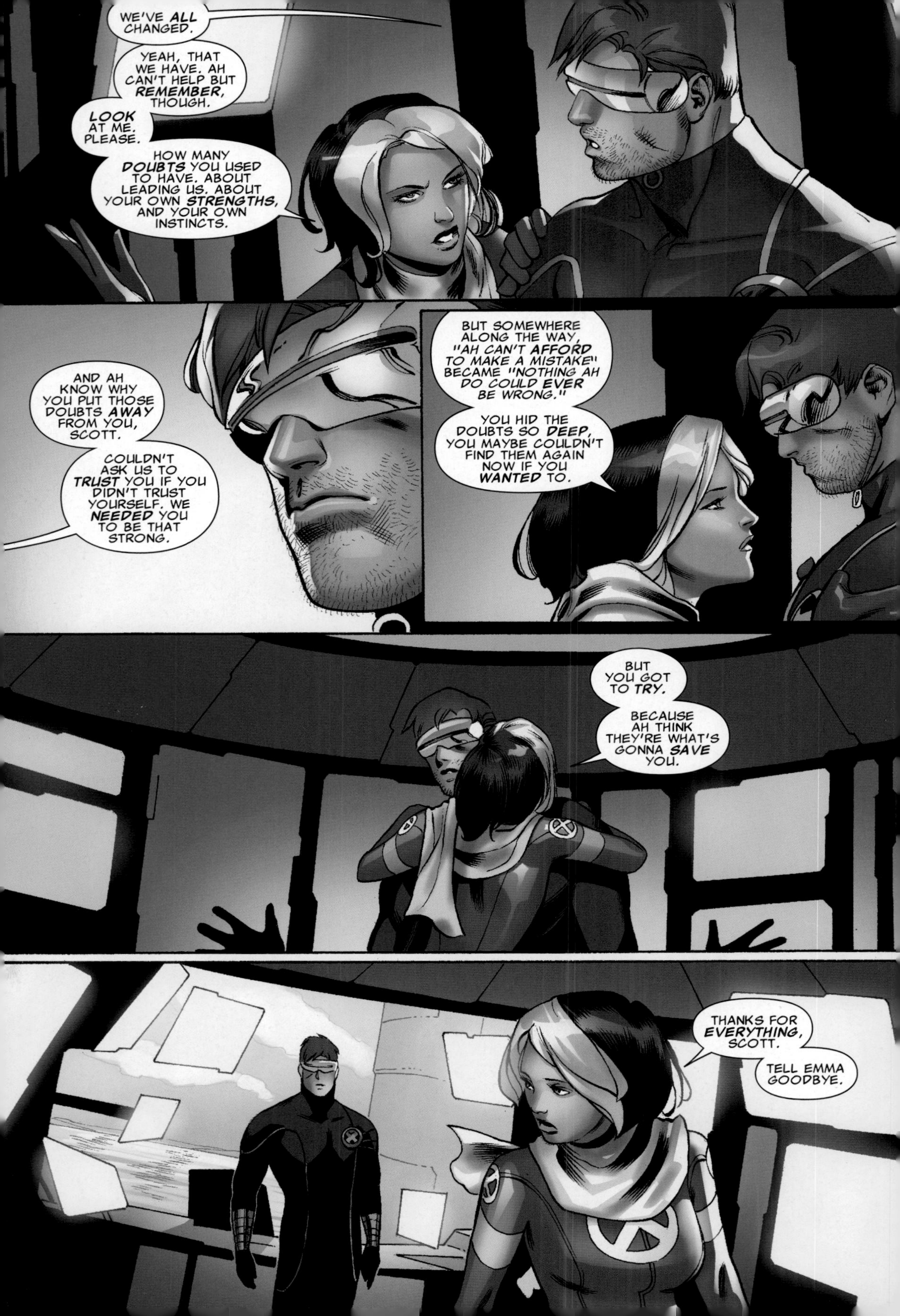
WE'VE **ALL** CHANGED.
YEAH, THAT WE HAVE. AH CAN'T HELP BUT **REMEMBER,** THOUGH.
LOOK AT ME. PLEASE.
HOW MANY **DOUBTS** YOU USED TO HAVE. ABOUT LEADING US. ABOUT YOUR OWN **STRENGTHS,** AND YOUR OWN INSTINCTS.
AND AH KNOW WHY YOU PUT THOSE DOUBTS **AWAY** FROM YOU, SCOTT.
COULDN'T ASK US TO **TRUST** YOU IF YOU DIDN'T TRUST YOURSELF. WE **NEEDED** YOU TO BE THAT STRONG.
BUT SOMEWHERE ALONG THE WAY, "AH CAN'T **AFFORD** TO MAKE A MISTAKE" BECAME "NOTHING AH DO COULD **EVER** BE WRONG."
YOU HID THE DOUBTS SO **DEEP,** YOU MAYBE COULDN'T FIND THEM AGAIN NOW IF YOU **WANTED** TO.
BUT YOU GOT TO **TRY.**
BECAUSE AH THINK THEY'RE WHAT'S GONNA **SAVE** YOU.
THANKS FOR **EVERYTHING,** SCOTT.
TELL EMMA GOODBYE.

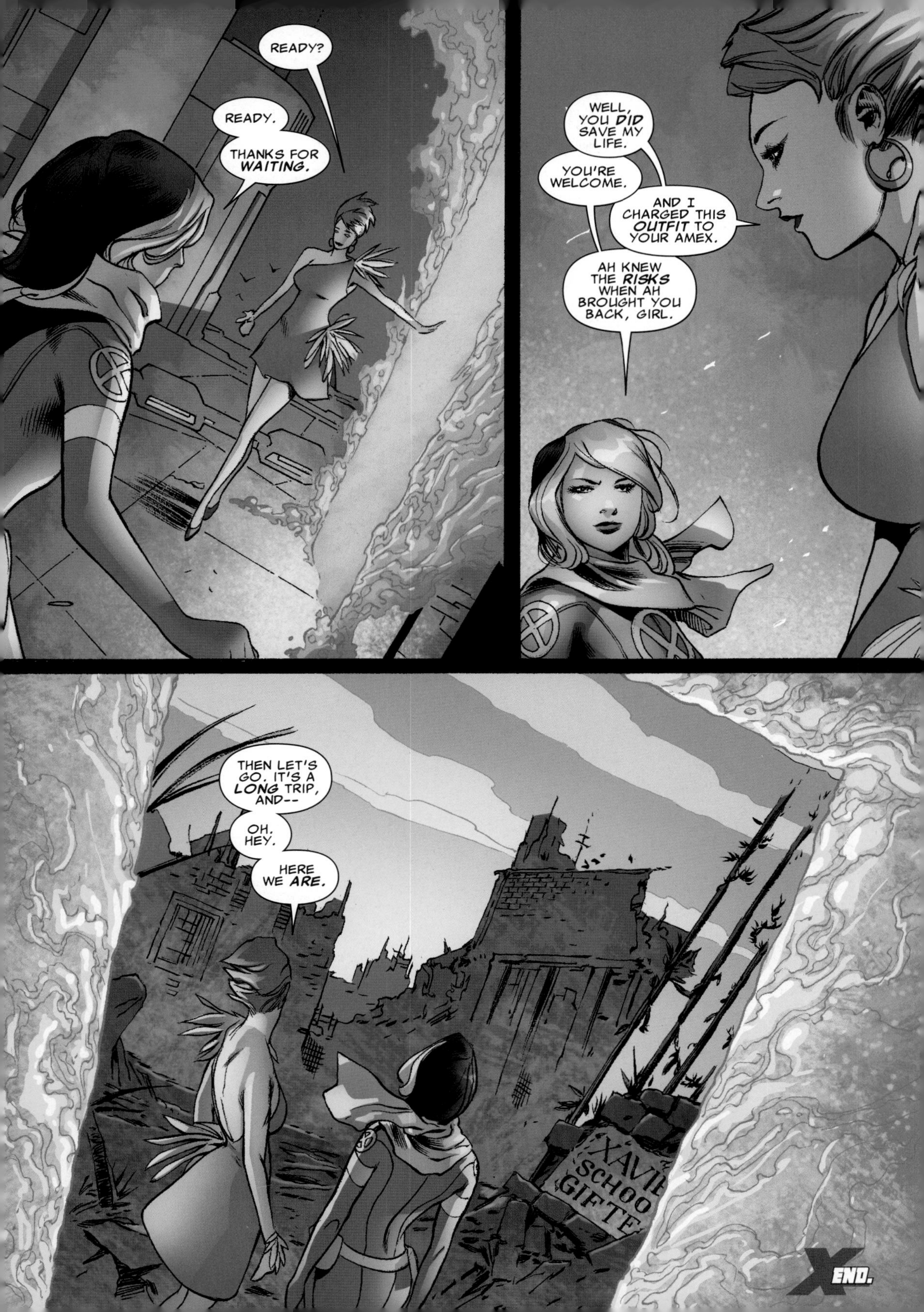
READY?
READY.
THANKS FOR **WAITING.**
WELL, YOU **DID** SAVE MY LIFE.
YOU'RE WELCOME.
AND I CHARGED THIS **OUTFIT** TO YOUR AMEX.
AH KNEW THE **RISKS** WHEN AH BROUGHT YOU BACK, GIRL.
THEN LET'S GO. IT'S A **LONG** TRIP, AND--
OH. HEY.
HERE WE **ARE.**
XAVIE
SCHOO
GIFTE
END.

UNCANNY X-FORCE #19, WOLVERINE & THE X-MEN #1,
X-MEN LEGACY #259 & X-FACTOR #230

COMBINED VARIANTS
BY NICK BRADSHAW & MORRY HOLLOWELL

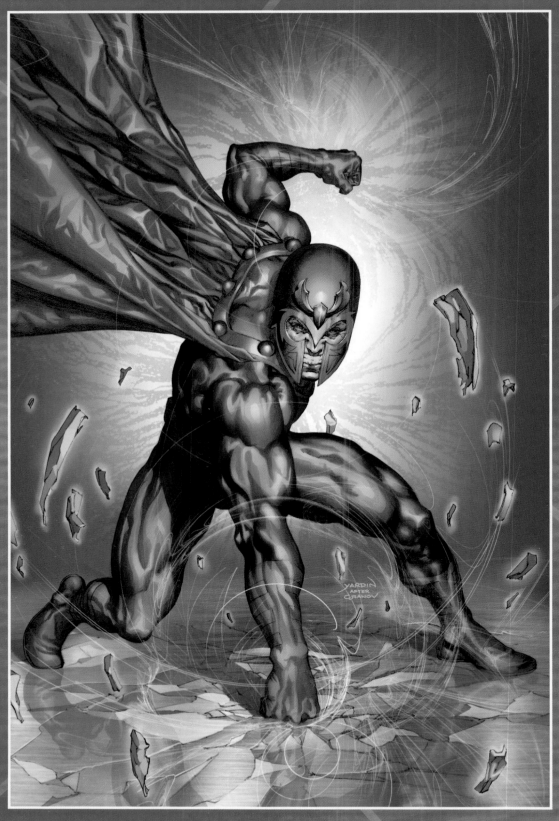

#259 MARVEL COMICS 50TH ANNIVERSARY VARIANT COVER
BY DAVID YARDIN